Merciless Eden

First Edition

Published by Ferry Media
Boise, Idaho
2013

ISBN: 978-0-9891910-0-5
E-book: 978-0-9891910-1-2

Copyright © 2013

Ferry Media
602 E 45th Street
Boise, ID 83714

DEDICATION

To Joe Zaunmiller

"You couldn't ask for a more honest, straight forward,
hard working guy than Joe Zaunmiller."
— John Crowe, 1989

Introduction

It has been seven years since our first journey to Texas to interview members of the Coyle family in pursuit of the history of Campbell's Ferry. Frances Coyle came to Campbell's Ferry in 1940 and dominated its life for forty-five years. She documented her life through over a thousand newspaper columns and hundreds of letters, photos and audiotapes. Frances was a notorious pack rat. Her interest in the past led her to keep not only her own correspondence, but also whatever record she could find of earlier occupants.

When Frances arrived, the Ferry had existed for more than four decades, so this story is much more than her life. The authors attempt to chronicle all of the pioneers who sought to forge a living from this bleeding edge of the boundary between civilization and wilderness.

Soon after William Campbell settled here the U.S. Government created the Forest Service to manage the forest reserves and their relationship to the many pioneers attempting to carve a living from their midst. That process included documentation of the status of the forests and the persons who were attempting through the Homestead Act to gain title to what they hoped would become their part of the public domain. Fortunately those records are preserved in the offices of the surrounding national forests and in the National Archives.

We have been able to contact many members of the families of Ferry pioneers – the Zaunmillers, Coyles, Cooks, and many others who knew those who lived here. Some are still living in the Salmon River Canyon.

Our greatest challenge has been the Frances years. She came to the Ferry while running from the law, and intentionally obfuscated her past. The authors had access to a few critical years of Frances' diary, but the full record is not available. As her career as a writer blossomed, Frances became a talented storyteller, seldom allowing the truth to get in the way of a good tale of backcountry life. The reader should keep that in mind when reading her direct quotes contained herein.

In 1890, just prior to William Campbell's establishment of his ferry on the Wild Salmon River, the U.S. Census noted the end of the American frontier. Officials declared there were no more large tracts of lands unbroken by settlement. They hadn't seen central Idaho. Approaching one and a quarter century since, little has changed here. Campbell's small plot of ground in the wild up and down of the Salmon River country is now on the National Register of Historic Places. It is surrounded by the largest block of untamed wilderness in the lower forty-eight states.

The homestead is an excellent example of the multi-century evolution in the way Americans view and interact with wild places. The first inhabitants of Campbell's Ferry were remnants of the early pioneers. Since the nation's founding these hardy souls had sought to conquer and push their wild heritage away. In the late nineteenth century Americans began to retreat from that effort, to allow the preservation of our wild heart. The nation established forest reserves, national forests, primitive areas and finally National Wilderness Preservation and Wild and Scenic Rivers systems. The lands and waters surrounding Campbell's Ferry have been all of these.

This transition in thought is embodied in Joe Zaunmiller. As Joe struggled to survive the Great Depression, he began to see the vast wilderness around him less as a source from which he could extract a living, and more as something he could share with an increasingly urban society. Joe, with his pioneer skills and knowledge of the backcountry, realized people from the city would pay him to reconnect to their rural, wildland hunting and fishing heritage.

During the century since William Campbell, the Idaho boundary between development and wildness was in doubt. Would the solitude of the Canyon of the Salmon be broken by a rail line or road through its heart? Would the thirst of the desert Southwest lead to the inundation of a wild river? The resolution of these and other challenges to Idaho's backcountry are told through the eyes of those who worked to save it for future generations.

And what of the homestead itself? Will the historic and cultural values on display here, evidence of the lives and lifestyles of backcountry settlers who dealt with the hardships created by the isolation and ruggedness of the Salmon River country be lost forever?

The owners of this property for the past quarter-century have stepped into the past and taken up the challenge of preserving it. A creaking, sometimes dysfunctional bureaucracy, charged with protecting the homestead has proven to be among its greatest threats.

Two hardy senior citizens, one a retired dancer and fine arts dean, the other a veteran of decades of connecting the public to wild rivers, move to a one-room cabin among the solitude of the River of No Return Canyon to battle the elements and bureaucracy to secure the preservation of this historic homestead.

Phyllis, my partner in life who shares my passion for this old homestead, is the author of our title, *Merciless Eden*, a tribute to the idyllic appearance, yet challenging reality of life in the Salmon River Canyon. She has contributed greatly to our research of the pioneers and writings about our life at the Ferry. Her journals and descriptions are essential to the story.

A timeline of events is included in the back of the book

The reader can find more about Campbell's Ferry online at mercilesseden.com and campbellsferry.org, including a larger catalog of images of the history and present day projects to preserve the homestead.

Doug Tims

Acknowledgments

Preparation of *Merciless Eden* would not have been possible without the helpful participation of many individuals:

The Coyle family – Tom Coyle, Frances' brother. Frances' nieces Becki Pollan Godfrey, Mary Key Eisenberg and Alice Brandt. Her nephews and great nephews Johnney Pollan, Doug Coyle, Steve Coyle and Glenn Coyle.
The Crowe family – Mary Crowe, Frank and Sandy Crowe, and Alison Crowe.
The Zaunmiller family – Stanley and Lynnette Zaunmiller, Paul Zaunmiller, and Bonnie Buccola.
The Warren Cook family – Warren's grandsons Dave Cook, Dan Cook and Sandy McRae
The Reho Wolfe family – Daughter Linda Karki and sons John and Dave Wolfe
Emma Sams Zaunmiller Family – Beck Sams, David Sams

Historians and river guides Cort Conley and Wayne Johnson. Historian and pilot Richard Holm, Jr. Historians Suzanne Julin and Dennis Baird, professor emeritus of history, University of Idaho.

Forest Service: Retired Slate Creek District Rangers Bob Abbott, Jack Carlson and Darcy Pederson. Retired Chief Jack Ward Thomas. Retired Forest Supervisor Steve Mealey; Payette National Forest: Larry Kingsbury, Gayle Dixon, Earl Dodds, Peter Preston. Nez Perce National Forest: Cindy Schacher, Mike Cook. Bitterroot National Forest: Mary H. Williams.

Friends of Frances – Alice Rickman, Zeke and Erlene West, Marlene West, Harold and Phyllis Thomas, Norm and Joyce Close, Omer Drury, Ray and Carol Arnold, Donna Henderson.
Also Carol Furey-Bryant, Jim Huntley, Gary Kraus, Lorrie Wilkes, June Miner, Mike Dorris, Bill Bernt, Norm and Kay Guth.

Acknowledgments

Campbell's Ferry Neighbors - Heinz Sippel and Barbara Eisenberg, Lynn and Mike Demerse, Sue Anderson and Greg Metz, Steve and Kathy Shotwell, Dick and Jodi Shotwell, Dave and Cornelia Shotwell, Jim and Gloria Mozingo, Jim and Jeanne Campbell, Mike McLain, Chip Dorroh.

Craig Vetter, review and editing; Dr. Robin Roberts, for help understanding Frances; Andrew McNab, Publisher, *Idaho Country Free Press*; Dave Hegeman, Oregon State Library; Peg Shroll, Idaho State Archives; Anne Schwartz, Salmon Public Library; Paul Franzmann, Fort Walla Walla Museum; Kathy Deinhardt Hill, author; Jim Bratt, Family Heritage Research Group; Paterson Smith, Antiquarian Bookseller and Publisher; Georgia Barker, Nez Perce County; Grace Knowles, Darby, MT; Mary Anne Davis and Tricia Canaday; Idaho State Historic Preservation Office; Falma Moye, for help with geology; Gaetha Pace, Idaho Heritage Trust; Keith Jones, AHJ Engineers; Craig Gehrke, The Wilderness Society; Vice Admiral Robert Monroe, retired; Bill Bernt, Grant Simonds, Al Bukowsky, Murray Feldman, David Stanish.

Campbell's Ferry Conservators - Brad and Patricia Janoush, Sam and Ann Langston, John and Beverly Janoush, Rex and Kelly Lyon, Lee Speakes, Leland Speakes, Joe and Peggy Denton, David and Ginger Head, Joe and LuAnn Corlett.

Linda Karki was a co-executor of Frances Wisner's estate. She preserved boxes of her records and shared them with Wayne Johnson, owner of Salmon River Rafting Company, who graciously shared them with the authors. They made an invaluable contribution to this story.

Images

Images

collection; Valentines Day 1941, Frances collection; Jim Moore and Frances Coyle 1941, Frances collection: Jim Moore circa 1930s, Nez Perce NF; Joe, Frances collection; Jim Moore note, Frances collection

Chapter 21 – Pfc Tom Coyle, Tom Coyle; Tom Coyle and Joe Zaunmiller, Frances collection; Rheo Wolfe and daughter, John Wolfe; Norman Wolfe, John Wolfe

Chapter 22 – Joe on Dan, Frances collection; Joe and Frances, Frances collection; Joe and Lloyd, Frances collection; Lloyd packing, Frances collection; Phyllis - Selway, author; Middle Fork, Eric Evans

Chapter 24 – Norm Guth pilots, Norm Guth

Chapter 25 – Porch and water and Great Majestic stove, Sam Meredith; Upstairs 1958, Johnney Pollan, Jr.; Texas watermelon, Johnney Pollan, Jr.; Becki and Joe, Johnney Pollan, Jr.; Harvesting hay, Frances collection; The ferry icebound, Frances collection

Chapter 26 – Tex Mott, Frances collection; Frances christening, Frances collection; Bridge dedication, Frances collection; The last ferry, Frances collection

Chapter 27 – John Crowe, Milling the lumber, Crowe Cabin under construction, Mary Crowe, Tractor photo, Crowe family collection

Chapter 28 – Vern, Joe and June, Christmas 1961, Frances collection; Vern, Frances collection; Verne and Frances, Frances collection; Zeke, Vern and Marlene, Frances collection

Chapter 30 – Gary Kraus, Frances collection; Kraus Cabin, author; Phyllis Thomas, Tom Close, Frances, Harold Thomas, Thomas family collection; The Blue Room, author

Chapter 31 – Frances 1980, Frances collection; Cougar, author; Black bear, author; Frances 1984, Frances collection; Tom Close and Frances, Harold Thomas; Frances and Gretchen, Glenn Oakley

Chapter 32 – Bob Abbott, Linda Karki; John and Mary Crowe, Linda Karki; Porch restoration, author; Foundation, author; Eric and Sam, Joe Denton; Tractor delivery, Salmon River Helicopters; Before and After, author; Clyde Smart and Doug Tims; author

Chapter 33 – Bell, author; Fire Pit, author

CONTENTS

Map Index

Map 1 – Campbell's Ferry in Idaho and Designated
Wilderness Areas

Map 2 – Gold Camps and Towns in Idaho

Map 3 – William Campbell's Trail from Dixie to
His Homestead

Map 4 – Trails: Lewis and Clark Route, South Nez
Perce Trail, Milner Trail

Map 5 – The First Route from North Idaho Gold
Camps and Towns to Thunder Mountain

Map 6 – Chamberlain Basin and the Three Blaze Trail

Map 7 – Roads into the Salmon River Canyon,
Campbell's Ferry, and other Homesteads
and Camps

All maps by Bill Reynolds, Lewiston, Idaho

Map 1
Campbell's Ferry and Idaho Wilderness Areas

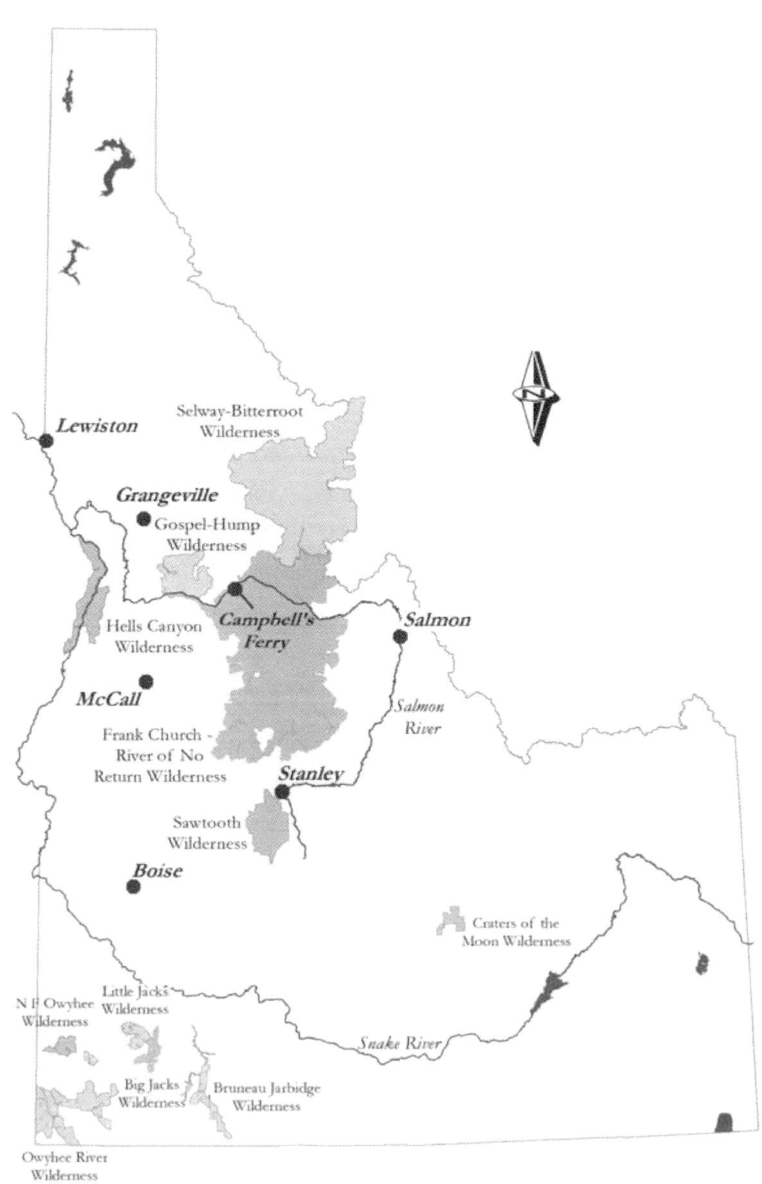

Map 2
Gold Camps and Towns

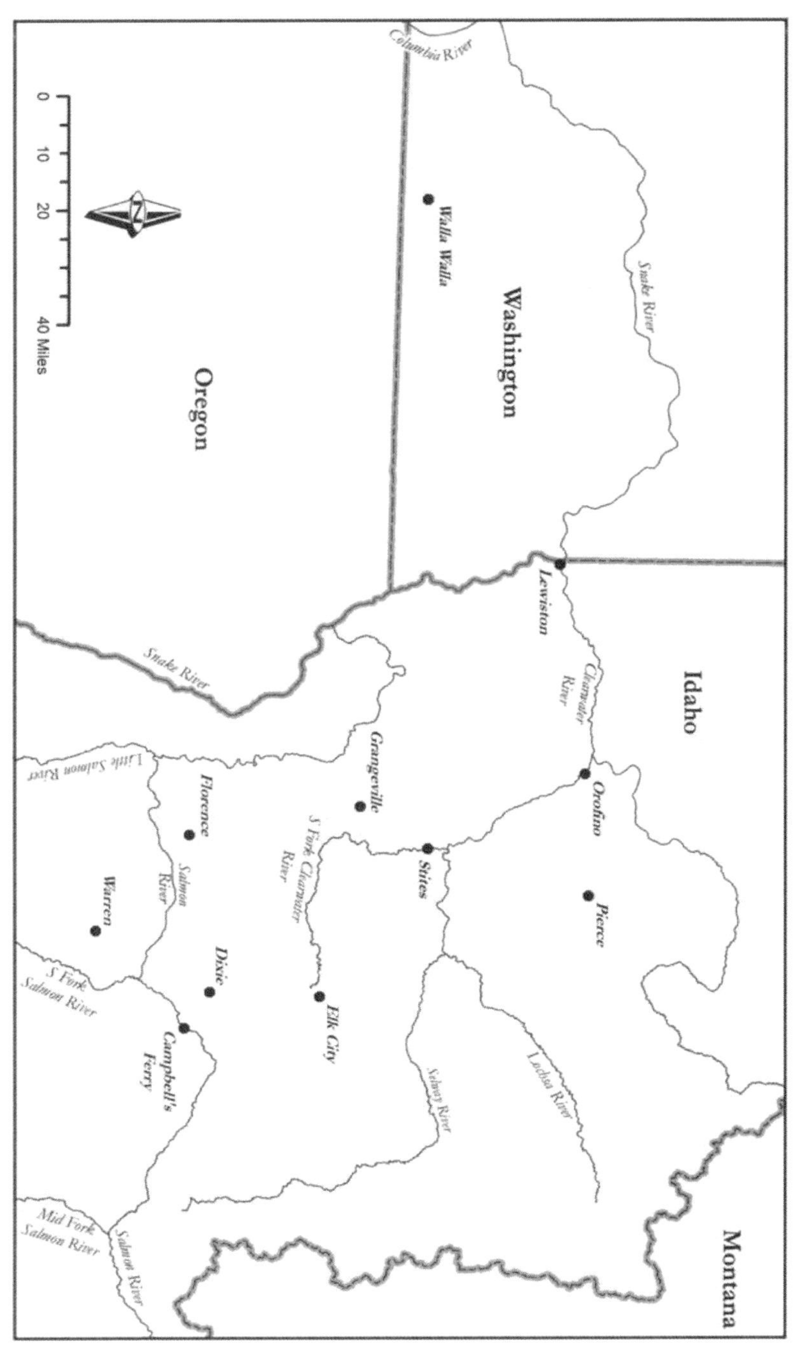

Map 3
Campbell's Trail: Dixie to Homestead

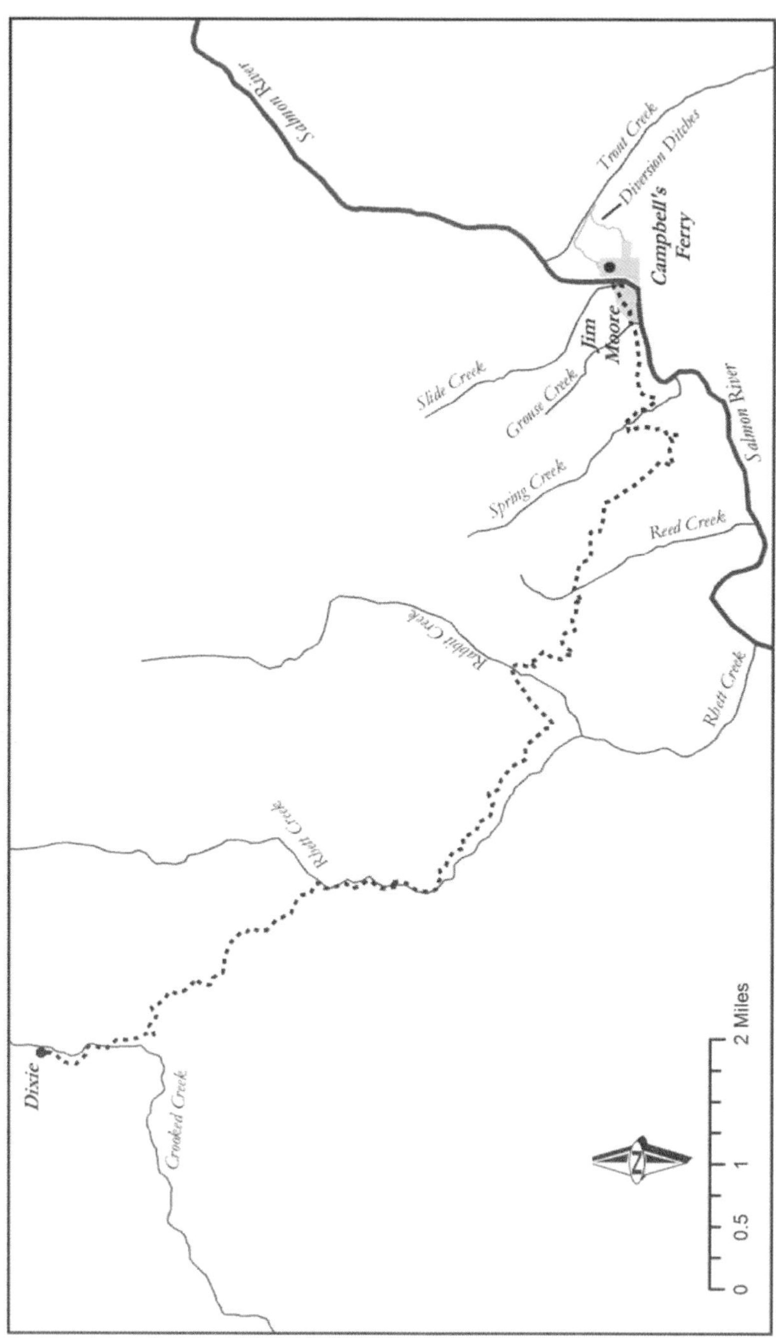

Map 4
Trails in Idaho

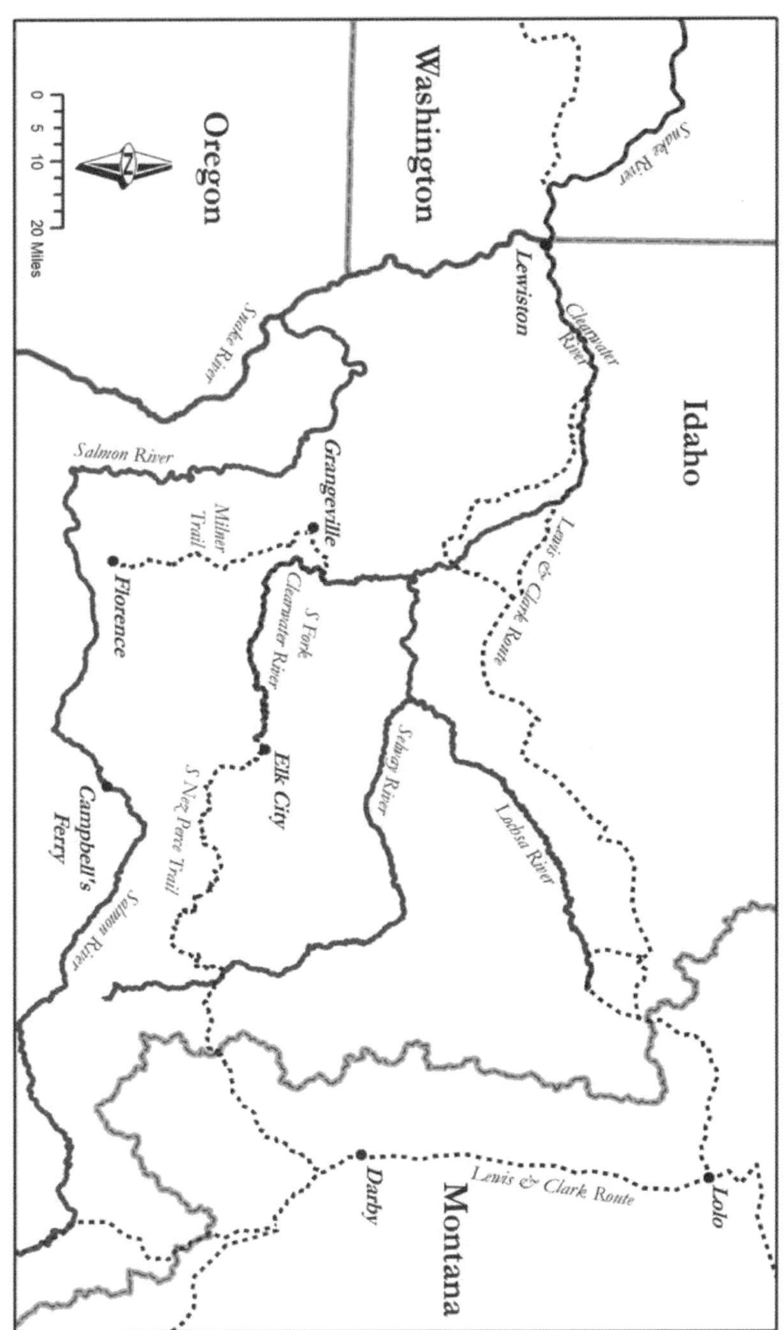

Map 5
First Northern Trail to Thunder Mountain

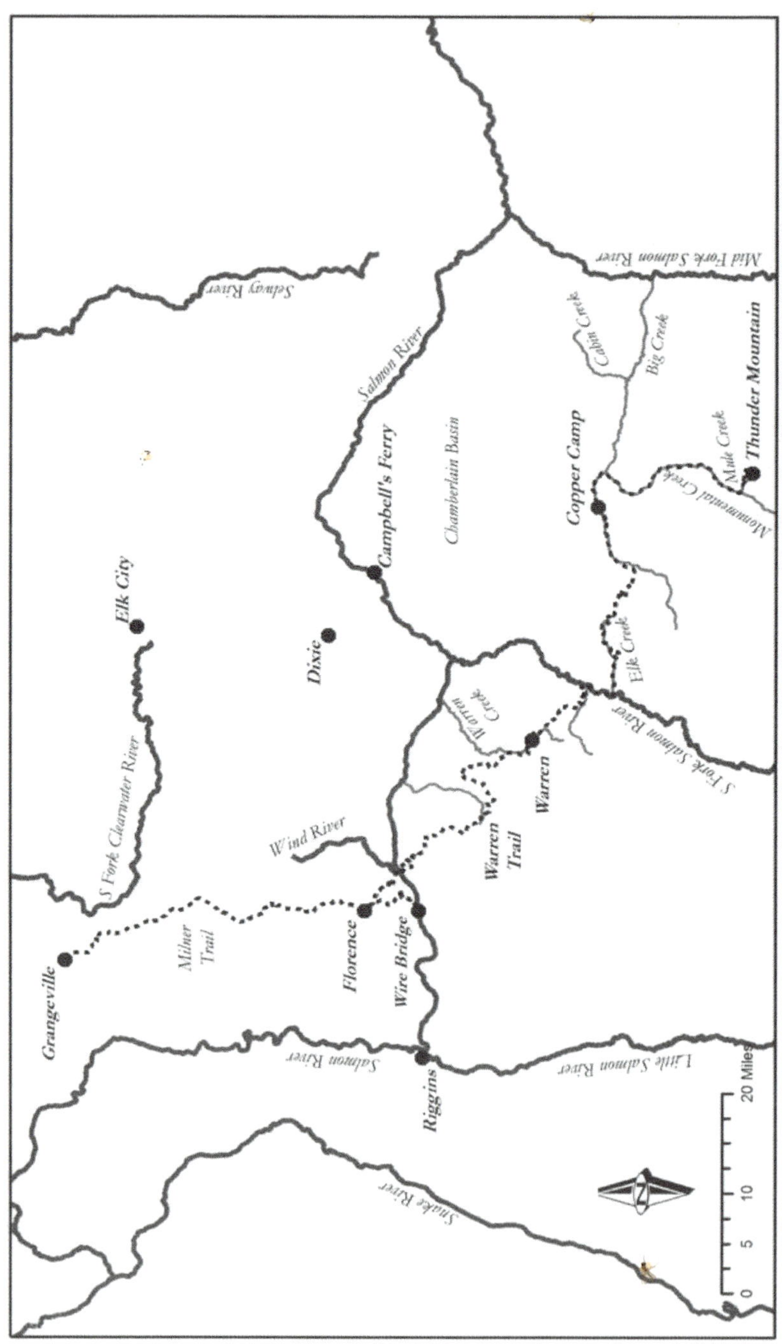

Map 6
Chamberlain Basin and the Three Blaze Trail

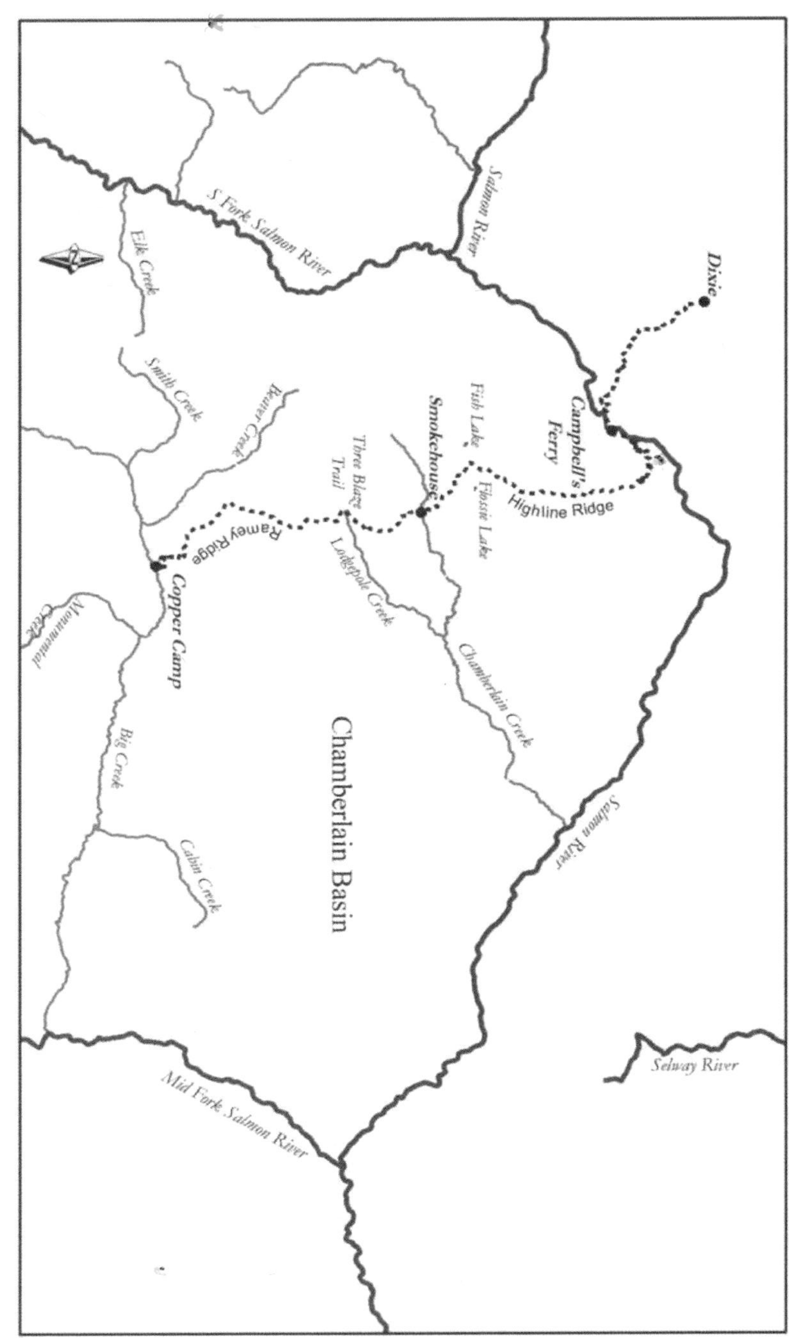

Map 7
Salmon River Canyon Homesteads, Camps and Roads

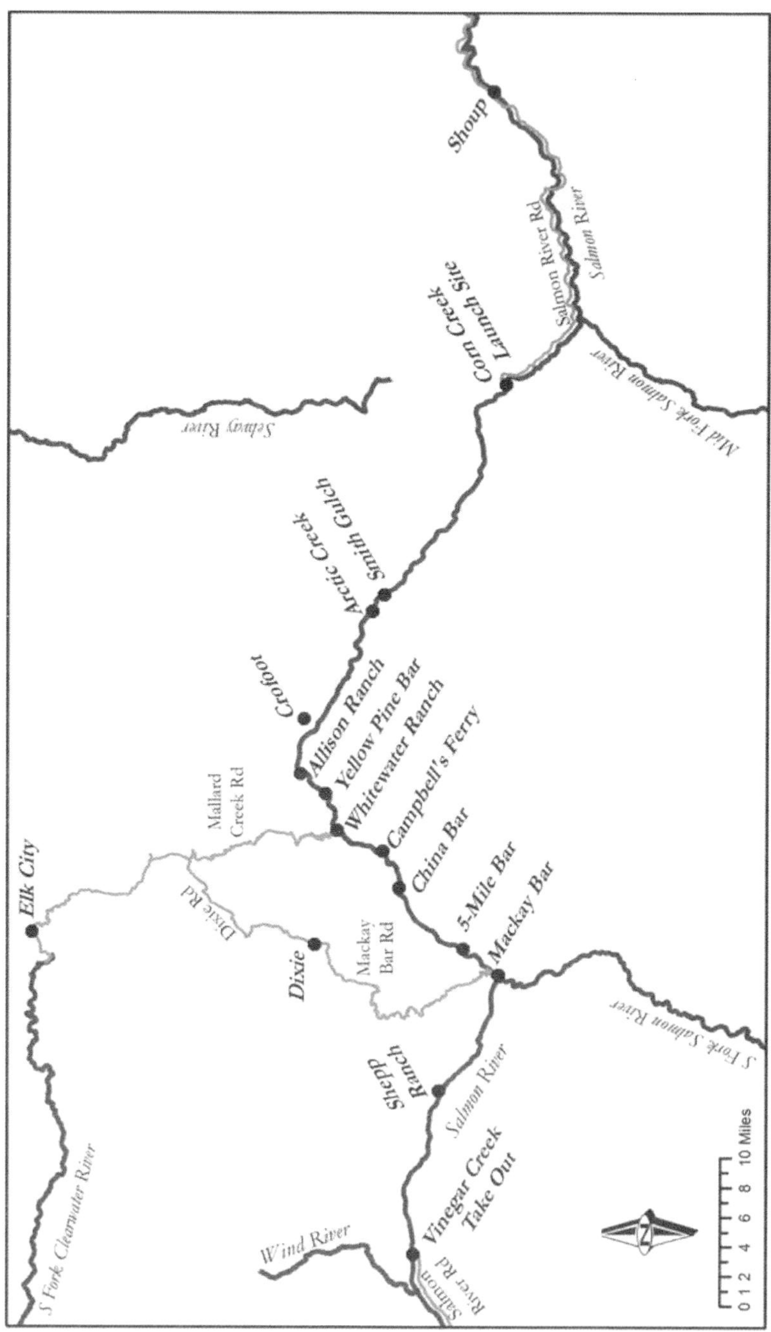

Chapter One

Alone

"Go confidently in the direction of your dreams.
Live the life you've imagined."
– Henry David Thoreau

I'm a licensed pilot. I flew my own plane for sixteen years, but I was glad not to be at the controls as we made the approach for this landing. It is stunningly beautiful. And scary: mountain peaks, canyons, strong, tricky winds, towering Ponderosa pines and Grand firs with a tight, short runway cut among them.

Ray Arnold, a veteran mountain pilot was in the left seat, I was in the right, Phyllis in the rear seat of the single engine Cessna 206. We were coming from Cascade, Idaho, had flown over 8,346 foot Chicken Peak and were looking down on two and a half million acres of the Frank Church – River of No Return Wilderness stretching for miles in all directions. It's a mountainscape that has always attracted tough men and women. A lonely Eden, and, for some, a garden of agony.

At about three thousand feet, Ray banked the plane steeply and finally put us down on the 800' runway that sits on a sloping meadow above the river crossing called Campbell's Ferry.

We thanked him, unloaded our twenty odd boxes of gear and watched as the little plane clawed into the air headed straight for the canyon wall across the river. The plane banked left to find the deep canyon opening downriver, banked again to follow the narrow cut, rounded the bend at Lemhi Point and was gone leaving only the sound of the Salmon River as it made its way past the historic homestead that would be our home.

Phyllis and I had heard the call of the river long ago. Now it would be the lonely voice of our only constant companion. We were alone. There was nothing around us but the rocks and trees and the vast River of No Return Wilderness. No neighbors. No roads. No phones. No electricity. Just a hundred year old homestead with a small one-room cabin: a relic of pioneer Idaho called Campbell's Ferry Ranch.

Its prior owners had resisted the modern world and left it primitive. A life here in 2006 would be the life of more than a century before.

We were exactly where we wanted to be, had planned to be. But now our enthusiasm for the solitude and serenity of the wilderness was shaken by reality. As we looked around, serious doubt hung in the air. Could we really do this?

Phyllis had first laid eyes on the place fifteen years before our arrival. She was on a raft trip down Idaho's Main Salmon River with friends from Salt Lake City. Phyllis had been running rivers since the late 1960s when her sister's romance with a river guide led to a family trip down the Salmon's Middle Fork.

Many years and river trips later she was teaching at the University of Utah and fell in with a group of boaters who invited her back to the Salmon, this time to the main stem of the great river.

Halfway down the wild roadless section of the river, the group camped on the north bank below another historic homestead, the Jim Moore Place. An after dinner hike took her to the pack bridge that crossed the river and up a trail to a high bench.

"The steepness of the trail kept us from seeing the homestead until we were actually upon it," Phyllis remembered. "As we topped the rise we found an open orchard of apple trees brightened by summer wildflowers blooming below their branches. On the edge of the bench above the river a large lush walnut tree partially obscured an old log cabin. Various weathered buildings and antique farm equipment spoke of those who had inhabited this isolated spot of Eden through the years. The beauty and nostalgia of the place were overwhelming. I felt as though everything went silent and time ceased."

Phyllis had entered the homestead of William Campbell. Gazing across the small orchard at the primitive buildings nestled in the deep woods she mused, "I wonder who is lucky enough to get to live in a place like this?"

Eight years later, in 2000, Phyllis was dating her own river guide, me, and visiting at my condo in Boise.

Emerging from the bathroom she asked, "What is that place pictured on the wall?"

"Campbell's Ferry Ranch," I said.

"Why do you have a picture of Campbell's Ferry?" she asked.

"Some friends and I own it."

In 2001 Phyllis answered her own question about who got to live there when we married and made plans for retirement that included spending half of every year caretaking the place.

Now we stood together at the edge of the little airstrip facing wilderness reality. It wasn't a question of immediate survival. We had gear and food enough to last a while. It seemed enough anyway. But how long is a while when the nearest grocery store is ninety-five miles away? When the first four of those miles is nothing but a narrow trail that leads to a road that is still blocked by last winter's snow.

What kind of muscle and wits was it going to take to dig in and begin to make a life in this remote patch of forest?

Our first job was to haul our pile of stuff downhill to a small structure: the sixteen by twenty-four foot shelter called the Crowe Cabin. John Crowe and friends had built it as a hunting cabin forty-six years before. It was all right for week long visits a few times a year, but whether we could make it into a full-time home was a question.

There was another, bigger cabin on the place, but it was even more primitive than the Crowe Cabin. Built in 1905, the Cook Cabin was built of hand-hewn logs and lacked even so much as a propane light. Or a sink. If you wanted to be polite you could have called it po-

Crowe Cabin – 2012

rous. The roof leaked. Gaps in the chinking provided daily access to an entomologist's dream of insect species.

Neither cabin had a toilet, which left us with a choice. From the Crowe Cabin you hiked up the hill to the outhouse, although *house* wasn't exactly the proper term for a fiberglass toilet seat perched on a platform with three-foot walls on two sides, no roof. If it was raining when you used it you got a shower in the bargain. The other choice was a bit more luxurious – a relative term.

Near the Cook Cabin was what we called the Blue Room (which made it sound like a nightclub which it resembled not at all). This was a real outhouse with four walls, a roof, one toilet seat and an exterior painted a garish blue. The color did nothing to discourage wasps and spiders from building their nests inside and just generally occupying the place as if it were a busy nightclub…for bugs.

We chose the smaller cabin because it kept the elements out better than older place. Built with lumber milled on the property it lacked the cracks the Cook Cabin had between the logs, and it had screened windows. There were propane lights and a simple water system. Simple meant a single marine battery under the cabin that powered a 12-volt pump mounted on the back wall.

The pump drew water from a plastic garbage can that served as a reservoir. The can was gravity fed through a pipe from an uphill irrigation ditch. It was better than hauling buckets of water from the ditch, but not much better.

When I tried to imagine the cleverness and the work it was going to take to make this our home, the only solace I took was thinking what must have faced the first pioneer to settle this beautiful, unforgiving place.

Chapter
Two

Settlement

"There is a history in all men's lives."
– William Shakespeare

Thirty-four-year-old William Campbell was the first to settle on this small patch of flat ground tucked into the relentless up and down of the Salmon River country. In 2006 Phyllis and I were rolling the clock back a century. In 1897 so was Campbell. He was trading the dawn of the twentieth century for the simpler life of one hundred years before when everything moved at the speed of a horse.

In the 1890s America was becoming an industrialized urban country powered by the labor of immigrants. A national railroad system was creating a unified continental economy, the largest and most productive in the world. Alexander Graham Bell had invented the telephone in 1876 and by 1900 America was using 800,000 of the devices. Thomas Edison invented the light bulb in 1879 and by 1898 there were 3,000 operating power stations in the country.[1]

Technology had begun its phenomenal surge and William Campbell decided to step out of its way. He needed no roads, no electricity, no motorized get-arounds. All he wanted was a flat place in a lonely jumble of mountains, streams and canyons. "Put some water on it and I can grow a garden," he must have thought. Game from the woods, fish from the river, a man can survive.

Campbell, the son of Scottish immigrant parents, was part of a flood tide of immigrants sweeping across America. One third of the 1890 population was either immigrant or the child of immigrants.[2] Born in October of 1863 in Scotland, Campbell arrived in America a six-year old. His school teacher parents, Sarah and William Sr. joined the gold rush west only to run up on the harsh reality that crushed most gold seekers – few got rich and the rest had to find other means of survival.

As the gold played out, the mining camps transitioned into communities that needed tradesmen, merchants and teachers to support those who remained. The Campbell family settled into a gold camp called Elk City, which was, and remains to this day, at the outer edge of Clearwater River country, part of what was to become Idaho Territory. Young William would spend the rest of his life in an area rich in gold mining history and rife with constant outbreaks of gold fever.

The first gold strike in Idaho had been in a part of the Clearwater River valley fifty miles north of Elk City (Map 2). Elias Pierce, an Irishman, had come to America in 1839. He volunteered to fight in the Mexican War and after that, like many veterans, responded to the lure of gold, first to California then to the Fraser River in British Columbia.[3]

Contrary to the general flow of settlement east to west in America, the north central part of Idaho was settled west to east. Eastern access to the area was difficult across the rugged Salmon River terrain and the Bitterroot Mountains. The initial flow of settlers to Idaho came from the Pacific Coast via steamboats up the Columbia River. Prospectors traveled upstream to the Columbia's Snake, Clearwater

1 George D. Moss, *The Rise of Modern America*, (Peason Publishing, 1995), p. 4
2 Moss, p. 2
3 Leonard J. Arrington, *History of Idaho*, (Moscow, ID: University of Idaho Press) pp. 183–86

and Salmon River tributaries in what was then Washington Territory.

A leasing steamer on the route was the *Idaho*, a name that had been proposed for Colorado Territory in 1859. So many of the miners rushing to Clearwater country had sailed on the *Idaho* that people began to refer to them as Idahoans, a name that proved to be prophetic.[4] In 1863, President Abraham Lincoln signed the Organic Act creating Idaho Territory, lands that included what are now Idaho, Montana and Wyoming.

In the fall of 1860 Elias Pierce and a few fellow California and Fraser River prospector veterans decided to check out rumors of color in the Clearwater River country. The area had been granted to the Nez Perce Indians in an 1855 treaty, a fact the prospectors ignored on their way to striking it rich. Word of their success drew many more miners than could make it in one camp. The overflow spread out finding more gold in what became Elk City on the South Fork of the Clearwater, then on to other camps named Florence and Warren in the Salmon River watershed.

The gold rush in those days resonated with faint echoes of the guns at Fort Sumter. Most of the country was engaged in the Civil War. Out West, sympathies were shown in the names of gold camps. Main Street often divided Yankee from Rebel sympathizers. Idaho had camps named Leesville, Grantsburg, Atlanta and Sesech. Dixie Gulch was the mining area that became the closest settlement to the homestead that would later become Campbell's Ferry.[5]

There is no record of William Campbell's early days in Elk City and Dixie. The search is confused by the common nature of his name. There were other William H. Campbells recorded in the 1900 census in nearby Grangeville and Florence. Our William is listed in Dixie Precinct in the same census. From a few extant descriptive passages written about him and from what we know about his lifestyle we might conjure up an image of him.

Campbell's body would have been honed to a lean muscular frame and his skin browned from a life dedicated to physical labor and outdoor living. He was described as being not too tall and very well liked, giving us insight into a man who must have had a strong

---

4 Arrington, p. 189

5 Marian S. Sweeney, *Gold at Dixie Gulch*, (Kamiah, ID: Clearwater Valley Publishing, 1982), pp. 1–3

work ethic, honest character, and a pleasant disposition. To create a homestead and devise a living in this wild place he would have been blessed with self-confidence, myriad physical skills and a lively spirit of adventure.

Young men growing up in this country had only to look around to see that success would come with the acquisition of basic skills. Because everything moved on your back or via packstrings of horses and mules you had to be a good wrangler. To move your packstring through this country required a passable trail. At first, game and Indian routes sufficed, but as the need to move equipment and supplies arose with each new mining camp, the skill to build improved trails became vital.

For shelter you needed logging, milling and carpentry skills. One needed hunting skills, too, for the meat to feed one's self and extra to sell to hungry miners. Most mines were in the high country where the growing season was short or non-existent. Gardening skills could lead to a ready source of income if one could find a place to put a garden.

****

In 1897 it was probably hunting and the search for tillable ground in the warmer environs of the Salmon River Canyon that first led William Campbell and others to build a trail down to the river. Dixie Gulch sat at 5,600' above sea level. The Salmon River flowed through a deep canyon seven miles to the south, some 3,300' lower than Dixie. Nights in the high mountain mining camps were rarely frost-free in contrast to a four-month growing season in the river canyon below.

Creating the first trail to the river must have been an enormous task in this unforgiving terrain. The center of present day Idaho is part of what geologists call the Idaho Batholith. Millions of years ago as the Pacific plate subducted under the continental plate a rising mass of magna, known as a pluton, broke through the continental plate. The hard granite substrate it formed is a primary reason why all human efforts since then to build roads and railroads through the area have been thwarted.

Though often capped by thick stands of pine and fir, what

passed for soil here is a layer of mostly decomposed granite extending just a few inches above the bedrock.

Dixie Gulch is just that, a gulch cut by Crooked Creek into the high plateau between the Clearwater and Salmon River watersheds. To traverse the seven miles to the river, Campbell would have to wind through and over a maze of creeks, mountains and precipitous slopes on a thirteen-mile route. Heading south from the Dixie Gulch gold camp he followed an existing trail over a 200-foot rise past the North Star and Dillinger Mines 2.5 miles into North Star Meadows, the headwaters of Rhett Creek.

Campbell built the first four miles of trail down Rhett Creek south and east as it drops 900' (Map 3). The slopes on either side are steep, running right to the edge of the stream. Periodic floods and the normal spring runoff have gouged out an irregular streambed choked by small to truck size boulders. Strewn among the boulders are the remnants of trees ripped from surrounding slopes or carried down from upstream.

In most places the only route for a trail is on the side slope. Location on the slope varied from a few to a hundred feet off the creek. Precise location depended upon the makeup of the side slope. Decomposed granite or broken rocks could be dug out. When Campbell came to a solid rock face he had to go up or down slope to make a passable route.

Campbell approached this task with the tools of the day – a pick, shovel, and a pry bar. He used them to cut a bench out of the slope, a bed for the trail. The greater the angle of the side slope, the deeper and wider the bench had to be. A man or a single horse with no packs can move along a trail not much wider than one animal.

To pack the supplies, tools and materials that would accompany future travelers the base, or tread, of the trail had to be wide. Travelers would have packs hanging off both sides of their animals and would need room to pass the uphill slope, trees, and protruding boulders.

Four miles down Rhett Creek the trail turns up Rabbit Creek coming in from the north. After a quarter mile it fords Rabbit Creek and switchbacks up to a ridge at the base of Rabbit Point. Switchbacks are a "Z" pattern where a trail doubles back on itself. Where a slope is too steep to go straight up, a characteristic of many slopes in the

Salmon River country, this technique allows you to spread large gains in elevation over a longer distance, maintaining a grade passable by humans and heavily loaded stock. On the climb up to Rabbit Point Campbell was working to gain 1,000' in just under a mile.

At the ridge top, he was back at the same elevation as Dixie – 5,600'. One mile below him and a three thousand three hundred foot drop in elevation ran the Salmon River. To get to the river Campbell had to traverse and switchback the steepest part of what is known as the Salmon River Breaks, where the relatively gentler slopes of the high country plunge over a short distance to the river.

The price of a mistake here would be high. Instead of a short slide to a creek bottom, a misstep here could end in a more than half-mile fall to the big river. Your loss could be a pack animal and its load, or your life, as a later resident of Campbell's Ferry would discover. The rope between each mule in the string was finished with a short thin line to prevent the slip of a single animal from taking down the entire string of animals. Packers call the short line a pigtail, designed strong enough to withstand the occasional tug as the string moves down the trail, but weak enough to break in a fall.

Campbell first took the trail down the canyon wall across the head of Reed Creek, a narrow rivulet that runs only in the spring during snow melt or after a rain. As he crossed the divide between Reed and Spring Creek, he followed a precipitous narrow ridge down a series of short switchbacks. Near the bottom he turned upstream, hugging the canyon wall just a few hundred feet above the river.

As he rounded a promontory jutting into the canyon between Spring and Grouse Creeks his destination came into view. Below him just above river level was a rare flat stretch of ground well situated for a homestead. Across the river, a slightly higher terrace of flat ground looked promising as well. Which would meet his needs?

Homesteaders seeking a place to settle looked for a few basic necessities: sun, water, tillable ground, and timber to build a shelter. Sun is a concern here because the Salmon River has cut a canyon that rivals the Grand Canyon in Arizona and Hells Canyon in Idaho in their depth between the river and surrounding mountains.

This depth, plus its location just north of the forty-fifth parallel (halfway between the equator and North Pole) often leaves the river bottom cast in the shadows of the surrounding canyon walls.

Flat terrain next to the river on the north bank catches more light as the sun arches across the southern sky. Flats on the south side are nestled at the foot of the south canyon wall and are shielded more due to the restricted angle of exposure to the southern sky.

The Salmon River generally runs east to west as it cuts across the state. But it is not a straight line. Between the two flats Campbell must have noticed that here the river was running almost due south. Both flats shared an equal opening to the south. Either one would have enough sun to support a garden and hay crop.

The ground of both is relatively flat. These flat terrac-

Campbell's first view of the homestead

es perched above the river were left here by conditions that are hard to imagine today. What William saw and we see today, is not the way it has always been. Over the past two million years, this area has seen multiple glacial and interglacial periods. The river system is dynamic and constantly changing. At times the climate has been much wetter, with widely varying flows in the river.

The material, rocks, sand and soil that make up the terraces were placed here in what is known as a fluvial process. In a gradual and sometimes dramatic manner water erodes the landscape upstream, collects the sediment and moves it to locations downstream where changes in flow cause the material to be deposited.

Long ago the river level was higher, before the natural process had cut the canyon to its present depth. When the river was at the level of these terraces, perhaps 150,000 – 200,000 years ago, there were multiple forces that influenced the amount of sediment brought to this site.

In an annual cycle the river peaks when the snow in the surrounding mountains melts each spring. The amount of snow varies with weather and climatic conditions. The amount of water flowing down river at the peak of the melt is also affected by the rate of melt. A high snowpack with high water content that melts quickly due to a temperature spike brings spring floods. The volume can be augmented if the temperature spike is accompanied by warm rain on snow hastening the rate of melt and adding more volume from the rain.

There were also times when the amount of sediment was influenced by landslides. The canyon walls along the river and its tributaries are steep. The walls rest in a semi-stable sloped state, their angle of repose. The steepness of the angle is determined by composition and substructure. Over time the substructure is influenced by water seeping in with cycles of freezing and melting, causing cracks and faults in the mass. Under the right conditions, such as rapid snow melt or heavy rains adding water and weight to the mass, the load on the mass changes, exceeding the angle of repose with a resulting landslide. These conditions were more likely during the wetter glacial periods of the past.

The slide can take the form of slabs, slumps, flows or torrents of moving material that bring a mass into the streambed below. Often the mass is absorbed by the normal flow rate of the river, but in some conditions it has enough mass to fill the entire streambed and dam the river or a tributary. The dam begins backing up water, filling a temporary lake. As the lake increases in size, the mass of water steadily increases the weight and force on the dam. Finally, the dam structure is breached, sending a sediment and debris filled wall of water downstream.

Where the riverbed is steeper, the flow of water accelerates, allowing more material to be carried. As the gradient decreases, or inside bends in the river, the flow slows allowing the water to drop some of its load of sediment and debris. Geologic processes similar to these are what created the terraces that William Campbell surveyed in 1897 as he tried to determine where he would make his home in the canyon.

Both sides of the river had adequate sun, tillable ground and plentiful supplies of timber for building shelter. The determining factor in his choice would be water.

The north terraces, later to be known as the Jim Moore Place, is 100' above the Salmon River. Bringing water up from the river was not feasible. But there are small creeks up and downstream of the flat. Grouse Creek on the downstream end has a small flow that begins with a spring just below the crest of the canyon wall above. The flow was insufficient to meet Campbell's hay and garden raising needs.

Slide Creek on the upstream end has a similar source but more flow due to a slightly larger watershed. But Slide Creek would require a diversion that would have to traverse a large scree slope that was not suitable to holding a ditch that could easily carry water.

The advantage Campbell found near the slightly higher terrace on the south bank was a robust year round stream nearby. Trout Creek begins high in the wilderness, thousands of feet up and miles into the backcountry. The watershed is expansive and holds enough snow in winter and ground water the rest of the year to dump a significant flow into the Salmon River throughout the year.

Getting water from Trout Creek to the south bank terrace is not a straight line, but the slopes would hold a ditch. It meant going a mile up the creek and following the contour of the sloping canyon walls, twisting along in a gradual down slope to the eventual location of Campbell's cabin and garden. Looking at this feat of primitive engineering today, one cannot help but marvel at the labor it took to establish the new water course.

The ditch is a constant struggle for us to maintain today, but to those who spent all their life scratching around in the earth for gold, digging shafts and hauling oar, it was just another task to be completed in the never ending struggle to fashion a life in the wilds of Idaho. Miner Joseph Boyd described a similar effort near Orofino, Idaho:

> I brought down a ditch of three miles in the fall of 1865… and built a dam to catch and divert the water. I surveyed the ditch with a triangle and plumb bob, the whole three miles being staked in a day…. In five weeks the three of us dug three miles of ditch, carrying 100 miners inches of water. We were out before sunrise, and started work by starlight, and worked until after sunset and went home by starlight. We worked all day, every day, rain or shine, and were often wet to the skin ten minutes after we had left our camp, and kept going in wet clothing all day. One partner went ahead with a broad ax or mattock cutting the brush, kinnikinnick, and sod and turning it

over down hill; the next partner followed taking a spadeful or two out, and I followed finishing up the ditch. I finished 105 rods [1,732'] of ditch in one day. I would get up at 5:00 A.M. and …..would walk three miles to the head of our ditch and turn the water into the ditch from the impounding dam which had collected it during the night, then walk back three miles for breakfast at 7:00 A.M.

At the end of the day I got dinner, and Ollie again got supper while I went to the head of the ditch and turned the water off again. Every Saturday afternoon we cleaned up our sluice boxes and Sundays we sort of rested up.[6]

Campbell started an extensive irrigation system with his original diversion from Trout Creek. Later pioneers worked to maintain and expand the ditches to water the meadows and supply the cabins. Now it was my turn.

6 William S. Lewis, "Reminiscences of Joseph Boyd," *Washington Historical Quarterly*, Vol 15, No 4, (University of Washington Press, 1924), p. 256

Chapter Three

To the River

"Eventually all things merge into one and a river runs through it.
The river is cut by the world's great flood and runs over rocks from
the basement of time. On some of the rocks are timeless raindrops.
Under the rocks are the words and some of the words are theirs.
I am haunted by waters."
A River Runs Through It
– Norman Maclean

Water. It was essential to Campbell first settling here. As the
first on the property each spring we faced the same need. Phyllis and
I gathered an armload of gear from the pile on the airstrip and headed
down to the Crowe Cabin. A diversion from Campbell's original ditch
flowed just uphill of both cabins. Or had flowed.

As was often the case, some time during the past winter the
flow had ceased. It could be a breach in the ditch, or a tree fall, or
maybe it was just clogged from falling leaves or pine needles. There
was only one way to find out.

After several trips with a wheelbarrow to the airstrip and back to move supplies, I pulled on my rubber boots, grabbed a shovel from the barn, and began to work my way along the ditch. Phyllis offered to come along, but we settled on her focusing on nest building in the cabin. I would sharpen my pioneer skills in ditch mucking.

Mucking is a term that fits the task. All around us was up. Up the creek. Up the mountain. Water moving downhill brings stuff with it: muck. You can hardly call it mud. There is not much mud around here. At least not much by Mississippi standards.

I grew up in a place called the Mississippi Delta. There is muck on a grand scale. My hometown of Cleveland was perched on the historic delta of the Mississippi River, three hundred miles north of today's outlet to the Gulf of Mexico. Farmers boast of topsoil forty feet deep. You could lose a pickup truck in a mud hole there.

In Idaho's Salmon River Canyon, what little actual soil exists has a tendency to be deposited anywhere the water slows down enough to drop the material it is carrying. At Campbell's Ferry Ranch, that means where the ditches from Trout Creek come onto the flat and deliver water to the cabins. The soil is mostly decomposed granite. Mixed with this grit is the duff fallen from trees: a mix of evergreens, mostly pine and fir, and the occasional deciduous tree. When deposited in the bottom of a ditch under water for a year the mix becomes muck.

Cleaning ditches is not all bad. Like every small boy who ever played in a creek, I find it fun. And satisfying.

Find the problem.

Clear it out.

Get the water flowing again.

I had come to Campbell's Ferry from a world where successes were longer term, less defined, not as easy to come by. I grew up an entrepreneur, a risk taker trying to sort through opportunities, building business plans and organizing employees to work together to make a living. Sometimes it worked and sometimes it did not. The struggles in between are the things that wake you in the middle of the night… worrying.

Here it is just a simple ditch, a simple tool, my shovel and a simple solution. Luckily, I find this time the flow is blocked by a single mass of branches that have collected pine needles into a perfect dam. The obstruction is a few hundred yards from the cabin: about halfway to Trout Creek near where the ditch flows under the main trail.

I clear the dam and rejoice as I watch the elixir of life flowing again toward our new home. As I hike back to the cabin I muse that what just occurred is what attracts me to life here in the wilds of Idaho.

****

The steps that brought me to Idaho began in the hardwood bottomlands that bordered the big Muddy – the Mississippi River. My father, Lowry, was an entrepreneur in a propane gas business serving the farms and small communities along the river. The son of a rural mail carrier, first in the Tims family to gain a college degree, my father exuded a knowing self-confidence. His stocky, slightly hefty build, pale blue eyes and responsible bearing belied an adventurous spirit willing to take risks in his business and his travels.

Lowry's norm was a daily routine of long hours away from home struggling to build a business from scratch. Even the brief times at home he was quiet, withdrawn into a focus on thoughts and subjects beyond the understanding of four young sons.

As an adolescent I watched my father's comings and goings. His behavior mystified me. He would show up at home in his usual casual business attire, change quickly into an odd, camouflaged look and disappear for days at a time. Returning home, his reserved nature was softened to a more open willingness to share stories of another world. He even smelled different.

What had happened? When I turned eight, he began to take me with him on journeys that solved the mystery and changed my life.

For fifty miles in every direction around my home in Cleveland, the terrain was flat. Unbelievably flat. If you left town driving west, the only hint of relief was a man-made structure, the levee. This long mound of dirt fifty feet high stretches on both sides of the river from Memphis to New Orleans. We lived on the protected side of the levee – protected from the spring floods when the river would top its banks and attempt to spread across a historic flood plain.

On the unprotected side, next to the river itself, was a hardwood timber bottomland rich in wildlife – deer, turkey, squirrels, wild hogs, ducks. The area was a magnet to hunters in the community who were fortunate enough to belong to hunting clubs that had purchased hunting rights to land along the river. Lowry belonged to a unique club: special due to its remote location and the extra effort involved in getting there. You couldn't just drive to the Ozark Hunting Club. You had to use the river.

Over time, the Mississippi River has meandered across the local landscape, creating the delta and leaving behind old river channels. The old channels were prime habitat for fish and other wildlife, and one, Lake Whittington, would be our passage to another world.

Leaving Cleveland, my father, two friends and I drove twenty miles west, topped the levee and descended to an old barge tied to the bank of the lake. The barge had been converted into a club and restaurant. Surrounding the barge were several floating docks. Attached to one was a flat-bottomed boat named the *Homewrecker*, a name representing the periodic separations it caused between men on their hunting trips and the wives left at home.

After loading a week's supply of groceries, guns and duffel Lowry steered the *Homewrecker* into the lake, following the sweeping arc it made to the west. The cold November air stung my cheeks as I watched the boat break the smooth surface of dark water. Our horizon was an endless wall of willows lining the banks into the distance.

A small crack in the wall of willows appeared at the end of the lake, growing to the width of two boats as we slowed and eased into a channel blocked by floating debris. Wayne Garrett, my father's right hand man, climbed onto the front with a pole and pushed the floating logs aside, gaining our passage into the swirling waters of a world I had known previously only through Tom Sawyer and Huck Finn.

The Mississippi River pulls water from almost half of the nation and measures its flow here in million cubic feet per second. Stretching at times to a mile in width, the waters from its myriad tributaries gather here to shape the landscape. At times clawing, tearing down the banks, at times building by depositing sand and soil, the river forms an evolving path for those who have used it as a route of travel for centuries.

Our small craft, the *Homewrecker*, shared the river with monsters of commerce – the massive towboats pushing grain, fuel and other goods up and down the river. Our greatest challenge, beyond the snags and currents of the river, were the tall wave trains kicked up by the barges.

It was not the first time Lowry had faced this challenge, and an hour later we pulled into a slough of still water behind a large sandbar on the Arkansas side of the river. We tied the boat to the shoreline adjoining a ramp that became a path to a small opening leading into thick woods.

After loading our supplies into Jeeps, we navigated a gauntlet of mud holes disguised as roads. Several miles later the camp appeared. Nestled among the trees, a group of small cabins were surrounded by a central lodge. The camp was enveloped by a large expanse of wooded land that rested inside the last sweeping loop the Arkansas River made before it entered the Mississippi.

The main clubhouse was elevated on stilts to allow the annual spring floods to come and go without destroying its contents. Here we gathered with friends from across the Delta. Inside, above a large round table hung a sign *Old Jack Drank a Keg, Fell Out of Bed and Broke His Leg*. Across the room a nude Marilyn Monroe calendar caught my wide-eyed gaze.

For hours I observed the men as they cooked, drank and swapped stories of past hunting adventures. It was the perfect setting where an eight-year-old could get lessons in male adult hunting rituals. And as the hours lengthened into the night, the lessons became less appropriate. Soon after dinner with a young son in tow, Lowry took his leave of the festivities, forgoing the poker game that often lasted until near dawn.

We retreated to our own small cabin and bedded down in anticipation of an early morning start to the first deer hunt of the season. Well before daylight we are back in the Jeep bouncing down rutted, muddy roads to hunt in an area my father had negotiated with his friends last night.

Cautioned to maintain quiet, I eased into the woods stretching my young legs in an attempt to place each foot exactly where my father's had just been. We settled in next to a tree and waited. Waited as the cold of a November morning soaked through the layers of insulated clothing. Waited until the quiet of the morning was broken by the distant howl of hounds.

Hours before the hounds had been released to begin their day-long run through thick woods. The hounds catch a scent, then track and follow the deer. By causing the deer to move, the hounds gave the hunter a greater chance of seeing game in the thick woods.

"They are coming around the end of Fish Tail Lake.
Crossing Washing Machine Ridge.
They must be near Whiskey Chute," my father said.
"What map is he reading?" I wondered.
"How could he possibly know where they are just by the sound of a hound's bark?"

I didn't dare ask. Just listened and absorbed the mysteries of the woods.

As the sound grows louder, the creeping chill is displaced by warmth from an increased heartbeat.

"Quiet now," he whispered.
"Be still when we see the deer.
The does will come first, but often, behind or to the side will be a buck."

True to his word the deer appear in the dim light filtering through the trees. A group of six run, stop, look back to the sound of the hounds, then move past some thirty yards in the distance.

A glint of white appears in a thicket to our left. Then a slight motion and we can see a cloud of breath in the cold November air. A buck slips through the undergrowth. In and out, a glimpse, then gone, then reappears. Lowry slowly raises his rifle, hoping the scope will provide a better view of the buck. But the brush is too thick.

The deer never shows that he has detected our presence. He slips through, manages to avoid giving us a clear shot, and then is gone.

Lowry
At the Ozark Hunting Club
1956

"That is how it works, sometimes. We will have another chance. Let's go to the river bank and see what's happening there," my father said.

I followed.

Stretching to match his footsteps.

Through the woods.

To the river.

To the River

Chapter Four

Thunder Mountain

"O accursed hunger of gold,
to what dost thou not compel human hearts!"
– Virgil

In 1897 William Campbell had come to the Salmon River to farm, to raise crops for his own use and provide enough to sell to miners in Dixie and Elk City. His ultimate goal was to make the property his home and gain ownership of it through the Homestead Act of 1862.

The Homestead Act encouraged men in the West to find cultivatable land and develop it. In Idaho, a succession of mining strikes in the cold high country had prompted many to seek out small plots to raise crops in the warmer low elevations of the river canyons.

It was challenging economic times. In 1890 forces beyond the state's control had begun to bring an end to the mining prosperity that had bolstered Idaho's development for thirty years. Idaho had been granted statehood that year and faced a depression greater than any experienced since the nation's founding. The decline had started with a bank failure in London.

A drain on U.S. gold reserves was followed by a financial panic in 1893. In March of that year the Philadelphia and Reading Railroad Company and National Cordage Company went bankrupt setting off the greatest selling spree in the history of the New York Stock Exchange. The market collapsed, banks called in their loans, credit dried up and a cascade of failed banks and bankrupt businesses swept the nation.[1]

The state was hit hard. In the northern Idaho town of Moscow, the largest mercantile in the state, owned by Governor William J. Mc-Connell, failed in 1893. Bunker Hill and Sullivan, the state's largest silver-lead producer closed, as did mines in Custer County. The state's leading newspaper, Boise's *Idaho Daily Statesman,* cut its pages in half.

Hundreds of unemployed men roamed the streets of the capital city. Wheat prices fell from $.82 per bushel in 1892 to $.36 in the fall of 1893. Some Idahoans joined the *industrial armies* of unemployed, destitute men who hopped trains and marched on Washington, D.C., demanding the federal government act to improve conditions.

The marches failed to get results, but by 1897 forces beyond Idaho's borders once again began to restore its economy. America's wheat prices rose as the wheat crop in India failed. Gold was discovered in the Klondike, and new methods of processing brought more efficient production of gold.

A war with Spain over Cuba and the Philippines gave more than a quarter million men, including hundreds from Idaho, lodging, three meals a day and a purpose.

Distant events helped the larger national and Idaho economy, but it was a local discovery that would change William Campbell's life and put his homestead on the map.

Among the thousands of men displaced during the depression were Ben and Lu Caswell, two brothers from Minnesota who tried their hand at prospecting in Colorado and Nevada before pushing into

---

1 Leonard J. Arrington, *History of Idaho*, (Moscow, ID: University of Idaho Press, 1994), pp. 449–50

Idaho in 1889.[2] Their route took them through the eastern portion of the state, ending up at a gold strike in Gibbonsville. Unable to find any unclaimed ground, the brothers likely followed the old Lewis and Clark route into the Bitterroot Valley where they took the South Nez Perce Indian trail, now known as the Magruder Corridor, to Red River and Elk City (Map 4).

Near Red River the brothers were driven into the river with all their belongings as a forest fire jumping a mile or more from ridge to ridge roared overhead. After visiting Grangeville, they turned south along the old Milner Trail, through Florence to where the Wire Bridge crossed the Salmon River. The men paid $.50 cents per animal for the crossing, leading them one at a time across the rickety structure.

Lu recorded in his diary, "The pack train was plenty spooky..... [The bridge] swung so hard it threw the horses from one side to the other but they couldn't get out because the guard rail was high enough. By leading each one over, this way they couldn't rear up."[3]

The fragile state of this bridge would later play a role in William Campbell's future.

The Caswells followed news of a strike near Yellow Pine, Idaho, along the East Fork of the South Fork of the Salmon River.

Lu noted, "While there we examined the country all around but proved to our satisfaction there wasn't anything to amount to anything."

They moved on to Big Bar on the Snake River near the southern end of the Seven Devils Mountains, where they filed a homestead claim and settled for the next several years.

In 1894 the brothers decided to prospect in the Big Creek area where mining activity was underway around the Smith Creek and Beaver Creek tributaries. They intended to work up Big Creek, but got lost and ended up downstream at Copper Camp. After spending a couple of days with Pringle Smith, Lu and Ben went farther down Big Creek and turned up Monumental Creek (Map 5).

As the two moved upstream they found increasing color in their pans, but it played out after they passed a creek coming in from the east. Heading up the tributary Ben noticed a jumble of rocks that

2 G. Wayne Minshall, *Wilderness Brothers*, (Inkom, ID: Steamside Scribe Press, 2012), pp. 21–25
3 Minshall, p. 26

The Caswell brothers, Ben, Lu and Dan in their cabin
at Mule Creek near the Thunder Mountain mine.

resembled an upturned mule, so he named the stream Mule Creek. Frequent storms that lashed the peaks and impeded their work prompted the men to name their location Thunder Mountain.

As the men approached the head of Mule Creek they found several promising sites – quartz outcroppings and places that could be worked as placer claims. Placer operations require water to separate gold from surrounding loose rock and soil. But it was August, the high snow was gone, leaving no ready source of water. The Caswells decided to return to Warren to file their first claims with the local recorder, a saloon keeper and gambler named Charles Bemis.

They needed equipment, supplies and a base closer than their homestead at Big Bar on the Snake River. Proximity was important because the brothers had encountered numerous other prospectors in the area, and feared that someone else might find Mule Creek before they could adequately assess its value.

They, like William Campbell, needed a place at a lower elevation where they could build a cabin, graze their stock, and raise a garden. They chose the mouth of Cabin Creek, a tributary of Big Creek, 4,000' and a one-day horseback ride from their new claims.

The full story of the Caswells' experience can be found in

Wayne Minshall's book, *Wilderness Brothers*, an excellent account of prospecting and frontier life of this period based on Lu Caswell's diaries.

Over the next several years the men gradually built up their capabilities at Thunder Mountain by hauling in pipe, whip sawing lumber and creating a water source to work several claims along Mule Creek. In 1895 their work netted $245.75 in gold. By 1896 their find was promising enough to justify four sluice boxes that produced $900.[4] The next year brought a similar amount.

1898 brought the biggest haul to date, enough to catch the attention of local miners and the newspapers of Idaho. The brothers and their partners showed up in Warren with close to $3,000 in gold. One can imagine the celebratory atmosphere in the local bar. The liquor flowed as the men unwound from months of hard labor in the mountains. The cat was soon out of the bag.

The August 19, 1898 edition of Grangeville's *Idaho County Free Press* newspaper ran the headline *Idaho Klondike*. The article reported from Warren, Idaho, that Ben Caswell, his brother Lu and others had made a rich placer strike at Thunder Mountain. "He bought a packstring of twelve horses and supplies for $1,300," the paper reported, and, "He reported panned out dirt of $8 to $10 per pan and invited all to follow since there was plenty for everybody."

The following week the paper included a report from the *Idaho Daily Statesman*, "Caswell bringing 10.5 lbs of gold from Thunder Mountain. The vein from which the gold is taken is from 150' to 200' wide. The entire body of ore averages more than $10 per ton in gold and can be mined and worked at nominal cost."

The news caught the attention of Idaho investor Colonel William H. Dewey, who in the fall of 1900 bought a $100,000 option from the Caswells. He sent a prospecting crew in the following year, which enthusiastically reported that the find was genuine and huge.

The enthusiasm was confirmed by the Idaho inspector of mines who wrote the Caswell claims contained "1,500,000 tons at a conservative estimate of $10,000,000.[5] The publication *Mines and Minerals* reported, "Thunder Mountain is a veritable mountain of ore, whose

4 Bob Waite, *To Idaho's Klondike*, (McCall, ID: USDA Forest Service, Payette National Forest, Heritage Program)
5 Martin H. Jacobs, *Report of the Mining Districts,* (Boise, ID: 1901) p. 39

estimated wealth throws the treasures of the Incas into the shade."[6]

Dewey was so impressed he rounded up more investors in Pittsburg, Pennsylvania, and formed the Thunder Mountain Gold and Silver Mining and Milling Company with $5,000,000 capital. They paid off the Caswell brothers ahead of schedule. The *Statesman's* coverage of the November 16, 1901 presentation of the check in Boise created a swarm of prospectors ready to try their luck. All would struggle with the problem of getting to the remote location.

While the harsh winter of 1901 stopped the rush to Thunder Mountain temporarily, it did not stop every newspaper, rail company, supplier, store-owner, outfitter and community leader from speculating on how they could benefit from the coming wave of prospectors.

The competition was on. Every small community rushed to report that those who had traveled to Thunder Mountain from their town were sure that it was the fastest and easiest route.

The truth was, every route was hard. Thunder Mountain was on an 8,500' ridge where the head of Marble Creek off the Middle Fork of the Salmon met the head of Monumental Creek. There were no roads, no improved trails – none anywhere near the strike.

The Mining Reporter, an influential journal, published an extensive account of Thunder Mountain in its April 10, 1902 edition, including information on each of five routes to the mine.[7] These included Boise, Ketchum, Mackay, Red Rock and Weiser. All were long, ranging from 142 to 190 miles in length, traversing some of the most rugged mountain terrain on the continent, but the perils did not stop the promotion.

Not to be outdone, the northern communities of Lewiston, Grangeville, Elk City and Dixie shamelessly promoted a local route. When area businessmen and miners needed a trail built from the north into the wilds of Idaho's backcountry, they knew where to turn.

William Campbell was known in the local community, having spent most of his adult life in Elk City, Dixie and Grangeville. He could move through the Idaho backcountry, even in challenging winter conditions although not without danger.

The December 20, 1898 edition of the *Idaho County Free*

6 William E. L'Hame, "Thunder Mountain," *Mines and Minerals* (July 1901), p. 558

7 Waite, *To Idaho's Klondike*

Press News reported in an article titled "Perils of the Mountain" that James Lynch had frozen to death. He died while looking for a deer while going to get "Campbell the hunter to kill one for him." Lynch had said he was going to "follow Campbell's trail."[8]

Later, the *Free Press* reported, "William Campbell had both feet severely frozen Friday night while he was bringing a doctor into Dixie from Elk City. The trail over the Moose Creek summit was badly drifted and they were five hours making the last four miles."[9]

Campbell made frequent trips out of his canyon homestead to Dixie and Elk City selling produce to the miners and picking up odd jobs. The news he heard among all the camps was of a new strike at Thunder Mountain. Imagine his sense of good fortune when Campbell realized the work he had done on a trail from Dixie Gulch to his Salmon River homestead turned out to be on the route to what the local newspaper had promoted as Idaho's Klondike.

Instead of just a place to live, hunt and raise produce, his homestead was perfectly situated to provide him with new business opportunities. Travelers to the Thunder Mountain Mine would not only use the trail he had built to the river, but would also need a way to cross the river and traverse the mountainous wilderness beyond.

8 "Perils of the Mountain," *Idaho County Free Press*, 20 December 1889
9 *Idaho County Free Press*, 27 December 1989

Chapter Five

Lucky Enough

"Luck affects everything.
Let your hook always be cast;
in the stream where you least expect it
there will be a fish."
– Ovid

My trail to Campbell's Ferry began in Mississippi. My father, Lowry, was an avid western traveler. For every vacation I can remember he loaded my mother, Marjorie, and the kids in the family car and headed west. Being the third of four boys, I was left behind for the early trips. I didn't complain. Much of my connection to the outdoors comes from the weeks I spent when they left me at Uncle Peter's and Aunt Mary Alice's dairy farm in rural east Mississippi.

By the time I turned sixteen my mother figured she had enough of marathon western travel adventures and I became my father's driver. Our first major trip was in 1963, driving his 1961 Cadillac Coupe de Ville to Alaska to see a total eclipse of the sun. In Edmonton, Alberta, we had car trouble that delayed us. We could not make it to Alaska in time for the eclipse, so we diverted to Hay River, Northwest Territories – the last 400 miles on a gravel road. We arrived in Hay River just in time to sit on the edge of Great Slave Lake and watch the eclipse shadow, like a massive black storm, approach across the water. Clear daylight changed to an eerie dark. Minutes later, when the sun returned, Lowry said, "OK, that's it. Let's head home."

He was that way. He had seen it. Now back to his work as an entrepreneur. I can remember coming up on him during hunting trips to the woods. He would be seated, his back resting against a tree with small pieces of paper lying around scribbled with notes he had made. He never could truly get away from his business. I was on the same path. As I had followed his footsteps through the woods, so did I follow his education route, travels west and life as an entrepreneur.

Lowry finished high school in the depths of the Great Depression. The son of a rural mail carrier, he had no chance for higher education until his uncle Austin, a newspaper man living in San Antonio, reached out and paid his way to local St. Mary's College. Two years later he transferred to the University of Texas at Austin where he got a business degree in accounting. After a short time as a liquified petroleum gas inspector for the State of Mississippi he borrowed money from a friend to buy his first truck. By the time I finished college he had dozens of trucks plus a business building ASME code pressure vessels – tanks, for propane. He also had an interest in a small life insurance company based in Jackson, Mississippi.

As soon as Lowry turned his first profit in the gas business, he started sending a monthly check to Uncle Austin. By his reckoning he would have gone nowhere without his uncle's priceless gift of an education. The checks grew as the business did, and did not end until Austin Tims' death at age ninety-six. He also honored his uncle by making his third son's middle name Austin.

I felt fortunate during my time at the University of Texas in Austin. As graduation approached, many of my classmates had no clear understanding of where they would end up. For me it was simple. I had a job waiting with my father. My business administration degree in finance would allow me to work by his side, learning how to operate in the real entrepreneurial world. I returned to Cleveland with a new bride, Loretta, and set out learning Lowry's gas and tank business, then the insurance business.

Several years later I began my own version of the western vacation routine. In 1972 I took a canoe trip on the Buffalo River in Arkansas. Loretta paddled the front while pregnant with our second child, Trudy. Our first, Angela, age two, sat in the middle dipping cookies in the river. I was not the only one being influenced here. Years later Angela would become a river guide. She is now chief operations officer of Maravia and Cascade Outfitters in Boise.

In 1974 I headed west for an outfitted river trip vacation on the Snake River through Hells Canyon on the Idaho and Oregon border with Martin Litton's Grand Canyon Dories. It fascinated me that people could make a living doing this. I became hooked on rivers and river running. I started taking friends on trips. Later I would organize an expedition to the Middle Fork of the Salmon River. Legendary river outfitter Dave Helfrich told me outfitters are like prostitutes. First they do it for fun, then for friends, then for money. I was headed that way.

In 1975 at age sixty-five my father's life was cut short by heart disease and a stroke. He had just begun to cut back his time in the business, spending more time at a cabin he had built in the woods he loved near the Mississippi River. It seemed terribly unfair to me that having just reached the point he could enjoy the fruits of his labors he was struck down. That realization would later influence my own decision on when to retire.

Seven years after our father's death, I sold my interest in the family business to two of my brothers. I took the capital I received and wrote all twenty-six outfitters who had permits to operate on the Middle Fork of the Salmon River seeking one who was interested in selling. That led to a twenty-seven year outfitting career on the Middle Fork and Selway rivers. But that was not enough. Just like Lowry, I expanded. In my case by investing in raft manufacturing and a river equipment catalog business.

While making a living taking clients on whitewater adventure trips, plus building and selling rafts, I regularly took the proverbial busman's holiday floating on and camping next to rivers. On those trips down Idaho's premier wilderness rivers, I passed several old homesteads, many of which had become guest ranches, fishing and hunting lodges. These places had been settled and homesteaded prior to the area being designated as wilderness by Congress. Floating by these old homesteads, I found myself wondering (just as Phyllis would years later), "Who is lucky enough to get to live in a place like that?"

When I had left Mississippi and moved to Idaho, a childhood friend, Brad Janoush, told me to save a place for him in my outfitting business as a raft guide. Brad is a bigger than life character, the smallest of four brothers at 6'5" and 205 pounds. We went to high school together. He left for the University of Mississippi while I followed my father's footsteps to the University of Texas at Austin. Brad came back to Cleveland and began a career in real estate, then appraisal work. When at thirty-two he got his MAI designation, the Ph.D. of the appraisal business, he called me and said, "Doug, I worked hard to get this and I'm giving myself a trip to the Bio Bio River in Chile. You are going with me." I could never say no to Brad. That trip to Chile was with an outfit out of North Carolina called the Nantahala Outdoor Center. It would be their first year to run the Bio Bio in 1982. They had a fleet of new rafts from a California-based company named Maravia.

Later that year, I headed west and bought my own outfitting business on the Middle Fork of the Salmon. With a new outfitting partner, Mike McLeod, we purchased rafts from Maravia and three years later bought the company and moved it from the Bay Area of California to Idaho – ever the entrepreneur just like the old man.

Brad took summers off from his appraisal work to guide for me, and three years later in 1986 made his own move to Idaho. Through his appraisal connections he heard about a homestead property on the Main Salmon that was for sale – Campbell's Ferry. Brad, his wife Patricia and our friends Joe and Peggy Denton flew on the mail plane to the property and camped overnight in the orchard. Returning to Boise, Brad and Patricia came over for dinner. Listening to Brad's tales of his trip, I blurted out, "Well hell, let's buy it!" Sight unseen, I was in. I had never floated the Main Salmon River and knew nothing about the details of the purchase, but it sounded good and I trusted Brad. The price was right. We were willing to gamble on this chance to get our own piece of wild Idaho.

Most of the lodges and properties grandfathered into the Wilderness and Wild and Scenic Rivers systems were outrageously expensive. Campbell's Ferry was on the market for much less due to a very restrictive easement that had been placed on it. Conservation and scenic easements are tools that the land conservation community use to control and restrict future uses of properties that possess unique natural or historic values.

Because of the easement, Campbell's Ferry, a property that might have sold for $750,000 was now on the market for less than a $100,000, a price Brad and I decided we could afford.

Buying Campbell's Ferry sight unseen was the beginning of the answer to my question, "Who is lucky enough to live here?"

****

Five years before, I had made a similar gamble. Several years after buying an outfitting business on the Middle Fork of the Salmon River I wanted to expand the river business. I asked Bob Campbell, one of my guides, what would be another good river to run.

"The Selway," he replied with no hesitation. "But you can't get it. There are only four outfitters allowed on the Selway and one has never come on the market."

That winter I was at a Western River Guides Association gathering in Salt Lake City, chatting between meetings with Steve Currey, one of the lucky four outfitters who held permits to operate on the Selway. In passing Steve mentioned that he had other expansion plans and might sell his Selway operation.

"Stop right now," I told him. "Don't talk to anyone else, I want to buy it. Name your price."

The next day we met again and struck a deal. I had never seen, much less floated the Selway, but I never looked back.

Both gambles turned out to be jackpots in the game of life.

Lucky Enough

Chapter Six

The Ferry

"A body immersed in a fluid is buoyed up by a force
equal to the weight of the displaced fluid."
– Archimedes

William Campbell couldn't believe his luck. He had worked
hard to establish his homestead on the Salmon River. He had improved
the trail to the river from Dixie. A few locals had started coming to the
canyon to fish, hunt, prospect and explore deeper into the backcountry. The news about the new gold strike at Thunder Mountain promised to turn those few into a swarm. Local merchants and miners were
anxious to promote a viable route to Thunder Mountain from the north
so they could all benefit from the flood of gold seekers that would use
it.

The businessmen and promoters turned to William Campbell
with his trail building skills and prime location on the route to the
mine. $3,000 was raised to pay for the new route. Time was critical.

The route would take advantage of an existing rail head for the Northern Pacific on the South Fork of the Clearwater River at the small community of Stites. Established trails from the end of the rail line went on to Elk City, Dixie and, thanks to William Campbell, into the Salmon River Canyon.

What was needed was a tie in to another trail thirty-seven miles away that ran down Big Creek and up Monumental Creek to Thunder Mountain. The existing route was already bringing miners in from another gold strike at Warren, Idaho.

Campbell needed help to first build a viable river crossing and later the longer trail through the high country. To build the crossing, a ferry, he could draw on his friend and neighbor, Jim Moore.

The 1900 U.S. Census lists Jim Moore as a servant and farm laborer with William Campbell as the head of household. This leads us to believe that Moore came to the canyon and helped get Campbell's place established before turning to work his own homestead across the river. At thirty-three he was three years younger than Campbell. Moore's skill as a builder is shown by the later work he did to construct nine buildings on his own place. Both men were familiar with the challenges of crossing the river here.

For individuals and small amounts of supplies, a skiff or boat would suffice. Stock animals could swim the river, but the heavy loads needed for work at the mine would need a more substantial conveyance. For over a hundred years as pioneers pushed across the continent ferries had been a key component of the nation's developing transportation system. Any time a travel route met a river, as soon as the volume of travel justified the investment, an entrepreneur would build a ferry. Such an opportunity was knocking on William Campbell's door.

Setting the exact location for the crossing was critical. The Salmon River flows over four hundred miles in a zigzag course from its headwaters in the mountains of south central Idaho to its confluence with the Snake River just below the Washington-Oregon border.[1] On average, the river drops 12' in every mile. Average is the key word here. In portions of the river near its beginning the gradient is constant, producing an almost continuous sequence of rapids. By the time

---

1 Jim Cassady, Bill Cross, Fryar Calhoun, *Western Whitewater from the Rockies to the Pacific,* (Berkeley, CA: North Fork Press, 1994)

it has reached the center of the state at Campbell's Ferry it has become a pool and drop river. Decades later river runners would describe it,

> The Main Salmon is a big-water river. Rolling rapids punctuate deep, calm pools which grow longer toward the end of the run. During peak runoff standing waves and holes can become monstrous, and only experienced boaters should attempt the run. Later in the summer, at moderate and lower levels, the Salmon is a perfect introduction to the pleasures of a long wilderness river trip: splashing through big but hardly terrifying rapids, camping on luxurious sandy beaches beside cold green water.[2]

What Campbell and Moore needed was a stretch of river lacking the threat that came with whitewater. A ferry needs stability, not boulders, waves, holes and large eddies. Water running down hill through an irregular streambed rarely moves uniformly in one mass. Often the main current will move only in the center or to one side, with part of the river still or even flowing back upstream, a feature river runners call an eddy. At the upstream end of the flat of Campbell's homestead was an ideal section of river where the current runs downstream uniformly from bank to bank through a section deep enough to be usable even in low water seasons.

A ferry is not pulled back and forth across the river. It uses the force of the current to move. It does this by adjusting the position of the ferry relative to the current flowing by. Look at the picture of the ferry on the following page. The river current is flowing from the right of the picture to the left. A heavy cable has been run across the river upstream of the ferry (out of view of this picture) and anchored on each bank to a tree or large boulder. The anchor point on the bank is called a *deadman.*

Two large pulleys have been placed on this main cable so they can run along the cable from bank to bank. A line is then run from each pulley to the ferry. One pulley is attached to a line running to the center, upstream end of the ferry. The second pulley is attached to a line running to an upstream corner of the ferry, through a small pulley with the line's end wrapped around a drum turned by a windlass. Look at the man standing on the right, upstream end of the ferry in the picture. He has a spoked wheel in his hands. By turning that wheel he

2 Cassady, et al

turns a drum that holds the line running to the ferry's corner and up to the main cable. As he turns the windlass one way, the line is taken in on the drum, making the distance between the upstream corner of the ferry and the main cable shorter. This turns the ferry so it is angled to the current, allowing the river's flow to push on one side of the ferry, pushing the ferry to one bank of the river. As the operator turns the windlass the opposite direction it lets this line out, making the line running to the corner longer, turning the ferry in the opposite direc-

Campbell's Ferry – 1900

tion, allowing the current to push it to the opposite bank.

This same principle of presenting one side or the other of a river craft to the current to move across the flow is used regularly by kayakers, canoers and rafters to maneuver their boat from one side of a river to the other. The maneuver is appropriately called a *cross stream ferry*.

Campbell and Moore would have had no trouble finding a model for the ferry they wished to build. As they traveled across the country in their journey to Idaho both would have seen many. The South Fork of the Clearwater below Elk City had a ferry, as did the

Snake River near Lewiston and lower on the Salmon River near present day Riggins. The hard part would be getting the hardware – the cables, pulleys and windlass to the homestead, and making the lumber.

Hauling parts was relatively easy for these experienced packers, but the cable was a unique challenge. One-inch steel cable weighs eight pounds per foot and they needed three hundred feet for just the main cable, making a load of more than a ton. To move this by mule required skill, patience, and a seasoned string of mules that could be relied upon to make the steep, narrow thirteen mile route intact. With this load the packer would not have the safety feature of pigtails – the rope between each animal designed to break if one mule went down. Joined together by the cable, if one slipped he would pull the next, and the next, and the next – the entire string plunging to the river thousands of feet below.

The cable would have to be stretched down one side of the packstring with loops formed at each animal, then brought back up the opposite side with another loop and equal weight of cable at each animal to balance the load. Allowing two hundred pounds of dead weight per mule meant they needed a string of twelve mules. No doubt the men chose twelve experienced mules: ones unlikely to be spooked by the task and uncertainties of a long challenging trip into the Salmon River Canyon.

Making the lumber for the ferry was also difficult. There was plenty of timber to turn into lumber, but the nearest mill was thirteen miles away in Dixie. Just like every other aspect of life here at the edge of the wilderness, Campbell and Moore would have to get lumber the way their ancestors had a hundred years before – cut it by hand.

The two men would be their own mill using a pit-sawing method.[3] First they would square a log using axes. The squared log would be placed over a pit. One man above and one below would lift and drag a crosscut saw down through the log and back up producing 100

3 Michael Williams, *Americans and their Forests: A Historical Geography (Studies in Environment and History*, (New York, NY: Cambridge University Press, 1989)

to 200 board feet of lumber per day.[4] This type of saw became known as a *misery whip*.

The ferry itself was a twin pontoon design. Each pontoon was twenty feet long with the upstream end angled up to meet the current. The pontoons were sealed except for an opening just behind the operator that allowed seepage to be bailed out. A ten by twelve foot platform was stretched across the two pontoons. Each side had a hinged gangway that was folded out to the bank to allow loading and unloading.

Approximately two feet wide and two and a half feet deep, the two pontoons would have displaced about eighty cubic feet of water when one foot of its height was submerged. According to Archimedes Principle, an object in a fluid is buoyed up by a force equal to the weight of the fluid displaced. Eighty cubic feet of water weighs four thousand nine hundred and sixty pounds, about two and a half tons. The ferry and rigging itself must have weighed close to a ton, leaving one and a half tons, three thousand pounds, as a useful load.

In the accompanying photo taken in 1900 by Al Stonebraker, a friend of Campbell's, the ferry is loaded with two horses, perhaps a thousand pounds each, and two men. We don't know for certain who the two men are, but given the time frame, it is likely Jim Moore and William Campbell. Campbell charged $1 per head of stock and $.50 per person to cross the river. Judging by the packstring waiting on the far bank, this looks like a good day for the ferry business.

---

4 Richard W. Massey, *History of the Lumber Industry in Alabama and West Florida*, (Nashville, TN, Vanderbilt University, 1960), pp. 174–81)

Chapter Seven

Three Blaze Trail

"Do not go where the path may lead,
go instead where there is no path
and leave a trail."
– Ralph Waldo Emerson

William Campbell had struck it rich. He had tried much of his adult life to find wealth among the rock and gravel of the mining camps at Elk City, Dixie and nearby Buffalo Hump. Now he found his fortune in his propitious selection of his homestead on the Salmon River. His location, plus years of work in the local area showing his talent for moving supplies and building trail, earned him the confidence and financial support of local businessmen and miners.

The locals raised $3,000, more than $200,000 in today's money, to hire Campbell to establish a viable route from the Salmon River across miles of virgin wilderness.[1]

Thunder Mountain was sixty miles to the south of his homestead. But Campbell's new trail would only need to traverse thirty-seven miles of backcountry and tie into an existing trail to the diggings from an earlier gold strike at Warren, Idaho (Map 5). The trail from Warren approached Thunder Mountain from the northwest, following Big Creek and Monumental Creek through the wilderness. Campbell would start at 2,400' at his ferry, build trail through country reaching to 8,400', then end at Copper Camp on Big Creek at 4,700'. Contrary to area newspaper's glowing reports of easy travel, it was anything but.

Today we call this high plateau in central Idaho the Chamberlain Basin. It is over 800 square miles of high country roughly bordered on the northwest and northeast by the Main Salmon River and its South Fork, on the southeast by the Middle Fork of the Salmon and on the south by Big Creek (Map 6). The terrain has been sculptured from the core of the Idaho Batholith, the massive granite pluton that broke through the continental plate here seventy-five million years ago. Throughout the area is evidence of volcanic activity, part of the process that brought the mineral wealth to the Basin's southern edge along Big Creek and Thunder Mountain.

A. F. Parker writing about the Sheepeater War of 1879 described the area, "What is known as the Sheepeater country is to this day the wildest and most impenetrable region of indescribable ruggedness and grandeur. Lofty mountain summits alternate with abysmal canyons thousands of feet in depth along whose depths the waters of mountain torrents dash along to free themselves from their rock-bound channels."[2]

Few humans had been there. A small band of Northern Shoshoni Indians, known as the Sheepeaters, periodically traveled to and through the Basin, but there had been no reason for a major route in the higher elevations. Though wildlife was plentiful, easier access to wild game and fish could be found in the low country. The closest ma-

---

1 www.measuringworth.com, a website produced by Lawrence Officer and Samuel Williamson, two University of Chicago economics professors, was used to calculate the current value of money

2 Sister Mary Alfreda Elsensohn, *Pioneer Days in Idaho County, Volume Two,* (Caldwell, ID: Caxton Printers, 1978), p. 277

jor Indian trails ran on the north side of the Salmon River. The Southern Nez Perce Trail was used by tribes to make seasonal treks across the mountains between the salmon runs of the Columbia River system and the buffalo herds on the Great Plains. Campbell's trail would be south of the Salmon River and plunge into terrain that had seldom been seen by whites.

A few prospectors looking for the next bonanza had penetrated Chamberlain Basin. Using only infrequent Indian and game trails, men who had responded to the 1860 gold strikes in Pierce, Elk City, Florence, and then Warren in 1862 traveled into the South Fork of the Salmon River Canyon that borders the Basin on the west. From there they travelled into the Big Creek drainage on the Basin's south side.

The first organized excursion into Chamberlain Basin was by the military soon after general unrest broke out in the region following the Nez Perce War of 1877. Earlier prospectors rushing to stake gold claims had ignored treaties giving Indians the rights to much of the Clearwater country. The government responded by trying to force the Nez Perce Indians, led by Chiefs Joseph and Yellow Bull, onto a new reservation near Lapwai. The Nez Perce resisted. They slew eighteen soldiers in a battle in White Bird Canyon on the north bank of the Salmon. The Indian success was short lived. The U.S. military led by General Oliver Howard drove the Nez Perce out of Idaho via the Lolo Trail and eventually captured them just short of the Canadian border on October 5, 1877.

In June and July of 1878 a band of renegade Sheepeater Indians attacked ranches, stole horses and killed settlers in the Weiser and Payette River valleys in southwest Idaho. The following winter brought an alleged attack by Indians on a gold camp at Oro Grande at the head of Loon Creek, a tributary of the Middle Fork of the Salmon River. In the spring of 1879 two men were found murdered at the Rains Ranch, a small homestead near the mouth of the South Fork of the Salmon River (twelve miles downstream from what would become Campbell's Ferry).

These events prompted General Howard to dispatch troops from Boise and Grangeville to find "who the murderers were; and, if Indians, apprehend them and bring them to Boise."[3]

It was not an easy journey. From Fort Howard near Grang-

3 Telegram to Brigadier General O. O. Howard, May 1879

eville forty-eight mounted infantry led by Lieutenant Henry Catley departed with Indian guides and a pack string of supplies. Leaving on June 4 it took over a month to travel the 100 miles to reach the Rains Ranch. First they had to traverse the high country to the gold camp at Florence sitting at over 6,000'. A winding trail took them down into the Salmon River canyon to 2,000', only to immediately head back up to over 6,000' to the gold camp at Warren. At one point they encountered a mile of snow five to eight feet deep.[4]

Arriving in mid July Private Edgar Hoffner, who served under Lieutenant Catley, observed the murder scene at Rains Ranch and noted in his journal, "From my observations I conclude that it was very convenient to have some Indians in one's neighborhood in case of a crime being committed. It gives one a chance to shift the blame on the Indians."[5]

Leaving the ranch July 17 the military column faced a steep climb out of the South Fork Canyon to Chamberlain Basin. On August 10, Hoffner noted, "Four mules were lost yesterday by falling over a precipice. August 17, A pack mule with load overbalanced went end over end down the mountain side like a shot, bringing up on the creek bed with a broken neck, after a fall of three hundred feet. Colonel W. C. Brown noted that the soldiers were in the field for three months in pursuit of the Sheepeater Indians and lost 45 pack mules and 18 horses."[6]

During that time they crisscrossed the Chamberlain Basin four times. After several skirmishes, the loss of one soldier and winter setting in, the military withdrew after capturing fifty-one Sheepeaters, Bannocks, Weisers and one Nez Perce who had surrendered. The prisoners were first taken to Vancouver, Washington, and ended up at the Fort Hall Indian Reservation in eastern Idaho, bringing the Indian Wars in Idaho to an end.

Twenty years later when word spread about the Caswell brothers' find at Thunder Mountain, prospectors would still be searching

4 James M. Hockaday, *History of the Payette National Forest*, (McCall, ID: USDA Forest Service Heritage Program, 1968), p. 3
5 Johnny Carrey and Cort Conley, *The Middle Fork and the Sheepeater War*, (Cambridge, ID: Backeddy Books, 1980)
6 Sheila D. Reddy, *Shadows in the Wilderness,* (McCall, ID: USDA Forest Service, Payette National Forest Heritage Program, 1995), pp. 17–18

for a better route through or around the Chamberlain Basin. The initial flood of men arriving from the north and northwest began the same way Lieutenant Catley had through Florence, Warren and into the South Fork of the Salmon River canyon. But instead of going due east from Warren into the canyon at the Rains Ranch and the hard climb out to Chicken Peak and Mosquito Ridge they went southwest into the South Fork, then west up a tributary called Elk Creek to its headwaters at Elk Summit and down into Big Creek. Although shorter than the military route, it was still a brutal slog to over 8,600' where the snow and ice lingered well into summer. There had to be a better way.

Or was there? Looking at the map today the route from Grangeville to Thunder Mountain through Campbell's Ferry is virtually the same distance as through Warren, 125 miles. The desire for a better route than via Warren was partially driven by the frequent failure of the crossing of the Salmon River between Florence and Warren.

A. F. Parker, founder of the *Idaho County Free Press,* described the river, "Partaking the character of the country through which it flows, The Salmon River impresses the beholder with the vision that it is a wicked, treacherous stream and as such it is respected with fear by all who have to do with it."[7]

Concerning the crossing, Parker wrote, "After leaving Florence, the trail descends along Meadow Creek into the canyon of the Salmon River to the Wire Bridge. The Wire Bridge itself is a structure four feet in width, built on the principal common to suspension bridges everywhere. The first bridge that ever spanned the Salmon was of the same character and was erected on that of the present structure in 1864 by Hon. Stephen S. Fenn, Gus Woodward and John Hunt. It afterwards passed into the hands of Johnny Wood from whom it was transferred to old man Baker who was killed at White Bird in the Indian outbreak of 1877. Since that time sundry other parties have temporarily owned it, and it was finally purchased of Bob Mansfield by the Carey brothers, the present owners. The old affair was washed away by the June freshet of last year and an entirely new and more durable bridge built."[8]

The new, more *durable* structure Parker described did not prove to be so.

7 *Idaho County Free Press*, 4 July 1881
8 *Idaho County Free Press*, 4 July 1881

This was the same bridge that the Caswell brothers had used for their first arrival in the Salmon River country. In 1889 the Wire Bridge was so precarious it allowed crossing by only one horse or mule at a time. Its days were numbered.

In the November 14, 1901 *Grangeville Standard News* it was reported, "F. F. Taylor, veteran packer had one delay on his trip back to Grangeville because of the collapse of the bridge across the Salmon river between Florence and Warren. The bridge was reported unsafe and in urgent need of repairs and Taylor was able to get his pack string over it dry shod one at a time instead of having to swim the river."

One week later the news was, "A sixty foot span has broken and collapsed Friday night." The primary route from north to south was cut off.

By January of 1902 the pressure for a viable route was building. The *Free Press* reported, "Storekeepers, hotel keepers, saloon and restaurant men and others have several hundred tons of freight already stored here. Some of them are employing dog teams to transport a portion of the freight over the divide into the new camp."

The county commissioners responded to complaints and "took up the matter of the state bridge across Salmon River and decided to advertise once more for bids. Should no bids be received by February 24 the county will turn contractor and hire men to do the work. The bridge is undoubtedly in precarious condition and is condemned unsafe."[9]

On February 13 the news was, "A large party came through on their way to the back country. Each of the men took about 150 pounds of supplies, fifty pounds of flour, thirty of bacon and the rest of the weight being made up of tea, sugar, beans and bedding. The party has one 25:35 Winchester and one .22 for birds and small game. Each man will pull his supplies on his own rawhide toboggan."

The lust for gold was leading men to risk travel through the wilderness in the grip of a harsh winter. That same month five men headed for Thunder Mountain via the southern and western route through Weiser, into the South Fork and up Elk Creek. The five "were caught in an avalanche and were overwhelmed by a snowslide at the head of Smith Creek on one of the cut-off trails instead of following the well-beaten winter trail through Warren. Two men faced it and

9 *Idaho County Free Press*, 30 January 1902

jumped and were carried some distance but three men were caught in it and entombed. The two men made their way as best they could to Warren and immediately fifteen big-hearted men were en route to the scene intent upon the rescue of the bodies, dead or alive."[10]

The same edition of the *Free Press* brought further bad news that although the commissioners were taking action to see that the Florence to Warren bridge was repaired, "It is possible that the actual work of reconstruction will not be begun until after high water in June…"

Just when they thought it couldn't get any worse the April 3 *Grangeville Standard* reported, "This afternoon the state bridge on Salmon river between Warren and Florence went into the river, only a few minutes after sheriff Dixon passed over it on his way out from Warren. The bridge fell before Mr. Dillingham could make any temporary repairs."

Packstring in Grangeville
getting ready for trip to Thunder Mountain on the Three Blaze Trail

10 *Idaho County Free Press*, 20 February 1902

The Three Blaze Trail switchbacks
up the ridge above Little Trout Creek

Chapter Eight

Boom Time

El Dorado

Gaily bedight,
A gallant knight,
In sunshine and in shadow,
Had journeyed long,
Singing a song,
In search of Eldorado.

But he grew old,
This knight so bold,
And o'er his heart a shadow
Fell as he found
No spot of ground
That looked like Eldorado.

And, as his strength
Failed him at length,
He met a pilgrim shadow;
"Shadow," said he,
"Where can it be,
This land of Eldorado?"

"Over the mountains
Of the moon,
Down the valley of the shadow,
Ride, boldly ride,"
The shade replied,--
"If you seek Eldorado!"

— Edgar Allan Poe

The misfortune of others meant opportunity for William Campbell. He had spent his adult life in mining country and was positioned to capitalize on the latest, and last, big gold strike in Idaho. To build the Three Blaze Trail he called on another experienced traveler in the Idaho backcountry, William Allen (Al) Stonebraker. Stonebraker was from Stites, Idaho, the terminus of the Northern Pacific Railroad located four miles south of where the South Fork of the Clearwater enters the Clearwater.

The Stonebraker family was known for their packing skills acquired from moving supplies and people from Stites and Grangeville to the mining camps at Elk City, Dixie, and Buffalo Hump. Al would later locate a homestead in the heart of Chamberlain Basin that today is owned by the Idaho Department of Fish and Game and still carries the name Stonebraker Ranch.

Stonebraker and Campbell pioneered the new route from Campbell's ranch south into the Chamberlain Basin, likely following a route they had discovered through trial and error. The hardest part was the first. The Salmon River has cut a steep canyon beset by canyon walls that rise abruptly from the waters edge at 2,400' to the high rim of the Basin's plateau. The Basin itself is not much higher than Dixie, but the elevation of the rim between the Basin and the Salmon to the north and Big Creek to the south rises to as high as 8,000'and more. The high points often hold snow into June. There are side canyons leading off the Salmon River into the high country, like Trout Creek, but they are narrow with unstable side slopes - not suitable for a trail. The best bet was to switchback up to a ridge that offers as gentle a slope as possible into the high country.

Moving upstream from Campbell's ranch the two men found an ideal location to begin their climb out of the canyon. It proved so suitable that today, over 100 years later, the primary Forest Service trail takes the same route. It is part of the Idaho Bicentennial Trail system that runs from the Canadian border with Idaho to its southern terminus on the Nevada border. From Campbell's Ferry to Big Creek one can still find trees along the route with the distinctive three blazes cut into the bark to mark the trail.

Using a sequence of switchbacks, Campbell and Stonebraker carved the trail into a slope, gaining 800' from the bottom of Little Trout Creek to the crest of Trout Ridge. From that point the trail follows the ridge in a five mile long sweeping arc gradually rising to over 7,000'. Today's Forest Service trail uses forty switchbacks to gain the highest point on the ridge. Campbell located the trail, "on open ridges for easier travel, as the ridges are not subject to blow-down timber and are free of winter snow for a longer period due to wind action."[1]

From Trout Ridge the trail drops into the head of Richardson Creek at Wet Meadows and continues south along Highline Ridge to the divide between Fish Lake and Flossie Lake; then southeast along the north ridge of Red Top Creek to a crossing point on Chamberlain Creek at the mouth of Moose Creek where a stopover cabin called *Smokehouse* was located (Map 6). The trail continues up Moose Creek to Moose Jaw Meadow, continuing south along the east ridge of Moose Creek to Hand Meadows, then south along Ramey Ridge to a steep descent (many switchbacks) to Big Creek at Copper Camp.[2]

At Copper Camp the Three Blaze Trail joined the existing trail from Warren, and traveled east along Big Creek to the mouth of Monumental Creek, then up Monumental to Thunder Mountain.

Was it a better route? It depended on your perspective. The newspapers of the day were not hesitant to carry the water for local businessmen who wanted travelers to pass their stores. In the *Lewiston Tribune* of January 27, 1902, E. B. Simmons of the Dixie Townsite Company made an attempt at objectivity, but concluded with a whopper:

With all the bluster over the various Thunder Mountain routes I am afraid the stampeder will not find a "hot air" line that will land him at that mecca, but with a personal acquaintance with the country north and west from Thunder Mountain and after making inquiry from the prospectors and mountaineers of that section, I am convinced that either of the northern routes is feasible. The Lewiston, Stites, Elk City and Dixie routes ensure one an excellent road lined with freight and mail teams all the way to Dixie with stopping places every ten miles. From Dixie to Campbell's ranch one travels a graded trail and then crosses the Salmon river at a safe crossing, either by skiff or on the ferry now being built. Then it takes on through Cham-

1 Peter Preston, *Chamberlain Basin's Historic Three Blaze Trail,* (McCall, ID: USDA Forest Service, Payette National Forest Heritage Program, 1995)
2 Peter Preston, *Chamberlain Basin's Historic Three Blaze Trail*

berlain Basin, crossing Big Creek three miles from the mouth of Monumental Creek; then up Monumental Creek to Thunder Mountain, leaving an altitude of 5,400' at Dixie and not crossing a higher point until the new district is reached.[3]

Ignoring the 8,000' ridges the trail crosses, Simmons went on to say, "This trip from Dixie can be made to Thunder Mountain in four days. The people along the line are awake to the advantages of the route and have already employed parties to carry the mail from Dixie to Thunder Mountain once a week….It is expected to reach its designation on the seventh day after leaving Lewiston."[4]

In early 1902 as the Grangeville papers were reporting the woes of the bridge collapse between Florence and Warren, they also broke the news, "There is a new roadway through Chamberlain Basin and Dixie into Thunder Mountain. This trail is the Three Blaze Trail, made by Campbell and Stonebraker."[5]

Campbell had spent enough time around gold camps to know that the good times would not last forever. He had been to Thunder Mountain and harbored doubts about its long term prospects. During a visit to Grangeville after completing the trail he engaged in some promotion of new ways to get to his homestead as a starting point for the trip to Thunder Mountain.

---

3 Marian S. Sweeney, *Gold at Dixie Gulch*, (Kamiah, ID: Clearwater Valley Publishing, 1982), p. 26
4 Sweeney, p. 26
5 *Grangeville Standard*, 20 May 1902

IDAHO COUNTY FREE PRESS
GRANGEVILLE, IDAHO COUNTY, IDAHO
THURSDAY, MAY 8, 1902

AN ALL RIVER ROUTE

**William Campbell Talks of Thunder Mountain
and How to Get There**

THERE ARE OTHER RICH CAMPS

Big Creek District Pronounced a Phenomenally Rich Territory

Among the numerous visitors to growing Grangeville this week was William Campbell, proprietor of the Campbell Ranch on Salmon River where the Dixie route to Thunder Mountain crosses that stream. Mr. Campbell has been prospecting in the Thunder Mountain country for the past six years and while he is satisfied that it has a great future, he believes the greatest future for that country will be found to lie in the country west of Thunder Mountain, in the great mines of Big Creek, Monumental, Government, Smith, Logan and the other streams which are tributary to Big Creek. He took in last summer W. H. Phelps, late of the Idaho Comstock, and C. P. Richardson, of the Moose Creek placers, and they made thorough tests of their samples from Thunder Mountain and while they got values they were not sufficiently high to justify them in making locations. This confirms the general impression among mining men that the Thunder Mountain district will eventually resolve into a number of low grade propositions carrying very large milling plants like the mines of the

Black Hills or Baranoff Island. But on the Big Creek country Mr. Campbell is very enthusiastic and says it is without doubt the most richly impregnated mineral country in the west and now that capital is being attracted in that direction he looks to see a number of big camps brought to light which will add enormously to the mineral output of this state.

Mr. Campbell also gives his impressions concerning the different routes into Thunder Mountain from the north and says that the business men of Grangeville should by all means look into the all-river route up the main Salmon River from the old wire bridge.

The Campbell crossing is 15 miles above the mouth of Crooked Creek where there was a mining district organized and considerable excitement in 1899-90 over the discovery of very large ledges of low-grade quartz. He says that for five miles below and for ten miles above his place there is a natural trail and from Crooked Creek down to the wire bridge there is a very good country on the south side of the stream where a trail can be built for not to exceed $100 per mile.

There are many bars along the river where no work at all is required, and from Crooked Creek to his place there is only one point where any considerable work would be required. The main expense would be in building the trail from the wire bridge to Crooked Creek, a distance of about 15 miles and with this opened to travel there would be a splendid route which at no point would be 100 feet above the high water level of the stream. Such a route would be of immense benefit to this section as affording a winter outlet to the great camps on both sides of the Salmon, with no snow, always dry and plenty of feed for animals and perpetual sunshine all year round.

This is the proposition which H. B. Brown submitted to our board of trade last winter and it is matter for regret that the information available at that time was not sufficient to justify our people in undertaking to look into its merits. If such a trail were open now all the travel to Thunder Mountain would use it, to the great benefit of our business men and the entire country besides.

Campbell was hedging his bets. He made note of the fact that Thunder Mountain was not the bonanza many had proclaimed and at best it might be a "low grade proposition." But he still promoted mining efforts on Big Creek, an area that would be served by his ferry and trail.

Eventually all western mining booms eventually had to face reality. The easy pickings faded fast, replaced by larger scale placer or hard rock industrial enterprises. Often the last to cling to hope were Chinese laborers who would invest more work for less return than the usual immigrant of European descent.

1902 was the peak year for travel on the Three Blaze Trail to Thunder Mountain. Jim Moore claimed that 1,800 men came through on the trail between 1900 and 1902. Considering that Campbell was charging $.50 per man and a $1 per head of stock you can calculate his gross revenue during that time was about $4,500. In today's money that would buy more than a quarter million dollars worth of goods! William was doing well. And he was doing it by making money from others, not the risky venture of digging for gold himself. By any measure he had become a successful entrepreneur.

Among those utilizing Campbell's handiwork that year was Robert G. Bailey, who chronicled his trip in his book *River of No Return* published in 1935. Bailey relates that a trusted national publication reported Thunder Mountain was so rich, "all one had to do was to go into the camp with a coal shuttle and a shovel, aided by the prospector's friend, the gold pan, stay a few days and return home with enough of the yellow metal to live ever after in ease and comfort,"

Bailey caught a train across the country and set out to Dixie and beyond:

> Twelve miles down precipitous trails landed us in the very bowels of the earth where we crossed the Salmon River on a crude boat at Campbell's Ferry. Ascending the steep sides of the canyon another fifteen miles brought us to Chamberlain Basin; here there were hundreds of acres of high mountain meadows, a most enticing spot, with big game to be had in abundance.

> Our outfit was not the only one on the trail. There was much travel in both directions. It was early in the spring and the highlands evidenced much snow. A few days ahead of us on the trail was a very large outfit consisting of several men, a number of women destined for the red light district and the dance halls, a complete bar, and a plentiful supply of liquor of various kinds.

> Farther along we climbed to what was known as Ramey Ridge, a high divide, 8,000' in altitude, and with the marks of many wind-swept winters to be seen on the stunted trees. Drift snow was piled up high in many places. In spite of the forbidding aspects of the country, prospectors were in evidence everywhere and several of them had nice specimens of gold-bearing quartz to show for their efforts.

We descended from Ramey Ridge to Big Creek.....Along Big Creek there were many prospectors at work, though the ore was base and held out little hope of being successfully treated in that faraway place. From Big Creek we headed directly south up Monumental Creek, going about twenty miles to reach the purported rich strike at Thunder Mountain.

Arriving at Thunder Mountain we found that hundreds of prospectors had preceded us and in every direction gleaming squared tree trunks proclaimed that all available land had been located, regardless of whether placer or quartz ground had been found. The object was to locate before the other fellow and then proceed to prospect. For some reason I was not impressed by the district, and though I prospected diligently in many directions I made no locations whatever.[6]

The boom at Thunder Mountain was accompanied by establishment of a town, Roosevelt, named for the popular President. In the November election of 1902 there were ninety-one votes cast at Roosevelt, almost equal to the ninety-nine at Warren. What was once an unpopulated wilderness canyon unknown to the outside world had in a few years become a bustling community. C. F. Neff described Roosevelt in an unpublished biography:

Beginning on the west side at the upper end and enumerating the business establishments the first buildings were the Fairview mine cabins, then (in order) Sam Heller's saloon and lunch room; Thompson's saloon; John Graham's Second hand Store; Pat McMahon's store "Everything Bought and Sold"; the Smith Hotel, run by George D. Smith, a Civil War veteran and his good wife Clara; a new and pretentious building being put up by Doc Cornell and two helpers; the saloon and gambling joint conducted by Klondike Kate and Bob Ward; a general store with a small but neat stock of merchandise and two thousand dollars worth of liquors. The three owners of this store for reasons not given to the public did not want to sell this whiskey. They would drink it up themselves within the next three years. Below them came the General Store of J. B. Randall and last on

6 Robert G. Bailey, *River of No Return*, (Lewiston, ID: Bailey Blake Printing Co., 1935), pp. 134–39

that side were the Surveyors and Assayers, Timm and Goodsell who had moved up from Thunder City when that town disappeared without trace overnight.

Coming down on the east side from the upper end was found first the Recorder's Office, Post Office and Fraser's blacksmith shop. Below the creek which crossed the street here came McAndrews and Richardson who were building but had not yet put in stock; the saloon of William Midgeley, a Klondiker, who was building and trading at the same time; Old Bart (Charles Bartholomew) who had some merchandise and whiskey and plenty of talk; the tent laundry of "Auntie" a giant negress; the restaurant of Pauline La Fontaine; the store of Ernest Pietzsch; the saloon of Sam Gillam, a refugee from Marble City and lastly, Johnny Conyers' saloon, the most pretentious in the town. Between many of these businesses establishments and behind those on the east side of the flat numerous tents had been set up and similar habitations were strung along the creek banks about the Fairview cabins.

All of Roosevelt was established without a single road to get there. Everything in the town except locally milled lumber was

Roosevelt in boom times

brought via pack train on trails through some of the most brutal terrain on the planet. At times the route was impassable through the extremes of the Idaho winter.

The initial excitement over the strike at Thunder Mountain began to wane as many of the prospectors returned to civilization. On the trail men had an odd reluctance to admit failure. As C. F. Neff noted, "We met a few men coming down the trail. They would invariably step out of the trail to let the horses pass. We, as was our custom, made an effort to interrogate these returning men about the trail ahead and always got civil answers to our queries. But when asked had they been in to the big thing and what did they think of it and what was it like, they would wave their hands, urge us to go on and see for ourselves, edge around the cavalcade and plunge on their way."[7]

Back in town something closer to the truth began to emerge in the newspaper. A July edition of the *Idaho County Free Press* stated, "The travel out from Thunder Mountain has been quite heavy for some days past. Some claim it is nothing but a first class fake, while others believe it will show up a number of big low-grade properties."[8]

The true test of Thunder Mountain would be sussed by the purchaser of the Caswell brothers' original find. Edward H. Dewey met the Caswells in Boise in 1900 and purchased a seventy-pound ore sample which he sent to his father in Pittsburgh. Based upon the sample he bought an option on the claim for $100,000. In 1901 Dewey sent a crew in to evaluate the claim and based upon their report exercised the option early. The report of this transaction in the Boise paper inflamed Thunder Mountain gold fever. The Deweys formed the Thunder Mountain Gold and Silver Mining and Milling Company with support from Pittsburgh financiers.[9]

The fever to get to Thunder Mountain was matched by the fever to sell stock in mining companies based upon inflated claims made about the area's prospects. The similarly named Thunder Mountain Consolidated Gold Mining and Milling Company placed an ad in the Boise newspaper stating, "Invest your money safely and profitably. Shares bought in our company….will net you thousands."

Such promotion prompted C. F. Neff to note, "Last winter a

7 C. F. Neff , Unpublished autobiography
8 *Idaho County Free Press* 3 July 1902
9 *Idaho County Free Press* 3 July 1902

weary prospector just back from the camp had come into the Overland Hotel in Boise and been immediately surrounded by men wanting to know about the difficulties of the trail." His reply had been, 'To hell with the trail to Thunder Mountain. Keep the trail to Pittsburg open. That's where the money is."[10]

Dewey mine development was originally accomplished with a ten-stamp mill shipped by rail to Nampa where it was dismantled and hauled via wagon through Emmett to Long Valley. Stamp mills are massive, heavy contraptions used to pound the gold ore, breaking it into a finer and finer consistency in order that it can be treated to extract the gold. A row of vertical steel rods, in this case ten, each with a heavy block of steel, the shoe, at the bottom are arranged in a large wooden frame. Each rod has a steel appendage attached to one side that rides on a camshaft. The camshaft is connected to a water wheel or other turning device. As the cam shaft is rotated, it lifts the appendage, shaft and shoe, which then drops onto the ore underneath. It is a noisy, dirty operation.

Given their purpose, the parts of the stamp mill had to be stout and heavy, making it even more remarkable that moving them fifty miles to the mine had to be accomplished on the back of a mule.

Later, a 100-stamp mill was ordered and shipped in forty rail cars to Emmett. By the time it arrived in 1904 a wagon road had been built to take it to the mine, but by then it was evident the claim did not warrant such an investment. The boilers for the mill were used instead in the Dewey Palace Hotel in Nampa and the rest was left to rust and was eventually sold for scrap at the rail head in Emmett.[11]

A second large development named the Sunnyside, located on the Marble Creek side of Thunder Mountain suffered a similar fate. Hundreds of thousands of dollars were raised via stock sales and a forty stamp mill set up for a test run. A cyanide processing plant was brought in. Yet total production for the Sunnyside from 1904 to 1906 was $5,000. The cyanide plant was never uncrated.[12]

As the fortunes of the mines dwindled so did the town of Roosevelt. The population shrank from thousands in 1904 to a few stragglers in 1909. The final insult to the dreams of the thousands who had

10 C. F. Neff, Unpublished autobiography
11 Craig Eldredge, "A Brief History of Gold Mining at Thunder Mountain, Idaho"
12 Eldredge, "A Brief History of Gold Mining at Thunder Mountain, Idaho"

invested money and labor in Thunder Mountain began on May 31. Craig Eldredge pieced together the story from various accounts:

> Miners along Mule Creek were aroused by a moving mass of earth 200 feet wide and 100 feet deep. Soggy conditions produced by rapidly melting snow caused a mudslide to break loose near the Dewey property at the head of Mule Creek, 2,000' above Roosevelt and two miles away. The slide moved slowly down Mule Creek, picking up boulders, snapping trees like matchsticks, and burying mining property in the rubble. The mudslide flowed across Monumental Creek, forming a dam which backed up the waters of that stream. The few remaining residents of Roosevelt, just upstream from the mudslide, moved their possessions to higher ground as the waters of Monumental Creek rose. Overnight the water level rose to twenty-eight feet, creating the present Lake Roosevelt. Outlines of buildings may still be seen beneath the water and logs from many of them have floated to the surface.

> The total production of all mines in the Thunder Mountain district was about $500,000. The Sunnyside alone spent well over that amount in the purchase of claims and machinery. When labor and transportation costs are added it seems peculiar that this company persisted for so many years. The Dewey mine and mill, in the hands of experienced and talented management, also failed to offset expenditures with production receipts. The people who suffered were those who purchased stock in these and other mining companies in Thunder Mountain. As Bailey said, there was vastly more money mined from the public than ever was taken from the ground in the Thunder Mountain District.

By 1904 the new road to the mine from the west and the struggles of even large well financed efforts to make the mine pay were beginning to put a pinch on the use of the Three Blaze Trail and Campbell's Ferry. That didn't stop the local business owners in Grangeville and Dixie from continued promotion of the route, but the writing for the last chapter was on the wall.

Roosevelt in flood

Boom Time

Chapter Nine

Missing

"The American dream has some nightmares attached to
it and this is one of the ways the American dream can
go. The American dream probably resulted in, for most
of the people who followed it, like a marsh light,
in disaster."
– Wallace Stegner

The collapse of the dream that was Thunder Mountain was
never seen by William Campbell. At the peak of the good fortune
brought by the trail and ferry he built he simply disappeared during
the winter of 1902–03. There are several plausible versions of his fate.
R. G. Bailey tells it thus:

William Campbell, a likable Scotsman, built and operated
a ferry across the Salmon River, on the trail to Thunder Mountain, when the camp was booming in 1902. Many pack trains
crossed at the ferry and Campbell derived a good income. In
the winter there was no travel, so Campbell stretched a trap
line to the high divide. One day some of his friends visited his

cabin, but found no one at home. Evidence seemed to indicate that he had been away for some time. The friends stayed at the cabin for several days, and when Campbell did not return started out to look for him. Their efforts were fruitless, and soon they had organized a man hunt, enlisting every person in the Salmon River Canyon. No trace of Campbell was ever found. He had gone out on his trap line when some disaster overtook him, and was never again heard from. Later it became known that another trapper, by name A. L McLaughlin, of Clarkston, Washington, had crossed the trail of Campbell and followed it to a high precipice, over which it was assumed the unfortunate man had fallen.[1]

The files of the Payette National Forest have a slightly different twist on this story. In this account, "Campbell progressed ahead of his party and became lost in a heavy snowstorm near the head of Lodgepole Creek; he was never seen afterwards. Search parties failed to learn what fate overtook him but the supposition was that a broken snowshoe spelled his doom in the deep snow."[2]

Johnny Carrey and Cort Conley would offer another view of Campbell's demise in their book of the same name as Bailey's *River of No Return*:

Bill Campbell mysteriously disappeared the winter after the trail was finished. He snowshoed to the Roosevelt mine where he worked, but refused payment of wages in gold, saying it was too heavy to carry. He took a check instead. He vanished on his way back to the river. He was never seen again and the check went uncashed. There are two likely explanations concerning his fate. One is that he froze to death in a snowstorm. The other seems more credible: Bill was engaged to Gene Churchill's adopted niece, Stella. He probably decided to stop and visit her. While crossing the ice, he fell through and drowned. (The niece later married Robert Bailey).[3]

1 Robert G. Bailey, *River of No Return,* (Lewiston, ID: Bailey Blake Printing Co., 1935), p. 451
2 Sister Mary Alfreda Elsensohn, *Pioneer Days in Idaho County, Volume Two* (Caldwell, ID: Caxton Printers, 1978), p. 457
3 Johnny Carrey and Cort Conley, *River of No Return,* (Cambridge, ID: Backeddy Books, 1977), p. 163

The Eugene "Gene" Churchill that Carrey and Conley reference was a Minnesotan who had come to the canyon at the same time as Campbell and Jim Moore. Frances Zaunmiller Wisner[4] said Jim Moore told her that Churchill stayed with Moore his first winter in the canyon to help him get his place going, then moved on to do the same four miles upstream. Today we call Churchill's homestead Whitewater Ranch. Churchill is remembered through Churchill Mountain just north of the canyon on the trail to Dixie, that bears his name.

As with many backcountry stories, numerous versions exist, and similar names add to the confusion. In a February 12, 1914, issue of the *Idaho County Free Press,* the story is told of a Charles Campbell who was, "lost ten years ago going through a snowstorm on 'his trail' to his wedding when he disappeared, labeling the story one of the mysteries of the mountains."

William Campbell was among many who died struggling with the dangers of this wild, remote country. He was the first connected to Campbell's Ferry Ranch to die. He would not be the last.

4 Frances Zaunmiller Wisner, Oral History, University of Idaho, 21 September 1976

Missing

Chapter
Ten

Cook

*"Pale Death with impartial tread
beats at the poor man's cottage door
and at the palaces of kings."*
– Horace

The disappearance of Campbell did not lessen the effort to promote the northern route to Thunder Mountain, but the locals were fighting a losing battle. Operation of the ferry was taken over by two men named Rudolph and Medaris. The two are mentioned in the *Elk City Mining News* as owners of the ferry in early 1904.[1] The 1900 census lists Mike Rudolph as a single forty-two-year-old farmer born in Illinois of German parents. At the time he was living in Nezperce, Idaho, a farming community twenty-one miles north of Grangeville. He and a friend named Medaris had purchased the ferry, or they may

1 Marian S. Sweeney, *Gold at Dixie Gulch*, (Kamiah, ID: Clearwater Valley Publishing, 1982), p. 26

have just been hired by Churchill, the executor of Campbell's estate, to run it until the property could be sold. The *Elk City Mining News* reported the two, "passed through camp on their way outside for provisions. They are so anxious to get the Dixie-Thunder Mountain trail in shape that they offered to put up work against $100 in contributions." Local merchants took them up on the offer.

The Commercial Club, an organization of Lewiston business owners, reported raising $325 in one day, over $8,000 in today's money, with prospects for more. A delegation was sent to meet with railroad representatives in Stites.[2] R. G. Bailey urged them on, claiming that Rudolph and Medaris, "deserve great credit for the manner in which they have cut out, widened and otherwise improved the trail. From the ferry to Chamberlain they cleaned the trail out and shortened it at least two hours." Charles Boii of Dixie went even further claiming, "Many of the turns and windings of the old trail have been eliminated, thereby reducing the distance by twelve or fourteen miles and the time by at least three-fourths of a day for loaded animals."

In October 1904 the *Elk City News* printed an extensive article calling the trail the "logical route" giving distances from the rail head at Stites to Elk City, fifty-three miles, from Elk City to Dixie, twenty-seven miles, Dixie to the ferry, twelve miles, ferry across Chamberlain Basin to Big Creek, thirty miles and another twenty miles to Thunder Mountain. The publisher assured the reader that Elk City was, "the mining center of Central Idaho where anything pertaining to mining can be purchased." Farther along in Dixie at the end of the road was a hotel, store and post office and the beginning of a trail, "well marked and absolutely free from snowslides and all danger to life incident to winter travel."

The *News* falsely reported the southern route through Placerville to be "abandoned" and discredited the Florence-Warren route by saying postal authorities realized the "utter impracticability" of this "so-called route." The paper claimed the people of Northern Idaho were doing what the government could not by, "placing the trail in such condition that any kind of freight, mail or machinery can be carried over it from Dixie....and brings the railroad about 35 miles nearer Thunder Mountain than any other."

The source of such inflated claims was undoubtedly influenced

2 "Money for Dixie Trail", *Lewiston Tribune*, August 26 1904

by local merchants promoting their businesses like this ad purchased in the same edition of the *Elk City Mining News* -

Charles Boii, Proprietor
Of the Cash Bargain Store
Dealer in General
Merchandise
And Miners Supplies
Try Us
Dixie, Idaho

The following spring of 1905 the Lewiston Tribune reported:

BRIGHT OUTLOOK
AT DIXIE

The travel over the new trail from this point in to Thunder Mountain promises to be much heavier this season than ever before, and many of the miners in the Big Creek and Thunder Mountain camps will make Dixie their trading point. The new trail affords a route 12 miles shorter than any other trail leading into the camp, and packers and miners will generally enter the camp from here.

A young miner named Warren Cook would have been privy to all the hype about the route and the homestead that was strategically placed where the trail crossed the Salmon River. Cook was a young Spanish-American War veteran who had come back from the war hungry for adventure and romance. He likely had a strong sense of patriotism and idealism. Photographs of Warren in his youth show a strikingly handsome young man with wavy dark hair, wide set eyes, and a generous mouth. He was strong bodied with large hands used to physical labor.

The 1900 census noted the twenty-four-year-old Cook living in Dixie working the mines as a day laborer and sharing a tent with Wade Blevens. His exact movements for the next few years are unknown. He may well have made the trek to Thunder Mountain and witnessed the boom and deflated hopes.

Living just thirteen miles up the trail from Campbell's Ferry, Cook would have known

Warren Cook
1st Idaho Volunteers

about the homestead and the opportunity that arose when its owner vanished. At some point he traveled to Elk City and met a 5'3" school teacher of Italian descent, Rose Bernardi Aiken. On June 22, 1903, forty-year-old Rose and twenty-seven-year-old Warren traveled to Grangeville and exchanged wedding vows before a justice of the peace. The next day they caught a stage to Elk City to fashion a life among the mining camps and wilderness of Idaho.[3] A year later Cook purchased Campbell's Ferry and moved to the river in March of 1905.

The couple did not have much to start with. The ferry was still operating, but, contrary to northern newspaper accounts, more and more the flow of traffic to Thunder Mountain was taking the southern route on a new wagon road. The route across Chamberlain Basin would soon be no longer necessary except for the occasional hunter. At the ranch his predecessors had left a primitive cabin and barn with a diversion ditch from Trout Creek running through the ravine behind the cabin. Built for a bachelor, Warren Cook needed to make the small

3 Kathy Deinhardt Hill, *Spirits of the Salmon River,* (Cambridge, ID: Backeddy Books, 2001), p. 67

72

cabin work for him and his new family. It didn't start well.

Soon after their arrival a tragedy took the cabin Campbell had built. When the fire began there wasn't a lot they could do about it. The only water on hand would have been via bucket brought from the ditch. There was no time for help from neighbors. The Salmon River separated Warren and his wife Rose from Jim Moore at his homestead. The choice he had was to fight it the best he and his wife could with buckets, or have one of them run to the river bank to shout for help from Jim. Even if Jim heard, the time it took to cross the river and climb the bank would have been more than enough for fire to overtake the small, wooden structure. The Churchills four miles upriver were even less of an option.

The origin of the fire is unknown, but the likely culprit was the flume. Heat for the one room cabin was a small stove, not much more than a metal box with a pipe off the back to take smoke and fumes up through the roof. Perhaps the jacket around the pipe wasn't thick enough, or had shifted to allow the hot surface to contact the roof structure. Or it could have been embers pushed out by the rising smoke, drifting back on dry roof shakes. What little time Warren and Rose had must have been used to save personal items.

Just a few short months after purchasing their dream, the couple was learning how harsh life in the Idaho wilderness could be. Their small cabin site had become a pile of ashes inside the rectangle of rocks that had once held the structure's base logs off the ground. Cook would have to work fast to build a new cabin. It would not be long before winter would arrive and they would be totally isolated. Inside the barn Warren set up a tent for the couple to live in and sent word out for help.[4]

No doubt, as it was then and remains now in the ways of the backcountry, neighbors would have rushed to help get a new cabin raised before winter set in. Friends from Dixie and Elk City likely came, as well as Moore and the Churchills. Rose had a large family in Salem, Oregon, including four brothers. Some of them may have caught the train to rail's end at Stites, hopped a stage to Dixie, and walked or rode horseback the last thirteen miles to help their sister and brother-in-law build a new home. With time to do it right, the new cabin would have used logs that were cut and left to air dry, but with

4 David Cook, Personal Communication, April 2007

winter on the horizon the men had to get something going.

The new cabin would be a temporary structure built with green logs. Warren and his helpers began felling trees dragging them to the new cabin site with horses. Using a crosscut saw they cut the logs to size, stripped the bark and fashioned corner joints with an ax. Green logs shrink, crack and move as they dry, making the new structure less than perfect. They could never have imagined their handiwork would still be here over a hundred years later.

Dave Cook, Warren's grandson, is the family historian, and tells of Warren's background and the origin of the Cook name:

Warren had known hard work. He was born in Dayton, Washington, February 26, 1876. Warren's grandfather was of Spanish descent, named Cusinero. He had come to the US and opened a slave trading business. He was an evil man. In one deal he bought all the slaves on a ship docked in Galveston. He threw the bodies of the dead overboard into the bay. He treated the sick ones, put them in iron shackles and branded them. As soon as he got them healthy he would auction them off. He made no effort to keep families together. He sold the young men for field hands, the old men for house servants, the old women for scullery maids and cooks and the pretty young girls for prostitutes.

He kept no records, just handled them like cattle.

When the Civil War came he fought for the South. When the Carpetbaggers came in during Reconstruction they came looking for him, Where's my sister, where's my mother? He was in trouble.

He put his family in a covered wagon and went as deep in the Rocky Mountains as he could go. In the 1860s there was no Montana, no Idaho, no Washington. This area was just Oregon. Outside of Grangeville was a huge blank space on the map.

Along the trail one night around the campfire, he asked his fellow travelers, "My name, Cusinero, what is that in American?"

"Cuisine is food," his companion responded. "Cocinero is a preparer of food. That's a cook."

"Well, I am Cook,' said Cusinero.

That is where the family name came from.

When he came into Grangeville under the name Cook he fixed up a big, thick Bible. In the front he had a genealogy showing how his family was traced back to Missouri. It is as bogus as a three-dollar bill. Every word of it. We still have the bible. But he needed it in case someone came after him, that is how you prove your genealogy, a family Bible.[5]

Warren's father, John Barrister Cook, was a farmer in the area around Walla Walla, Washington, when Warren, their first child was born. John later moved with wife, Clara, to Grangeville where he set up a blacksmith shop. Two other children followed in close order.

Clara suffered from a mental disorder that caused her to walk out one day leaving her husband to raise the three kids. She was never seen again. Warren's father brought a Nez Perce woman into the home to help, but the burden of it all led to an unstable family life. At age ten, Warren was sent to live with a Nez Perce family, and after eighth grade set out on his own, working in the local farming communities.[6]

In the spring of 1898 in response to President McKinley's call for 125,000 additional men for the war against Spain, Warren joined Company C, Grangeville, First Idaho Regiment of infantry volunteers as a quartermaster Sergent. He boarded a ship in San Francisco in June and upon arrival in the Philippines in August spent the first six months on duty guarding supplies during the battle for Manila.

In February an insurrection ensued and the Idaho volunteers saw action in the Battle of Santa Anna. A force of 1,500 Idaho and Washington troops brashly charged 10,000 well-fortified and well-armed Filipinos.

When commanding officer General Charles King realized the emboldened troops could not be called back he shouted, "Go it, you damned Idaho savages, go it!"

Settling back into his saddle he remarked, "There goes the American soldier, and all hell can't stop him."[7]

By noon Santa Anna was captured. The troops saw action on three other occasions before returning to the U.S. in the fall of 1899

5 David Cook, Personal Communication, April 2007

6 Sandy McRae, Personal Communication, April 2007

7 Leonard J. Arrington, *History of Idaho*, (Moscow, ID: University of Idaho Press, 1994), pp. 438–40

minus thirty-seven who had died in the effort.

Rose Bernardi Aiken was born in Salem, Oregon, in December, 1862, the daughter of an Italian father from Switzerland and a German mother. The couple had immigrated to the California gold fields in 1848. By 1860, Joseph Bernardi had given up the life of a miner and moved to Oregon where he worked as a saloon keeper, then liquor dealer.

Rosa, named after her mother, was the second of eight children in this large Catholic family. In 1881 the dark-skinned, 5'3" 130-pound Rose[8] married Joseph Aiken who had a young daughter, Bliss, from a previous marriage. Bliss drowned in the Snake River in 1899, followed by Joseph's passing by pneumonia in 1900, leading Rose to move back in with her widowed mother and siblings.[9] What brought her to Idaho is unknown, but three years later, while working as a school teacher in Elk City, she met and married Warren Cook.

Bernardi family dinner – Rose third from the right
Salem, Oregon – 1900

8 Kathy Deinhardt Hill, *Spirits of the Salmon River,* (Cambridge, ID: Backeddy Books, 2001), p. 66
9 www.ancestry.com, 1860-1900 Census records

Warren built his new cabin a hundred yards downstream from the ashes of the Campbell Cabin. Perched on a high bank overlooking the river, he could see traffic on the trail on the other side from his new location and make the short hike downhill to greet visitors and operate the ferry.

Experiencing their first year in the wilds together, the Cooks must have been nervous after a rough start. The struggles with a cabin fire would have softened as the small family reveled in the wonders of spring in the canyon. On the canyon floor snow normally lingers through February, but by March the snowline starts to recede up the canyon slopes.

In April, fresh green shoots appear and wildlife is abundant. The howls of wolves echo off the canyon walls as they emerge from their dens with new litters of pups. The packs begin their annual trek up the sides of the canyon following the deer and elk, preying on their young. Occasional storms march through the canyon, spitting snow pellets and sleet in the last vestiges of winter, soon to be replaced by daffodils and robins.

By late May the Cooks would have their first garden in, looking forward to mid-June and the beginning of its bounty of fresh vegetables. The heat of late spring, early summer brings the snow melt from the high country, turning small rivulets into rushing streams, combining to bring the mighty Salmon River to its peak. The quiet of the canyon is replaced by a constant, dull moan as the rising tide picks up floating debris, tearing at the banks as it rushes by.

Rose had adapted well to life in Idaho. Working in Elk City she had developed friends and according to the local news was, "well and favorably known." She told friends that since coming to Idaho she, "led an ideal life."[10]

Warren's projects at the property would have been much like ours – get the garden in, water flowing in all the ditches, plus a new ditch to bring water in front of the new cabin site, caring for the new fruit trees in the orchard, perhaps he even started to fell the trees needed to add an extension on the front of the new cabin. When summer arrived it would be good to get the heat of the kitchen into a room separated from their sleeping quarters.

As spring arrived it brought blooms to the fruit trees, new

10 *Idaho County Free Press*, 26 October 1905

growth to the garden and the promise of more new life in the canyon. Rose was expecting Warren's child.

The due date would be during the Cooks' first winter at Campbell's Ferry. There must have been discussions between the two about a critical issue. Would the child be born at the homestead? Perhaps they should spend the winter in Grangeville or even with Rose's mother in Salem where Rose would have constant attention and access to a doctor. The decision would be made in the context of medical knowledge at the turn of the century.

It wasn't until the late 1800s that scientific advances in bacteriology occurred and were applied to surgery. In 1894 the first cesarean section was performed in Boston. By 1900 physicians were attending about half the nation's births, including nearly all births to middle and upper class women. Less than five percent of women gave birth in hospitals. Midwives took care of women who could not afford a doctor.[11] In rural America it was the norm for women to deliver with the help of other women, and the Cooks felt fortunate to know that their closest female neighbor, Ella Churchill, just a two-hour hike upstream, was a midwife.

The decision may have been complicated by Rose's experience with another child. Family knowledge on the subject is foggy, no doubt complicated by Warren's reluctance in later years to talk about what must have been a tragedy nearly impossible to endure. One of Warren's grandsons recalls a story that a five-year-old son from Rose's earlier marriage had been born with great difficulty and the doctor had advised against future child bearing.[12] Sandy McRae, another Cook grandson recounts, "At some point a five-year-old boy shows up – don't know if Rose was a guardian or what. We can find no definitive record of the child, and an extensive court-ordered search years later when Warren Cook died also failed to locate the boy."[13]

We don't know if it would have made a difference that winter if Rose's labor had occurred in town, but the suffering would have been less. Whatever the circumstances, the final decision to stay in the canyon would seal their fate – a cruel saga to be played out that winter

11 Adrian E. Feldhusan, *The History of Midwifery and Childbirth in America: A Time Line*, www.midwiferytoday.com/articles/timeline.asp
12 David Cook, Personal Communication, April 2007
13 Sandy McRae, Personal Communication, April 2007

in a small cabin in the wilds of Idaho.

At some point after labor ensued on October 7, Ella Churchill was summoned. The trail along the river to Churchill's ranch was often passable for long stretches during the winter due to its low elevation. It is often possible to move within the canyon even as travel to the high country is hampered as snow from the approaching winter builds to block roads and trails.

With Ella in attendance it became evident that Rose's delivery was not going well. As the hours of effort changed to days, the small group began to realize something was horribly wrong. For three days the women struggled to deliver the baby. They may have recognized that the child was in breech position. The midwife would have tried to manipulate the pregnant belly to get the baby to flip to a normal head down position. As the local news related, Mrs. Churchill, "did everything for the unfortunate sufferer that kindness and matured judgment counseled."[14]

A last desperate attempt was made to secure a doctor, but the trip out and back took days. It was thirteen miles via trail to Dixie, the last ten being in the high country where snow was encountered. From Dixie to Elk City was another twenty-seven miles at high elevation. Mrs. Pete Campbell and Dr. Cullen responded to the call for help, "making the long ride in a day and night, but did not arrive until after the Angel of Death had claimed its own."[15]

Rose's struggles throughout the ordeal were without the aid of anesthesia and pain treatments that are so familiar today. Jim Moore later told the story, "First we prayed that she would have the baby. Then we prayed for it to be over soon."[16]

Rose Cook had lived a tragic life, losing one husband and a stepdaughter five years earlier in Oregon. Now her dreams of a new life, nestled in the idyllic beauty of the Salmon River canyon with her young loving husband Warren, ended in a six-day ordeal of agony and isolation. The scene in the small log cabin, lit by kerosene lanterns, heated by the small woodstove would have been hard to bear. The small group of Warren, Rose, Ella, Gene Churchill and Jim Moore

14 *Idaho County Free Press* obituary, 12 October 1905
15 *Idaho County Free Press* obituary, 12 October 1905
16 Kathy Deinhardt Hill, *Spirits of the Salmon River,* (Cambridge, ID: Backeddy Books, 2001), p. 67

were engrossed in the harsh reality of nature's absence of mercy to those who choose to live close to her wild heart.

Warren selected a gentle slope among the pines above the garden for the final resting place for Rose and the child. Today a simple redwood marker on the grave with a brass plaque reads, *Rose Aiken Cook and Her Child, Died in Childbirth, Fall 1904.*[17]

Through the years, those who lived at Campbell's Ferry must have felt linked to Rose as we do now. We have collected stones to lay as a mosaic on her grave. We imagine she would find pleasure in

the two old fashioned rose bushes we planted nearby in her name, a pink one for Rose and a white rose for her child.

****

Warren's life with Rose surrounded by the natural beauty of Campbell's Ferry had become a nightmare. He found he could no longer stand the place. It just held too many sad memories. According to his grandson, prior to pursuing a new career, he had to deal with Rose's child by a former marriage. Dave Cook relates, "The child had some bad disease. He would never speak of it. We have never known what it was, but it was a serious disease."

According to Sandy McRae, another of Warren's grandsons "Warren decided to leave the ranch, built a raft, floated to Riggins with the boy, and asked someone in Riggins to raise the boy with Warren's financial help. I'm not sure where the boy was taken, maybe to Lewiston for education, or maybe moved to Portland. Nothing was ever verified. When Warren died in 1951 the state needed to know that

17 The date is wrong by a year. The actual date of October 12, 1905 is confirmed in an obituary in the *Idaho County Free Press* newspaper.

this boy wouldn't have a claim on Warren's estate. The Judge finally accepted that the family had tried all that was possible to find the boy and allowed the estate to be settled."

Warren's father had struggled to raise his kids when their mother had "lost it" in Grangeville years before and fled. Perhaps Warren as well was unable to deal with the loss of a wife and the challenges of raising a child with disabilities.

He turned his attention to finding a new job and signed on with the newly created U.S. Forest Service as an assistant ranger. Warren had learned survey work, perhaps self-taught as his family later found books on the subject in his library. His job with the agency would be to survey an area including Chamberlain Basin, Big Creek, and Elk Summit, which was then part of the Payette Forest Reserve.

Cook was later assigned to Hay Station near Warren, just beyond the breaks of the South Fork of the Salmon. While there, he met Helga Peterson who had come to Idaho from teaching in the iron mining country of Michigan. Helga secured a new position that opened at the small school in Warren. In 1908 the two were married and had a daughter, Dorothy. Soon after she turned four, tragedy struck the Cook family again when Dorothy died of diphtheria. The funeral was held in McCall.

In an effort to console Warren, his supervisor spoke to him saying, "Warren, this is a terrible tragedy, but she is in a better place." Warren never was much for religion. All he could think was once again he was placing his child's body in the cold ground. In anger he replied, "What do you mean she is in a better place?" In a state of rage and grief he picked up a nearby two by four and hit the supervisor in the head. That was the end of Warren's Forest Service career.[18]

Helga would later become the postmaster at McCall with Warren working as an assistant. They went on to raise two more children. Warren ultimately found success in real estate in McCall, owning and developing lots around Big Payette Lake. By 1940 he had acquired a lease on a cabin at the mouth of Allison Creek just upriver from Riggins. He moved there in his retirement, gardening, developing new strains of roses and baking Indian bread in a rock oven he built. He only left the place three times – for medical reasons to McCall and once on a vacation to Mexico. He lived out his years on the Salmon

18 David Cook and Sandy McRae, Personal Communication, April 2007

River, dying of cancer after a life as a smoker. A sign hung on the porch of his Salmon River home that announced, "Let me live in a house by the side of the road and be a friend to man."

Two of Warren's grandsons still live on the Salmon River, just upriver from Riggins, retired after military careers in service to their country.

Warren Cook's Cabin
after more than 100 years

Chapter Eleven

Artists

"You can dance anywhere,
even if only in your heart."
– Unknown

The next inhabitant of Campbell's Ferry was a performing artist named Ernest Frederick Sillge. He would not be the last.

Bustling Idaho mining camps attracted hordes of gold seekers from every walk of life from around the globe. A thirst for the yellow treasure was their primary focus, but a similar thirst for artistic fulfillment is shown by the establishment of theatres for performing artists in many of the raw mining camps.

In Idaho City an opera house was built that was frequented by companies touring the West. Dixie was too small for opera, but the local citizens did support the arts. By a process called subscription, funds were raised to pay for George Otterson's travel by wagon to Elk

City to procure a piano for the community.[1]

The local newspapers frequently mentioned the professional quality performances given by Fred Sillge. Sillge was a highly educated German musician who had played in some of the cathedrals of his homeland. In his late teens, he was brought to America by his father so that he would not be drafted by the German army.[2] A hard worker, during his time in Dixie he secured a contract to make 10,000 roof shakes for the Majestic Gold and Silver Mining Company.[3]

In addition to Fred's reputation for musical talent he was also known for his fondness for drink as Margaret Trader, a neighbor in Dixie, recalled, "He could sit down and play almost anything on the piano. He loved to play *Humoresque*. He was German and quite well educated. He had the house just below us. He drank a lot and sometime he'd lay out there after too much to drink and my mother would give us a little bread dough and we'd bake it on top of the stove – bread for Fred."[4]

Sillge's time at Campbell's Ferry was spent gathering fruits and vegetables from the garden and expanding the system of irrigation ditches. He operated the ferry for the few still passing through to diggings in Thunder Mountain, Big Creek and the Chamberlain Basin. The ferry was not a year-round operation. The river would freeze over in the winter and run too high for safe operations each spring. Under these conditions the ferry itself would be tied off to the bank. A pole would be attached between the ferry and the bank to hold it away from damage caused by the surging water pushing it against the rocky shore. The main cable would still be stretched across the river. A basket or seat would be hung below, attached to a pulley on the cable, allowing one or two men to sit and pull themselves from one side to the other. It was not without risk, as noted in the June 16, 1921 *Idaho County Free Press*:

1 Marian S. Sweeney, *Gold at Dixie Gulch*, (Kamiah, ID: Clearwater Valley Publishing, 1982), p. 26
2 Johnny Carrey and Cort Conley, *River of No Return*, (Cambridge, ID: Backeddy Books, 1977), p. 142
3 Sweeney, p. 25
4 Sweeney, p. 25

WILLIAM SORROW AND FRED SILGE PERISH IN TREACHEROUS STREAM

William Sorrow, 22 of Grangeville and Fred Sillge, 58 of Dixie were drowned at Sillge's Ferry 15 miles south of Dixie on Wednesday of last week. The men were crossing Salmon River in a basket suspended from a cable. A log, which was floating down the river hit the basket and the men were upset in the water. Silge sank immediately and was seen no more. Sorrow came to the surface once and attempted to swim ashore, but is believed to have been caught by the undertow and sucked into the whirlpool. The river at the time the men were drowned is said to have been the highest in years.

Allen Stonebraker, who resides in Chamberlain Basin, south of the Salmon, a Mr. Flower and a Mr. Butler of Mabton, Washington were in the party. The drowning occurred more than 75 miles from Grangeville and is in a veritable wilderness. Silge was unmarried…. He is believed to have a brother in Baker, Oregon…While the bodies may be found near where the drownings occurred, it is pointed out that they also may wash many miles downstream before the river gives up its dead.

The bodies were never found. The wilderness had taken another pioneer soul. There would be more.

Artists

I couldn't believe she was willing to do this. Her friends in the art world would gasp in amazement. The Ferry's newest performing artist had retired in 2005 as the dean of the College of Fine Arts and Associate Vice-President for the Arts at the University of Utah. Every day at work she showed up dressed to kill. To this girl St. John was not a religious term. Or was it? She could make the case that finding just the right fine knit outfit to fit her 5'3" 103 pound dancer's body was a religious quest. Who was I to argue?

Now, I couldn't help but smile as I looked at her, crouched in a number three wash tub in front of a primitive one-room cabin, the Salmon River Canyon stretching off in the distance. She deserved a hot bath. I had drawn two buckets of water from the newly restored ditch, heated them on the stove, and fixed her bath the only way I could figure. And she loved it. They would never believe this in Salt Lake City!

While I was off being a little boy playing in the ditch, she had tackled squeezing our clothes and supplies into one sixteen by twenty-four foot room. It all had to fit. The kitchen, the bedroom, the closets (there are none), the cabinets (none of those, either), dining table, chairs, wood stove, small office table. We had one cooler with ice to last a week. After that, the only cooling would come from placing things in the ditch. Actually, this time of year, the water flowing through is just removed from snow, so it did well for now. By the time summer got here we would need another solution.

Phyllis did not decide to be a dancer until she was three. Living in Santa Barbara, California, with her grandparents while her father served in World War II, her mother took her to a performance by a ballet company that had come through town. The child was enthralled.

Fortuitously, living half a block from her grandparents was a Russian immigrant, Madame Maria Kedrina who had performed with the Diaghilev's Ballets Russes alongside Anna Pavlova and Vaslav Nijinsky.

Phyllis remembers, "Madame took a look at me and asked my mother, How old is she?"

"Three, my mother answered."

"She's too young; bring her back when she can skip."

So her mother took her home, taught her to skip that afternoon and brought her back to ballet lessons the next day. Two years later Phyllis made her auspicious debut on stage, dancing the role of a lettuce.

Madame Kedrina was extremely well trained and particular about every detail. "She always scared me," Phyllis said. "Until I was probably in my thirties – she was all of five feet tall and weighed no more than eighty pounds. But she was very strict."

"There would be times when my fear overcame me and I would say, I think I want to stop going to ballet."

"My mother would answer, You can stop anytime you want, but if you stop, you can never go back."

Phyllis had no doubts of her mother's sincerity. "I would think about the joy of moving through space and the high I felt performing on stage, so I kept going back."

By the time Phyllis was in high school she was dancing lead roles and even doing some professional work.

Phyllis was introduced to Modern Dance at the University of Arizona where she continued to have opportunities to perform as she finished her degree. After moving to New York and, later, San Francisco, she continued to study and perform. In 1969 she entered the University of Utah where she completed her Master of Fine Arts degree in Modern Dance. By now her resume included professional work in ballet, modern dance and musical theatre. She danced *The Kiss Dance* (a duet with Joel Grey) in the original version of *Cabaret*, appeared with Barbara Eden in *The Unsinkable Molly Brown*, and in *Funny Girl* with Marilyn Michaels.

At thirty years of age Phyllis assumed her performing days were behind her, but soon after receiving her graduate degree she joined Ririe-Woodbury Dance Company in Salt Lake City. The Company had just been listed on the National Endowment's Artist Touring Program and what followed was a whirlwind eight years touring the U.S. and abroad, dancing in some of the world's most prestigious venues.

Eventually the gypsy life takes its toll, so when Phyllis was offered a teaching position at the University of Hawaii she reluctantly left the company but happily moved to Honolulu for eight years. In Hawaii she taught and developed a passion for choreography, while still performing on occasion.

During her final year as an associate professor at the University of Hawaii, Phyllis took a year's leave of absence to be a guest artist at the Hong Kong Academy for Performing Arts. While in Hong Kong, she was offered the opportunity to return to the University of Utah, this time as chair of the modern dance department.

Thus began the next phase of her career, arts administration. In her new position she not only taught, choreographed, and performed from time to time but also, most importantly, took on the leadership of one of the country's most prestigious university dance programs. It was an honor and a challenge.

Ten years later Phyllis was tapped to be dean of the College of Fine Arts overseeing the departments of art & art history, ballet, film, music, theatre, as well as modern dance. Two years later she added the title of associate vice president for the arts, incorporating oversight of the Utah Museum of Fine Arts, Kingsbury Hall performance venue, and Pioneer Theatre Company to her duties as dean of the college.

How does one go from dancing around the world, leading arts entities in academe, to a life of bathing in a number three wash tub surrounded by millions of acres of wilderness? It was not such a stretch as it might seem

From the age of five, Phyllis was raised on a family ranch on the edge of Santa Barbara, California. Though Santa Barbara had its posh reputation even then, the ranch was fairly remote. If you got a flat tire on the road into town you could end up spending most of the day there before someone came along to help. There was a beach right below the property and rolling foothills above it, acres of room and freedom to roam....alone. Her brother Mike and sister Patty were considerably younger. There were seldom other children around for playmates.

Although not nearly as remote as the Ferry (they did have electricity and running water), the family lived close to nature. Coyotes sang in the barrancas, there were horses to ride into the hills and along the beach, the family always had a garden and orchard which required the children's help.

Phyllis' first job as a nine-year-old was caring for the family chicken flock, about forty Rhode Island Reds, who shared their extensive complex of coops with a variety of exotic game birds and two peacocks that roamed the grounds. Perhaps in lieu of playmates, the children were allowed all manner of pets. Besides the usual dogs, cats, horses, parakeets, fish, rabbits, hamsters, and guinea pigs, at various times the menagerie included: a pet goat that found all landscaping delicious, horned toads, a variety of snakes and lizards that fell victim to child ambush and were released once their novelty wore off, a pet crow named Rowdy that would come when summoned to eat from your hand and took delight in tormenting the cat, a pet owl named Ed who lived in the fireplace, and a very large pig named Hershey who roamed the premises with the dogs.

Raccoons, skunks and possums pressed their noses against the windows to ascertain that the family was busy inside, giving the varmints opportunity to steal avocados off the trees. Summer days were spent on the beach, body surfing, swimming, and exploring along the cliffs. By the time she entered high school the family had acquired a cattle ranch about twenty miles north.

Phyllis' mother, Phyllis The First, had been raised by her own father to hunt a variety of game. It was not unusual for her mother to ride off alone, shoot a deer, hang, gut and quarter it, then pack it home. Her father, Eldon, had joined the family engineering business when he returned from Germany after World War II.

Although family vacations were rare, they generally involved some sort of adventure, traveling and/or camping somewhere remote. One adventure took Phyllis and her mother on a four-day camel ride through the Escalante area of Southern Utah. She went scuba-diving in Hawaii, Palau, Australia, Borneo, and Thailand. It was on one of the family vacations that she discovered whitewater rafting.

In 1969 younger sister Patty was in college and dating a young man who guided for Hatch River Expeditions. Phyllis and her parents signed on for a five-day Middle Fork rafting adventure. For Phyllis it was love at first rapid; she was hooked. She went on to raft rivers throughout Idaho, Utah, California, Arizona, Oregon, as well as Chile, Costa Rica, and Australia.

Although she had never lived in a spot quite so remote and primitive as Campbell's Ferry, she had grown up with an affinity for nature and experience in living close to it.

Phyllis

Chapter Twelve

Forests

"I recognize the right and duty of this generation
to develop and use the natural resources of our land; but I do not recognize the right to waste them, or to rob, by wasteful use, the generations that come after us."
– Theodore Roosevelt

William Campbell, Warren Cook and Fred Sillge were gambling that the land they settled and purchased could some day be legally theirs. Until the nation and states sorted out the concept of public
domain and how portions of it could pass into private ownership, their
claim to what became Campbell's Ferry was tenuous.

When Cook, devastated by the loss of a wife and child, left
the Ferry in 1905, he applied for work with a newly formed federal
agency, the Forest Service, which had just been given management
authority over the millions of acres surrounding the Ferry. The agency
had little knowledge of the character and boundaries of their new do-

main. The first order of business would be to hire men like Cook to map the nation's newly established forest reserves.

Today, as we cross the boundary between the eighty-five acres set forth in the deed to Campbell's Ferry and the bordering lands that are now Idaho's part of the national forests and national wilderness preservation systems, we traverse a landscape managed by policies with their genesis in our nation's founding.

The federal lands surrounding Campbell's Ferry are remnants of a public domain created as the United States grew from the thirteen colonies of its infancy to the coast-to-coast nation it is today. Shortly after its founding the fledgling United States was beset by huge war debts and an uncertain basis for funding growing federal operations. The nation needed money and it had at its disposal what was then deemed an almost endless supply of land.

In 1785 and 1786 the Continental Congress passed two ordinances that set forth policies on public lands. The ordinances created a rectangular surveying system, determined the procedures by which territories would become states, spelled out the principles of land sales and public reservations, and in general laid down the public land philosophy still in use today.[1]

The concept of western lands first meant the area west of the Appalachians and east of the Mississippi River, but through acquisition, negotiation and war, western became the vast land mass stretching all the way to the Pacific Ocean. Congress created the General Land Office in 1812 to manage the process of transferring much of this land to private ownership. The Office operated under the core principle that the land must be purchased.

In 1849 the Interior Department was created and the Land Office became part of it. Thirteen years later a significant exception was made to the principle that the land had to be bought. The Homestead Act of 1862 allowed pioneers to acquire 160 acres through sweat. By living on and improving the property over a period of five years, title to the land would be granted to the pioneer. The only monetary cost was a small filing fee.

Congress, with a majority of members engaged in agriculture, viewed public lands through the eyes of a farmer. They saw land in

---

1 Harold K. Steen, *The U.S. Forest Service, A History,* (Seattle, WA: University of Washington Press, 1976), p. 4

simple terms; it was either suitable for agriculture or not. The not portion received little attention. Encouraging homesteading was seen as a way to facilitate the growth of agriculture.

Another major component of the process that moved land from public to private use was the drive to extend a railroad infrastructure from coast to coast. In the early 1860s massive land grants were given to the Central Pacific and Union Pacific railroads to encourage the construction of the first transcontinental rail line. Even larger grants followed to the Northern Pacific Railway. [2] The total of these and other government efforts would eventually result in a nineteenth century transfer of half the nation, over a billion acres, to the private sector.

As might be expected such a large scale transfer and expansion came with widespread abuse. The pioneer was focused on survival and conquering a wild landscape that seemed endless. He needed timber to build a house for his family, put up his fences, and keep his fire burning but often had no legal way of getting it. The choice was to steal it from public lands or let his family suffer.[3]

Such small scale thievery with survival at stake might be forgiven. A much larger problem was wholesale for-profit exploitation by large-scale lumber operations that were taking millions of feet of Government timber without the shadow of right.[4] This large scale thievery set off alarm bells within the Department of Interior Land Office. Their reports to Congress complained of theft and destruction of the nation's forested land.

A man often quoted in these reports was America's first conservationist, George Perkins Marsh. Marsh was the first to challenge man's impact on the natural world in his landmark 1864 book, *Man and Nature*. Marsh wrote, "Man is everywhere a disturbing agent. Wherever he plants his foot, the harmonies of nature are turned to discords."

Marsh's writings had significant impact on Franklin Hough, a physician, historian and statistician who wrote an 1873 paper for the American Association for the Advancement of Science, *On the Duty of Governments in the Preservation of Forests*. This became the basis for the first of three reports he would author for Congress over the

2 Steen, p. 5

3 Gifford Pinchot, *Breaking New Ground,* (Washington, D.C.: Island Press, 1947), p. 83

4 Pinchot, p. 83

next decade. The first was funded by what is called an earmark today, inserted as a rider in an appropriations bill for the Department of Agriculture. The second report in 1881 prompted Congress to establish a Division of Forestry, a one man operation in the Agriculture Department headed by Hough. In his third report Hough put forth the recommendation, "that the principal bodies of timber land still remaining the property of the government ....be withdrawn from sale or grant."[5]

Hough was active in the American Forestry Association (AFA), an organization founded in Chicago in 1875. The group's purpose was to bring together the best minds in the nation and publish materials to advance the knowledge and practice of forestry. AFA, the nation's oldest citizen conservation organization, is based in Washington, D.C., today. In the 1990s I had the pleasure of serving on its board of directors for six years. During that time the name was changed to American Forests.

In 1888 AFA's law committee presented a bill to Congress, "for reserving and administering the public timberlands."[6] The bill never passed but Section 24 of it, authorizing the President to use proclamations to, "set apart and reserve" public lands in any state or territory bearing forests was made part of an 1891 act that revised multiple existing land laws. With little fanfare or public attention this presidential authority to designate public lands as forest reserves became the basis of the entire national forest system we know today.

Less than four weeks after authorization to create reserves passed Congress, President Benjamin Harrison began creating the system with the Yellowstone Park Timber Land Reserve. By the end of 1892 he had created fifteen reserves totaling more than thirteen million acres. His successor, President Grover Cleveland, added five million more acres, and then put a halt to the process until Congress acted to provide a means to protect the reserves.[7]

Over the next several years AFA and others advocated a commission under the National Academy of Sciences to study the reserves. The study's purpose was to determine whether fire protection and permanent forests were practical in the public domain, to estimate the influence of forests on climate, soil and water and to recommend

5 Steen, p. 18
6 Pinchot, p. 84
7 Steen, p. 18

specific legislation.[8]

The commission consisted of members of the Academy, plus one non-member, Gifford Pichot, a young forester. Throughout 1896 Commission members traveled the west examining the existing twenty million acres of reserves with an eye to adding more. Pinchot was often accompanied in his travels by America's most famous naturalist, John Muir. The two had met four years prior and developed an instant bond based on their appreciation of the natural world.[9]

In August of that year Pinchot hired an outfitter to take him, an Army officer named George Ahern and Henry Graves into the Selway country. The party traveled west from Hamilton, Montana, up Lost Horse Canyon into the Bitterroot Mountains, over the divide into Bear Creek, a tributary of the Selway River. The country they were in was among the wildest in the contiguous United States. It remains so today.

Ninety years after Pinchot's venture I would spend twenty-five of a twenty-seven year outfitting career taking the public on six-day rafting excursions down the Selway River through the heart of the Selway-Bitterroot Wilderness. Among our favorite stops on the forty-seven mile trip was a haven perched on the edge of the pristine river. The small flat with a canopy of centuries old cedars, firs and Ponderosa pines is named Pinchot Camp.

The Commission's 1896 report to President Cleveland included a recommendation that he use Washington's Birthday in 1897 as an appropriate date to double the size of the existing reserves, adding thirteen more that covered twenty-one million acres. The President agreed and acted on February 22, 1897. The largest among the thirteen was the Bitterroot Forest Reserve, a 4,147,200 acre swath of undeveloped land stretching from the Selway to the north bank of the Main Salmon River immediately across from a flat of land soon to be settled by William Campbell. The land south of the river, surrounding Campbell's future homestead would be added as the Payette Forest Reserve in 1905.

The President's 1897 action was taken with little public awareness. As his action became widely known it created a furor of criti-

<hr>

8 Pinchot, p. 89
9 Timothy Egan, *The Big Burn, Teddy Roosevelt and the Fire that Saved America*, (New York, NY: Houghton Mifflin Harcourt), p. 32

cism, mostly from Congressional representatives of western states. Thus began a distrust of federal control of public lands that festers to this day. What was missing in the eyes of the critics at the time was any provision for local citizens and communities to draw upon the forested lands for timber, mineral and water resources to support their lives.

The reserves were established, but there was no law in place setting out how they would be managed. Congress scrambled to fashion a solution, but time was short. President William McKinley's inauguration was just a week and a half away. An appropriations bill headed to President Cleveland's desk was amended to create a division under the Department of the Interior with the task of managing the reserves and allowed for sale of the timber on them to the public. On inauguration day Cleveland met with his cabinet to consider the bill, but with McKinley literally at the door of the White House, Cleveland threw the bill to the floor and refused to sign it.[10]

Entering office with no appropriations in place to fund the government, President McKinley called the Congress back into session and soon had a new appropriations bill on his desk. An amendment was included that set forth water protection and timber production as the criteria for designation of forest reserves and included a provision for free timber and stone for settlers.[11]

Seven years after the Division of Forestry had been established, Gifford Pinchot was appointed to lead it. This one man's impact upon the profession of forestry and management of the nation's forest would be profound. Pinchot's interest in forestry had begun at a time when the concept of professional foresters did not exist in America.

Pinchot's path to the profession began in 1885 when his father's knowledge of forestry in Europe led him to encourage his son to take up its study at Yale. In his college years Pinchot wrote a term paper on the nation's lumber supply. He studied abroad in Europe and after graduation went on to make two excursions into America's western forests, managed thousands of acres of woods on Charles Vanderbilt's Biltmore estate, established a forestry consulting firm

10 Steen, p. 34
11 Steen, p. 35

and interacted with leaders in the field as a member of AFA.[12]

As Director of the Division of Forestry Pinchot had a bully pulpit to convince the American public through pamphleteering and publicity that the nation's forests could be scientifically and intensively managed for the public good. There was one problem. His Division of Forestry in the Agriculture Department had no forests to administer. The forest reserves were under the Interior Department.[13]

A cooperative agreement between the departments was struck that allowed Interior to call on Pinchot for his expertise as the government worked to fashion a strategy for administering these little known vast stretches of land. Interior Secretary Cornelius Bliss appointed Pinchot a confidential agent and asked him to study the reserves and recommend a structure for a managing agency. His report contained the basic elements found in today's Forest Service.[14]

Pinchot's desire to move the forest reserves from Interior to Agriculture made no headway under President McKinley, but he did manage to grow his Division from a score of men to over five hundred. Budgets doubled and then tripled. He spread men across the nation to map the reserves, opened offices and began to structure relationships between users of the reserves and its government managers. The prospects for full implementation of his ideas on forest management improved dramatically in 1901 when Theodore Roosevelt moved into the oval office after an assassin's bullet stuck down President McKinley.

Pinchot had known Roosevelt since his time as governor of New York. During a visit to the governor's home, the two discovered a shared concern that the nation's forests needed protection from unchecked industrial logging that both thought would create a timber shortage. They were witnessing a tipping point, where the original two-billion acres of public domain had been cut in half. Over a billion acres had been given to companies, states and private landowners for their own use.

The two men wondered when it would stop; would there be any left? While discussing the issue over tea, Roosevelt proposed a wrestling and boxing match between the two. It was Roosevelt's way

12 Steen, p. 53
13 Pinchot, p. xvii
14 Steen, p. 56

of testing the mettle of the rising star of forestry. The match ended with a split decision. T.R. won at wrestling and the taller Pinchot triumphed at boxing.[15] The two outdoorsmen had found the basis for a lifelong friendship rooted in their shared love of the outdoors; the beginning of what we now refer to as a conservation ethic.

When Roosevelt became President he called on Pinchot to be the nation's forester and a special presidential advisor to help write his speeches. In 1905 with T.R.'s help, Pinchot finally gained control of the forest reserves. He hired an even larger cadre of professional foresters to manage them, and saw the name of his organization changed to United States Forest Service.[16] Two years later Congress passed an act declaring, "The forest reserves shall hereafter be known as national forests."

In 1908 President Roosevelt changed the name of the portion of the Bitterroot Reserve north of Campbell's Ferry to the Nez Perce National Forest. The lands surrounding the Ferry to the south of the river were first the Payette Forest Reserve, then the Idaho National Forest and later the Payette National Forest, the name they retain today.

15 Egan, p. 32, 18
16 Egan, p. 32

Chapter Thirteen

Homestead

The Homestead Act
May 20, 1862

Sec. 2. That the person applying for the benefit of this act shall…… make affidavit….. that he or she is the head of a family, or is twenty-one or more years of age, or shall have performed service in the Army or Navy of the United States, and that he has never borne arms against the Government of the United States or given aid and comfort to its enemies, and that such application is made for his or her exclusive use and benefit, and that said entry is made for the purpose of actual settlement and cultivation, and not, either directly or indirectly, for the use or benefit of any other person or persons whomsoever; and….. on payment of ten dollars, he or she shall thereupon he permitted to enter the quantity of land specified [one quarter-section: 160 acres or less] ….. no certificate shall be given or patent issued… until the expiration of five years from the date of such entry; and…..at any time within two years… the person….. shall prove by two credible witnesses that he, she, or they have resided upon or cultivated the same for the term of five years immediately succeeding the time of filing….. the purchaser shall acquire the absolute title… and be entitled to a patent from the United States….

Homestead

Warren Cook was the first to formally apply for homestead status for Campbell's Ferry. Through the application process he would also find his future employer. In May of 1906, eight months after Warren lost his wife and child, Forest Ranger David Laing, newly appointed to the Chamberlain District of the Payette Forest Reserve, visited the property to examine it for suitability for homestead status. In the *Report on Agricultural Settlement of Warren E. Cook in the Payette Forest Reserve,* Ranger Laing described the property as a "squatter location."

A squatter was someone who occupied a piece of land with no legal authority. Such illegal possession was a common occurrence in the new forest reserves, especially anywhere there was land with the potential for agricultural use as William Campbell had determined on this piece of ground in 1897.

Sorting out the legality of such occupation was a primary duty of the new Forest Service. It was not an adversarial process – more like a determination of the claimant's true intent. Were they really trying to make a go of it? Was it "actual settlement and cultivation*"* as the Homestead Act said, or was the claimant acting for the benefit of others?

A major abuse of land laws at the time was companies or individuals paying persons a small fee to claim smaller segments of land, later to aggregate them into larger, more valuable holdings. "The basic scheme was to find 160 acres, patent it with a shack that could be labeled a home on 'agricultural' ground, and then sell the land for a big profit to one of the timber companies, which were prohibited from homesteading. These claims were neither homes nor farms, but in this way, big sections of the new national forests were nibbled away… in the Bitterroots nearly 90 percent of the homesteads were frauds set up by agents of industry…"[1]

Ranger Laing also wanted to know if the property was a mining claim. Had it been, the claim would have fallen under the Mining Act of 1872. Under that act prospectors used a self-initiation system under which a person physically stakes the claim, posts a location notice and places stakes or piles of rocks known as, *monuments,* around the boundary. After filing notice of the location with county authori-

1 Timothy Egan, *The Big Burn, Teddy Roosevelt and the Fire that Saved America,* (New York, NY: Houghton, Mifflin, Harcourt), p. 32, 80

ties he could set about *proving* the claim by working it on an annual basis. After a sufficient period of time accompanied by demonstrated economic value and mining success, the claimant would be issued a *patent* to the claim, the equivalent of fee simple title.

When Ranger Laing designated Cook's application as a squatter location, it meant that he wanted to know what buildings were on the property and what agricultural work had occurred. Warren Cook reported the existence of a log house, 28' x 14' with two rooms. There was also a 12' x 16' barn, a 12' x 14' store house and a 10' x 20' hen house and shop, all constructed of logs. Cook and William Campbell before him had been busy.

Cook stated that fifty of the 160-acre squatter location was suitable for tilling. He had fifteen acres under plow, forty acres under fence and twenty-five acres under ditch. Agricultural output was reported as twelve tons of hay, two tons of fruit and six tons of vegetables. Cook noted that there were fifty acres of timberland on the property. One-third of the forest had been cleared to make the ground suitable for general agricultural use.

The ranger noted that Cook had three head of cattle and three horses that were being grazed on Big Trout Creek, and that a grazing permit had not been obtained. The lack of a grazing permit would not have been unusual. The Forest Service was just beginning to get a handle on how grazing use of the forest would be managed. Devoting the majority of the agricultural output of the place to hay demonstrated how much of the effort that went into these homesteads had to be devoted to sustaining your stock. Without enough hay to feed horses and cattle through the winter, one would end up starving out your stock, and then one's self.

Cook also reported that he was living on the property continuously and he had no other claims – Campbell's Ferry was his only home.

Based upon his examination of the property and meeting Cook, Laing ended his report with the recommendation, "that claimant be given title to land at the proper time."

Laing was impressed. He saw a young war veteran who had invested a lot of hard work to make a go of the place. It was just the kind of talent the fledgling land management agency needed. Later that year Cook, disillusioned by the tragic loss of his wife and child, dropped his homestead claim on Campbell's Ferry to accept the job of deputy ranger. He moved twenty-three miles up the Three Blaze Trail to a small cabin Laing had built for the Forest Service – the beginning of what would become today's Chamberlain Ranger Station. Cook filed a new claim on 158 acres near Laing's cabin, but later dropped it. The ground he had filed on is now part of the north-south landing strip at the Chamberlain Ranger Station.[2]

The challenges Laing, Cook and other new rangers faced in the newly formed Forest Service are best described by J. B. Lafferty's account of his work in the Weiser Forest Reserve in 1906:

I went to Weiser, which was made headquarters, rented a two-room building. With typewriter, home-made table, two chairs, some official forms and the Use Book, I began organizing the new Reserve…. My salary was $1,000 and my field force was two Assistant Rangers. For $60 a month, a guard had to furnish two horses, saddle, pack outfit and board himself and his horses. In 1907 I had a field force of ten men…. About 150,000 sheep and 25,000 cattle and horses grazed on the Reserve…. Had to prevent grazing of unpermitted stock along 400 miles of unfenced boundary – look after applicants for timber and protect the Reserve from fire. At one time had twelve small sawmills on the Reserve and many small sales to farmers and settlers.

When Cook left the Ferry to become a ranger, he sold the place,

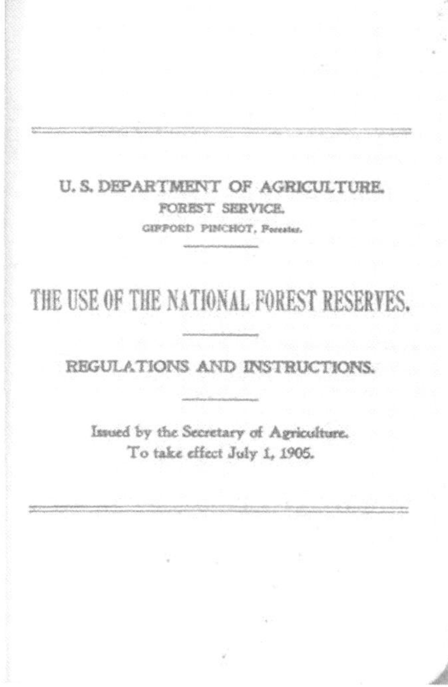

The 6"x4" 140 page Use Book
Issued in 1905 by Gifford Pinchot

2 Peter Preston, *An Outline of the Cultural History of the Frank Church – River of No Return Wilderness,* (McCall, ID: USDA Forest Service, Payette National Forest Heritage Program, Nov. 2001), p. 25

or to be legally accurate, sold the improvements on the property, to a land speculator named Oscar Eakin. Eakin had come to the gold fields of Idaho from Tennessee. Over the years he bought and sold many properties in the Salmon River Canyon. For a while he lived on and built a cabin at Lantz Bar, twenty-nine miles upstream. He also claimed Jersey Creek Bar where he built another cabin that contained an improvised pigeon-hole post office for canyon residents.[3] Jersey Bar, eight miles downstream from the Ferry, would later become the Painter Mine.

Eakin also patented a claim at China Bar, four miles downstream from the Ferry, and settled the flat across from China Bar known as Gaines Bar. Eakin was the canyon's early equivalent of a modern day developer and real estate agent.[4]

After Cook left and sold the place to Eakin, he grew to distrust him. As the new deputy ranger in Chamberlain, it was now Cook's responsibility to review homestead applications. When Eakin filed on the Ferry in 1907, Cook's investigation revealed that Eakin had quickly sold the place to Fred Sillge. Cook noted on the application, "this transfer was not ascertained by the F.S. until recently…. Applicant is a very unsettled man…. Since applicant has transferred all title and right on improvement on this land, and since applicant has stated he was going to Alaska in the spring, I recommend that this case be closed."[5]

Cook's reference to Eakin's "unsettled" state may have been related to Eakin's taste for alcohol:

Residents of Dixie remember him as a small man with a little moustache. As he got older his rheumatism became almost unbearable and he'd periodically relieve the pain with a good binge. About midnight he'd return to his Dixie cabin, stand on his porch for half an hour or so and serenade the residents in a high-pitched, tuneless voice.

Dorrie recalls that one night Oscar Eakin died in the Dixie Tavern and his friends sorrowfully laid the body out on the tav-

3 Johnny Carrey and Cort Conley, *River of No Return,* (Cambridge, ID: Backeddy Books, 1977), p. 174
4 Carrey and Conley, p. 171
5 Homestead Application #9, (McCall, ID: USDA Forest Service, Payette National Forest)

ern table. In the morning they were flabbergasted to see the body up and looking for breakfast, unaware of the fuss his heavy drinking had caused.[6]

Sam Myers

The third homestead application for Campbell's Ferry was made in 1917 by Fred Sillge. As noted before, his effort to complete the five-year residence requirement was cut short by his drowning in the Salmon River in 1921. The county appointed his friend Sam Myers administrator of Sillge's estate.

Myers was born in Pennsylvania in 1831. At age nineteen he joined the horde of forty-niners who headed west to the California gold fields, returning to Pennsylvania prior to the Civil War. Inspired by the battle at Gettysburg near his home, Myers enlisted and ended up serving under General Sherman for his march through Georgia. After the war he came west again to prospect. After trying his luck in Colorado and Montana, Myers settled in Dixie where he was remembered for his story telling and fondness for drink. On more than one occasion he fell off his horse in a drunken stupor on the way home and slept where he fell.[7]

In 1903 Myers partnered with Sillge and staked a claim at what was later named Myers Creek ten miles upstream from Campbell's Ferry. Today the Myers Creek property is known as the Allison Ranch.

After hearing about Sillge's drowning in June of 1921, Myers moved to Campbell's Ferry. According to Kathy Deinhardt Hill's book, *Spirits of the Salmon River*:

> On October 19, 1921, Myers left Campbell's Ferry bound for Dixie on horseback. He was leading two pack horses to bring back supplies for the winter. A day later, Myers' saddle horse returned to the Ferry alone. Louis Schroeder, who had been staying with Myers at the Ferry, saddled up and rode to Dixie, expecting to find Myers somewhere along the trail, but found no sign of him. Once in Dixie, Schroeder learned that

---

6 Marian S. Sweeney, *Gold at Dixie Gulch*, (Kamiah, ID: Clearwater Valley Publishing, 1982), pp. 92, 114

7 Kathy Deinhardt Hill, *Spirits of the Salmon River*, (Cambridge, ID: Backeddy Books, 2001), pp. 59–63

Myers had never arrived there. He and Bob Hilands then back tracked in their search.

On October 22, they found Myers' body resting on a ledge in the Salmon River Canyon, well below the pack trail. From the condition of the body, they surmised that he had been jerked from his horse by the pack horses and fell to his death. Schroeder and Hilands took the body to Dixie for burial the next day.[8]

Sam Myers had died one month shy of his ninetieth birthday.

According to a 1923 report on the homestead claim in the files of the Payette National Forest, "In the spring of 1922 Bob Hilands was appointed administrator of Sillge's estate and has resided upon the land to date of this report."

The *Three Year Report on Homestead Claim* was the result of a status report process that had been put in place by the recently formed Forest Service to get a handle on the large numbers of claims on national forest land.[9] The report noted, "This residence was in trespass in as much as Sillge purchased the improvements from one Oscar Eakin. Mr. Eakin having come into possession of such improvements upon the death of the previous owner, Mr. Wm. Campbell, who squatted upon the land in 1897 and was lost in a snow storm… This purchase of improvements and subsequent possession of this area being made after tract was included within a national forest. The Forest Service took no note of this trespass prior to the application for this area by Sillge."

Walter G. Mann, the deputy forest supervisor, had made a personal inspection of the property on September 15, 1922. He liked what he found. "Soil is a deep sandy loam capable of producing almost any farm crop. This land is one of the best suited for the production of crops and fruit in the whole of this country and its agricultural possibilities are simply limited to the small area."

Mann noted the same buildings that Ranger Laing had seen in

8 Hill, pp. 59–63

9 National forest land is the correct way to reference land within a national forest. Stan Tixier, retired regional forester for Region 4, Ogden, UT, always made it a point to correct anyone, especially his own employees, when they used the term Forest Service land. The agency owns no land. The agency is in the employ of U.S. citizens through their elected representatives tasked with managing the public's national forest.

his visit with Warren Cook sixteen years before. He also found one-half mile of pole and wire fence, all in first class serviceable condition and placed a value of $1,000 on all the improvements.

Alfalfa, clover and timothy hay was being raised to support six horses and ten cows. The garden was more than an acre and the orchard was producing peaches, plums, pears, apricots, apples and grapes.

Robert Hilands, the new owner, was one of five children of David and Emma Hilands of Pennsylvania. In 1900 at age twenty-four he was living with his parents and working as a railroad lineman. By 1910 he had found his way to Idaho and was working with five other men on a gold mine at Concord, about ten miles west of Dixie. The 1918 draft registration lists Hilands as medium height and build with blue eyes, gray hair and very deaf. Carrey and Conley report that he placered[10] at Shorts Bar, near Riggins, before moving to the Ferry. Bob had an old friend, Oscar Waller, who stayed at the ranch with him.[11]

According to a story later told by Jim Moore, Hilands was among the group of men present when Fred Sillge had drowned crossing on the ferry cable. Sillge had tried to convince Hilands to ride the cable with him and another man. Both men laughed at Hilands and called him coward. In Moore's telling:

> Bob stayed on the Ferry side of the river and we were all on my side of the river watching them come over and the carriage did have too much of a load. The cable sagged when it got close to the middle of the river. When it hit the water, the current just tore the carriage out of the irons and they never did find the two men.
>
> So Bob just stayed there until after the river was down, and then he made a trip to town and filed his claim on the place. A lot of people got mad at Bob that year, cause they tried to work their tricky schemes on him and he just the same as told them to go to hell. Those chiselers started showing up. Each one had a claim on something Fred had left or else they said that Fred

10 Placer mining involved diverting a water source into a ditch or flume that fed a hose which sprayed the water on hillsides to wash the dirt, gravel, and hopefully gold into sluice boxes or other devices to separate the gold.
11 Carrey and Cort Conley, p. 163

owed them money and they had a claim on the ranch. Bob just looked them in the eye, gun handy, and told them to bring him a note or letter in Fred's handwriting and he would pay the claim. Of course with Fred in the river, he wasn't writing any notes, and those chiselers hated Bob until the day they died.

Bob Hilands at the Dixie store. It was a thirteen-
mile trip from the Ferry, on foot or horseback. Note
his Depression era footwear - wrapped in burlap and
tied with cord.

The next Forest Service three-year report solidified the case for granting Hilands homestead rights. Ranger Dan LeVan reported that, except for a brief three and a half month period when claimant was working a mine in Elk City, he had occupied the land continuously since November of 1922. Thirteen acres were producing crops, and the orchard was now twelve years old with all trees bearing fruit. He concluded with, "The claimant shows good faith and works on claim all the time…. And has qualified in all homestead laws and is entitled to patent the claim."

On July 29, 1927 the U.S. General Land Office formally recognized Hilands' claim.

Homestead

...mpbell's Ferry was now private land. All Bob had to do was ...iving. It wasn't easy. As glowing as the Forest Service reports hau ...en, it was still a very small piece of rough land a long way from any market. Mine work was scarce and ferry traffic was infrequent at best.

Hilands may have been the first at the property to try his hand as a fishing and hunting guide for spending money, but he was also making whiskey.[12] Hilands friend Lee Hida told of coming upon the moonshine production:

> Came in the house at the Ferry once, it was after the walls had been put on the woodshed and a kitchen made of the room. Doc Byam was staying with Bob. Those two were making barley whiskey and they had the kettle on the stove and the coil got plugged and the lid was raising on the kettle. When I opened the door and started into the room there was Bob poking wood in the stove. Doc had a pillow on top of the pot and was sitting on it like a banty chicken on one egg. He was just sitting up there holding his feet out. I took one look and backed out, closed the door, put my pack down and just waited for it to happen. After the bottom blew out of the pot and Doc got down from his pillow I opened the door and went back in. Neither one had noticed when I entered the first time.[13]

In 1931 the Corral Creek fire burned the area around the property, including Hilands' hay crop. The fire, "turned into an awesome conflagration with an eighty-five-mile front of flames. It jumped the river in places, noticeably at Elkhorn Creek. When it was over, the Forest Service decided it was started by Bob Hilands – probably by his still. They were preparing to prosecute him when Everett Van Arsdale came down from the lookout on Sheep Hill where he watched fires for 31 years, bringing his records of lightning strikes. He pointed out that he had logged lightning hitting Trout Creek that day and the case was dropped."[14]

Federal revenue agents heard about Hilands' still and made an effort to catch him, but the backcountry grapevine saved him:

12 Peter Preston, *Campbell's Ferry,* (McCall, ID: USDA Forest Service, Payette National Forest Heritage Program, August, 2002), p. 6
13 Frances Wisner personal files.
14 Carrey and Conley, p. 160

One time some revenuers came in to Dixie. They stopped at the Caldwell station [in Elk City] to have dinner before they come on in. They had a pretty good Buick car, but they were wearing bib overalls, like farmers. Mrs. Caldwell, she was quite a hand at getting all the information, and she found out who they were. After they left, she got on the crank telephone and called in to Dixie and told Les Powerlson. He broke the news to everybody around, and when they came, everybody acted like they didn't know what was going on.

Doc Byam was the veterinarian and a packer, and he was hired to take 'em down to the Jim Moore ranch, and then over to Bob Hilands', 'cause somebody reported they was bootlegging down there.

Max Hovey was 'bout seventeen, eighteen years old then, and Doc gave him a horse and says, "In the morning I'll start out with the pack string. You sort of hold back 'til we get out by the North Star. I'll take 'em around the old road where it makes a horseshoe bend. You take the new trail that cuts straight across, cut through ahead of me and tip those guys off." So that's what they did, he tipped 'em off – Jim Moore and over at Bob's. He rode on up the river to Floyd Dale's place and stayed overnight. The revenuers knew somebody'd got there ahead of 'em 'cause Jim Moore had a still, but he'd dumped it all out. They couldn't find any evidence. They were pretty upset because they'd gone all that distance and somebody beat 'em to the draw. One of 'em complained, "There's faster horses in this country than the ones we rode."[15]

When the Great Depression set in it overwhelmed Hilands' attempts to make a living at Campbell's Ferry. Making whiskey, raising cattle, and selling vegetables were not enough. According to Jim Moore, Hilands was not cut out for the job:

Some ways Bob was smart as a firecracker, but he had too much education for the Ferry ranch. First thing he did was get a bunch of fancy Hereford cattle. I begged him to get the ground into hay first. Bob had not been on the river those winters when the squirrels starved. He thought it was just the talk of an igno-

15 Sweeney, p. 78

rant placer miner. That first winter he turned the cows out. They had to find their feed or starve. He lost every head he owned.

In 1933 Bob's finances were in a heck of a mess. The taxes had been neglected until it was almost up for tax sale. The grocery store had refused further credit, and Bob was scared and broke. Joe Zaunmiller had been in the mountains since 1926, but always on someone else's place. Bob propositioned Joe that if Joe would pay up the taxes and all the other debts, Bob would deed him half interest in the ranch. Joe paid and got the deed. Then Bob told Joe if he and his wife, Emma, would move to the place, Bob would see that Joe got the other half interest when he died.[16]

Joe and Emma took Hilands up on the offer. They moved to the Ferry and Joe set out to do whatever necessary to make the new deal succeed.

16 Frances Zaunmiller Wisner personal files. Her account of the story told her by Jim Moore

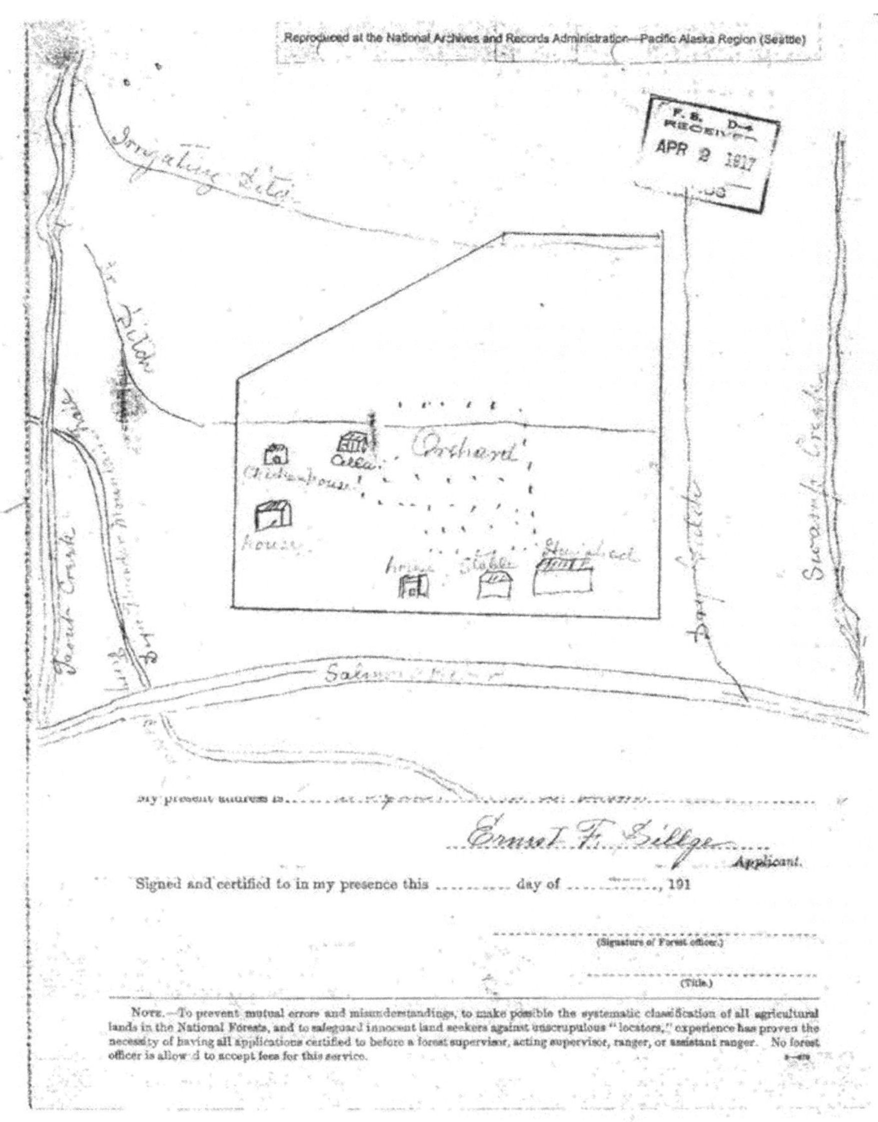

Fred Sillge's drawing of the property
submitted with his homestead application in 1917

Homestead

Chapter
Fourteen

Zaunmiller

"Joe was a great guy. You couldn't ask for a more honest, straight forward, hard working guy than Joe Zaunmiller."
– John Crowe

Joe Zaunmiller was born August 11, 1891, in Walla Walla, Washington, one of three sons of John and Anna Zaunmiller. The Zaunmillers were German immigrants who had arrived in America in 1883. John was in the brewery and mercantile business. Anna ran a boarding house, a large home where sons Joe, Albert and Harry grew up surrounded by more than a dozen working men boarders, mostly fellow German immigrants. There were a baker, two carpenters, a saddler, salesman, two stone masons, painter, two teamsters, and a distiller – the type of men who were building Walla Walla into a thriving agricultural and supply center. The Zaunmiller boys were surrounded by positive role models, no doubt a contributor to the serious work ethic they would demonstrate in later life.

Walla Walla's main street was built on the old Nez Perce Trail that stretched from the nearby Columbia River to the Bitterroot Mountains, a traditional Native American route between salmon fishing areas on the Columbia River and buffalo hunting on the Great Plains. It became a banking and supply center during the late 1800s due to its strategic position on the trail to the gold rushes of Idaho and Montana.

Young Joe Zaunmiller

Wheat farming was the center of life in Walla Walla throughout Joe Zaunmiller's youth, primarily due to the invention of the side-hill harvester. The rich soil in the area was ideal for wheat, but prior to this innovation the contours of the land had made it impossible to economically raise and harvest the crop. The vast area of rolling hills was characterized by forty-five degree slopes of random humps and hollows.

By the time Joe was a teenager, the side-hill harvester had grown to become a massive piece of farm equipment drawn by thirty-three horses or mules that required a team of five men to operate. A day of work on Walla Walla area farms with the complex machinery was an education in important skills – harnessing and tending to the stock, operating, maintaining and repairing the machinery, and cooperation among the crew to efficiently harvest and transport the crop to market. This was experience that would serve Joe well later in his life in the wilds of Idaho.

At twenty-five, Joe signed up for the World War I draft. His registration shows him as a farm laborer working in Prescott, Washington, another small community just north of his parent's home in Walla Walla. The military rejected him due to "leakage of heart," a diagnosis proven unlikely by the following forty-seven years of an active, physical life. The young man is described as having a heavy build, medium height, light hair, blue eyes, and unmarried.

By 1920, twenty-eight-year old Joe was back in Walla Walla, working as a truck driver hauling wood and coal and married to Bertha, a twenty-seven-year old midwesterner from Kansas. Bertha had a six-year-old son that Joe adopted, or at least gave him his last name. Bertha and son Neil were out of Joe's life by 1924. We don't know why. But by then he had married Emma Sams, a twenty-year-old woman who had grown up just a few blocks from Joe's family home in Walla Walla. All we know of what happened to Bertha and her son Neil is that she went on to marry twice again – in 1938 in Oregon and 1940 in Seattle.[1]

Emma was the seventh of eight children of Samuel and Lattie Sams. Her parents came from Missouri where her father had been a shoemaker and coal miner. The family moved to Walla Walla in 1903 after Samuel had served two years in the Missouri state penitentiary for killing a man. According to relatives a man had attempted to rob Samuel and the man's death from a knife wound was an act of self-defense.

Emma, born in 1904, had an older sister, Addie, who, like Emma, would marry a man who would take her to a life on a Salmon River homestead. Addie's new husband, Tom Newsome, a local mechanic who had come west from Tennessee, was twice the age of the sixteen-year-old.

In 1926 the two couples, Joe and Emma, Tom, Addie and Addie's seven-year-old daughter, Bernice, followed the old Nez Perce Trail into Idaho. It wasn't gold drawing them. Joe's motivation was more likely built on his independent streak, a desire to make a place of his own. He could have stayed in Walla Walla where family and business prospects were good. One brother, Albert, had gone into the brewery business like their father, and the other, Harry, became a successful nurseryman. But Joe's sense of adventure drove him to look for a place in the wilds. It wasn't an easy trip.

In 1926 getting to the Salmon River Canyon was still a

Emma Sams Zaunmiller

1 www.digitalarchives.wa.gov, State of Washington Digital Archives

struggle. From Walla Walla there was a passable road to Lewiston. From there the road followed the rail line up the Clearwater River to Kooskia, then a few miles up the South Fork to Stites, the starting point for a rough fifty-three-mile wagon road into Elk City.

Beyond Elk City the Zaunmillers were able to drive another seventeen miles before trading their car for a packstring. Their destination was eight miles to the southeast – the Harbison Ranch at the head of Mallard Creek. It is hard to imagine a more idyllic backcountry setting. Perched in a shallow canyon, the ranch was set in a large meadow surrounded by foothills gradually rising a thousand feet over three miles south to the edge of the Salmon River Breaks. Mallard Creek meanders for a mile through the meadow, producing a lush green carpet that brushed the bellies of the horses, mules and cattle it sustained.

Vic Bargamin and Ed Harbison originally settled the place in the 1890s. Bargamin's interest was trapping. Using a string of burros he would go out each year to the railhead at Stites to secure supplies that he would cache at a series of cabins built along the ridges between the Salmon and Clearwater Rivers. Spaced about a day's travel apart by snowshoe, each cabin was outfitted with bedding, camp stove and firewood to support multiple mid-winter trips to check trap lines.[2]

Harbison was of a phlegmatic disposition and tended cattle on the two homesteads the men had staked along the creek. A residence, barn, chicken house and milk house supported the men's effort to provide a living trapping and supplying the nearby mines with meat, dairy and eggs.[3] Ed was friends with Sam Myers, his neighbor seven miles away in the canyon. Sam and Fred Sillge had homesteaded the flat on the river that is now Allison Ranch.

It was Ed Harbison whom Sam turned to for money when he ran up gambling debts in Dixie. After Sam died in 1921 while packing from the Ferry to Dixie, Elmer Allison acquired the homestead by paying off Sam's thousand dollar mortgage held by Harbison.[4] Allison then raised money to cover the purchase by periodic trips out of the canyon to work at the mines. While Allison was away working the

2 Robert G. Bailey, *River of No Return,* (Lewiston, ID: Bailey Blake Printing Co., 1935), p. 473
3 Bailey, p. 473
4 Carrey and Conley, p. 140

mines he asked the Zaunmillers to come down from Harbison Ranch and take care of his stock and homestead on the river.

To get to Allison's place from Harbison Ranch the residents took a trail four miles to the edge of the canyon, then switchbacked three precipitous miles down to the river. The route developed a reputation; local settlers came to call it Horse Killer Trail. Tom, Addie and Bernice continued two miles upriver from Allison to another homestead called the Crofoot Ranch. This property had been settled by Bruce Crofoot, a Scotsman who had come into the canyon in 1910.

It wasn't long after the two couples settled in that they experienced the cost of living so far from civilization. Addie's husband Tom Newsome developed a serious dental problem and had to leave the canyon and travel to Grangeville to have a tooth extracted. After he returned to Crofoot he developed blood poisoning and died far from medical care that was readily available in town.[5] Tom was buried on the property, another casualty of the pioneer canyon lifestyle. Addie and Bernice moved in with Emma and Joe, helping them care for Elmer Allison's ranch on the river.

In May of 1927 Emma wrote a letter home telling Joe's parents about her life in the canyon.

Elk City, Idaho
May 4, 1927
Dear Mother and Dad,
I haven't received a letter from you since I came down here, but will write just the same. How is everyone and the weather down there? We are all well and happy. There has been rainy weather off and on for a week now. Mr. Allison has a ranch down here and he lives alone and has asked Joe and I to live with him. He has 13 head of cattle and some will be sold this fall. Joe gets half of them for staying on the place this summer while he goes out and works. After Joe and I stay with him a year Joe gets half interest in the ranch. After we stay this summer we will have papers made out. Elmer Allison goes to work this summer and Joe goes out to work next. We have a new cabin started on the place and will fix it up. Elmer shot a last year buck this morning out the cabin window. It

5 Carrey and Conley, p. 138

was at the salt log eating salt. I wish you could come up and eat some fresh meat.

Two weeks ago we had fresh fish nearly every day for a week. Joe put a throw line out with four hooks and I looked after it. I took some nice ones off of it, too. None was less than 12 inches long and some was 20 inches. I caught a 22" Bull trout with my fish pole and it weighted 2 ½ lbs dressed. I was wishing you and mother was up here then. The river is up and muddy now so I can't get any fish for a while.

Joe went up to Crowfoots place this morning and I hiked up to Bargaman Creek a mile and a half from home. I thought I would meet him but he was too late so I came back home and had supper ready and was waiting on him, Adda and Bernice. Joe and Elmer is going over to Caldwells so Adda came down until they come back. Dad stayed up there because Elmer gave them a cow to milk. We milk two cows now. All we need is chickens and Mrs. Harbison is hatching us off a few. We have plenty of butter and milk.

Dad, will you get a Pinochle and a plain deck of cards for Al and send them up. Al hasn't answered my letter or I would ask him.

Harry ought to be answering my last letter before long.

Well folks, I will close for this time.

Love to all,
Emma

The Zaunmillers were doing what most of the hardy pioneers who settled the canyon did. Between their own fierce determination and support from the canyon community, they pulled together whatever it took to survive. They overcame the loss of their brother-in-law by taking in his widow and child. They pitched in to help a neighbor during his necessary trips out to make some money. Emma's father, Dad Sams, came in as well, helping out where he could.

Later Joe himself would go out for work and the family would go back to Walla Walla to live with Emma's mother during his absence. Every trip in and out was never just about a single task. Life in the remote canyon required supplies from town. Each trip included

Emma and Joe Zaunmiller
1938

a shopping list for the homesteader and their neighbors. If, as Emma wrote, you needed chickens your friend, Mrs. Harbison (Ed's widow) would raise a few extra chicks at her home in Grangeville to send in. The bonds among families and neighbors were strong out of necessity to make ends meet at the edge of civilization.

The arrival of the Great Depression in the early 1930s drove even these hardy pioneers to forego their fierce self-reliance and seek government help.

Doug Eier of Idaho described the times:

There was nothing. No jobs. Nobody had any money. Families were on relief. My stepfather was a good electrician but there wasn't any jobs for anybody. I remember the relief food we used to get. The cans had white labels with black printing – tomatoes, noodles and stuff like that. It was tough. When the CCC's came along that was the greatest thing that ever happened. We got a dollar a day, food, clothing, a chance to do some work, learn how to work, how to get along with other people. Twenty-five dollars went home. That was great. That saved the family. Bread was a nickel a loaf, hamburger was two pounds for a quarter. Milk was ten cents a quart. Taylor made cigarettes were ten cents a pack. I smoked Bull Durham, five cents a bag. Times were tough. The CCC's gave me a chance to grow up and really find out what life was all about,[6]

The Civilian Conservation Corps (CCC), was established by

6 Doug Eier, *CCC in Idaho,* Idaho Public Television, 2001

Congress in 1933 for, "unemployment relief work in forestry and related fields on federal and state lands…." Over two and a half million men participated nationwide. In Idaho, 109 of the 163 CCC camps were built on national forests. The majority of the young men in the camps were from urban America and lacked basic skills and education. The men were taught to plant trees, build trails, bridges, roads and also participated in educational programs.

Joe's earlier opportunity working for Elmer Allison to earn half interest in Allison Ranch had not worked out, but he had found a new chance for ranch ownership with Bob Hilands. Under the deal, Joe needed enough money to pay Campbell's Ferry's back taxes and some outstanding bills Hilands had run up with merchants in Dixie and Grangeville. There were no other places to earn a wage in the Depression, so he signed up with the CCC.

It turned out a good fit. Joe already possessed the skills to work in the woods. And the Forest Service needed experienced local men to help them manage the thousands of young greenhorns arriving from cities across America. Joe became a foreman at the CCC camp at Headquarters, Idaho, on the Nez Perce National Forest. Letters between Joe, Emma (Joe affectionately called her Muzzy) and Bob Hilands tell of the struggles of surviving the Depression.

July 18, 1934
Headquarters, Idaho

Dearest Muzzy,
　　Received your welcome letter yesterday and sure was glad you got home alright. I am always

Joe and his fellow foremen
at the CCC camp near Headquarters, Idaho

worried until I hear you get back. I expect the check tomorrow and will send you a money order as soon as I can and it won't be long before I have another check.

The new rookies will be here the 23rd and then I will catch hell again. They will be 75 and all from New York and that will tell if I can make it if the rest of them come. Tell Bob I will bring him in something this fall that will fix his stomach up. Tell him not to work too hard for there ain't a hell of a lot to be made down there until the road comes up and then we will give them hell.

Don't you and the rest of them work too hard either for we will have something to eat this winter and something to wear and a radio, too. Everybody says times are going to be worse this winter than they was two years ago. Nobody seems to be able to get a job. I sure am glad I got one.

Your Loving Husband, as ever,

Joe

A week and a half later Joe writes that he has found a box of tools he will send to the Ferry along with a money order for $100. He reports that he is developing "a good rep" with his supervisors for his hard work as foreman and, "My old belly has sure went down." Joe longed for his sweetheart and was tortured by her regular reports of all the fresh fruits and produce turned out by the Ferry garden.

"Now my stomach has sure been giving me hell. This damn grub would kill anybody. Some of the other foreman had the same thing but not quite so bad. I thought sure I had the appendicitis for a while. But I guess it was just my old guts. No fresh fruit and the grub ain't seasoned. Any way that is what the doctor said and I guess he knows."

In September, 1935 after another year working at Headquarters Joe wrote his partner, Bob Hilands, complaining about the youth being sent to the CCC camp and to say he would be back to the Ferry soon, "I hope it won't be long. I am getting damn tired of herding these kids. This is the hardest bunch of kids I ever had anything to do with. They sure are a bunch of alley rats."

At the Ferry Bob Hilands health was failing. He had problems with his hand, stomach and legs. He was struggling to survive by selling off some of the stock at the ranch. In 1938 he gave up and went to live with his sister in Pennsylvania. Hilands was no longer able to deal with the most basic of challenges brought by living in the canyon. He could no longer walk the trails. "The pain is often long." he wrote, "I will never be able to travel the hill again."

CCC boys lining up for mess hall

Over the next two years Hilands frequently sent letters to Zaunmiller attempting to sell his interest in the property. But Joe was barely getting by himself, both financially and personally. The scarcity of money in 1939 is shown by the price Hilands was trying to extract for his interest.

In February he wrote, "I don't think that $235 was too much to ask. You offered $152.50 without the cow and calf and mule teams. But I will never be able to get out there again. If I get much worse I will not be able to use my legs. If you will pay me $5 down and a mortgage for the balance we will call it a sale. As I don't expect ever to see Idaho again."

Zaunmiller

****

An objective look at Campbell's Ferry would have led Joe Zaunmiller to realize that what had gone on before at the property was not enough to support him and his family. The mines in the area as always were a boom and bust proposition. He could sell produce to the miners, but there was increased competition from the merchants and farms of the outside world. Competitors had the advantage of mass production and a constantly improving transportation infrastructure.

Campbell's Ferry Ranch had a small tillable area and everything produced here could only be moved at the speed of a horse over miles of difficult trail.

Joe needed to find his own advantage. What did he have that folks in the growing towns and cities did not?

Since his birth in 1891, Joe, now forty-two, had witnessed the industrialization and urbanization of America. A rural society had evolved, pulling millions of men and their families from the farm into city environments, seeking new opportunities and jobs. The move took them away from a life formerly immersed in nature.

The childhood and lives of the parents of Americans had been closely connected to natural places. The woods had been all around them. Flowing streams were a common source of recreation and sustenance in rural America. But the move to the city severed that connection. Woods had been cleared for housing and farms. Streams became sewers, useful for hauling away urban waste but no longer suitable as a swimming and fishing hole.

The move to cities had robbed the public of the benefits of nearby natural recreation opportunities, but at the same time it created the financial and transportation resources that allowed them to travel to seek them out. Joe could see this happening in his and Emma's families. Photo albums of the day show the families loaded into cars and trucks, headed out of town to the remaining favorite camping, fishing and swimming spots.

When Joe looked around at Campbell's Ferry what he saw was the largest, wildest remnant of the natural world left in the lower forty-eight states, literally teaming with the fish and wildlife that most Americans had grown up with. Yes, it was a long way from anywhere, and hard to get to, but that would be part of the allure.

In October of 1935 Joe bought a two dollar hunting license in Dixie. It lists him as a 5'8" 175-pound rancher. Joe had plans to add to that occupational status. He knew how to travel in the backcountry, how to secure supplies and how to take care of people and stock in the wilds. He had an idyllic base, a homestead set among mountains, streams and rivers of incomparable beauty. He would become an outfitter.

As a startup business, what Joe was lacking was a way to let the public know about his services.

Fortune was about to visit Campbell's Ferry again, not in the form of passing miners looking for gold, but a gold mine of publicity brought when an expedition from the National Geographic Society ran aground in Growler Rapid at Joe Zaunmiller's doorstep.

Chapter
Fifteen

River Visitors

"There is an eternal landscape, a geography of the soul;
we search for its outlines all our lives."
– Josephine Hart

The National Geographic Society was formed in 1888 in Washington, D.C., for "the increase and diffusion of geographical knowledge." In 1935 its search for knowledge of the geography of the U.S. instigated an expedition to the wild core of Idaho, an area still very much a mystery to most Americans.

The stated purpose of the trip was to study the Idaho Batholith, the granite mass that broke through the earth's mantle seventy-five million years ago to become the formative geologic feature of the central Idaho wilderness. The trip included Dean A. W. Fahrenwald, a metallurgist and educator who was director of the Idaho Bureau of Mines and Geology; Idaho Congressman D. Worth Clark, who was interested in the forests that some were now referring to as primitive areas; Dr. Maynard Williams, on the magazine's staff as a photographer and writer, and Howard Flint, the regional forest inspector of the Forest Service's Missoula regional office. Flint's role was to study the plants and animals of the river environs.

The Society accessed the country by boat, hiring an outfit for the trip headed by a man Cort Conley called "the most magnetic and knowledgeable man on the river, Harry 'Captain' Guleke."[1] 'Cap' Guleke himself did not make the trip. At age seventy-two he was nearing the end of a forty-year career that had dominated the art of navigating the Salmon. For this trip Guleke turned the navigation task over to top hands Monroe Hancock and John Cunningham.

Guleke had learned his trade from men who in the 1880s had figured a better way to get mining equipment and supplies to mines at Shoup, a small community thirty-eight miles downriver from Salmon City. The miners had developed flat bottom boats to haul heavy stamp mill components on the river and hired the young, muscular Guleke as a bailer and swamper.[2] After the mine equipment was set up the miners went to work in the mine, leaving the river trade to Guleke who developed the river's dominant freight hauling business. He made his first of many complete transits of the canyon in 1896. At the end of each trip he would sell his boat for the value of the lumber in it, buy a horse, ride back to Salmon and do it all again.

The first to consider accessing this wilderness via the river were Lewis and Clark in the summer of 1805 (Map 4). Having crossed the continental divide at Lemhi Pass, the Corps of Discovery descended the Lemhi River, a tributary of the Salmon, meeting the main river at the present day site of the town of Salmon, Idaho. After consulting with the local Shoshone Indian band, Captain Clark made a scouting trip into the canyon in the area below the present town of North Fork. He reported in his journal, "many other Indians tell me that the mountains close and is a perpendicular cliff on each side, and continues for a great distance and that the water runs with great violence from one rock to the other on each side foaming and roaring through rocks in every direction, so as to render the passage of anything impossible."

<hr>

1 Johnny Carrey and Cort Conley, *River of No Return*, (Cambridge, ID: Backeddy Books, 1977), p. 23
2 Swamper, a term applied to the extra hand hired on freight boats to perform the grunt tasks of loading, pushing off rocks, and tying up.

The explorers wisely decided to abandon any hope of navigating the challenging river in dugout canoes and proceeded to purchase horses for an overland route through the mountains to the north over Lost Trail Pass and the Lolo Trail.

In March of 1832 a fur trapping brigade of the Hudson Bay Company led by John Work sent a crew of four men "in a small skin canoe to descend the river and hunt their way down."[3] Their destination was the fort at Walla Walla, but they never made it. In July Work learned that two of the men had drowned and the other two had proceeded on foot until rescued by Nez Perce.

Transit of the canyon was finally accomplished in 1872 in two separate and vastly different efforts. The first was John McKay, a native of Scotland and skilled millwright by trade. McKay had come to the Salmon River Canyon after the tragic death of his wife involving a piece of equipment fashioned by his own hands. McKay invited his young wife to inspect a large mill he had constructed for a company. During the visit her skirt was caught by a flywheel and she was dragged to her death before the machinery could be halted. McKay retreated to the solitary life of a placer miner and recluse to salve his broken heart.

Every spring in Salmon City, McKay would build a small wooden scow with a sweep blade at each end and work his way downriver, placering for gold from sandbars and side creeks. He often built small cabins and wintered in the canyon, eventually reaching Lewiston where he sold his boat and used the gold he had found to pay for another round of supplies and gear. He accomplished more than twenty round trips in this manner.[4]

The same year McKay was making his first descent through the Salmon River Canyon the Northern Pacific Railroad Company was looking for the shortest and most cost-effective route to create a northern transcontinental rail line linking Montana to Washington through Idaho. Just three years earlier the first transcontinental railroad had been completed through Utah. For the northern link, three plans were under consideration. The front runner was through northern Idaho alongside Lake Pend d'Oreille. But the board of directors thought a course following the Clearwater or Salmon River might be

3 Carrey and Conley, p. 5
4 Carrey and Conley, p. 9

better. They sent Colonel W. W. Delacy to Salmon City to build four boats and hire twenty-five men to survey the Salmon River route.

The local newspapers, just as they would later shamelessly promote Thunder Mountain, focused their rose-colored glasses on the Salmon River option. The path along the Salmon, "is so much better than has heretofore been supposed, that even the most difficult portions of it may be considered trifling compared with our previous conceptions."[5] The railroad's chief engineer had a different perspective, no doubt because his boss's money would ultimately pay for the route chosen.

In his summary of the exploratory survey taken down the Salmon he reported, "This survey down the Salmon River may I think be the most difficult instrumental survey ever made in the United States….. when this remarkable and hazardous survey was finished….. it proved to be 12 miles longer…. and vastly inferior in every element through a region with a much higher summit, heavier grades, more curvature, much greater cost, and running through a region so utterly forbidding as to afford no hope of any local business… In every reasonable sense it is an impracticable route."[6]

Thank goodness! Today we have a near pristine free-flowing wild river in the canyon instead of a rail bed carved from its flanks to carry an endless procession of locomotive drawn metal pythons snaking their way among the canyon walls.

In 1935 the vessel that Hancock used for the National Geographic trip was called a sweep boat or scow.[7] The design had been used for a century on the Mississippi and adapted well to the big waters of the Salmon. The writer for the expedition described it as, "an antediluvian ark sired by some prehistoric mail-order packing case."[8] Cort Conley describes the craft in his book, *The River of No Return*:

> These boats, which could be built in three days, were roughly eight feet in width and thirty-two feet in length, angled up at the ends. The double hull was made of longitudinal green lumber planks, with interior planks running athwart the barge,

---

5 Carrey and Conley, p. 19
6 Carrey and Conley, p. 50
7 Carrey and Conley, p. 22
8 Philip J. Shenon and John C. Reed, "Down Idaho's River of No Return," *National Geographic Magazine,* Volume LXX, Number One, July, 1936, p. 98

while elevated floor boards prevented wave-water from wetting supplies. The gunwales were generally three feet high, double walled to facilitate grocery storage. The seams were calked with pitch or tar.

The steering devices were two twenty-eight-foot poles fitted with fourteen-foot blades which rested in the water, one at the bow and the other at the stern. These "sweeps" were pinned at a pivot point. A sweep exerts and experiences considerable leverage in whitewater. For that reason they were sometimes counter-balanced with green wood or stones near the handles and it took two men to run a large boat. Boatmen stood on an elevated deck, usually with hobnail boots for traction, and operated the sweeps above the passengers. The captain took the front sweep, reading the water and calling his decisions to the rear pilot....

The sweep boat was an efficient craft, often carrying tons of freight to the mines, while drawing only fourteen inches of water. Its only shortcoming became apparent when docking: it was necessary to bump along the bank until someone could get a bowline around a boulder.

The critical position, the front sweep, was manned by Monroe Hancock. Hancock had grown up on the Snake River, the son of a commercial sturgeon fisherman. Hancock's wife described his fellow guide, John Cunningham, as "fit only for a rear sweep, since he could never make up his mind which way to go."[9]

Picking the correct and safe path among the boulder-strewn river was indeed critical. A sweep boat travels slightly faster than the river current. Not only does one have the force of the current pushing the boat along, but the surface of the river is tilted downhill, creating additional forward momentum. The sweeps on a scow allow the operator to change the direction the boat is pointed, but cannot slow its pace. This fact places a heavy burden on the front sweep man to anticipate where the boat needs to be positioned long before he gets there.

Consider a thirty-two foot long, eight-foot-wide box loaded with tons of people and supplies. Position the craft on the surface of

9 Carrey and Conley, p. 50

a moving mass of water. Also, imagine how many times in more than a hundred miles of river that craft and that mass of water might encounter an obstacle in the current – a smallish boulder just under the surface, or a large rock projected well above and plainly visible. Both can cause a problem.

Riding up on a rock just under the surface can puncture the bottom or halt the boat in a position with deep water on each side, leaving no place to stand for leverage needed to free the craft. The preferred course in both instances is to pass on one side or the other of the obstacle. Failure to move the craft and avoid the obstruction invites a disaster whose scale is mandated by the masses and forces involved. At the worst, the boat can be overturned or smashed to pieces.

On a normal October day the Salmon River is known to flow at a rate of around four thousand cubic feet per second. A cubic foot of water contains seven and one-half gallons. A gallon of water weighs eight pounds; meaning a cubic foot represents sixty pounds. On that normal day you have a 240,000 pound mass of water moving downstream at an average speed of four miles per hour. That is average. The speed more than doubles in the rapids where most of the obstacles are encountered.

Think of it this way. An average bull elephant weighs about five tons – ten thousand pounds. The mass of water the guides were dealing with was the equivalent of a herd of twenty-four bull elephants rushing by…. every second!

Hancock was charged with steering his craft on the backs of the herd. If he encountered a rock, causing the boat to stop in the midst of our imaginary elephant stampede, he, along with the passengers and supplies would be trampled by the near quarter of a million pound mass.

The thought of this had taught Hancock to think ahead. He had to initiate any maneuvers well in advance of trouble so the entire boat would have time to move to one side. If he waited until he was at the rock, he would only have time to move the bow of the boat, causing the side of the boat to hit the rock. This would turn the entire craft across the current and result in a broach on the rock. The full force of those twenty-four elephants passing each second would then be directed against the full length of the boat, snapping it in two and committing all of its contents to the savage whims of the river.

Detecting the proper course in advance takes hard-won skill. It did not take long for the National Geographic crew to appreciate their guides. "If there was a channel, our inexperienced eyes could not detect it. But on we went; there was no turning back. A quick surge, a rush of water, a few strokes of the sweeps, and we were through! At one moment a huge rock blocked our path. Then it lay behind. With each rapid our respect for the boatmen grew. Their timing and precision were perfect."[10]

Hancock and Cunningham had acquired their skill by parlaying their many previous trips down the river into a mental map. The markers on the map would be the shape or composition of the canyon wall, a particular outcropping, a stand of trees, side creeks, established camps, boulders, rapids – all combined into position keys that told the boatmen where they were, and what to expect ahead. Their mental map had to be fluid as the water level changed from trip to trip. As it did rocks were covered, or exposed and the shoreline changed profile. As the flow was altered preferred routes changed.

The second and equally important component to the boatman's skill set was interpretive – what boatmen call *reading* the water. As water flows over an irregular stream bed the surface becomes a painted canvas of clues the practiced eye can study to gain an understanding of what is happening below. At the upstream *top* of a rapid the guide might observe one or more tongues – v-shaped slicks of water with the narrow point downstream. Here is where the deeper flow leads into the rapid. Further into the rapid he might see a mound of water rising above the surrounding surface, telling him that a rock is below pushing the water up as it rides over the obstruction.

Downstream of the obstruction might be an area of white, frothing water, lower than the surrounding surface – what boatmen call a hole. Here the water in front of an obstruction has been pushed up by an encounter with a rock or ledge. As the water passes over it plunges down, pushing out a hole in the surface if the river. As downstream water cascades back upstream into the hole, it will strike a boat with a force counter to its downstream momentum. Larger scows like Monroe's would easily punch through and be unaffected by any but the largest of holes. The smaller one's craft, the more danger that a hole will trap and swallow the boat.

10 Shenon and Reed, p. 105

The trip ran into trouble at Salmon Falls. The jumble of rocks blocking the channel had long been a problem for boats leading to several applications of dynamite to create a navigable route. Just two years before Cap Guleke had almost lost his life here. In the low water conditions of October, Hancock chose the lesser of evils, steering the scow down the right channel where it slid up onto shallow rocks and stuck. With the help of nearby placer miners the crew was able to pry its craft loose and proceed downstream to Barth Hot Springs.

The springs were a welcome relief. Since the beginning of the trip both Hancock and Flint had been suffering from colds. The hot water made Flint feel momentarily better. That night he placed his bed on an uneven slope and during the night rolled out from under his protective rain fly. A cold rain thoroughly soaked him, leaving Flint in such a weakened condition that the primary goal of the trip became getting him out of the canyon to the hospital.

One member of the party was sent ahead to a Forest Service phone.[11] Arrangements were made for a plane to come in from Missoula to Mackay Bar thirty-two miles downstream, the only landing field in the canyon at that time. But it was two day's travel to Mackay Bar through some challenging rapids. Despite unloading all but Flint and one other passenger to lighten the load, the scow caught a rock in Split Rock rapid that drove the boat onto the shore before spinning and sliding back into the current.

As the group approach Campbell's Ferry it had to deal with a rapid that in low water conditions is feared by boatmen to this day – Growler:

With Flint confined to his sleeping bag, we could take no chances. Hancock chose the safer but shallower channel, toward which the heavy boat plunged at top speed. Then a sickening creak and groan, and we were stuck, this time on a three point suspension that held with viselike tenacity.

For two hours we pried and pulled, to no avail. The dean cut a long pole while the rest of us tediously unloaded the boat, over a slippery bridge of saplings. Then with a rope tied two feet or so from the bottom end, we applied the tree-trunk lever

11 Several of the homesteads along the river were allowed to tie into the Forest Service lines running between fire lookouts and ranger stations in exchange for maintaining portions of the line.

Stuck in Growler Rapid
Unloading to lighten the boat

and, led by Representative Clark, pulled as never before.

The boat moved inches. Again we pulled. It moved a foot, then two feet, then slipped free. Though darkness was upon us, we pushed on to the hospitality of Joe Zaunmiller's ranch, where Flint was given broth and placed in a warm bed.

In the cold dawn we carried Flint down to the scow on an improvised stretcher. On through the rapids and polished water we hurried…. The moment the boat touched shore at Mackay Bar, we climbed to the landing field to find Dick Johnson, who had just landed, looking for us…. We arranged an improvised bed in the front cockpit, bundled Flint in his sleeping bag, and fastened two safety belts securely over all. As he bade us farewell his last words were, "Well fellows, if the doc lets me, I'll join you at Riggins."[12]

The ride out of the canyon and high altitude flight over the Bitterroot Mountain range in an open cockpit biplane accompanied by the cold October weather was too much for Flint. He died two days later in the hospital in Missoula.

The story of the balance of the National Geographic trip on the

12 Shenon and Reed, p. 118

Salmon is an interesting and ambitious one. It can be found in your local library in the July 1936 edition of *National Geographic* magazine. The article is a remarkable forty-three page promotion of the adventure and beauty to be found in Idaho's Salmon River Canyon, accompanied by forty-five stunning photographs and maps.

Outfitters have very small marketing budgets, restrained by the inherently small, family-size businesses that they are. None could ever imagine affording the purchase of such exposure, but this came to Joe Zaunmiller as a gift, a boost for a man, a pioneer of an outfitting industry that would one day grow to be an important economic engine for many of the small rural communities clinging to the edge of Idaho's wild core.

Better days would come, but in the short term Joe and Emma struggled to make ends meet deep in the Great Depression in the depths of the Salmon River Canyon.

Howard Flint is loaded into a biplane for the trip to Missoula.
Joe Zaunmiller is on the far left. Monroe Hancock is on Flint's left.

Chapter Sixteen

Struggles

"Adapt or perish, now as ever,
is nature's inexorable imperative."
– H. G. Wells

While many were trying to deal with the Depression by finding gold, Joe Zaunmiller was more focused on turning Campbell's Ferry into a working ranch. He raised a few cattle, grew hay and vegetables and picked up what jobs he could, using his packing skills.

Joe had plans to build new, better structures to support an expanded outfitting and ranch operation. A valuable commodity for any building project was sawn lumber. In the early days on the property William Campbell had resorted to whip-sawn lumber to make the ferry, but it was a back-breaking, laborious task too difficult to produce the volume needed for the new barn, blacksmith shop, wood shed, and chicken coop Joe wanted. His upstream neighbors at the Ayers place on Richardson Creek and Allison Ranch had mills, but it was hard to transport lumber the seven and ten miles along the river. Two challenging rapids between the Ferry and Ayers made floating the lumber impractical. Joe looked for an opportunity to get his own mill.

His nearest neighbor at the time was Bill Randall at Elkhorn Bar three miles upstream. Bill was learning it was not easy to carve a living out on the Salmon. "Many people came to the Salmon River looking for gold," said Randall. "They thought all they had to do was turn over a rock and pick up the gold; it wasn't that way at all. It took hard work and know how to get any gold."[1]

Randall's first effort was at the mouth of Mallard Creek, just above the place four miles upstream of the Ferry now called Whitewater Ranch. He took over a claim and cabin that had been developed by Toll Lowe. Randall rolled rocks into Mallard Creek to raise the level enough to divert water into a flume leading to a sluice box on the river bank. He spent a week shoveling dirt and gravel into the sluice box. Then he turned the water off to do what was called a *cleanup*. He found eight dollars in gold for the week of effort. The tests he had done with a gold pan told him there had been more gold among the material, but due to the poor design of his sluice box, it had just washed into the river.

Discouraged, Randall considered giving up and leaving, but a neighbor told him that an experienced older miner was due soon and he might want to wait and ask him what he was doing wrong. The man was Oscar Eakin, the same Eakin who had tried to stake a homestead claim on Campbell's Ferry in 1906. Eakin's twenty-eight years of prospecting in Alaska and up and down the Salmon had provided many valuable lessons. Eakin arrived and suggested that Randall move his claim a mile downstream to the mouth of Elkhorn Creek. To catch the gold he was washing away Eakin told him to line his sluice box with burlap and metal lath, to slow the flow and allow the heavier gold to drop from the rushing water and collect in the burlap. Using this process Randall increased his take to one or two ounces a week.

Salmon River gold from this type operation is called *flour* gold – very fine and about seventy-five percent pure. Local miners would send their gold to the assay office in Boise. The price was set by the government at thirty-five dollars an ounce. Randall's weekly take

1 Marian S. Sweeney, *Gold at Dixie Gulch,* (Kamiah, ID: Clearwater Valley Publishing, 1982), p. 81

would have been in the twenty-five to thirty dollar range, less transport and processing fees. He was encouraged enough by the improved results to build a cabin to replace his tent and send for his family to join him.

Lumber for Randall's new cabin was purchased from Charley Ayers who had built a water-powered sawmill at his place four miles upstream at Richardson Creek. Ayers would mill the boards and tie ten together in a bundle and toss them in the river. Randal waited below in a boat and collected his purchase as it floated by. He sent his wife and son upstream to pry loose any bundles that lodged among the rocks. Suddenly all the bundles seemed to be arriving at once when Randall looked up to see the reason. Clyde and Don Smith had been floating the river when they saw Randall's wife and boys at work, so they pitched in and created one large moving mass of lumber.[2]

The improved prospects at Elkhorn Creek did not last, so Randall and his family moved to Dixie where he built his own mill. He used an old Dodge car motor and ordered a saw and mandril from a mail order house. He fashioned a windlass at each end so one man could pull a log through the saw and another pull it back. Though a crude mill, it produced enough lumber to build a thousand foot flume and structures at two mines.

Joe Zaunmiller had befriended Randall when he lived at Elkhorn Creek. When Randall finished his projects in Dixie, Joe purchased the mill, disassembled it and packed it to Campbell's Ferry Ranch. The deal was that Joe would use it and when Randall returned to the river, Joe would cut whatever lumber he needed, but Randall never returned.[3] Remnants of the mill including the large circular saw blade remain at the Ferry today.

When Joe got his new mill going it became a source for his own needs and new downstream neighbors. Rex and Clara Coppernoll from Minnesota had just settled two river miles below on, "a nice little bench opposite Fall Creek where we built a cabin and made a garden spot." The Coppernolls built a log cabin, placing horizontal logs for the first four or five courses, then cut shorter logs and stood them on end to complete the walls. Rex had friends to help and, "they went up to Joe Zaunmiller's sawmill and got slabs and rafted 'em down the

2 Sweeney, p. 82
3 Sweeney, p. 82

river to our place. We drug 'em up there and I shaped the edges with my axe so we could fit em into a floor. They fit pretty snug until they got dry and then we had to watch that the kids didn't fall through!"[4]

In the late fall of 1936 Joe got involved in a search and rescue effort that centered on his new neighbor's place. Rex Coppernoll had left for the winter and eighty-year-old Jack Swazey was staying at the cabin. A husky twenty-two year old miner, Bob Hemminger, had left Dixie when winter shut down mining activity. Bob decided to go hunting in the canyon. Wayne Nickell, who became part of the search party, tells the story in *Gold at Dixie Gulch*:

One day in late fall when someone from Dixie stopped in to see Jack Swazey, Jack inquired whether anyone had seen Bob Hemminger. No, nobody'd seen him. He left here about a month ago to go up to get some meat, Jack said. He went up on the side of the hill towards Chamberlain Basin. He didn't have a coat on, just in his shirtsleeves, and he has never come back.

Jack was wondering if something had happened to him or if he'd decided he didn't want to winter in there and had gone back to Dixie. Word got up to Dixie that Bob Hemminger was missing. A bunch of us went down to the river to look for him, about eight of us. There was Bill Randall, Eck Ramey, Carl Fuller, Joe Zaunmiller and myself, and some others whose names I don't recall.

Bill Randall was going up along the old slide where the side of the mountain had slid out and left a deep canyon along the hillside. He kept seeing coyote tracks in the snow leading off the cliff into that deep canyon. Pretty soon he looked down and saw the skeletons of two bighorn sheep and then he saw Bob Hemminger's body layin' there. He came back to camp that night and told the rest of us that he'd found him, but that it was going to be an awful job to get to him.

In the morning two of the fellas stayed down at the river and dug a grave, and six of us went up after him. Carl Fuller had a little Eswing Hatchet and we took some rope and canvas. We were going to bring him down and bury him on a little grassy flat, close to the river.

It took us from eight o'clock in the morning until about

4 Sweeney, p. 101

three o'clock in the afternoon before we fought our way up there and got him taken care of. The ground was covered with frozen ice and a new skiff of snow fell during the night before we went up there. It was awful steep and awful slippery. It took us a long time and we just hung onto the brush to keep from slidin' back down. But we got up to where he was layin' in the bottom of this canyon.

He was layin' down in where the water had been runnin' and it froze as it come down and he was froze in that ice, all except one arm, his chest and his head. So we had to chop him out of the ice with that little ax.

The sheep layin' nearby were completely eaten up, all except their bones. The coyotes and the varmints had eaten those two sheep, but they hadn't touched this boy. The only thing that had eat on him were the mice, you could see where they'd nibbled on his lips and nose and ears.

You've heard stories about coyotes killin' people and eatin' 'em – well, that's not so, because this fella had laid there for thirty days and they had completely stripped those bighorn sheep. The body was within ten feet of those two sheep and there wasn't a coyote track within three feet of Bob Hemminger's body. That should tell you something. Seeing the trouble we'd had getting' in we began to wonder how we were ever going to get him out of there. Joe Zaunmiller says, "If we try to pack him out of here we might all slip and kill ourselves."

So we decided the best thing to do was to bury him right there. There was no place to bury him except in the side of this cliff. So we sharpened sticks and pried out the rocks until we got a little shelf built in there. Then we wrapped his body in the canvas, wrapped rope around that. Four of the guys held onto that rope and I took him by the head and Eck Ramey took him by the feet and we just lifted him in there. Then we put rocks back in to kinda seal it up, so the varmints wouldn't bother him too bad.

The next spring Jimmy Daufman, the forest ranger, got some of the men and Pick Ward and they went up, took him out, brought him down and buried him. They also pieced out what happened.

Hemminger had killed three bighorn sheep up on the rim of this cliff, above the slide. He decided he would kick 'em off over the cliff and then he could drag 'em down to camp. He had kicked two of 'em off and evidently lost his footing. He slid and fell down over the cliff right close to where the sheep had landed. He left his gun leaning against a tree and it was still there. And the other sheep was still there.

Today a tombstone marks Hemminger's grave in a beautiful stand of Ponderosa pine on a gentle slope above Rush Creek.

In addition to his periodic work on adding new buildings at the ranch, Joe worked with the Forest Service supervising and training young men at the CCC camp at Headquarters, Idaho. Another CCC camp was set up in 1936 at Red River with a spike camp at Trapper Creek to begin construction of a road that would come into the Salmon River Canyon from Elk City to the north, meeting the river at Whitewater Ranch four miles upstream from Campbell's Ferry.

We do not know what, if any role Joe had in this project, but it would change life at the ranch forever. Instead of the difficult thirteen-mile pack out to Dixie via trail, a short four-mile pack to Whitewater was all that was now necessary to reach vehicles that could come into the canyon by road. The new route would turn Whitewater into a terminus where fuel, food, materials, supplies and increasingly important outfitter clients could be brought.

In 1938 Joe secured a contract from the Forest Service to construct a landing strip high in the Chamberlain Basin ten miles from the Ferry. The location was Hida Ridge, a 7000' ridge running through the northern section of the Chamberlain Basin south of the Salmon River Canyon high above the Allison Ranch area. Access to the construction site was best achieved via the Three Blaze Trail up to the head of Richardson Creek, then cross country to the ridge. The 2000' x 150' landing strip was cut from raw wilderness.[5] Joe and a crew of three used horses, mules and hand tools to cut virgin timber, dig stumps and move tons of rock to make a usable landing surface. The purpose of the strip was "to facilitate, the use of aircraft in forest fire protection and particularly transport of men and supplies to remote areas

5 Richard H. Holm, Jr., *Bound for the Backcountry: A History of Idaho's Remote Airstrips*, (McCall, ID: Cold Mountain Press, 2012), p. 262

and dropping of supplies directly to fire camps from the air."[6]

Twenty-one years prior to tackling this ambitious project Joe had been diagnosed by army doctors as having a "leaky heart." Other reports mention that he had, "bad lungs because he froze them one winter."[7] Projects like Hida Ridge and photos of Joe from the period show no signs of physical infirmities. He was a stout, bull of a man willing to tackle any physical task necessary to secure a living in that most difficult of times.

Joe and His Nephews
Richard, Stan and Paul

Joe had become an expert packer with skills honed since he started working around stock as a teen on farms near Walla Walla.

It takes special people to work with stock. Over my twenty-seven years in the outfitting industry, many of them in leadership of an organization that represented both packers and boaters, I developed a keen appreciation for the hard-bitten individualists who made a liv-

Joe with his packstring in the orchard at the Ferry

6 *Landing Strips in Central Idaho*, (Ogden, UT, USDA Forest Service, Region 4, 1943)
7 Sweeney, p. 83

ing leading strings of horses and mules through the backcountry. It was not uncommon for them to be challenged when it came to human interaction, yet blossom around their stock. It takes an almost angry strength to manage the strong will that many of these large equines possess.

The professional packer's relationship with his stock is not the sweetest, almost human, loving interaction you might find among individual horse owners. It is more that of a dominant pack leader, backed by a firm voice and often profane vocabulary. The packer has a sound respect for these thousand-pound creatures, mixed with a view of them as beasts of burden, a critical tool in the tasks of the wilds. And there is a profound respect for how stock can hurt one, invariably born of experience.

During my tenure as president of the Idaho Outfitters and Guides Association I knew very few older packers who did not walk with a limp or set off metal detectors at the airport. After years of being stomped, bent and broken by their stock, their bones were riveted with metal screws strategically placed to hold them together. And the packers paid for this knowledge, literally – beyond their broken bones. All outfitters are required to carry insurance, and the liability cost for those who run strings of horses and mules is twice the cost for those with fleets of rafts.

A common cause of accidents with horses and mules is an encounter with the unfamiliar. Pack outfitters like to run experienced stock. Often when queried about the age of an animal in his string the answer would come back, "old enough to vote." When you are going to put untested greenhorns on stock headed along often precipitous trails in the wilderness, it is good to use a horse or mule that has already seen everything they might encounter. It is the unfamiliar smell, sight or sound that can cause trouble.

When hikers first began to bring llamas into the backcountry it caused consternation among the old experienced packers. The site or smell of these unfamiliar creatures often caused their stock to bolt; bad enough when they are carrying gear, but potentially deadly when the cargo is human.

At first there were the grudging jokes, "How do you pack a llama? Just like you do an elk. Gut and quarter it." But gallows humor was soon replaced by packers seeking out the llama owners and offering free pasture next to their stock so familiarization could occur prior to hunting season, long before an encounter along narrow, steep backcountry trails.

We don't know exactly what caused the horse that Emma Zaunmiller was riding to bolt, but one November day in 1938 she found herself suddenly being carried at full gallop across the orchard at Campbell's Ferry. When the horse ran under a tree, Emma was raked from its back and tumbled to the ground. It could have been a tree limb striking her head, or perhaps the ground itself or a rock.

Head injuries are challenging to diagnose even in today's advanced medical environment. In 1938 the prescription for Emma was to return to Walla Walla to the family home and rest. After a week attended by her mother, Dr. Montgomery was called, and an hour later Emma died. The doctor listed the principle cause of her demise as convulsions of undetermined origin or cause. Once again the angel of death had visited Campbell's Ferry.

After Emma's death, Joe was alone and in need of someone to help care for the property and his outfitting business. The 1940 census shows that Joe took in Phillip Murray, age twenty-eight, as a partner. Phillip's wife, Dorothy, was the cook, and a seven-year-old stepdaughter, Mary Helen Skinner, was present.

In 1941 Jim and Pearl Chittick came to lend a hand. The couple had left North Dakota and come to Dixie just two years before. The Chitticks were miners, but they took a year off to move in with their new friend, Joe. Zaunmiller's fellow Forest Service packer, Pick Ward and his wife Lillie visited often, taking time from their four children in school at Dixie to make sure Joe was comforted and cared for through his grief. In a show of sympathy, Jim and Pick shaved the top of their heads to match Joe's balding dome.

A year later Joe put the word out that he was looking for help, a caretaker, preferably a woman, to tend to the homestead while he traveled on his periodic Forest Service jobs or took clients hunting and fishing for his growing outfitting business.

Zaunmiller was wise to the ways of the backcountry and he knew what it took to care for a homestead.

Fifty years later when we came to Campbell's Ferry we were clueless.

Joe Zaunmiller, Jim Chittick, Lillie and Pick Ward

Chapter Seventeen

First Year

Two roads diverged in a wood, and I –
I took the one less traveled by,
And that has made all the difference.
– Robert Frost

When Joe Zaunmiller was looking for a caretaker in 1939 he had worked on homesteads for fourteen years. In 1990 when we first purchased the property Brad and I knew little of the task we had taken on. Both of us had growing businesses with family and employees to support. We couldn't spend the time needed; nor could we just throw money at the problem of getting someone to stay and do the necessary upkeep. We decided to bring in four more partners. Our goal was to get enough people with an interest in the place to achieve a critical mass of the energy and effort it would take to spend time to halt the decline the property had experienced in the prior two decades.

First Year

After Joe Zaunmiller the homestead suffered from neglect. The later occupants proved to be less industrious, endured medical issues and faced the reality that the Ferry's task list was not suited to aging residents.

Caring for a home in the wilds is a fight even for the young and fit. Natural forces have the upper hand. Open space left unattended at a homestead in the canyon will gradually revert to the wilds. The edges of the orchard, pasture and runway are in a constant state of creep. Grass grows, then brush, mixed with small trees – eventually the forest takes back what the pioneer worked so hard to clear.

The buildings suffer, too. Nothing here has the advantage of a modern foundation. The structures are built of wood sitting on rock. Over time, the rock works into the ground until the wood makes contact with the soil, hastening the inevitable process of decay and rot.

Water is the enemy of a wood structure. A leak in a roof allows moisture to enter the core of the building. Wind tugs at the tin panels. Snow piles up in the winter, adding a load that presses down on the rafters and walls, then retreats each spring. It slides off the roof, piling up around the walls, pressing in and wetting the boards and logs. Wind drives rain under the eaves and drips from the roof, splashing up against the base of the structure, gradually weakening the critical sill logs.

After the last resident left in December of 1985, the property was unoccupied for four years – except for rodents. Given the chance, field mice, pack rats and marmots prefer a structure. For four years there had been no one to challenge the horde of rodent homesteaders who took up residence at the Ferry.

My first visit to Campbell's Ferry was via river. Brad and I and a few friends floated the forty-two miles from road's end at Corn Creek down the Salmon River, taking two days to make the trip. We were ecstatic, reveling in the knowledge that now we had our own backcountry dream – one of those wonderful places we had often passed in the wilderness and mused, "Who is lucky enough to live there?" Campbell's Ferry was ours. Soon after arrival we began the process of washing the shine off our rosy perspective, dampening our enthusiasm with buckets of our own sweat.

The eighty-five acres of the Campbell's Ferry homestead stretches almost a mile along the south bank of the river. There are several places you can pull a boat over to unload. Coming from upstream the first is the old ferry site. A small sand beach on the left is nestled among large boulders. From the river's edge a trail winds a quarter-mile up the hill, through a draw, past the site of William Campbell's original cabin, through the orchard to the Cook Cabin. You are walking on a well beaten path worn down by decades of the footsteps and hoof prints that began with miners headed to Thunder Mountain. The elevation gain to the orchard is 140 feet, an easy walk. Carrying a load makes it harder.

It is also possible to pull over a half mile past the old ferry site and take a steep switchback trail up the bank just behind the blacksmith shop. Your last chance is below the suspension bridge that crosses the river. At the top of a large sand and rock beach is a wagon road built in the mid-fifties to move supplies down to the crew that was building the bridge.

We chose the last and headed up the hill with an armload of gear. A barbed wire fence in a serious state of disrepair ran beside the road on the uphill side. I say a road, but really it was just two side by side paths running the short distance to the edge of the orchard. As we reached the top of the rise the glory of the orchard of apple, pear and peach trees in the blush of spring bloom was breathtaking. It was green, lush and doing a pretty good job of hiding a mess. As we walked toward the Cook Cabin, on our left was a gaudy, out of place chain link fence surrounding a 12'x12' enclosure that once held a weather station. To our right were several stacked rows of wooden rounds, half a winter's supply waiting to be split for firewood. The last resident had left the wood four years earlier – a December trip to see the doctor from which she never returned.

Next on the left was the blacksmith shop. Entrance to the shop was blocked by piles of junk, left in stacks of disarray as if tossed in with no thought of ever being seen again. It looked threatening. Broken windows with shards of glass strewn below, odd, rusty, protruding pieces of metal of unknown origin and use were everywhere. Looking in made one immediately wonder if your tetanus shot was up to date.

Wall boards ran right to the dirt with rotten, decaying bottoms. A work bench looked as if a century of rusted, broken tools had been randomly thrown across the top and into shelves below. A bed pan sat on a shelf encrusted with almost two decades of dust accumulated since its last use. We stood at the entrance gazing, taking a mental inventory, imagining what might be found if one dared step in and begin to dig in the piles – it looked hopeless.

The list that would never end began. Item number one – move everything out of the shop, find what is worth keeping, what not, and what to do with it. Timeline for the first entry on the project list – someday. It would be a long time before we would complete a survey of the property – not a measuring survey – just a look at what was there and what needed to be done. Later we would learn a truth of the backcountry. Every homestead has such a list. A list that is never complete, always growing from new additions as fast or faster than the removal of checked off, completed tasks.

Turning towards the Cook Cabin we encountered an odd assortment of fences and gates, constructed in a patchwork of periodic repairs. It was hard to see what had been the original fence. Every few feet wire of a different description filled the space between an odd assortment of posts. Some gates hung by hinges, others were just wired in place. The reason for it all was evident. Two sides of the cabin had been enclosed to protect a garden that stretched around a flat yard on the south and east.

On the north side of the cabin the ground dropped sharply into a ravine. The ravine was filled with an endless morass of cans, bottles, barrels and debris tossed into the latest of what we would discover were five dumps on the property. The west side of the cabin was a back room projecting off the flat, supported by posts and beams, suspended above a slope that ran down through the woods to the river.

A stately mature English walnut tree, fifty feet in height with rich, green foliage, stood shading a seventy-foot-diameter circle in the cabin's front yard. The edge of its canopy just touched the roof of the front porch. Below, a few feet from the floor of the porch, ran a small ditch with no water.

We walked onto the porch half expecting at any moment it might fall around us. The floor was rotted wood, sunk into the dirt, an uneven surface stacked with buckets and boxes with trash strewn about. The door had a lock on it. We had been given a key by Donna McBain from the Trust for Public Lands. Pushing the door open left a semi circle of cleared space on the floor. When pulled back the door left a pile of chewed pieces of paper mixed with rodent droppings pushed against a cabinet.

We entered a compact kitchen. To the left was a small propane stove, beyond that a massive Great Majestic wood-burning stove. On the opposite wall were more cabinets, a door and a counter with shelving on one end and drawers below. Every surface was covered with one to three inches of debris. The majority of it consisted of clumps of dark, dried, crumbling marmot scat interspersed with packrat droppings and a myriad of materials they had chewed up. For years the resident rodents had worked their way into every drawer, shelf and box containing newspapers, magazines, books, quilts, and clothing, ripping pieces to be used to make their nests. It was everywhere; in every room, in the ceiling, and we would later find, in every building.

Under the buildings looked like the tunnels of Cu Chi. In Vietnam the Viet Cong had built underground living complexes to hide from their enemy. When a threat arrived they retreated to safety, later rising up to wreak havoc in the dark of night or whenever opposing troops were absent. So it is in the backcountry. Millions of acres of wilderness are the home of a near endless army of rodents. When humans move in, it is a never ending war between those above and those below ground. After four years of free reign the rodents held the upper hand. The question hung in the air, "Who will occupy, who will survive on this old homestead?"

We had brought reinforcements. Joe Denton had shared the same small hometown in Mississippi with Brad and me. The three of us had developed a passion for running rivers in canoes, making marathon drives to rivers in the Arkansas Ozarks and southern Appalachians of Tennessee and North Carolina. We had pitched in with a couple of other friends to buy land on the Mulberry River in the Ozarks and built a log cabin together, a base camp for our weekends exploring the rivers and hollows of northwest Arkansas.

Joe was the oldest son of Joe Sr., owner of Denton's dairy and family farming interests. He grew up rising at 4:00 A.M. to get a fleet of milk trucks on the road to serve a network of grocers and small food stores stretched across the Mississippi Delta.

Brad and I had an acknowledged weakness when it came to mechanical or motorized equipment and were quick to turn to Joe. He never flinched or hesitated, always ready to jump headfirst into any task. He brought a high school football lineman's build and strength and a can do attitude that saved our bacon on many a cross country venture.

I had just descended the steep, narrow stairs from the upstairs of the Cook Cabin. All the mess we had seen below was just as bad up above, even worse. I looked across the room at Brad and recognized both of us were beginning to wonder what the hell we had gotten into, our smiling enthusiasm faded to frowns cast in a sweaty, dusty reality. Not Joe. His enthusiasm was undiminished. The deeper we got into the filth and clutter the bigger his smile and determination. He couldn't wait to get after it.

Joe had come to Boise in 1984, the second Mississippi immigrant, followed later by Brad, all of us from the same small town of Cleveland. Joe bought a printing business and dived headfirst into what we all viewed as life in an outdoor lover's paradise. His goal in the nineties was to organize his business to allow him weeks, hopefully months, spent on the Salmon River in a sweaty grin of never ending projects.

For now our challenge was just getting gear and supplies up the hill. We returned to the rafts to bring up our gear. It was a lot.

We river rafters are spoiled. A raft will haul a lot of weight. Unlike a backpacker, keeping it light is not normally an issue. A raft lets you take with you all that is necessary to eat, drink and sleep well while tackling the task at hand. We had large aluminum boxes full of food and kitchen gear. Usually it was only necessary to move part of it a short distance to a river side, river level camp.

It was all the better if you follow the *Bob Campbell rule* – never place your kitchen further from your raft than the length of your bow line. At Campbell's Ferry it was a quarter-mile hike up a hill to the homestead. The trip up and back became a brutal chore.

As we looked around to see how the pioneers had done it we saw several tractor tires lying on the ground, remnants of a 1953 Farmall Super C tractor that a later resident had brought in to ease the work load at the Ferry. The tractor had since been removed from the homestead. Our options for moving materials and supplies were limited.

Looking around we found what the last resident had used. Her preferred method of hauling supplies had been a pair of kid's plastic sleds with ropes tied to the front. She simply wrapped the rope around her waist and pulled the loaded sled across the ground. We did the same. It worked for the periodic run to the river and back for personal supplies, but how would we move the heavier materials we needed to repair and maintain the buildings?

Horses and mules were not an option since none of the new owners were experienced with stock and what would we do with them the rest of the year? Our plans were to come in for days, or weeks at a time, but full time occupation was not an option. None of us were at a time in our personal lives to make that commitment and a provision in the new easement forbade year round occupation. There was also a prohibition against the use of motor vehicles. For now the closest thing to horsepower on the place would be the two-legged variety.

First Year

Chapter Eighteen

Fire

"The only time you learn from the mistakes of another
is when they end in tragedy."
– Chaytor Mason

When we first laid eyes on Campbell's Ferry in 1990 the beauty of the place was enhanced by a thick, verdant cloak of Ponderosa pine and Douglas fir covering the surrounding canyon walls. We knew that these same lush stands of trees that enhanced the property's beauty also represented the greatest threat. The Ferry stood a fifty-fifty chance of surviving the Big One when it came.

The forests were in an overgrown condition because of a successful program of fire suppression that began in 1905 with Gifford Pinchot and the newly created Forest Service. In those days fire was seen as the enemy, a villain that destroyed valuable timber resources. Few had the notion that fire might be part of nature's plan for the woods. The concept of an ecosystem did not exist.

Fire

Pinchot had a plan for fires in the forests. "The one secret to fighting fires is to discover your fire as soon as possible and fight it as hard as you can and refuse to leave it until the last ember is dead," he told the New York Times. He and President Roosevelt believed that forest fires could be controlled.[1] Pinchot's plan would evolve to the 10 A.M. Policy. Under this approach all of the Forest Service's resources would be marshaled to get fire fighters on a fire by ten o'clock the morning after it was detected. In the early stage a fire could be attacked with fewer men and stopped before it had a chance to grow.

To facilitate the detection and suppression efforts the agency set about putting fire lookouts on peaks throughout the national forests. Each was equipped with a firefinder, a round mapping board that the lookout operator used to sight the compass direction of the fire. Using a similar sighting from a second lookout and a process called triangulation, the exact location of the fire could be determined. To communicate between the observation points miles of telephone line was strung from lookout to lookout and to ranger stations. In later years radios would replace the phone lines. There are still many lookouts in service, supplemented by aerial patrols and satellite imagery.

To get an army of firefighters to the fire the agency became one of the largest owners of horses and mules in the country. It created Remount Depots, modeled after the U.S. Cavalry, to support fire fighting efforts. The Ninemile Remount Depot outside of Missoula, Montana, had hundreds of trucks and men ready at a moments notice to draw from a herd of more than a thousand mules. When the call came in men, mules, fire fighting equipment and supplies would be loaded in trucks and transported to the trail head closest to the fire.

In 1940 a newer, quicker method, the smokejumper, began when Earl Cooley and Rufus Robinson parachuted out of a Travel Air 6000 to fight a fire on Marten Creek on the Selway River.

Over time as equipment and techniques improved, the agency would get very good at fighting fire. Today we see the results of their success in changes in the frequency and intensity of fire activity. Prior to the suppression efforts it was the norm to have frequent low intensity fires set by lightning. Fire would occur every ten years or so and creep through the forest, burning underbrush and small trees. Large

1 Timothy Egan, *The Big Burn: Teddy Roosevelt and the Fire that Saved America,* (New York, NY: Houghton Mifflin Harcourt), p. 71

trees, especially fire resistant species like the Ponderosa pine would flourish in open, widely spaced stands.

Infrequently, natural conditions of high fuel loads, drought, lightning storms and low humidity would converge to ignite a rare high intensity wild fire. That is what happened in 1910 when the great Idaho fire burned millions of acres from the Salmon River watershed north to the Canadian border.

Today it is far more common to have large high intensity fires. Thanks to decades of successful fire suppression efforts, the circumstances that created the 1910 fire in north Idaho had grown by the 1980s to exist in a much wider swath of our forests nationwide. Forests had accumulated large amounts of brush and small trees, fuel for the fires, at ground level. *Ladder* fuels grew to more frequently allow fire to move from the ground up into the branches of the larger trees. Fire moves into the canopy in a process called *crowning* and engulfs entire stands of trees on a broader scale. Now when fires occur they tend to grow more quickly in scope and intensity.

The 1988 fires in Yellowstone National Park were a prime example of the problem. For the past several decades similar massive fires in the overgrown wild forests of the Idaho backcountry have been so large they frequently overwhelm the resources the government is able to bring to the fire battle. Massive expensive shows are put on, but the big fires are usually not contained until the weather turns to bring lower temperatures with rain to aid the suppression efforts.

Federal land management agencies have recognized their error in past fire policy and are adapting. We are in a transition period that will some day restore the forests to a more natural condition. Now, when fires occur in wild areas the goal is to allow them to play their natural role. Emphasis is on protection of human lives and structures in the woods while allowing the fire to burn and thin the forests.

By the time we purchased Campbell's Ferry in 1990 the forests on and around the property looked nothing like they had when William Campbell first saw it. Open widely spaced stands of Ponderosa pine with pockets of Douglas fir had become overgrown. The property was surrounded by a perfect example of large stands that were too thick with too much fuel load, waiting for the right conditions to explode in a massive wildfire.

The Big One did arrive in 2006. We had a front row seat to

a show of the latest fire policies in action. A mix of firefighters, organized in groups called the Black Hills Fire Use Module, McCall Smokejumpers and Lone Pine Hot Shots showed up to protect Campbell's Ferry. We knew the risks they would be taking would not just be with taxpayers dollars. The firefighters were putting their lives on the line to defend our historic homestead.

To me and to them, it was all too personal. In 1993 after my five-year term as president of Idaho's outfitter organization a friend, Jim Thrash, took over the position. For years Jim had been building his own outfitting business and as with many outfitters, had taken a second job to support the effort. Jim's other job was as a smokejumper.

In 1994 Idaho's outfitting and smokejumper communities were stunned to hear that Jim, one of their own, was among fourteen firefighters who lost their lives while fighting a fire at Storm King Mountain near Glenwood Springs, Colorado.

Our common loss quickly established a bond between us and the professionals who showed up to protect the Ferry from fire.

To document the efforts they would make and our experience with the fire Phyllis kept a journal for the next two weeks.

<u>August 7, Monday</u>

Around 6:30 P.M. a weather front moves over the canyon with significant thunder and lightning but virtually no rain. Dark clouds roll through quickly and by 7:30 Doug and I sit out in front of the cabin having a cocktail. Doug notices a column of smoke rising up high on the ridge at the head of Slide Creek across from the Ferry in the Nez Perce National Forest. He calls the sheriff's department on the satellite phone. By eight there is a spotter plane circling the site.

A lone hiker comes past the cabin about 8:30, having come all the way from Chamberlain Basin that day. He tells us he saw two plumes of smoke on our side of the river in the drainage of Little Trout Creek

<u>August 8, Tuesday</u>

Doug is scheduled to go out to Boise today on the mail plane. Just about the time Ray Arnold with Arnold Aviation arrives in his Cessna at 8:30 A.M., a helicopter with a water bag checks out the Nez

Perce fire from which smoke is still rising, then crosses the river to fly over Trout Creek. Doug flies out with Ray. Rita, our Vizsla puppy and I walk down to watch the chopper dip water from the river just below the bridge.

Gayle Watt, the owner of a fishing lodge upriver, jet boats under the bridge and pulls up on the beach river right. He and some guests join us on the bridge watching the copter dip water and fly up to drop it on the Nez Perce fire. The group follows Rita and me up to the Ferry where I tell them a history of the place and take them through the Cook Cabin. They leave to visit the Jim Moore place.

About an hour later (11:30 A.M.) I am walking up from the garden when for the first time I notice a large plume of smoke rising above the Trout Creek ridge. As I turn to walk back down to watch it, Gayle comes back up from the river to point it out to me. The helicopter had flown off around 11:00 and the Nez Perce fire was showing very little smoke.

The smoke on our side of the river continues to grow and fill in the canyon. Around 3:00 P.M. I put the satellite phone and my wallet in Doug's backpack and take Rita, our Vizsla puppy. My thought is to walk up the trail on the opposite side of the river towards Whitewater Ranch to see how close the fire is. By this time a spotter plane had been circling over the smoke for about an hour. A float party arrives at the bridge just as I approach. I ask them what they have seen. They report that the fire is about two miles up river, high on the ridge. They could see some flames. Two miles seems a fairly safe distance to me so Rita and I return to the Ferry.

Around 4:00 P.M. a big tanker helicopter comes in to suck water out of the river, right at the old ferry site. It drops some on the Nez Perce side but concentrates on our side of the river at the Trout Creek site.

<u>August 9, Wednesday</u>

Rita and I sleep well, considering, and Ray flies Doug back in at 7:30 A.M. They could see the fire up Trout Creek from the air. As we eat breakfast a plane flies over the Nez Perce fire dropping seven smoke jumpers and their gear, one pass for each jumper and double drops for gear. Wanting to see for ourselves how close the fire had come, Doug and I hike as far as the ridge on the downstream side of

Little Trout. The smoke is rising beyond the upstream ridge but we can see no flames.

Later in the day, around 4:00 P.M., the tanker helicopter returns to drop one load of water on the Trout Creek fire. Soon after, a smaller helicopter is over Trout Creek. It circles back over the Ferry and lands in the grass just below the road up to the Crowe Cabin. Seven fire fighters from the Black Hills Fire Use Module disembark with personal gear. We speak with them briefly before they hike off to survey the situation on the ground. Three of them return around 7:30 smelling very smoky and looking tired. They have run out of water so I take them down to the Cook Cabin. The fire is on the move but they hope to contain it in Little Trout. They leave to hike up to Whitewater to pick up additional gear that has been trucked in and to spend the night. The remaining four follow about an hour later.

August 10, Thursday

When we awake it appears that the Nez Perce fire is completely out. Our firefighters are back at the Ferry by jet boat at 9:00 A.M. with additional gear and personnel. They drop their personal gear in the orchard near the Cook Cabin where we have invited them to camp and set off up the trail towards the increasingly ominous dark smoke.

Doug's daughter Trudy, her husband Svein and their children Perry and Cecelia are due to arrive tomorrow and we are thinking of calling to cancel their trip. It would be exciting for the kids to be here with all the firefighters, helicopters, planes, etc. but if the fire should get worse we wouldn't want them in harm's way. We will wait to get a report back from the firefighters. In the meantime I spend the day cleaning and getting ready for Trudy and her family.

As the day progresses things look worse. The wind, which has been coming up everyday around 4:00 P.M., starts in again. Our firefighters straggle back. They have not been able to hold the fire. It has burned down into the upper part of Little Trout. Doug calls Trudy and cancels. During the night I hear the ghostly sound of trees falling in the distance,

August 11, Friday

Over night we had been questioning our decision to cancel the kids' trip but now we are glad we did.

Fire

The firefighters head off again. Doug and I hike up the trail about a mile and a half toward Whitewater Ranch to look at the fire from across the river. We can see smoke coming up from Little Trout but we cannot see flames.

Back at the Ferry in mid-afternoon we notice the smoke is appreciably thicker with high plumes rising beyond the ridge above Trout Creek. Then, suddenly, the fire crests the ridge and starts running down towards the creek. We watch it through binoculars as it burns down into the draw. The firefighters come back. They cannot stop it and will no longer try. Their plan now is to stay here and defend the Ferry. They have called for more water from the helicopter and for water hoses, pumps, a water reservoir, and building wrap to be brought in. I talk with Brandon from Flagstaff. His parents live in Tubac. He gets into his duffle bag and pulls out a card which he gives me. It is a watercolor of a desert scene, really lovely work. His mother is the artist. He is obviously and appropriately proud of her.

As we wait and watch the fire I remark to Doug that we are lucky that the fire is on a fairly open hillside so that it is only grass and bushes burning. The words are scarcely out of my mouth when three large trees on the ridge erupt in flame. It is suddenly very clear to me what *burst into flame* really means. The noise is like a flight of F-14s coming over the hill. The conflagration is sudden, dramatic, and just as quickly it is over. The three trees are left dark skeletons with bright orange-red edges.

The crew starts moving everything away from the building structures that can be moved. The crawl spaces under the Crowe Cabin are boarded up.

Around 2:00 P.M., Doug and I decide to pack up the few things we would want to take out with us should we need to evacuate. Now things are beginning to feel surreal. Although it is hard to get your head around it we just have to choose something, so we do. It feels arbitrary and odd. Doug takes our selected bags down to the river with some of the firefighters' gear.

The tanker helicopter comes back around 7:00 P.M. One man, Mark, has been left at the fire to direct the drops. After about eight drops it flies off. The chopper was called from another fire it was working and probably was running low on fuel. Just after the helicopter left (around 8:00 P.M.), a red and white C-47 flies overhead.

Sanya, one of the firefighters with the Black Hills unit is talking to him on the radio, directing parachute drops. We think he will be using the runway but to the surprise of all of us, including Sanya, he chooses the orchard. We huddle under the walnut tree as he drops twenty-one boxes of the requested gear, three at a time. Three drop into

Supplies are delivered by parachute

tall pines trees, one lands in the pear tree and one just misses the garden. Orange and white parachutes are everywhere. One lands in a tree next to the river. Eventually, when they cut it down, the tree falls into the river, too far out in the current to retrieve the parcel, which unfortunately contains gasoline.

Eric Allen is in charge of the Black Hills Fire Use Module. Doug asks him if he thinks we should leave. He says we will be safe here with them, but of course it is our call.

After the plane leaves, there is a flurry of activity. Boxes are unpacked, chutes are rolled up and the first pine tree is cut down so that the gear can be retrieved. We are not sorry to see it go down since it is one of the approach hazards for landing at the ferry. Hoses are unrolled and laid out until darkness prevents anymore work. The firefighters set up the kitchen down at the river. So far as we can see they haven't even started cooking so all will be done in the dark. We have let them use the four-wheeler and we see its lights going up and down the river trail.

<u>August 12, Saturday</u>

Doug gets up at 6:30 A.M. I can hear Eric out in the field by the Crowe Cabin talking on the satellite phone. Doug brings him in the cabin and they study the map, talking about the fire's location and speculating where it might go. Eric says he believes it will burn through the trees above the Crowe Cabin and the runway. He believes the Ferry is defensible with all the hoses. They did not receive the building wrap they had ordered but he thinks they can defend the buildings. Nevertheless he goes on to tell us how the buildings would burn should they not be able to protect them. As I listen I look around the cabin and imagine it happening. We again talk briefly about leaving. Eric says, "The orchard should be the safest place. That's where I am going to be." We decide to retrieve our bags from the river to the orchard.

The chainsaws starts up and three more trees come down. When we go to the river parts of pine trees are laying on either side of trail. The big tanker helicopter comes back and makes many trips from the river to Trout Creek. Out on the bridge three men are laying down hose and setting up sprinklers to protect the structure. As we talk to Mark I can overhear the conversation coming over his radio. Eric is telling the helicopter pilot where to make the drops.

Earlier this morning Doug and Rita walked up to Trout Creek with Eric. Doug reported the fire was down low in the drainage.

We bring our stuff back up to the orchard, dump it in the middle of the field and transfer it all into our waterproof bags. Suddenly I am imagining us standing next to the bags while the fire burns around us. I must look worried 'cause Doug kisses me, holds me and tells me he loves me. For the first time I feel like crying, but I don't.

Instead I come back to the cabin and do dishes. Whatever I do feels pretty useless but I must do something so I keep doing ordinary things as an antidote to an extraordinary day. The firefighters are relentless. They started at first light and never seem to stop. There are two women, Sanya and Dafna. Dafna is Israeli, from Haifa. I watched her lug the big pump down the long steep bank to the river below the Blue Room outhouse by herself. Both women are attractive with lovely smiles and, needless to say, both are strong and fit. The crew seems very nice and congenial, not only with us but with each other. They have moved their kitchen and all their gear up from the river to the camp in the orchard. One or two tents are set up but mostly they just throw their sleeping bags under the trees.

Around 1:00 P.M. two river patrol rangers, Rob and Matt, came up to check things out. They talk with Sanya, take notes and walk around the site. They have managed to rescue the fuel carton that fell into the river but the chute is still underwater, caught in the felled tree. The fuel can was intact and no fuel was spilled in the river.

By now a big, orange plastic reservoir is being set up in the orchard. Water is being pumped up from the river into the *pump-*

kin and then pumped out through the network of hoses around the property.

The heli-tanker,[2] or sky crane (as I learn it is called), returns at 4:30 to make runs at the fire once again. Earlier we had another cargo drop, this time seven cartons from a Twin Otter. One chute tangles in the peach tree but all arrive safely in the orchard. A

A plastic reservoir, the pumpkin, and hoses are set up to move water from the river to the historic buildngs

much smaller helicopter lands across the road from the orchard about 5:00 P.M. to drop off a fire-behavior expert named Irene who has been looking at the fire from the air. She does a quick survey of the place while Eric is taken up to look over the fire from the air. Our crew has opened the building wrap which was part of our latest delivery and is wrapping the back side of Frances' cabin in what looks like heavy aluminum foil. They have cut back all the bushes around the cabin to create a clear barrier. Dafna and Zack take a roll of building wrap up the trail to cover the Trout Creek Bridge and the small bridge over the irrigation ditch.

Doug goes to the river to meet Mike McLain who is bringing in the beer we ordered for the fire crew. We know them all by name now, where they are from, and at least a few details of their lives. Eric, back from his chopper ride, and Doug climb in Mike McLain's jet boat to check out the fire from the river. Doug brings back pictures. The fire has burned down Trout Creek to the river.

<u>August 13, Sunday</u>

At 3:15 A.M. the smell of smoke is heavy in the cabin. I can feel it in my throat. Even in the darkness you can see that the canyon is filled with it. I lie awake until Eric knocks on the door to retrieve

---

2 Large helicopter that carries a 2,000 gallon reservoir that can be filled with water or slurry to be dumped on a fire.

his satellite phone that we have been charging. Doug goes out for a report and returns to say that ten more firefighters/smoke jumpers are coming in this morning. The smoke is so thick that you cannot see across the runway. It will be awhile until anyone can land here. Soon after we hear a chopper passing back and forth overhead but it is impossible to see it.

Fire on the river

Since they could not land at the Ferry, the seventeen smoke jumpers were dropped off at Whitewater Ranch. Heinz Sippel and Mike McLain pick them up and bring them to us. Doug drives the 4-wheeler down to pick up their gear. A small helicopter does make it in to deposit a new boss, an "operations specialist." It lands right next to the garden, blowing all the plants so wildly that I am sure they will be uprooted. The new arrival is in marked contrast to the seasoned, dirty crew we have grown to know. He looks like he just stepped out of a catalog with a clean, pressed shirt and pants and cute little shovel without a scratch on it.

He and the helicopter will stay till evening to assess the possibility of dropping PSDs[3] along the ridge to start a small burn to contain our fire. I ask the helicopter pilot if it is possible to not land so close to the garden next time.

For the past few days we have heard trees crashing in the forest when the wind comes up around 4:00 P.M. Precisely at 4 the wind starts to blow and a tree falls. The sound is much closer. From where we sit under the walnut tree, we can hear occasional shouts from the firefighters.

Rita, who at first was unnerved by the helicopters, is now thoroughly bored with them. She barely opens her eyes when one lands.

We now have twenty-five people on our fire. They have called for assistance from a heli-tanker but there are so many fires around,

3 Device installed in a helicopter that drops flammable spheres to igninte fires on the ground for prescribed or wildland fire application.

we get put on a list to ration available resources. From The Cook Cabin I can see at least a dozen plumes of smoke rising. Smoke is filling the river corridor, all along the drainage, and upwards clear to the top of the eastern-most ridge.

The big ridge above the Crowe Cabin has not started to burn, yet. Suddenly we hear the heli-tanker. It is back and dumping water just inside the perimeter of our woods. The water in the small ditch at the Cook Cabin now tastes like smoke. Doug and I make preparations to sleep in the orchard *if necessary*. We make hasty decisions about what to have with us, some strategic and some arbitrary. Again, it all feels very unreal.

Every day Eric has told us that the fire is coming here. It is not a question of <u>if</u>, but <u>when</u>. It turns out that when is tonight. The new boss who came in today completely changed Eric's plan from defense to offense and sent everyone out to stop the fire. The crew seems skeptical of the new plan but quickly accept.

It did no good. Eric was right. The firefighters straggle back to the ferry, very sooty and tired. The new boss flies back to McCall in his helicopter. Doug contrasts the clean air-conditioned motel room he will have with our crew's conditions sleeping on the ground. He compares the situation to a grizzled experienced military unit that is suddenly forced to follow a green first lieutenant — an FNG, F***ing New Guy. We are glad the FNG is gone.

Eric goes back to his defense strategy. The whole experience strengthens our bond and faith in *our* crew. The fire is approaching fast so everyone is moving very quickly. They are amazingly efficient and well coordinated. The sprinklers are started. The big hoses are manned. The perimeter of the back-fire has been marked.

At 8:30 P.M. part of the crew walk the perimeter with drip torches.[4] In the darkness we can now see the wild fire approaching through the trees. The firefighters start the drip torches and the set fires start advancing towards the wild fire. Everything is moving fast. The crews are cool, quiet, and efficient but the scene is undeniably dramatic. With our backs to the river, we are surrounded on three sides by fire. Earlier a fire lane was cut down to the river in hopes of stopping the fire from burning in between us and the river. Everyone

---

4 Drip Torch – A hand-held device for igniting fires by dripping a flaming mixture of diesel and gasoline on the materials to be burned.

is counting on it to hold. The fires around us are all in the under story, very few trees are burning. We are very, very fortunate that the winds were mild and died down early. We have ideal conditions for the defense of the Ferry. Doug and I walk along the fire line in the darkness, watching the crew silhouetted against the firelight.

Except for the crackling of the fire and the occasional tree crash, there is an eerie silence and serenity. Around 1 A.M. Doug and I go to bed in the Crowe Cabin while, about forty feet away, the back fire burns through the forest towards its wild relative.

<u>August 14, Monday</u>

At 6:30 A.M. the air is once again thick with smoke, the hillside across the river barely visible. Doug rises and goes out to talk with the firefighters and survey the scene.

The barn and firefighter silhouetted by the backfire

Some of the firefighters have been up all night, watching. Eric sends them down to China Bar with Mike McLain so they can sleep undisturbed. The rest are already up and working, cleaning up, checking hot spots, widening the fire lane.

The *Hot Shots* and smokejumpers start back-burning up Moore Creek, the first drainage downstream from the Ferry. During the day more supplies and equipment are air dropped — twenty-one packages.

Eric called for a heli-tanker to drop water around the Moore Creek back burn. Unfortunately the heli-tanker arrives at the same time as the supply drop plane so there is a thirty minute delay in getting water onto the site. It also means we only get half the commitment allotted to our fire before the helicopter has to return to base. Doug is now calling Eric *The Maestro*. He tells me that Eric's work on the fire is like great choreography. I guess Doug has been paying attention at all those dance concerts he has attended with me in the past five years.

Around 4:00 P.M. the wind increases and the hills behind the Ferry erupt. This is the hardest moment so far for me, watching the huge beautiful old pines flare up and die in seconds. A whole portion of the hillside ignites as quickly as a match strike and almost as quickly dies out. Then, another section ignites. You can easily understand why you can not outrun a fire. There isn't enough time to take a deep breath, let alone run anywhere and, of course, the air is suffocating. At one point a huge fat column of apricot-colored smoke rolls around itself like a tornado as it arcs across the sky. The trees on the ridges blow wildly in the winds that the fire generates on its own.

Eric comes to talk to us. I think he sees that this is hard for me and just wants to check in. He tells me next spring the hills will be green and this will make for a better, healthier, forest thirty years from now as the new trees grow up. All I can think about is how beautiful these trees were and that for the rest of my life I will be looking

Eric Allen,
Maestro

at their black skeletal remains and missing them. I think, what if….. What if they hadn't started the back burn up Moore Creek? What if the helicopter had been able to give us a full hour of water support?

Doug and Eric go off while I continue to watch the flames and mourn. Although I can't help grieving the loss of this beautiful forest, I begin to suspect that my perspective is selfish and shortsighted. Thirty plus years from now some woman will stand where I am and love the new trees just as much.

The fire erupts

All the rest of the evening and throughout the night the fire runs wild over the ridges. We can tell from the eerie back-lighting illuminating the smoke that the back sides of our hills are burning hard in the night.

We go to sleep breathing smoke.

<u>August 15, Tuesday</u>

The morning is still dark with smoke when Doug checks in with the crew and comes back to tell me that our Black Hills gang is leaving within the hour for China Bar. This is unwelcome news. We thought they would be with us for at least a couple days more. Rita is very sad…she has fallen in love with Dafna. We go down to the river to see them off and thank them again. They thank us too. Doug had beer brought in for them, loaned them the 4-wheeler, gave them fuel when their deliveries were short, gave them our ice-cream. They saved Campbell's Ferry for us all. We feel close to one another and know it is unlikely we will meet again. Doug takes individual photos of each and gets their email addresses. Then, they are gone.

The smoke jumpers are scheduled to stay till tomorrow and ask what they can do for us. They chop several of the downed trees into rounds for firewood. They clear out remaining trees and brush around the buildings and take out the big nasty Hawthorn bush at the far end of the orchard. Brush debris is piled up for spring burning. Steve, the leader of the McCall smokejumpers, has a tree trimming business in the off season so we have a true expert on hand for this work.

Around 11:00 A.M., Cornelia, our neighbor from up river at Whitewater Ranch shows up at the Ferry. She and Copper, her dog, hiked down to see how the fire is progressing towards them and to check on us. She joins us for lunch while Rita and Copper play, then catches a ride back home in the jet boat that is taking a couple of the firefighters to Whitewater, which has the only road in to this part of the canyon.

In the late afternoon we plan to go with the crew to the river for a swim when, as now seems usual, plans change again. They will be picked up at 6:00 P.M. to go to China Bar where they will rendezvous once again with the Black Hills crew. Quickly they pack up. We are sorry to see them go too although we did not have as much time to get to know them. They were very good to us. We owe them all our deepest gratitude. The Ferry is safe and intact.

Doug and I see them off then walk up from the beach to see the orchard deserted for the first time in a week. We sit outside only briefly before the smoke drives us in. The smoke downriver is lit from within, letting us know the fire is still alive and moving on.

<u>August 16, Wednesday</u>

There was considerable thunder and lightning last night, and some rain, but in the morning we are still smoked in. Ray cannot land for the mail delivery. He leaves mail and groceries at Whitewater. If a jet boat is coming by it will deliver our things to us. Doug and I feel like we have been chain-smoking twenty-four hours a day since Sunday.

It feels odd to be here on our own without the people and bustle of the past week. We are finally coming back into our own lives. Doug moves our stuff out of the middle of the orchard and puts it away. I putter in the cabin, putting it back into some semblance of order.

After lunch we walk down to the beach. There is fuel left there for Heinz and for China Bar but no mail or groceries. Yesterday Ryan found where the back burn had come up again and had crept inward toward the barn. He extinguished it, of course, but Doug and I walk the fire's perimeter just to check. There are a number of small smokers but nothing close to the edges. We also climb down to Frances' fishing spot where the pump still sits ready to pull more water up if the fire should return. We start moving some of the rounds cut from the downed trees up to the cabin to be split for firewood.

At 5:00 P.M. I see two firefighters walking up the road. It is Chris from Lone Peak Hot Shots with his boss, Donny. It seems eighteen of them are coming back into the Ferry to check the movement of the fire. All these firefighters are a flexible, unpredictable, and improvisational crowd. Plans change at a moment's notice. They take it all in stride.

6:30 P.M. and the second wave of firefighters arrives via Mike's jet boat. Doug jumps on board to go up to Whitewater and retrieve our mail and groceries. At 7:30 P.M. the third wave of firefighters comes in, greeted by thunder and lightning. Doug returns with the mail, groceries, and a map of the fire. It has burnt over 5,000 acres. Campbell's Ferry stands as a very small peninsula outside the fire's perimeter. We have a cadre of smart, brave people to thank for our enclave of safety.

<u>August 17, Thursday</u>

When we get up the Maestro is once again back from downriver. He and Donny (head of the Lone Peak crew) hike up to look at the leading edge of the fire burning upstream from us. Most of the Lone Peak crew start clearing the trail up to Trout Creek. We can hear the hum of their chain saws.

Two of the men left behind start splitting the rounds of the downed trees for firewood and stack it near the Crowe Cabin to dry. Then they chop up some of the dry rounds in the barn…they have used up the wood we had stacked at the Cook Cabin.

When the trail crew returns for lunch, Ryan asks what chores we might have for them. It is amazing the level of energy the firefighters have. They can hardly stand to sit still. Even after a before daybreak start and hours of digging and fighting fire, they come back, dirty and tired, eat a meals-ready-to-eat (MRE), then ask, "Do you need anything done around here?" I mention the irrigation ditch and he is immediately into it. Grabbing shovels, he, Luke and Doug head out, soon followed by Bob.

After lunch it appears that all hands have been called to hike up to meet Eric and Donny at the fire's edge. Rita tries to go with them but they bring her to me. It is well after dark when they return. We see their headlamps snaking down the trail behind the barn as we are preparing for bed.

August 18, Friday

At 9:30 A.M. Doug leads a group of twelve back to the ditch. They have volunteered to help clean and repair it. By 10:30 seven of them are back, called to jet boat up river to a new fire that has broken out between here and Whitewater Ranch.

The air quality has been improving for the past two days. Our throats are still raw but feeling better. With the clearing air it is getting easier to assess the extent of the burn on the east/southeast hills above the runway. It appears that about 90% of the trees are dead. Some still stand but their needles are brown. Eric has told me any trees with that color are dead although they may not drop their needles for several years. I think about a conversation I had with a friend who underwent a mastectomy. She said, "The scar is ugly, but I am alive." And, so is Campbell's Ferry.

At lunch we hear that our guests will depart tomorrow morning for Vinegar Creek, the end of the road forty miles downstream. Doug hauls our extra fire supplies down to the river where Heinz and Mike transport them to China Bar for the Black Hills crew's use. Eric, who had come up again for a few hours, returns with them. It seems that operations for the fire have been transferred to the Nez Perce and Eric now answers to an unusually taciturn individual who is camping with his crew of Blackfoot Indian firefighters at the Jim Moore Place across the river. On our way down to the river we meet Lyle, one of the Blackfoot group, who spends several hours visiting the Ferry.

The crew working on the ditch returns around 6:00 P.M. They have made remarkable headway. Water is running freely. We drop off a cooler of beer for the crew before heading to the beach for a swim. Doug is as dirty as any of the crew because he has been working side by side with them all day as a swamper, as well as directing their work.

Talk about elegance in dining! Promptly at 8:00 P.M. the Lone Peak crew has a hot meal delivered by helicopter. It hovers over the orchard and lowers until the two net bags hanging below it gently touch down.   The crew releases the bags while the wind from the blades blows like a hurricane through our garden, sending all the flowers on my tomato plants blowing across the meadow. Oh well, we don't need many tomatoes. Matt comes up to invite us to have dinner with them but we have already prepared our meal. After dinner we take ice cream down to them.

August 19, Saturday

They pack up and leave this morning. More sad goodbyes for us and especially for Rita who has been the recipient of lavish attention. Some canned goods and the two net bags with last night's food containers are left behind so I suppose we will have someone coming to get them with another helicopter. Poor garden!

We met Lyle (Blue Cloud) yesterday from the fire crew of twenty Blackfoot Indians camped across the river. Today he is back with three others to pick up supplies left by Lone Peak. We talk for awhile under the walnut tree. I tell them the history of this place and they tell me the history of their fire crew and their tribe. In the evening they come back again to attach the cargo nets to the helicopter, carrying Lone Peak's empty food containers and trash out. Doug and I come back from a swim at the river around 7:30 P.M., just in time to see it all take place. Rita is very excited…running over the nets as they attach them. We almost have an airborne dog.

August 20, Sunday

At 7:30 A.M. we see a Life Flight helicopter land at Jim Moore. We hear later that one of the fire crew was taken out, likely a case of appendicitis. Rita and I walk over to ask if a crew can come to the Ferry to put out some spots that are still smoking in the back burn. Lyle and several of his crew come to deal with it.

A helicopter is still dipping a bucket in the river and dumping it at the mouth of Ruff Creek, just below the Ferry. We can see it all from the Crowe Cabin.

At 6:00 P.M. when Doug and I come up from our evening dip in the river we are surprised to see there is no smoke rising from the back burn up river of the Cook Cabin but by 8:00 P.M. it is definitely back and going strong.

August 21, Monday

4:30 A.M. I awake to see a glow through the window down river. When I get up to look I can see flames and fire-lit smoke in the vicinity of Ruff Creek. Nevertheless, most of the day is quiet. A Blackfoot crew comes over late morning to walk the perimeter of the fire. I take them down to where it was smoking last night.

When Doug and I go down to river around 6:30 P.M., there are little flames and smoking spots along the corridor. Mike McLain pulls his jet boat up to the beach to talk and we hear Dafna on his radio saying that there are sixty-mile-an-hour winds down river at Mackey Bar. As we cross the bridge an hour later we see a tree suddenly catch fire at the river's bend just below the bridge. The big winds hit the Ferry just about the time we reach the cabin. We have also seen major flare-ups on Trout Creek ridge. This fire is not dead…not by any means. Sanya had told us last week, "This fire won't be out until the first snowfall." It seems her prediction will be right.

August, 22, 23, 24 (Tuesday, Wednesday, Thursday)

Days are falling into a recurring pattern as far as the fire is concerned. Hazy smoke continues. Small to medium smoke columns appear down river and in the hills. Occasionally we see flames sparking in the night. Spotter planes circle overhead. Bucket helicopters dip in the river and head off in all directions. Jet boats scurry up and down the river transporting supplies and personnel. A crew from the Blackfoot Spirit Mountain crew comes through every morning checking on us. Living with the smoke is the hardest thing to endure now.

August 25, Friday

Two of our Campbell's Ferry partners are scheduled to fly in this morning to survey the aftermath of the fire. Joe Corlett flies his own plane and he is bringing Joe Denton. Doug and I wake to the sound of a steady rain. The canyon is foggy and the sky dark and cloudy. We are glad for the rain but afraid that it will keep the Joes from their visit. But, at around 8:30 A.M., we hear the plane and watch it slip below the clouds onto the runway. We show them around the place and tell them the fire stories over coffee and cake, and later lunch. The rain continues soft and steady but it lifts a little around 1:00 P.M. and we watch them take off into its haze. Precipitation slows down in the evening.

August 26, Saturday

The rain is gone, the sky is blue but morning mist hangs over the river. Doug finds that our upper ditch is pouring down onto the road in front of the cabin, creating a water feature of its own design. He takes a shovel and sets off to modify it. We have planned to hike seven miles up to Yellow Pine Bar today, stopping to pick up Cornelia at Whitewater. I pack our things for an overnight since we will only come back as far as Whitewater tonight. The hike will give us an opportunity to see the fire damage up river.

We arrive back at Whitewater around 5:30 P.M. Cornelia and I visit while Doug rests. We have a late dinner and sleep very well.

August 27, Sunday

Cornelia shows us the Whitewater hydro system before we hike back to the Ferry. We meet two firefighters on the trail. We note there are still many hot spots smoking up on the hills. While at Whitewater we saw a fire report on the computer that said the fire was about twenty percent contained. Once back at the Ferry, Doug starts drawing designs for a sprinkler system.

Epilogue
Spring 2007

May 21, 2007, Monday

We arrived back at the Ferry on April 26. During the flight in Doug and I both watched out the windows for signs of last year's fire. While obvious in a number of places, the effects are clearly muted from last year. After our touch down on the landing strip, we watched Rita cavort happily across the brilliant new green of the runway. I raised my eyes to the hills where the fire had run rampant and decided to wait awhile to write about its aftermath.

In the meantime Doug and I edited the journal. He pointed out my reference to "our" firefighters, saying that, we don't "own" them, and I agreed to change the reference. But the change did not feel right to me and after several days I changed it back. No, certainly, we do not own them but in my mind the word represents closeness, like our family, our friends and it better represents my feelings for these wonderful people who saved Campbell's Ferry with its history and legacy intact.

Today a steady rain keeps us indoors and I am no longer able to distract myself with the many chores on our list. It is time to write this last entry. I have been looking up at the burnt hills daily for over three weeks now The black, spiny skeletons of the dead trees still stand, rimed by the red-brown needled trees that have died but were on the edge of the conflagration. The hills look like the humped backs of huge porcupines with black quills poking at the sky. I had wished that the dead trees would all fall, to be less obvious so I could be less reminded.

But instead the dead trees stand as their own grave markers. It will be decades until they are all down. In today's rain, wisps of mist form and float among them. When I first notice it I feel my heart jump. The mist brought back images of last August's smoke and for a moment I imagine that somehow the trees are burning again in the rain. As I watch the mist form and vanish I see that, just as Eric had told me, there is green emerging underneath. It is pale and sparse but undeniably there. So I pin my hopes on that new, fragile growth and wish it speed and strength to survive.

****

Another Big One, threatened the Ferry in 2007. The Forest Service named it the Rattlesnake fire after a creek near its origin. It began on July 7, 2007, with lightning near Warren, Idaho — twenty miles from Campbell's Ferry. Over the next four weeks the fire moved into and up the Salmon River Canyon, reaching Campbell's Ferry on August 3. When it reached the area on the south side of the river burned by the 2006 fire it laid down, then jumped the river to threaten the Jim Moore Place. The firefighters set up fire protection and used a backfire at Jim Moore just has they had for Campbell's Ferry the year before. We watched for days as the fire burned across the face of the canyon opposite Campbell's Ferry.

The Rattlesnake Fire approaches from down canyon

Our Maestro in 2007 was a seasoned veteran named Terry Mc-Shane. Again, soon after meeting the firefighters, I established a bond to the fire crew due to my friendship with Jim Thrash. When I mentioned this to Terry he grew somber, reflective, then said, "Sometime later, we can sit down and talk about it. Right now, I have a job to do."

Forty or so, Terry had a commanding look to him. A piercing glare from his chiseled, scruffily bearded face made me want to snap to and salute. He just oozed strength. The many trips he would make up or down the surrounding mountains would be of no concern.

I watched Terry over the next several days. It was clear that the usual focused competence of a firefighter was at a different level with him. He had all the talent we had seen in Eric, but with Terry, there was an edge to his supervision of the crew. He lacked the ability to wrap his leadership in the easy congeniality that had made our time with Eric so enjoyable. He wasn't harsh, just intense.

Five days later Terry and I found ourselves with some time while sitting at the top of the runway, so I asked if he would tell me about knowing Jim. He didn't know Jim. Not the way I had known him. But he did.

Fire

In 1994 Terry was stationed in Colorado when the Storm King Mountain fire took Jim and the lives of thirteen other firefighters. Terry had been one of a small crew of fellow firefighters who first located the bodies. He began to tell me of the experience, first reflecting on what had happened, the mistakes that had been made leading to the group being overcome by the firestorm. It came down to poor communication - bureaucratic bungling with a tragic cost.

When Terry's story turned to the details of that day, what he had discovered at the scene, I had to stop him. I had long struggled with the loss of my friend and could not deal with more intimate knowledge of what a consuming fire does to the human body. My mental images of Jim were of him alive, sharing our passion for Idaho, wilderness, and outfitting. Terry's images were those of nightmares. I couldn't deal with them, and for a time, neither could Terry.

The experience had caused McShane to end a two-decade career in fire fighting.

He just quit.

Walked away.

"So why are you here now?" I asked.

Three years after quitting, Terry had received a call from a friend, pleading with him to return.

"Why would I want to do that?" Terry asked.

"So there will be no more Storm King Mountains," was the answer.

So here he was. Intense, focused, competent — nothing more important than the safety of his crew. If that meant not as fun or friendly, so be it. His crew would leave here alive.

Chapter Nineteen

New Arrival

"The beginnings and endings
of all human undertakings
are untidy."
– John Galsworthy

In 1938 when Joe Zaunmiller lost his wife Emma in a horse accident, friends from Dixie visited to help him cope with the loss. But he needed a full-time companion to help him realize the dream of turning Campbell's Ferry into a viable business. It was impossible for one man to manage the myriad tasks necessary to survive at the primitive homestead in the canyon. Someone was needed to mind the place when Joe was off doing trail or other contract work for the Forest Service. When outfitting clients arrived, it took more than one person to lead the hunts, wrangle the stock, and provide the food and supplies necessary to support the crew.

One would think the answer to his needs would come from

among the friends Joe had made in the canyon, or Dixie. He could not have anticipated that criminal activity unfolding in far away New York, Mexico, California and Texas would conspire to resolve his problem in the wilds of Idaho.

In January of 1938 a woman walked into the Plaza Linen Shop in San Antonio and handed the clerk a crisp, ten dollar bill to pay for a $1 play suit, "for my little boy, " she said. The clerk handed the bill to her manager who looked the customer over and thought, "How could this be?" Just five minutes before an agent from the San Antonio branch of the Secret Service had left the store on his rounds of local merchants, warning them that a wave of counterfeit bills that had swept the country during the preceding three years had now reached Texas.[1]

As the agent had warned, the fresh bill in the manager's hand looked good, but closer examination revealed a less than distinct image of Alexander Hamilton, points on the Federal Reserve seal that weren't sharp, and the serial numbers matched a pattern of 8's, 3's and one each of 4, 7 and 9. The manager caught the clerk's attention and asked her to call the police while he engaged the customer in small talk. Minutes later police detectives, followed closely by the Secret Service, arrived to arrest Elsie Gersbach.

Gersbach protested her innocence, but good detective work by the agents led to the arrest of her accomplice who had been holed up in a local hotel. Michael La Centra under the alias David Weiner, had met Gersbach, a young hostess from New York, weeks before while she was vacationing in Mexico. La Centra was in Mexico freshly released from a fifteen year term in Sing Sing prison in New York. He was a four time loser with a record of extortion and holdups. When he came up for parole he had convinced authorities that if they released him he would return to his native Italy.

Once free, La Centra went to San Salvador instead, then Mexico, where he hooked up with Gersbach. The couple re-entered the U.S. through California, where La Centra contacted David Krakauer, an old cellmate from New York prison days. Krakauer had been released years earlier and while living in New Jersey became the head of one of the largest counterfeit operations the U.S. had seen. La Centra

---

1 William Mangil, "Counterfeit Blonde and the Conspiring Three," *True Detective Magazine,* Vol 33,(New York, NY: Macfadden Publications, March 1940), p. 22

convinced Krakauer to ship him a shoebox full of counterfeit ten dollar bills which he and Gersbach proceeded to spread along a trail from California to Texas.

Now sitting in a San Antonio jail, La Centra befriended a fellow inmate, Joe Cain, who was due to be released on bail soon. La Centra told Cain of his get rich quick scheme and that he was convinced it was a way to find easy wealth in Depression times. But he warned Cain to avoid the mistake that got him caught. Don't get involved with the underlings passing the bills. Acting as a distributor was the way to go. Let others take the risk of actually passing the bills.

Upon his release Cain brought a couple of gambler friends from Houston into the scheme and all three drove to New York to obtain the fake bills that would become the basis for the south Texas component of the nationwide counterfeit ring. The three men brought in more underlings to a criminal enterprise that grew to include an estimated 300 *passers* of the fake bills.[2]

Among the passers was Charles H. Gamble, the son of a San Antonio pharmacist.[3] Gamble was born in Ohio in 1903 to Roy and Edith Gamble. Roy had worked his way up from clerk to owning his own drug store, moving the family from Ohio to West Virginia, finally settling in San Antonio. When the Depression hit, son Charles turned to criminal activity, joining the rush of the easy money crowd to the relative boomtown atmosphere that erupted around Houston and the small towns situated close to the East Texas oil fields.

In one such town, Beeville, Gamble met an attractive blonde, Lydia Frances Coyle, working as a switchboard operator in the local telephone office. They may have met at a local *honky tonk* of the type Frances described in her later writing where she loved to dance with typical youthful exuberance. Judging by Gamble's character, we doubt it was in church.

Frances was born in Bruceville, TX (near Waco) May 19, 1913. She was the fourth of nine children. Frances would later serve as caretaker to the three youngest while she was growing up.

Her father, John Arthur Coyle was from Arkansas. As a young man breaking horses for an Oklahoma rancher he was told the only escape from his family's poverty was an education, so he worked as

2 "3 Suspects Linked to Counterfeiting," *New York Times,* 19 May 1938
3 Steve Coyle, Personal Communication, June 2009

a janitor to pay his way through Weatherford College in Fort Worth. After college John found work as a carpenter, building wooden rigs for oil drilling companies. He later moved to the Waco area, working as a rural mail carrier with a small farm and garden to help support his growing family.

Frances' mother, Rebecca Bottoms Shook, was from Missouri. Rebecca's father, grandfather and several uncles were Methodist ministers. At age twenty-six while living in Waco, she met and married thirty-two year old John Coyle. During her thirty years of marriage and child bearing Rebecca displayed an iron will and skills that she passed on to her children, especially her daughters. She was very skilled in the needle arts and taught them to Frances and her sisters.

Throughout the family's frequent moves Rebecca always put in a garden, reasoning that if they were not there to enjoy the harvest, the next family would have food – a charitable and giving perspective of great value among families trying to survive in the Great Depression.

Rebecca was an excellent marksman; a skill honed protecting the family's chickens on their Texas farm from snakes and other predators. By the time Frances was twelve years old she had been taught to catch, kill, clean and fry a chicken. Soon she could can food, run a house and take care of a family. The Coyles struggled, but succeeded in making ends meet in a life in south Texas that was relatively primitive. The rural areas of Texas did not receive electricity until 1946.[4]

In late childhood Frances suffered three times with injuries that left her bedridden for periods ranging from ten to eighteen months. During that time she was encouraged by her grandfather and parents to read, and passed the time in bed in a small hot room of their Texas farm house taking imaginary trips to exotic destinations through *National Geographic* magazine. Later, reading the tale of the 1935 National Geographic expedition on the Salmon River may have influenced her ultimate decision to settle in the wilds of Idaho.

During Frances' childhood her father moved the family often, periodically trying his hand at farming and working in jobs connected to the oil field supply business. The Depression engulfed the country just as her older siblings reached maturity, married and started their own families. Frances was now the oldest child at home and therefore

4 Alice Brandt, Personal Communication, April 2010.

called on to be surrogate mom to her three younger siblings while her parents worked to make ends meet.

Arthur and Rebecca expected compliance from their children. Frances' rebellious nature led to a rocky relationship with her family. The young woman felt unappreciated and used. Frances thought her parents looked down on her, at times viewing her only as a sitter, then a chauffeur who could be brought along on family outings to wait in the shadows until she was needed to drive them home.

Frances had a stubborn streak, a strong will that would serve her well later, but at home, as she faced demands brought on by her parents' efforts to support the family, she grew angry. She felt she was never allowed to settle and feel comfortable and began to harbor ill feelings that she did not get her due for being pretty or having a good singing voice. She was restless.

In 1937 John Arthur Coyle died and Frances' mother and younger siblings moved in with one of the older children further south near Corpus Christi. Frances' older brother Sam had developed a unique oil derrick design and had a thriving business supplying the oil industry. Frances, now twenty-three, left and found a way to start a life on her own in the small south Texas community of Beeville, just three miles from the family farm. In 1920 Beeville had a population of just over three thousand and no paved streets. The population doubled in the 1930s as the community benefitted from economic activity related to major discoveries of oil in southeast and east Texas.

These were wild times and the opportunities for trouble for an attractive outgoing newly independent young blonde were many. Oil wildcatters were roaming the area looking for their chance at the riches of black gold. The boom brought a criminal element with it including Charles Gamble. When Charles hooked up with the pretty young telephone operator from Beeville, it set in motion events that would change Frances' life forever. He was living high, in sharp contrast to Frances' hardscrabble upbringing. He had money to burn. The only problem was, it wasn't real.

On March 30, 1938, Charles and Frances were married in Dallas, Texas, but the marriage was on shaky ground from the start. We do not know how much Frances knew of Charles' involvement with the counterfeit ring, nor do we know of Frances' involvement, if any. Perhaps she was another pretty blonde who charmed retail clerks during small purchases used to turn fake $10 bills into real change. Or she could have been an innocent observer of Charles' illegal ways, gradually growing suspicious and nervous about her future.

In any case, events were out of their control. Two months after Charles and Frances' marriage the Secret Service was able to track the Texas branch of the counterfeit ring back to its source in New Jersey, leading to the arrest of all of the higher ups in both states.[5] The arrests set off a scramble among the hundreds of *passers* involved in spreading the fake bills.

Charles and Frances fled the state, entering Mexico through Nuevo Laredo, the border crossing closest to San Antonio. When their money ran out in Mexico, her sister pleaded with Frances to return to Texas to the Corpus Christi area where help was available from the family. But the couple didn't want to be near where local law enforcement was focused on rounding up the rest of the counterfeit ring.

Eventually the Gambles re-entered the United States and found a job at the remote Kohl Ranch outside of Payson, Arizona. "I know you have been wondering why in all creation we should winter here," Frances wrote her sister. "You know why we went to Laredo. But did I tell you that Laredo was no good? Rather than go back broke, we kept on trying. We have a job as winter caretaker on a ranch. It doesn't mean much,but there is plenty of work, no cash salary, a warm house, wood, and staples in grub."

She invited her sister to join them, but warned them cigarettes were expensive in Arizona, "so bring plenty. I smoke a pipe. And if you bring the canning outfit, we can can a couple of deer."[6] It was hard times indeed.

The couple was poaching wild game to survive. Frances wrote her mother, "Mr. Kohl left his guns with us to take care of. Bob [an alias for Charles] made a gun case for them. If the deer come up tonight how I would like to get one. But it will be about one more week before we can. You see, the game warden lives about 1/4 miles from us, but in the next few days he will move to the fish hatchery - when he does he will be snowed in until spring."

Charles and Frances did not leave much of a trail during the two years after they left Texas, but it had to be a turbulent time. Years

<hr>

5 "3 Suspects Linked to Counterfeiting," *New York Times*, 19 May 1938
6 Frances Zaunmiller Wisner, personal correspondence, 16 December 1938

later in a letter to the author of a book about her life, Frances revealed that she had two still born children.[7] The exact circumstances of those pregnancies and their loss are unknown.

At some point in those two years the strong willed young woman from Texas made a crucial decision. She and Charles had left the ranch in Arizona and traveled north, visiting Durango, Colorado, Seattle, Washington, and other western locations before settling in Salmon, Idaho, in September of 1939. At the time Salmon was a small, struggling agriculture, ranching and mining center located at the junction of the Lemhi and Salmon Rivers. It was perched on the eastern edge of the largest contiguous undeveloped land mass in the U.S. A spur of the Northern Pacific railroad had been built to the community from Montana in 1909. The year the Gambles arrived the railroad shut down after a three-decade effort to secure its economic footing.

The town was hit hard by the Great Depression and gainful employment must have been hard to come by for the new arrivals from Texas. Charles resorted to his criminal ways which led to his arrest for poaching game. The local sheriff delayed Gamble's incarceration due to his wife's illness, perhaps the first of her two miscarriages.

When Frances recovered, Charles was introduced to the Lemhi County jail. Frances was fed up with her husband's criminal activities and feared for her life. In the summer of 1940 with Charles in the Sheriff's custody, she took the opportunity to flee, heading west to the small mining community of Shoup, the last stop for those heading into the Idaho wilderness. In August of 1940 Frances wrote her sister Billee who relayed the message to Mary, another sister, "I got another letter from Frances," Mary said, "But she asked me to keep her whereabouts secret on account of she is afraid Bob may find out where she is. Bob seems to have gotten mixed up in some more crooked business and she left him, but he is probably looking for her in order to shut her up about what she knows."[8]

When Frances left Charles, she fell into the company of Bert Rhoades, another man with a checkered past. The two did have one thing in common. Both had a prior marriage they would just as soon forget.

7 Carol Furey-Werhan, *Haven in the Wilderness: The Story of Frances Zaunmiller Wisner of Campbell's Ferry Idaho,* (Kamiah, ID: Carol Furey-Werhan, 1996)
8 Billee Coyle, Personal Correspondence, 7 August 1940

Rhoades, born in 1883 in Spokane, Washington, was one of three children of Daniel Boone Rhoades. The family moved to a farm near Cottonwood, Idaho, where his mother died when he was two. He only managed four years of education, and went to work on the local wheat farms as a common laborer. He developed a reputation as a skilled rider and trick rope artist, likely learned from a neighbor, Jack Hoxie, who later went on to Hollywood and a career in movies.[9]

Bert's later notoriety in Idaho was chronicled in the Lewiston and other local papers when he and two accomplices were arrested and convicted for robbing the general store in Denver, Idaho. Rhoades always maintained his innocence, a common point of view among the hundreds of inmates he joined in the Idaho State Penitentiary. He served a five-year sentence from 1904 to 1909. A couple of years after getting out, Rhoades was in Riggins, Idaho and married Sylvia Irwin. Sylvia had a local reputation as a *hellcat.* The honeymoon was soon over and Sylvia, the jealous type, had the local blacksmith make a wicked-looking knife she carried around inside her skirt, telling anyone who would listen she planned to "cut Bert's heart out" if she had the chance.

Bert Rhoades 1904

Understandably, Bert decided it would be safer to spend his time in the wilderness, so he began a thirty-five-year career that included working for the Forest Service as a packer and other ranch and wrangling jobs – anything that would keep him away from Riggins and his knife-wielding hellcat wife.

In 1939 Bert was doing work for Harry Donahue at the Stonebraker Ranch in Chamberlain Basin and Joe Zaunmiller at Campbell's Ferry. At some point his path had crossed that of Frances Gamble, most likely in Salmon or Shoup. We can only speculate, but somehow a young twenty-seven year old woman on the run from an outlaw husband and the law in Texas made an arrangement with Bert

9 Donna Henderson, *The Denver Debacle of 1904, 103 Years Ago, An Outlaw Gang Roamed Idaho County*, (Post Falls, ID: Henderson, 1995)

Rhoades, an ex-con, to take her into one of the wildest places left in the nation, the heart of what would later be known as the River of No Return Wilderness. For someone who had been raised on the flat, dry plains of south Texas, the journey into the Idaho backcountry must have been remarkable.

The couple left Shoup and followed a gravel road that ended abruptly where the CCC was engaged in an effort to blast a road through the Salmon River Canyon clear across the state to Riggins. At the end of the CCC-built Salmon River Road, they switched to horseback. It was a two-day ride from that point into the heart of the Chamberlain Basin. Following a trail thirteen miles downstream they crossed the Salmon River on the Horse Creek Pack Bridge. Their destination was a homestead that had been established by William Allen "Al" Stonebraker around the time he had helped William Campbell build the Three Blaze Trail through the area in 1902.

The Stonebraker Ranch had been located to take advantage of the large meadows surrounding the West Fork of Chamberlain Creek. The free feed for grazing by cattle and stock made it a financially feasible operation during the short growing season as long as mines provided a not too distant market. The Stonebraker family built cabins, corrals and barn facilities as a base of operations. They were joined in similar ranching efforts nearby by others, including August Hotzel, a German immigrant. The U. S. Forest Service also established a ranger station in the area.

When Frances arrived in 1940, she found a cluster of activity. About a dozen part time inhabitants in the small settlement were surrounded by millions of uninhabited acres. The ranger station had just completed a new warehouse-storeroom facility to support the original cabin and living quarters built in 1906. Using funds appropriated to fight the Depression under the Emergency Relief Act and Emergency Conservation Work program, the agency was solidifying its administrative presence in the backcountry and expanding a nearby airstrip to improve access and support for fire fighting efforts in the area.

Frances found the Stonebraker Ranch being run by Harry Donahue, an old-timer wise to the ways of the backcountry. Harry was from Texas also. As a youth he had hired on as a wrangler on trail drives from Texas to Montana of the type featured in Larry McMurtry's epic novel *Lonesome Dove*. He, like Frances, was captured by the beauty of the forests and mountains of Idaho and stayed to use his horse packing skills to make a living.

Harry took the energetic young woman under his wing and began to school her in the art of survival and self-sufficiency on a wilderness ranch. Soon after her arrival at Stonebraker Ranch, Frances started a diary telling of her daily activities.

July 21, 1940 – "Bert returns dead tired after fighting a forest fire. Planes and men fighting fire, " she began.

Over the next few weeks Frances chronicled the myriad chores and comings and goings of a typical summer at the high country ranch. Horses were being shod. The roof, corral, stove, saddles and doors were repaired. Hay was harvested and irrigation adjusted.

The young Texan explored the surrounding country on foot and horseback. She traveled up nearby Lodgepole Creek to a cabin on Hand Creek and later visited a ranch on the South Fork of the Salmon River. She was delighted to find wild, ripe huckleberries. Frances showed her culinary skills by putting up dozens of quarts of jam in the kitchen and used her needle arts to mend the men's shirts. Fish were plentiful, including salmon spawning in Chamberlain Creek and trout from Flossie Lake.

There was a garden to tend, but output was limited by the short growing season due to the 5,600' elevation of the ranch. She visited two other women at the ranger station and a nearby ranch, no doubt a welcome opportunity to hear how others coped with life in the wilds among so many men. And she found time to write a letter to her older sister Mary telling of her new status – a woman on her own in the wilds of Idaho.

In mid-August Frances' diary notes a gift of fresh tomatoes and cantaloupe sent by a man living far below along the Salmon River – Joe Zaunmiller. A few days later the local forest fire near Stonebraker that had absorbed so much attention that summer was finally suppressed, giving Harry Donahue some free time to venture into the canyon and visit his friend at Campbell's Ferry. Joe, as noted earlier, had lost his wife two years before. He needed help at his ranch and he and Harry must have discussed the young, capable, attractive woman who was making an impression at the Stonebraker Ranch.

Joe had a contract with the Forest Service for trails and pack work that required travel throughout the backcountry. He scheduled a stop at Stonebraker on his next trip. At the same time Frances notes in her diary that she is gathering potatoes, peas and fish for dinner and on August 26 notes, "Joe Zaunmiller up for a visit. I dress up." Five days later Joe made a second visit. And a third four days later. The attractive young woman's culinary skills had made a good first impression.

On September 6 Joe showed up a fourth time, but this time he brought an extra saddle. The following day Frances borrowed a horse named Buck and tried her own hand at wrangling. The two left for Campbell's Ferry, taking two days to make the twenty-three mile ride. Years later Frances would describe her first sighting of the homestead, "From up there above the barn, the way the timber is, you don't see the ranch coming down the trail from Chamberlain until you are just above the barn, and then a spot opens up. I stopped my horse and looked. To me it is the most beautiful place in the world. I said, I don't know how you are going to do it Frances, but you are going to drive a nail in the wall of that house and hang your toothbrush on it. You are through traveling."

Barely five feet tall with an hour glass figure, Frances was small only in stature. With her glittering blue eyes and mischievous smile, her arrival in the canyon registered at least 9.5 on the Richter Scale with the resident male population. Women were a scarcity in the backcountry – especially women as pretty as Frances. She liked men and liked seeing herself reflected in their eyes. The feeling was mutual.

By any standards Frances was a beautiful woman who delighted not only in her femininity but also her ferocity. Even in the wilds of the Salmon River Canyon she made a habit of dressing for dinner in the evening. Numerous photographs show her standing out in the fields or orchard wearing dresses and high heels with her hair elaborately coiffed. But she was no Barbie Doll.

Frances' cooking skills were legendary; by her own admission she was less fond of house keeping, especially in her later years, but there is no question she was a hard worker willing to learn to do whatever it took to hold *her* Eden together. Her family upbringing had resulted in many of the skills she needed to live in the backcountry. Not only could she cook but also sew, knit, garden, can and preserve, care for animals, and shoot. In her early years in the canyon Frances cultivated her relationships with women friends of whom she had many. Her nieces and nephews remember her as generous but strict, stern but loving, and as a straight-talking, gifted teacher.

Frances received a warm reception at Campbell's Ferry. Since Emma's death, Joe had been helped by his friends Jim and Pearl Chittick and Pick and Lillie Ward from Dixie. When Frances arrived they were getting the homestead ready for the hunting season. Joe's friends welcomed the new arrival who was not feeling well (Frances noted these monthly events in her diary). Lillie and Pearl took Frances in and told her to rest up for a couple of days.

The day after her arrival the men left for Dixie, allowing the three women a chance to relax and get acquainted. When the men returned it would mark the beginning of three months of constant cooking, cleaning and caring for the needs of clients coming and going – clients who had paid to have Joe and Bert Rhoades take them into the high country to pursue elk, deer and bear.

The bounty of fruit and vegetables from the Ferry orchard and garden impressed Frances. She set out to prove her worth to the common effort, preparing cherry preserves and apple, grape and mint jelly. It took some time getting used to the small wood-burning stove, but soon she was turning out pear butter, strawberry and raspberry preserves, elderberry jam and canning pears to fill the pantry for winter.

Joe and Bert were back and forth to Dixie – twelve times in the next three months. And there were trips up the Three Blaze Trail to hunting camps that had to be set up, stocked, and maintained for a constant flow of hunters. The real work started when their hunting clients succeeded in their pursuit

Frances Coyle at her new home

of game. The carcass had to be processed – internal organs removed, skinned, quartered, packed on a mule and transported to the ranch to a log cold storage building Joe had built to hold the meat. When the hunt was over, the hunters, all their gear plus the meat, hides and any trophies were taken across the river on the ferry and thirteen miles to Dixie.

Frances quickly became a key component of the support team for the outfitting effort. There were chickens to tend to, eggs to gather, cows to milk, butter to churn, fruit to harvest, a ferry to operate, plus prepare meals for those at home and pack lunches for day use by the hunters. She was washing, house cleaning, sewing and even found time to make a quilt.

Many years later on a visit back to Texas to interview her family, the authors asked what it was like for Frances to go from Texas to a primitive lifestyle in the Idaho wilderness. "It was the norm," was their answer. She grew up in poor, rural Texas with few amenities. That experience and the skill set taught her by her mother served her well at Campbell's Ferry. Joe and his friends had no training to do. Frances already knew the basics. During the time with Harry Donahue at Stonebraker Ranch she had been a quick learner. There were chores unique to the homestead, like keeping the water flowing in the ditches and tending to the ferry as the river level rose and fell, but there were plenty of mentors around to help.

Among the many wonders Frances would experience in that first year in Idaho were the unique weather patterns of the canyons and high country. Growing up in southeast Texas She was used to heat accompanied by humid air masses from the nearby Gulf of Mexico. When it rained, it rained buckets. Average annual rainfall was thirty-two inches and ninety or hundred degree temperatures would be accompanied by ninety percent humidity. At night little relief was gained by opening the windows, just more muggy, sticky heat.

In Idaho, riding across the high country Frances experienced cold nights and dry air, even during the summer. For a child of the coastal plain she would have marveled at the western weather phenomena known as virga, where rain or snow falls from the clouds but evaporates before reaching the ground. In August at Stonebraker Ranch she would awake to ice in a bucket in the yard, then, in early September after descending thousands of feet into the canyon, have another two months of temperate weather known locally as Indian Summer. At the Ferry she would see winter arrive in the high country, coating the canyon rims with snow while the canyon bottom received only light rain or none at all. As the weeks passed the snow line on the canyon sides gradually progressed lower. She wasn't in Texas anymore.

By mid-November winter arrived in earnest bringing snow to the flats and mornings with temperatures in the single digits. Fires in the woodstove were welcome and a morning of fresh hot coffee heated on the stove top became a welcome start to each winter day. The hunting season ended and with it the flow of visitors. Joe still had work to do, packing out camps and supplies, moving stock and trail work. Frances began to learn one of the greatest joys of the Ferry, especially for one of her temperament – the joy of solitude with nothing but the wildlife, changing weather patterns and murmur of the river.

Chapter
Twenty

Reinvention

"If I have any intelligence in the way I live, a little of it I was born
with. Most of it was drummed into me by that little
handful of old timers I was lucky enough to know."
– Frances

Frances Coyle's first attempt to reinvent herself wasn't a total failure. Her marriage to Charles Gamble had allowed her to leave
Texas. She was traveling, no longer under the control of her parents,
free from the constraints of their frequent moves, their Depression era
struggles, caring for their children. But she found life with Charles
was an equally uncomfortable, controlling environment. She had trad-
ed control by parents for control by a husband, one who turned out to
be mean and a crook. Those with less determination might accept such
a mistake, but not this warrior. Stubborn and strong willed, Frances
would try again.

For her second reinvention she abandoned everyone she knew,
every sense of the life she had known, and disappeared into the wil-

derness. Frances was looking for a life to live on her terms, where she was in charge, where she could create her own romantic version of a new person. She couldn't have known exactly who that new person would be. But, as master weaver of spells, she would invent the new Frances: one who would become, in her writings, *the woman*: author, dispenser of wisdom, arbiter of all that was right in what she asserted were "My Mountains, My Canyon" – and yes, a legend. The men in the Salmon River Canyon didn't know it, but they were about to meet their match and have their world turned upside down.

At Campbell's Ferry, Frances landed in the midst of a cluster of restless men – some of whom were fleeing their own demons. They were, like Frances, freedom seekers, pursuing a life free from the tyranny of someone else managing their life – the tyranny of schedules, gadgetry, authority. They needed a sanctuary, something tangible, with a measurable manifestation of their success in getting away from the constraints of life in town. And what could be a clearer measure of reaching that sanctuary than a wilderness homestead – a place that was difficult, sometimes impossible to reach – no electricity, no cars, no roads, no authority present, surrounded by millions of acres of trackless wild lands.

To this point in her life, Frances' writings had been limited to letters home. Later, she would become a columnist and author of several decades worth of stories about life in the canyon. In this, the beginning of the new story of Frances, it is not hard to figure who, among the three main characters at Campbell's Ferry, the willful newcomer would choose for the titular role of lead in her reinvented life. The outcome may be obvious, but the joy of observing the scenes written by a master weaver is worthy of our attention.

Before Frances' arrival, Bert Rhoades, Joe Zaunmiller and Jim Moore were close, yet separate. They would spend hours, days, weeks both together and alone. After Frances arrived, their comings and goings would allow each opportunities for one-on-one chances to make their case for the lead role in Frances' new life. They were all old compared to the pretty, talented, vivacious twenty-seven year old. Bert Rhoades, who was Joe Zaunmiller's partner in his outfitting business, was fifty-seven. Joe's neighbor and friend, Jim Moore, just a ferry ride across the Salmon River, was seventy-two. Joe was the youngest of the potential suitors at forty-nine.

Life in the canyon would allow the men the occasional chance to see women who visited or passed through, but those women were usually spoken for. The nearest opportunity to find single women was Dixie, thirteen miles away. Given its status as a dwindling mining community the pickings there were no doubt slim. Their ages didn't mean they weren't paying attention when Frances arrived. The men's bodies may have been old, but their minds could remember a youthful exuberance. The testosterone began to flow.

Frances didn't make it easy for them. She was not content to let the rough life away from ready access to the usual accoutrements of womanly charm wear down her feminine aura. Dinner time at the Ferry meant a dress, and if there was no store to acquire one, she had the skills to make her own. It might take a long time for catalogs of the day to make it into the remote Salmon River Canyon, but she still enjoyed keeping up with style. When finances permitted, she placed an occasional order. Her sisters helped out, too. Once they learned of her new life and address at the Ferry, trips out by the men to pick up mail would often mean their return with a care package sent by Frances' sisters in Texas.

Bert Rhoades had been the first of the three men to spend time alone with Frances. He had brought her from Salmon into the backcountry. Frances hints in her diary at a relationship with Bert dur-

Joe Zaunmiller, Jim Moore, and Bert Rhoades

ing their time at Stonebraker Ranch. She keeps constant track of his whereabouts and after a trip to the garden and a visit with the neighbors notes, "Bert home, waiting for me." Later when Harry has gone to Big Creek she tells of showing Bert her "private path." After moving to the Ferry she makes a shirt for him and speaks of being homesick for both Bert and Harry.

And why not Bert? Tall, broad shouldered with wavy dark hair and light colored eyes, Bert was the kind of handsome that looks like trouble coming down the road. His photos display a cocky nonchalance that has the self-assurance of a performer. Bert had a calculated awareness of his appearance. His square-shaped face and heavy eyebrows were typically hidden under his tall crowned cowboy hat. No doubt he had a graceful physicality and astute coordination to compliment his lean muscled body. In her diary Frances describes his sweet,

Valentines Day, 1941
Joe Zaunmiller, Jim Chittick, Jim Moore, Frances Coyle, Bert
Rhoades
"Jim came over. Looked dandy. Played cards and took some pictures."
Frances' diary

gentle nature but there must have been another side to a man who could rob a general store and cause his wife to threaten his life.

That late fall of 1940 Bert spent a lot of time at the Ferry and helped with the seasonal end of fall outfitting activities. He removed shoes from the stock, getting them ready for winter. He also struggled with an illness, exactly what, we do not know.

At Thanksgiving Frances notes Bert was not well. In December he was bed ridden, then up, finally going out to Grangeville, presumably for medical help. On December 20 Frances noted, "Wonder if Bert is hurting tonight. Please, I don't want him to hurt. He is too good and kind and gentle. I do want him not to hurt – and I want him."

As the pace of life eased with the onset of winter, snow and cold brought changes to the river and gave Frances time to get to know her across-the-river neighbor. In 1897 when William Campbell came to what became Campbell's Ferry two other men, Eugene Churchill and Jim Moore, were with him. Churchill ended up settling a homestead four miles upriver from the Ferry.

Jim Moore and Frances Coyle
1941

Moore took up the flat just across the river from Campbell's Ferry. To this day it is called the Jim Moore Place. Perhaps Jim's role when he first came to the canyon can be explained by what he told the census taker in 1900. He listed his occupation as *servant* of William Campbell. He spent his first year or two helping Campbell get his homestead and the ferry started. Then he settled on the second choice of homestead sites.

As noted earlier it was second choice due to the greater challenge to get water. Jim solved the problem by building a lengthy wooden flume across large scree slopes to bring water from Slide Creek. Then he turned his attention to a root cellar and almost a dozen sturdy log structures, all hand hewn from nearby trees. Many of them remain today.

We have no early photographs of Jim Moore. The few we have show a man with a shaved head, jug-eared, sporting a Groucho Marx mustache. He looks wonderfully fit for his age but not imposingly handsome. His posture is erect and his body is honed to a recognizable toughness. Fashion was clearly not his concern. He wore bulky jodhpur-style britches held inches below his arm pits by wide suspenders, the narrow legs of the pants typically tucked into the tops of calf-high lace up boots.

Nonetheless Moore's clothes were scrupulously clean and his flannel shirts were closely buttoned at the neck and at the wrist. Frances would later speak of Jim's fastidious care of his possessions and affairs. Mostly self-educated, he was obviously bright, energetic, and highly focused. Like his friends Joe Zaunmiller and William Campbell, Jim was the kind of man who thrived among the challenges of the backcountry.

From their first meeting in the fall of 1940, Frances would know Jim for barely a year and a half, but he had a profound effect on her. During the times Joe and Bert were away, she found that Jim was a source of strength and knowledge about the old ways. Frances respected the old timer and was eager to learn from him, much as she was during her short time with Harry Donahue. Decades later, Frances would sit down with a visitor from the University of Idaho and leave a loving oral history of Jim Moore, a man she called Justice Jim:

He was all man, not merely male. He was gentle unless the situation called for a different approach. If

Jim Moore – circa 1930s

need be, he could be aggressive, too. Not everyone liked Jim. But everyone did respect him. He had an old medical book, doctor book, and one part of it went on about a correct diet. Jim observed that. Until six weeks before that man became sick and died he was as hearty and as keepable as most men in their 50s.

He told me many things because I was a city girl determined to live in the mountains until I died. And so I had to learn. The way of the early people was the way of the mountains, as it had been in the beginning. There were many things for me to learn and Jim was one who taught me. I had helped my parents in the garden in Texas but I had never had the responsibility of a garden and I learned both from his verbal instruction, also from the books which he had bought, for when he came to the mountains he had worked on farms and ranches as a hired man.[1]

Jim told Frances his own history. Born August 20, 1867, in Carmine, Illinois, Jim and his sister were orphaned and taken in by relatives. Jim ended up with an uncle and as Frances tells it:

This uncle was an ultra religious, shall we say so-and-so, who had heard somewhere if you spare the rod you spoil the child. He could not tolerate a spoiled child. When Jim jerked away from one of the uncle's frequent beatings the back of his shirt stayed in his uncle's hand, but the rest of the shirt stayed on Jim and Jim ran. And he kept running – west. He didn't say from where, but I got the impression Illinois, Indiana, farm district. He hid by day and he moved at night. I asked, 'How did you eat?' He was absolutely disgusted with my question. How do you think a little boy is going to eat when there's nobody to feed him? Jim stole to keep his belly, not necessarily full, just to keep himself alive.

Jim's story skipped from the day he ran from his uncle until he was mature and working on a wheat farm – Nebraska, Kansas, in that part. And at the end of harvesting time everyone had to sign their name for what they'd been paid, Jim made his X. That evening the rancher talked to his wife about this young man – he's a good worker – he seems like a fine young man

2 Frances Zaunmiller Wisner, Oral History

but he wrote an X. So they propositioned Jim and he accepted to stay the winter and help the husband with the chores for his keep and the wife would instruct him in reading, writing, and numbers.

That was the beginning of Jim's education. When I knew him you would talk with him and you would wonder what university did he go to. He went to Jim's school. What he wanted to know, once he'd learned to read and to write, he found a book on that subject and he absorbed the book. He worked on the railroad when it went through northern Idaho. And when he left that job he came into the mountains to hunt a home, a place where he could build and never have to move again. And he did it.

He was a very special man and yet not the only one like that on the earth. I loved him. I still love him as a very dear friend. And many, many times since Jim was gone and I've had something which must be done and I didn't quite know how I'd think, what would Jim tell me.[2]

Frances' own decision to leave the terrible mistake she had made by marrying Charles Gamble and fashion a new life in the Idaho backcountry can be seen in her description of Jim Moore's motivation to live in the canyon. She starts telling the story as his, but slips into possessing the dream as her own:

He was one of the few men on this earth that fulfilled his ambitions. When you compare an ambition with a gob of money in the bank, try to balance it on the scale with a home where I will have a roof that does not leak. My walls will turn the winter's cold and the summer's hot. My bed will be as comfortable as I want. And I will have a table and chairs, not just for me, but for my visitors. I will have all the food I can eat and a little more. All the things I need to work with and I will work with them. And I will never move again. I don't even want to go to town. I begrudge the time that is spent away from my place. And when a man has that ambition and has attained it, I think if that and a pile of money were put on a balance scale the pile of money would go clear up in the air for it has no real value at

2 Frances Zaunmiller Wisner, Oral History

all. The pile can be replaced with more money but a home, my walls and my roof and my table and my cellar and all the things I work with, they cannot be replaced. The food you have raised yourself, fat bugs and hot weather and an early spring frost or a late spring frost, that is not the same as food you take from the shelf in a grocery store. Jim had it. He still has it because he's still there.

Jim wasn't concerned with a lot of money. He wanted to be able to provide himself with the necessities and a little bit extra for fun. But to get rich – no. He had no desire for it. It did not fit in what he wanted for life. He wanted acres of ground that would grow things to eat and just to look at. He wanted trees for his fruits. There was something about a man who works honestly for what he has that leads to his quiet statements of fact being very forceful. Jim never ranted and raved. He had a very strong sense of moral conduct. He did not legislate toward your or my morals. He assumed that everyone is what they are for reasons of their own and it was none of his business. For himself he was very rigid but since it was what he wanted to be he wore that moral code like you wear an old, treasured jacket. It fit him and that's all there was to it. Everyone knew no matter what you do in your own house you behave yourself at Jim's. He'll ask you to leave and when he asks you to leave you want to.[3]

Joe

It is likely that Frances' love of Jim Moore was like the love a woman has for a grandfather. Later events would show that perhaps he hoped for a different relationship.

Frances' relationship with Joe Zaunmiller began as his employee. She was there because, just like her father, John Coyle, she went where the jobs were. Frances would

3 Frances Zaunmiller Wisner, Oral History

soon learn that Joe Zaunmiller's character embodied everything the ideal *western* man should be: strong, loyal, capable, more action than words. Compact and muscular in stature, his body was a coiled spring, quick and efficient, but he carried himself with an easy grace and a quiet sense of self-assurance. He was sun-weathered handsome, a man carved by his environment.

Well liked and admired by both men and women, Joe engendered a deep loyalty in his friends. There was much to admire. Tireless in his work ethic with a deeply ingrained sense of responsibility, Joe did whatever it took to get the job done. He was a respected leader who also had a sense of fun and whimsy. His nieces and nephews would remember him with deep affection for his gentleness, high standards, and personal warmth. Despite the physical, emotional and economic hardships of the Eden that was Campbell's Ferry, Joe was the individual who was able to make the place work.

During the first months after Frances' arrival Joe was often absent caring for his outfitting clients, but when winter came, he joined in a running game of cribbage between Frances, Jim, Bert and the occasional visitor. Sometimes he pitched in on home chores, cleaning the house and fixing the occasional meal. He had grown up in a German household where these were traditionally women's duties, a perspective Frances would eventually come to know as his true belief.

As the winter of 1940–41 progressed, Frances began to explore her surroundings with a hike up the Three Blaze Trail to relive the epic views of the canyon she had experienced on her first arrival. She climbed Moore's ridge to the south to gain additional perspective on the homestead. She did some hunting, missing two shots at a cougar she had spotted. But mostly it was domestic chores that consumed her days – cooking meals, pies, cakes, cookies, donuts, ice cream, sewing, quilting, making dresses, washing and ironing. And she tended to all the men's aches and illnesses. There were mustard plasters for Bert and Joe, hot water bottles and massages for Jim's arms, legs and foot cramps.

The place benefitted from a woman's touch. As spring arrived she was able to put her own plan in place for the garden, add flower beds and build a pond in the draw behind the cabin. On the first day of May she notes in her diary, "Place very different from last fall. Flower beds, clear back porch, paths, etc. Me like."

Her first summer at the Ferry brought a growing appreciation for the expanded garden that the low elevation, good soil and ample water made possible. It was an annual event to *spring tooth* the orchard with a horse-drawn harrow used to turn the earthen surface. Fertilizer brought from Dixie was spread to enhance hay production to be stored up for the following winter. June would bring the first cutting, and another in early August. By mid-August the fruit in the orchard was ripe and the annual parade of bears, conditioned by four decades of regular access to a ready food source, would arrive and be a constant presence through September.

On September 22, 1941, Joe Zaunmiller made his move to settle the question of who would gain the hand of Frances in marriage. She notes in her diary, "Can pears, Joe gave me ring. Charge batteries. Men hay."[4]

It seems odd, doesn't it? No all caps, exclamation points, bold, shouting – just one of the four entries on what happened that day. Joe proposed. Wouldn't it be interesting to know how it happened? What information was exchanged? Did Joe know about Charles Gamble?

He probably did. Frances never talked about it, but years later Johnney Pollan, who was married to her sister Doris in Texas, told that soon after Frances came to the Ferry there was a visitor at the Wildt Ranch (now Whitewater Ranch) four miles upstream. Lew Wildt was surprised to find a man calling himself Charles Gamble show up at his door, claiming to be the husband of Frances.

Gamble wanted to know where Frances was. Wildt was suspicious, so he told Gamble where the trail downriver was, but also added that as soon as Gamble left he intended to get on the hand cranked phone and let Frances know he was coming.

Wildt also told Gamble when he got to the river across from the homestead, it was necessary to fire a warning shot to summon the ferry. He added that Frances had become dead-eye shot with a hunting rifle and was likely to return fire. Gamble gave up his pursuit and left.

When the CCC built the access to the Wildt place deep in the canyon it was a spur of a road that ran from Elk City and Red River, east across the wilderness to Darby, Montana. This leads us to believe that Charles left the Salmon River and took that route east, for eight years later, he was in Missoula, Montana, getting married to a woman

4 Frances Zaunmiller Wisner, diary, 22 September 1941

from Darby.

Gamble gave his own residence at the time as Conner, a community just a few miles south of Darby. The woman he married, Sue Williams, was a widow of a man killed in a logging accident, leaving her with three children. A year later she sued Gamble for divorce claiming abandonment. The last record one can find of Gamble is at age forty-seven in 1950 in Butte, Montana. Where he had spent most of the 1940s and where he ended up after Sue divorced him, we do not know, but he never again entered Frances' life.

When Frances got the proposal from Joe, she undoubtedly knew he was widowed, but did she know he had been married twice? Frances never said, and Joe left no record that he told her. We can only imagine how they sorted it out. We do know Joe's proposal brought reactions from both Jim Moore and Bert Rhoades.

If you discount the twice a year trips Jim Moore made to Dixie for supplies, he almost never left the canyon. The only time was when, as Frances wrote, "His teeth were just giving him fits. He came to Grangeville and stayed until all his teeth were pulled, his mouth was healed, and the new teeth were ready, and then he came home." That was it, except when Jim found out Joe had given Frances a ring. Jim left again. A few days later, he came back, but was upset. Frances tried to call him on the backcountry telephone line. Her diary's one word description of the conversation, "Rebuffed." It is a full three and a half weeks later that she reports a thaw, "Jim more cheerful. "

Bert was upset, too. He remained at the Ferry helping with the outfitting business, but on October 24 Frances notes, "Bert back. Partnership over." The next week it is obvious she and Joe had settled some issues, because she announced, "I will marry Joe next year." Four days later, "Bert and Joe finally talk."

So it was settled. Frances would become Mrs. Joe Zaunmiller. But there remained a problem – not a minor one. Frances was still Mrs. Charles Gamble. On November 6th Frances and Joe left the canyon and made a ten day trip out that included a stop to see Thomas Madden, an attorney in Lewiston. The couple then went to Joe's family home in Walla Walla where he introduced his prospective bride to his two brothers.

On the trip back to the Ferry, they stopped and paid Madden his $80 fee for handling the divorce. Since the whereabouts of Gamble was unknown, the process would be lengthy. It included checking with the Department of Defense to be sure Gamble was not in the military and publication of three notices in the Lewiston paper. It took a year for the divorce to be final.

Soon after the couple returned to Campbell's Ferry news came over the radio that changed the lives of every American, even those sequestered in the wilds of Idaho. On December 7, 1941, the Japanese attacked Pearl Harbor. The next day President Roosevelt formally declared the U.S. entry into World War II. Joe and Frances didn't know it at the time, but the war would have a profound impact on their dream of making a life at Campbell's Ferry.

That winter life seemed normal. When the weather was clear, Joe was able to go to Dixie to pick up mail and packages. The arrival of Christmas brought many packages from Texas. Christmas Day was spent at Jim Moore's. The routine of keeping the ferry clear of ice, tending the stock, baking, and occasional trips to the neighbors continued. The radio kept them informed of the nation's buildup to war. In February Frances noted reports of the first action of the U.S. Fleet. It had been engaged in action off Borneo in the South Pacific.

In early March Jim Moore's health began to fail. On April 8 he was brought over to the Ferry so Frances could care for him. For a week she fed, shaved and doctored him as best she could. On April 15 he was able to take a walk outside in the sunshine, but it would be his last.

The next day Frances treated Jim for choking and troubled breathing. She rubbed crystalline into his chest. She administered Paregoric to ease his abdominal pain and help him sleep. She notes, "Jim had me write letters for him. Made chicken broth, gave it to him by tablespoon. Can't breathe. Massage chest."

For the next week there are no diary entries, then this sad note, "Been too busy to write. But Jim was so sick. And he needed me. The boys did the housework. Let the outside stuff go except for chores. Jim died last night, April 25, 1942, 3:25A.M. I took word downriver today and Fred will take word to town. Now I'm going to sleep."

The following day Jim was taken across the river and buried as he had instructed. He had drawn a map, and at one time taken Frances to the spot to be sure she knew his exact desire for a final resting place. When they dug the grave they found nothing but clean dirt, no rocks. Jim had pre-dug his own grave and refilled it to be sure his friends would have it easy when his time came. The location of the grave is up a gentle slope above the flat that held his cabin. He told Frances that someday there might be a road built through the canyon, and when they did, it would probably be on the flat. He wanted to be able to come out periodically and watch the cars go by.

Bill Gaines, Jim's neighbor four miles downstream, built a coffin for him. Frances had crocheted a pillow. When they laid him in the coffin they realized something was not right – he didn't have his teeth. Frances went back across the river to fetch them, but they were unable to get them in his mouth. They placed the teeth under his pillow and joked that some day, an anthropologist would find Jim and wonder what strange ritual was being followed where one's teeth were placed under the head of the deceased.

In addition to his gravesite, Jim left instruction on how to locate a two by three foot rock, under which, "you will find a red tobacco can." The can containing his treasure has never been found.

Jim left his placer claim on Slide Creek to Frances. According to the transcript of a later hearing on the status of the claim, Frances said she located the claim on Slide Creek Placer in 1942 . She believed she deeded it to Bert Rhodes in the fall of that year because she couldn't maintain it.

Bert would later have a heart attack in 1944. Just as with Jim Moore, Frances nursed him and got him to town. Bert sold the place to Sub Woods in 1945. Frances later found that Bert, who died in December of 1945, had never filed papers on the sale to Sub, so she deeded it to Sub at the time he decided to sell it to Jack Wenzel in order to document his ownership. The poor job of record keeping eventually resulted in the place being taken by the Forest Service.

Joe took the loss of Jim Moore hard, and was unable to help with his burial. Frances thought it odd that Joe couldn't participate. Instead he spent the day on chores and with his stock.

Two weeks later on May 11 Joe went to town and registered for the draft. He was listed as being 5'8" tall, 165 pounds with blond hair and gray eyes, employed by the U.S. Forest Service. His effort to join the military was rejected again, just as it had been during WWI. He was fifty years old, had a leaky heart and a hernia – a diagnosis hard to believe given the hard work he undertook everyday at the

Ferry.

A few days later Frances' diary ends. With the war on and outfitting clients scarce, the Ferry had lost its viability as an enterprise to support Joe, Frances and their employee Bert. The couple made the difficult decision to leave the Ferry and seek a living in the outside world. The ranch was left in Bert Rhoades' hands, but without any pay, he would have to find other work as well. After a while he left the garden and hayfields to the wildlife and the stock to fend for itself.

On November 9, 1942, the court in Lewiston issued an order formally ending Frances' marriage to Charles Gamble. Ten days later, Joe and Frances were wed in Walla Walla, with Joe's brother Harry and his wife Ellen acting as witnesses.

One might be tempted to think of Frances' choice of Joe as a financial one. Of the three suitors, he was the property owner. He owned the Eden that prompted Frances, upon first sight, to declare, "I am through traveling." He also had the best prospects for long term financial support. The country was just exiting the Depression and hadn't Joe made it work through the worst of times? But it wasn't just a financial calculation.

Years later, after Joe had passed, Frances would write her sister about Joe and declare, "He was my husband, my lover and my baby. Joe was my teacher, too. In the role of husband Joe wore the pants in our house. He was not mean or nasty about it either. Perhaps it was as much my own thinking on that subject (I've never admired skirted husbands). So when we disagreed and discussed some items which would or would not become a part of our way of living, as soon as I understood his view and desire, then that view and desire became my own. Joe, as my lover, was a great pleasure to be with."

Now in Walla Walla, the newlyweds moved into Joe's family home at 117 West Poplar. Joe took a job as a civilian worker for the U.S. Army. He became a patrolman on a project building the McCaw Army Hospital. Beginning in April 1942 the facility was quickly constructed to accommodate the wave of casualties coming in from the grueling effort the United States had undertaken to capture a series of stepping stone islands leading to the Japanese homeland. The carnage from Guadalcanal, Tarawa, Iwo Jima, Okinawa and more had overwhelmed U.S. military medical facilities. After two and one half years and treating 14,000 casualties the facility would close in November

1945.

Joe's initial pay was $1,860 per year, but within months he was promoted to senior patrolman with an increase to $2,040. Joe had a small amount taken out each pay period to buy war bonds. He also worked security for the Marcus Whitman hotel in town. Joe Zaunmiller, ever resourceful, had found a way to support the war effort, generate an income for him and his new bride, and to save money for an eventual return to the Ferry. Although it was not certain that they would return.

During their absence, Joe and Frances had made the difficult decision to list Campbell's Ferry for sale. Maude Pratt in Dixie had the listing and wrote them in June 1943 with a report:

Dear Folks,

Just a line today not very encouraging news though, as the river remains the same. It has not gone down an inch. The ranger says the high country snows haven't begun to go yet. This unusual cold weather is holding the snows back. Therefore the river hasn't reached its peak yet.

Bert is working on the forest. He has been on Rabbit Point trail and was able to let us know how things were down on the ranch. He said yesterday the stock were all in. They have broken through the fence. I do not know what the results will be now. They are all OK as far I know they would come in for salt. I carried down salt and gave them a good salting before we came on this last trip. I'm just a little sick over the way things turned out.

Bert has been sent on another job. I do not know where but he will not be on the river until after fire season. He says he is going to winter his stock outside. The elk and deer are cleaning his hay up.

Harold Beacham came in the other day. He said there's a man and his wife who are interested in taking the ranch. We are sending a letter to them and telling them to get in touch with you folks. Their address is Mr. Louis Wedekind, Kennewick, Wash. General Delivery. If you get in touch with them I am sure they will be the party you're looking for. It'll be quite some time before any one can cross, but its worth looking into.

Mrs. M. D. Pratt

Nineteen forty-three was a very unsettling and challenging time for the couple. Joe had a job, but a war was raging and their dream in doubt. It is likely that this is the period when Frances suffered through a second lost pregnancy.

During the year they received more bad news from the Ferry. In their absence a horse had been killed by a falling tree, and two cows had starved to death after being left unattended in the barn. When Frances filed their taxes for the year she took a loss of $100 for the horse and $80 each on the cows, telling the taxman the loss was due to "a careless caretaker."

The sale of the Ferry did not materialize, and in 1944 the Zaunmiller's relationship with their realtor turned sour. Through comments or letters, Frances made disparaging remarks about Dorolitta Pratt and her mother, Maude. When word got back to Maude in Dixie it prompted a stern rebuke:

Joe and Frances,

When I came to Dixie today I was surprised and hurt when I found out the cruel and unjust things you said about Dorolita. Whatever your grievance is against others is none of my affair but I am Dorolita's "Mother" and it is My duty to protect her both from slander and harm.... I have tried to work with you both to the best of my ability. I have done my part so far, even took two months of my mighty scant rations to keep my word. Your appreciation is only shown by abuse of my girl....

If I should hear one more remark about her character or my inability to raise her right I'll make no idle threats, but will take advantage of the protection that Dorolita's father made possible for us, that we be spared abuse and slander, after his death.... It is too bad that good things can't be said to me directly ...... as the cruel and mean things in my absence.

Mrs. M. D. Pratt

Other than the employment and financial records for Joe in Walla Walla and the communications with Maude Pratt, we have no record of what Frances was doing during that period. A year and a half later the couple would return to Campbell's Ferry.

Note found in Frances' papers
titled
Jas Moore to Francis Cole

Chapter Twenty-One

1945

"Sorrow makes us all children again
destroys all differences of intellect.
The wisest know nothing."
– Ralph Waldo Emerson

Joe's plan to go to Walla Walla and earn enough to get the Zaunmillers back on their feet financially had worked. The couple decided against selling the Ferry. The war wouldn't last forever. They could return to the canyon they loved, pick up some trail work with the Forest Service, raise a few cattle and get by until the conclusion of the war ended gasoline rationing.

When the public was able to travel again hunters would return to Joe's outfitting business. Beef prices were good, but there were other challenges. Rationing of sugar made it difficult to can and put up enough food to last the winter. Everyone in rural America was dealing with the same shortages, so at the Ferry, as was the norm, they just made it work.

Joe's reputation as a skilled, reliable worker with supervisory skills served him well through these tough times. When looking for work in Walla Walla or back in Idaho he carried with him a sterling recommendation from his days with the CCC.

Even when the war ended and the job market flooded with veterans given preference for Forest Service jobs, Joe's work ethic and understanding of forest ways served him well. Frances wrote her sister, "Joe has been home a month but Monday he goes back to the Forest Service. They tried to get someone to take his place, but no go, so the USFS gets Joe and I'll be alone again. The Ranger has been trying to place discharged veterans – but they can't take the quietness of the hills. The last one pulled out about 9:00 P.M. -- just started walking -- didn't even take time to pack his clothes or turn in his time or anything."

Another event in 1945 brought Frances an opportunity for a new career, one that could be pursued from the small cabin in the wilds. Early in the year, among the letters she wrote to family members, was one to her brother, Tom Coyle. Tom was a Private First Class in the Army Air Corps stationed in Assam, India, where he was loading and fueling planes that were flying supplies over "The Hump," the eastern end of the Himalayas to China. Coyle was part of a unit of the U.S. military that President Roosevelt had directed to help the Chinese Nationalists, led by Chiang Kai-shek, in their war with the Japanese.

Pfc Tom Coyle

Frances wrote to tell him of her life at Campbell's Ferry and in reply he wrote, "This is really a small world." Tom had discovered that the same mailbag containing his sister's letter had also brought a letter from Idaho to his unit's Master Sergeant. The Sergeant's friend, a Mrs. Bert Hayes, was the daughter of the publisher of the *Idaho County Free Press* newspaper in Grangeville, Idaho.

Half a world away in remote India Tom Coyle and his Sergeant were both corresponding with friends less than fifty miles apart

Tom Coyle and Joe Zaunmiller, on the ferry in 1945

in a remote region of Idaho. This chance occurrence would become the genesis of a more than thirty-year career for Frances as a columnlist.

Sergeant Hodges was impressed with Frances' vivid description to her brother of life in the wilds of Idaho, so he suggested that Pfc. Coyle tell his sister to visit Hayes' father, John Olmsted, the publisher. Frances rarely went to town, so months later she wrote Olmsted a letter that he printed in his paper:

Let me introduce myself – and chatter as I would – should I meet you and Mrs. Hayes. I'm from the Texas coast where the water is chemically purified and hard; where the only thing that keeps you from seeing all the way to China is the horizon; where the blue bonnets and purple sage fill the air with a heady perfume that is intoxicating. When I was a child I loved it – but before I was even grown – people started clearing the land; plowed up the blue bonnets, dug out the sage and cactus; they cut the land up and fenced. There should be no cotton shortage – certainly enough of Texas has been put into cotton to cover the world with 12oz. canvas. Anyway, I finally got the courage to leave that wonderful farming country and think now I am in a place I was born to be. All the good things I knew as a child are here – and more!

Here (Campbell's Ferry, Salmon River, Idaho Nat'l Forest)

we farm – raise nearly all our own food. We did that in Texas, too, but here there are trees. People who have lived in Idaho most of their life have no idea how truly beautiful this country is. I have a mountain for my backyard; black bear visit me and steal apples and peaches; nine cow elk have declared squatters rights on the alfalfa field; the deer don't bother to leave the salt log when I go to the barn. I have been here since 1940. In hunting season my husband Joe takes the hunters a day's trip from here.

You see, we live on the south side of the Salmon River, which means we're marooned by ice in winter and high water in summer. I could not visit with my neighbors even if there were any. Joe works for the Forest in the summer so from May 1st to Sept. 30th I am alone, except for the wild things. They have learned to trust me and my dog, and we have a lot of fun watching the deer and elk. Gosh, but I'm long winded. That comes from being alone so much. When I start writing I pretend the person is in the room and then the only thing hard about letter writing is to stop, particularly if I am telling about the beauties of the primitive area.

Years later when John Olmsted was looking for a new voice to add to his local paper, he would remember Frances. He figured that his readers in Idaho County, a place with a population of only twelve thousand in an area larger than the state of New Jersey, might appreciate regular reports from one of the county's wildest corners. Olmsted contacted Frances Zaunmiller and gave her a simple mission — tell us of your life on the Salmon River. She would do so until her passing in 1986. In the process Frances created a priceless record of a place the modern world had left behind. In her unique third-person style Frances introduced the *Idaho County Free Press* readers to her corner of the natural world, her friends, visitors, life and death.

In a later column titled "Life in Mountains Rugged in Winter," Frances describes what life must have been like the winter of 1945.

CAMPBELL'S FERRY, March 6 - You ask me to tell you of life in the mountains? Sometimes it is all peaches and cream and sometimes – but let the first few days of March tell their own story.

The woman who lives at the ferry is blessed in that she needs very little sleep. So before morning is here, she builds the fires and sips hot tea while waiting for the day to begin. She likes that quiet time, and would hardly trade it for any hours of sleep. The morning of March first was no different from any other, until day came and she could see outside. Snow – gobs of the wet sticky stuff. She did have control enough not to yell and disturb the sleeping, and she also took the shovel and made a path to the woodshed, where the snowshoes are kept.

Sixteen inches of new snow is a bit much to shovel all the paths, snowshoes did a good job of trail making – to the chicken house and barn and that all important path to the plumbing. There are times when the plumbing would be more convenient were it in the house, and this morning, with a total of 31 inches of snow was one of those times. Then it was time for breakfast.

There is just time enough between breakfast and the morning gossip time to put the house in order. After gossip time the stock need be fed. Again she wore snowshoes, the straps had been cut on his, so she made trail for both of them. The haystack is almost a quarter of a mile from the house – a nice waist-slimming distance – and they shoveled the snow off the hay. It is too hard to dig the hay out when so much snow is on top of it. The man digs hay out of the stack and throw it over the fence, she scatters it so that the horses that like to eat quietly can do so – and the ones that like to go from hay pile to hay pile can do so without too much bother to the other stock.

Back at the house and she could not stay in the house – so she snowshoed over to the creek. Nothing over there but more snow, so home again, where the cookstove looked so lonesome that she put it to work. In a little while no one was hungry.

The next morning there was only seven inches of new snow, but it was the same old story so far as cleaning trails was concerned. Light snow kept falling until the evening of the fourth and it turned clear and cold.

The morning of March 5 was a cool 18 below zero – these are the days when everyone's stove is just like Monroe Hancock's – in cold weather Monroe says that his stove draws so good, it draws him right up against it.

A bunch of elk have taken over the Jim Moore place. The woman was so busy watching them when they moved in that she like to never got the dishes washed. They are so cautious and moved slowly, two big cows were scouting the bar, and after they gave the all clear then the younger stuff, calves and two year olds, came too. She watched them on that ridge above the flume. There is salt out at Jim's and snow may be on the ground, but it is March and the four-legged people are hungry for salt. Salt is the reason the Ferry people keep the trail open to the creek. The big salt ground for the ferry is on the Flat across the creek.

Despite her idyllic public representation of life at the Ferry, Frances did have doubts. She wrote her sister, "Sometimes I wish we didn't have this place. It seems like the place belongs to Joe and I belong to the place. But that is only cabin fever that makes me feel that way. Guess its lack of sleep more than anything else. I don't get much sleep anymore."

The lack of sleep was mostly a summer problem. Idaho is known for having four distinct seasons and summer can bring temperatures of a hundred degrees or more. The geography of the homestead helps explain. The property is located on the south side of the Salmon River, but in a stretch of the canyon where the river itself is running due south. This opens the bottom of the canyon up to more sunshine. Running a wood-burning stove in a small kitchen with outside temperatures in the hundreds with sun beating on the cabin walls was unbearable. Frances had begun to do her cooking and canning at night. Daytime chores did not go away, so sleep became a luxury – one more example of the couple doing whatever it took to make life work at the Ferry.

****

The daily routines of life in the canyon that summer of 1945 were interrupted by a tragedy among neighbors that the Salmon River delivered to Joe and Frances' doorstep.

Allison Ranch is ten miles upstream from the Ferry. Almost

twenty years before, Joe Zaunmiller and Emma, his wife at the time, had worked the place for Elmer Allison. Now it was being tended by George Wolfe, with periodic stays by his wife, Reho and other family members.[1] George and Reho, both Idaho natives, had met in 1935 in Kamiah where she was in high school and he part owner of a local sawmill. George's true desire was to be a musician. After marrying in 1936 and nearly losing a finger in the mill, George applied for and won a job as a music teacher in Missoula, Montana.

As World War II approached, George worried about being taken from his family, despite being too old for the draft. They might not take him at age thirty-eight, he reasoned, but later they would probably take anyone they could get their hands on, so he decided to end his music career and take his family to the wilderness. He found an abandoned cabin at Crofoot Ranch, just two miles upstream from Allison Ranch, and began to work a trap line for furs and hunt for food. In 1943 Elmer Allison's cabin burned, resulting in Elmer leaving the homestead to care for his wife in Lewiston. George Wolfe took on the task of rebuilding the cabin and caretaking Allison Ranch.

By 1945 George, Reho, four-year-old son Norman and one-year-old daughter Carol had settled into Allison. That spring Reho had invited her father, John Bergman, to come live with them, but it would be necessary to wait until high water had receded to bring all of his belongings from the trailhead at the Dale (later Whitewater) Ranch. The problem was the crossing of Big Mallard Creek, a large, robust stream that flowed from the mountains into the Salmon River a mile and a half upstream of the trailhead. The creek had to be low enough after the spring runoff to allow a loaded packstring to wade across. A foot log ran from bank to bank.

On June 30 it was determined the creek would be passable so George and Norman set out on the six-mile route with a packstring to fetch Reho's father's possessions. On the trip out, Norman was able to ride one of the pack horses himself. Father and son made it to the Dale Ranch for lunch, packed the horses and headed home. John Wolfe tells what happened next:

When they reached Mallard Creek, Dad told Norman to wait while he took the horses across the creek, then he'd come

1 John A. Wolfe, *Reho Wolfe, The End of a Salmon River Era*, (Viola, ID: Rhett Creek Publishing, 2002), p. 16

Reho Wolfe and daughter Carol, followed by Norman
On the trail between Dale Ranch and Allison Ranch
1944

back for him. As Dad was tying the horses to a tree on the far bank he heard Norman screaming. Norman had attempted to cross on the foot log while Dad was busy with the horses. Dad turned just in time to see the boiling torrent drag his little boy into its powerful grasp. Frantically running along the bank trying to save him, Dad witnessed as it dumped Norman into the river. He went under and did not resurface.

As Dad jumped from boulder to boulder along the river bank, desperately hoping to find his son, he fell and severely sprained his ankle. He didn't notice though. No doubt his panic and emotional pain must have overpowered the agony of his injury.

Finally, after scouting the river all the way down to the Dale Ranch, he struggled, making his way back to the horses and headed home. Mom had to help him off the horse and into bed, because he was unable to use his injured ankle.

The next day it was obvious that Dad could not resume his search for Norman, so Mom headed out on her own. When she reached Charley Ayres' place,[2] Monroe Hancock was there. She told him the bad news and asked him to help her search. She wanted to search all the way to Campbell's Ferry, a crossing six miles downriver from the mouth of Big Mallard.[3]

For a mile and a half Monroe and Reho walked along the bank of the river searching every eddy and drift pile for signs of Norman. When they found an old wooden rowboat along the bank Monroe used a small hand ax from his backpack to fashion oars and with a five gallon oil can as a seat, continued their search downriver. At Elkhorn Rapid, Monroe thought better of trying to run the major rapid in high water in such a small craft, so they resumed the search on foot.

As evening approached they came to Campbell's Ferry. Joe and Frances brought the ferry across to get Reho for the night while Monroe went on to Dixie. The next day Joe took Reho back to Dale Ranch. From there she went back to Allison to take care of John Bergman, her ailing father, while others continued the search for Norman.

Two weeks later Reho's father's health took a turn for the worse and she decided it was time to leave the canyon to seek medical help. John Wolfe picks up the story:

When they reached Yellow Pine Bar, John told Mom he had to stop, he couldn't go any farther. She helped him off the horse and let him rest against a tree while she went to the river to get Charley Ayre's attention. Charley crossed the river and took Mom and her father back over to his house. John was so weak that he had to be piggybacked up to the cabin where they got him into bed and as comfortable as possible. The next day, July 14, John asked Mom to get his checkbook out of his car. He had one thousand dollars in the bank, and was going to give it to Mom. So Mom hiked the four miles down to the end of the road to get the checkbook. By the time she returned, her father had died.[4]

Reho returned to Allison and she and George packed up their belongings and daughter Carol. The couple left the river with the in-

2 At the mouth of Richardson Creek, across the Salmon River from what is now Whitewater Ranch.
3 John A. Wolfe, *Reho Wolfe, The End of a Salmon River Era*, (Viola, ID: Rhett Creek Publishing, 2002), p. 24
4 Wolfe, p. 26

tention of never coming back. The loss of two close family members in two weeks was too much for them to bear. It caused a wound in Reho and George's relationship that would never heal. As son John would later report in his book, "I think Mom blamed Dad for Norman's death. She told her sister Olga, I am never going to let George do this to me again." Their saga had not ended. On July 19 while visiting with George's sister in Kooskia they got a call from the Forest Service. Frances Zaunmiller had reported that Norman's body had been found.

In Frances' personal papers she left an account of finding the body using her usual style of referring to herself in the third person:

She was making raspberry jam, early in the morning, before the sun came over the hill, for it was July and the days were hot. Standing over a woodstove was not the most comfortable place to be. Joe was in the upper meadow, trying to get finished with raking hay before it got too hot.

She heard her name being called from across the river. She started not to notice, but to finish the jam first. As she listened there was an urgency that was almost panic in the voice that called. So she went into the yard and looked across. There on a saddle horse was a man,[5] shouting like someone demented, 'Frances, come over!' She pulled the jam off the stove and went to the river. As she cast off the mooring ropes on the ferry she could see the river had dropped about three feet during the night. She was glad. High water had lasted long enough and it would be good to be able to cross the river whenever she wanted. Across and the boat tied securely, she walked up the trail to where the man was sitting on his horse. He had ridden to meet her. He was sure the body he had seen on the river bank just below where he had called was the missing child. When asked why he did not go closer and make sure, he said he could not for 'dead people make him sick.' So the woman turned her back on that man and walked down the river bank from the ferry boat. And she came to this thing that had frightened the man and stood there looking at what had been a little boy.

It was difficult to identify the body after almost three weeks in the river, but Reho's earlier description of his clothing and a missing

---

5 Sub Woods, who lived at the Jim Moore place at the time.

tooth convinced Frances that it was indeed Norman Wolfe's body the man had found. She crossed the river again, stopping at the house to call the ranger. Then Frances continued:

She walked up to the meadow where Joe was raking hay and it seemed strange that the morning was still young. She had been on the river bank less than an hour but it was as tho two years had passed. She was very tired. Her husband went back to the river with her and the man who could not look upon a dead person came to help move the child. They wrapped him in a piece of canvas, tied him securely and lashed the body to a long pole. The men took the ends of the pole on their shoulders, carried him to the ferry and brought him across the river to the place of burying.

While waiting for the parents to arrive, Joe and Sub Woods dug a grave and built a coffin. There was a discussion about sealing the coffin or not, whether they should wait for George and Reho. Frances was determined that the parents would not see what she had seen. She settled the discussion, closing the coffin herself and covering it with a blanket and flowers from her garden. It was near midnight when the Wolfes arrived. In the moonlight prayers were said over the open grave. Frances led the couple back to the house while Joe and Sub filled the grave.

The next day the Wolfes left. Reho checked into the hospital in Grangeville, emotionally and physically drained by the experience. There it was learned she was pregnant, another burden this strong, remarkable woman had carried through the entire ordeal.

Frances told of the next night at the Ferry:

The day after we buried the baby boy, Joe went to town. He was gone overnight. That night I was in the living room, writing to Joe's nephew when the most awful noise started. It seemed like the souls of all the damned were mourning their sins. My hair stood straight up. The source of the sound was on the river bank where we found the body. I never finished the letter, though I did finally get courage to go to bed and slept.

Two nights later Joe was home and Bert Rhoades was here, too. Just after we went to bed it started again. I grabbed handfuls of bed and just lay there. Joe got up and went outside. So did Bert. I tucked my pride in my pocket and asked them what was wrong. It was a wolf and I hadn't mentioned the other night because I was afraid I was hearing noises that were not real. Had he not howled when Joe was here to listen and tell me what it was I would always believe it to be the first real manifestation of my being batty. No wonder novelists always use blood curdling to describe the cry of wolves. Joe had heard them before in Montana and Bert spent two winters in the Great Slave Lake country of Canada. I'll still be frightened when I hear it, but not like the first time. I'll be glad when it rains, then maybe the scent will be washed off the rocks and they won't come around any more.

There were now three people buried at Campbell's Ferry – Norman Wolfe in 1945 and Rose Cook and her child from 1905.

Norman Wolfe

Chapter Twenty-Two

Outfitters

When determining the value of a property, real estate appraisers use a concept known as highest and best use. The approach is to look at the property in terms of what one is physically able to do at the location – activities that are legally allowable, financially feasible and produces the maximum benefit. Joe Zaunmiller was not an appraiser, but when he began to use Campbell's Ferry as the base for his growing outfitting business, he had found the property's highest and best use.

Joe and Frances' outfitting operations would support them financially for more than a decade. In the process of building their own success, they would also play a role in fashioning a profession that ultimately would be the economic cornerstone of the wild lands and rivers that surrounded them.

The greatest challenge associated with making an outfitting business work at the Ferry was also a significant asset. Campbell's Ferry was extremely hard to get to. Only those with the skill, knowledge and equipment necessary to overcome that inaccessibility could visit the area. They were few.

The nation was rapidly becoming more urban, industrialized and dependent on modern conveniences. Few could still manage a packstring of horses and mules. Few could throw a diamond hitch to secure days and weeks of supplies on the back of a pack animal headed into the wilderness. The vast majority could not. The farther that vast majority got from their pioneer heritage, the farther they were from a connection to rural landscapes, mountains, free flowing streams, and open spaces.

The farther they were, the more they valued opportunities to return to revisit them. For many this included keeping their hunting heritage alive. To do so they needed help. They needed Joe and Frances.

Joe Zaunmiller was a vestige of an earlier time. He possessed the skills and knowledge that had first allowed early explorers and pioneers to access America's wild places. Joe had acquired these skills as a young man working on farms around Walla Walla. During his years at the Harbison Ranch, Allison Ranch, and now Campbell's Ferry he nurtured those pioneer skills. When he became an outfitter he found a way to tap that reservoir of pioneer savvy and turn it into a viable business.

Of course another major asset the Ferry had to support an outfitting business was the wildlife. Deer, elk, bear, bighorn sheep, moose, mountain lion, fish, all thrived in the millions of acres of prime habitat surrounding the Ferry. Joe's years of hiring out to the Forest Service to work and maintain trails had taken him throughout the surrounding wilderness. His many trips into the backcountry gave him valuable knowledge of the location, habitat, life cycles and characteristics of the wild creatures his hunting clients wished to find. He had a mental map and an understanding of wild places that those who lived in urban America lacked. So they turned to Joe and paid him for his knowledge.

Perhaps the most critical asset in Joe's outfitting operation was his wife. Even today if you study the successful outfitting operations in Idaho, virtually all are run by a couple. Outfitters are many things – guide, logistics manager, transportation provider, purchasing agent, supply sergeant, educator, entertainer, cook, nurse, and baby-sitter. And who at the Ferry filled most of those roles? It was the savvy, talented woman from Texas.

Together, Joe and Frances would draw on the resources provided by the homestead and forge them into the critical components of a successful outfitting business. Caring for the stock, providing their food and assuring their health was the task that took most of the couple's time and energy. Without stock, nothing else worked. They were the source of transportation and provided the ability to move people and supplies from the trailhead to the homestead and beyond to the hunting camps in the wilderness.

Most of the year the stock got its feed from the meadows on the ranch and the open, grassy slopes of nearby Trout Creek and Little Trout Creek. The areas off the homestead were national forest, which required the Zaunmillers to acquire a grazing permit from the Forest Service.

In 1944 Joe paid $20.16 for a ten-year permit to graze eleven head of stock between April and November of each year. The forage needs of the stock for the balance of the year were met by an annual multi-month effort to raise, harvest and store enough hay to feed the

Joe on Dan — 1946

stock through the winter.

Water was critical to the effort. The same ditches that brought water a mile from Trout Creek to the homestead for human consumption also fed a myriad of supply ditches used for periodic flood irrigation of meadows. The water was not under pressure so there were no sprinklers. On a regular, rotating schedule Joe, using just a shovel, would divert the water into ditches covering different segments of the meadows, opening and closing overflow points along the ditch to allow gravity to disperse the water across the ground.

Harvest meant time-consuming, back-breaking labor. Initially the hay was cut by hand with a scythe. Later a No. 7 McCormick Deering sickle mower drawn by mules would do the bulk of the job. A dump rake pulled the cut hay into piles which, when dry, were loaded into a wagon and stored in the barn.

The stock at the Ferry was an evolving mix of horses, mules and cattle. One or two milk cows were kept, providing fresh milk, cheese and other dairy products. Mares and cows were occasionally bred to provide young to be raised and sold. All the stock required periodic veterinary care, which was provided by Joe, Frances or their seasonal help.

To feed themselves and their clients the Zaunmillers relied on their garden, orchard, cows and chickens. Staples, like flour, sugar, coffee and spices came from the periodic trips to Dixie, but the majority of food was local from their huge garden. It had to be big. Not just because of the number of people being fed. A significant amount was taken by marauding wildlife despite their constant efforts to maintain fences. A balance was struck.

Frances loved having wildlife around the homestead for viewing and company. She took ownership of them, calling the various species *mine,* but she had her rules. "Most of my coyotes are well behaved. They eat the deer and once in a while an elk. Woe to the coyote who develops a taste for chicken! There is a lot of space in my canyon, but even the canyon is not large enough for a thief."

She knew the bears that were regular visitors to the orchard. Generations had brought their cubs to the annual fall food feast, and were tolerated, "as long as they observed the rules of good conduct." Those rules were broken during a hunt when one of their hunting clients had taken a nice bighorn ram. It would be days before all the

Joe and Frances with hunting client and two rams

hunters were ready to leave, so the carcass had to be stored. Joe had built a stout log building on the homestead for just such occasions. The building had an exterior made with eighteen-inch diameter logs. An interior wall was constructed of concrete, built with material Joe had packed in from town. The entire structure was built on top of one of the irrigation ditches. The gable ends of the roof were open for ventilation with sawdust piled on top of the ceiling and periodically wetted to provide an additional evaporative cooling effect.

Frances tells what happened, "Next morning before breakfast the men checked on the meat – what meat? The outside door was open – the screen door on the cement cooler room was torn and broken, hanging by one hinge. Inside everything was a mess. The wood block where I keep my butcher tools was turned over – knives, whetstones and a saw were scattered all over the floor and the ram was gone."

The men tracked down the offender and took a shot at it, but missed. They were able to salvage the trophy head and little else. That night they took turns sitting watch over the remaining stored meat, occasionally waking everyone at the Ferry with gunfire used to run off the returning bear.

Joe and Frances could not do all the work associated with

the outfitting operation. They needed good guides. Hunting outfitters faced a unique challenge in this area. First the guide had to be a skilled packer, experienced in handling stock. He had to be an accomplished hunter, familiar with the territory and habits of the game being pursued. He had to have camp skills – the ability to set up, sustain and take down a base camp from which the clients could operate.

Since hunting season spanned the transition from fall to winter the camps often faced challenging weather conditions. And finally, the guide had to be strong and willing to engage in strenuous physical activity from before daylight until well after dark. Finding such talent was not as hard in Joe's and Frances' time. The nation was still primarily rural and agriculture based. Most of the youth raised on farms and ranches of the era left home with many of these necessary skills. However, as the nation would become more urban and family farms declined, hunting outfitters would find the ready supply of talent diminished.

For years the Zaunmiller's primary guide (the Idaho term is Lead Guide) was Bert Rhoades. Bert had all the requirements of a good guide, but he had heart problems and was aging. And there is reason to suspect that his relationship with Joe and Frances had suffered during the period the property was in Bert's care during the Zaunmiller's stay in Walla Walla. Two cows had died of starvation when left unattended in the barn.

So Joe and Frances began to look for a replacement, and as luck would have it, one that met their requirements showed up on the Chamberlain Trail.

In 1949, twenty-four-year-old Lloyd Lindholm came walking into the Zaunmillers lives. He had all the skills of a guide, and appeared to be a perfect fit for their long range plans for the Ferry. Lloyd was tall with blonde curly hair, carrying his Norwegian heritage in high cheekbones on a handsome chiseled face. The stocky, broad-shouldered, long limbed youth was built for the difficult tasks of wrangling stock in the backcountry. Born in Minnesota, in 1930 four-year-old Lloyd, two sisters and their mother, absent his father, were living with their mother's sister, brother-in-law and their three children in Crookston, Minnesota, a rural, agricultural community. He served in the U.S. Navy for four years during World War II as an aviation mechanic.

Joe and Lloyd Lindholm at the ferry

Frances later wrote of him as, "another of those trail travelers that stopped at the Ferry for a meal and overnight, but his stop was longer. Lloyd Lindholm was such a nice young man. He really liked the rough life in the mountains. He came and went as he liked, working for the Forest Service, making trips to visit his mother or just walking though the mountains. He wanted to make the Ferry his home."

The couple took the young man in and formed a very high opinion of him. So high, that when a need to find a buyer for half the ranch arose, they turned to Lindholm. In 1933 Joe had bought half interest in the ranch from Bob Hilands. When Hilands died in 1939, he had left his half interest to a brother and sister back east. Bob's relatives made an initial overture to Joe about buying out the interest, but at the time Joe was in no position to do so. So Hilands' family just held on to it.

When Bob's sister, part owner of the interest died in 1952, the heirs approached Joe again. This time, Joe, now sixty-two, saw an opportunity. It would be good to have a young man around with more than just a paycheck's interest in the place. Lloyd had demonstrated an ability to take on any task that arose. Joe and Frances felt it was a good match, so good that they personally loaned Lloyd part of the money to make the purchase.

The price was $1,800. Lloyd had $300 of his own money. His mother loaned him $1,200. The Zaunmillers loaned Lloyd the last $300.and the deal was done. It seemed to work well. The outfitting business was thriving. Lloyd was energetic and often made trips to town that had required Joe's effort in the past. At one point, he and Joe went in together to buy a new motor for the sawmill. If the business continued to grow there was no limit to

Lloyd packing supplies

what they could do with the place, perhaps even build a second cabin on the place for Lloyd.

But the partnership and good relations did not last. The story of what happened was contained in a sealed note we found in Frances' personal papers. The envelope was titled, "this is to be opened only if the occasion merits. Frances Zaunmiller Nov 6, 1954," and it was addressed to Bill Dee, the Zaunmiller's attorney in Grangeville.

Inside, Frances wrote:

Tonight I am nervous – shouldn't write – but must for my piece of mind – this is to be used only if Joe or I die an unnatural death – for I have become afraid – afraid of Lloyd – of all people.

He is the nicest person, next to Joe, I know. Because we think so much of him we took him into our home, made him a part of us. It's true he bought the Hilands' part of the ranch – but just because he owns half the place is not the reason we made our wills, so that should we both die together, Lloyd would own all the ranch. We did that because we think enough of Lloyd to want him to have what Joe worked so hard to get and since I've been here I have worked to help keep it.

When Lloyd is drinking he is not the same person as when

he's sober. He has been drunk – I mean viciously drunk here – one time I will relate here – it is the reason I am afraid. The night I'll tell you about – he started drinking – there was supper – but he drank instead of eating – Joe went to bed – so I had to stay up and be sure the cigarettes were not left laying all over the place. Lloyd talks when he's drunk – he knows the answers to all the problems in the world. Also he goes through stages. First he is wise. Second he must find something to cry about. Then he must be big and argue. Then he gets mean.

This particular night he decided that Frances is a bitch. He took a lot of time and very carefully explained how much better off Joe would be if she would leave. He even had the guts to say that Frances was doing her best to kill Joe by working Joe to death. He took a lot longer to say it than it takes to write this. Frances couldn't take much more of that so she went outside for a couple of minutes. When she came back inside Lloyd was putting bullets into the 38 pistol and roaring that if she had the guts to kill a man now was her chance.

Frances didn't wait to find out just who she was supposed to kill. She took the gun away from him and threw it into the closet. Then she got the quilt and whipped that drunken fool 'til he was half sober, telling him to get to bed. He went to bed. Later when he was sober he swore he did not remember acting that way. Maybe he does not remember, but a person who will act that way drunk or sober is not to be trusted. I truly expect that some time when Lloyd gets lousy drunk it will enter his mind to get rid of Joe or me or both of us. Of course he will succeed, else you will not be reading this.

In that case, he will probably say he did not do it, or else plead temporary insanity. I believe now 6 P.M. November 6, 1954, that he is actually wondering how to get rid of us without paying for murder.
The note was signed, Frances Zaunmiller.

The incident prompted a confrontation between Lloyd and Joe. Joe insisted that Lloyd sell his interest and leave. Lloyd didn't want to, but finally agreed. He knew the business couldn't work without Joe's support. Knowing how determined the Zaunmillers were to end the partnership, Lloyd took advantage and placed a $2,600 price on his half of the property. It was more than Joe and Frances figured it was worth, but they had no choice. They borrowed the money from R. S. Edwards, one of several men associated with the Goodman Oil Company of Boise who were frequent outfitted clients of the Zaunmillers. The loan was paid off several years later.

****

Joe and Frances would not be the only outfitters to live at Campbell's Ferry. As noted earlier, I got into the business myself in 1982, purchasing a rafting operation on the Middle Fork of the Salmon River. In 1985 I expanded, adding an operation on the Selway River, another pristine wilderness river in the Selway-Bitterroot Wilderness area just north of the Salmon River watershed. By the time Phyllis and I showed up at the Ferry in 2006 I had sold the Middle Fork operation and was just doing four trips per year on the Selway. Three years later I would sell the Selway operation as well and end a twenty-seven year outfitting career.

In some very obvious ways river outfitting is different from pack and hunt outfitting, but at its core it is the same – taking the public into the wilderness for hire. Joe and Frances used horses and mules. I used rafts. We outfitters put ourselves in a unique position with our customers – by law we are responsible for their health, safety and welfare. But taking on the risk was worth it for all the positives you get back.

I often compared taking guests into the backcountry to trips my first wife, Loretta, and I would take with our two daughters into the Arkansas Ozarks. With friends we had built a log cabin on the Mulberry River in the Ozark National Forest. It was a three hundred mile drive to get there from home in Mississippi, and after a while, the kids grew tired of it. So we began letting them take a friend with them. Each time, what had become mundane to the girls was relived and revived as together with a friend they explored the rope swing, trails, swimming holes and surrounding forests.

In outfitting, a river that you may have seen on dozens, eventually a hundred trips before, is seen again through the eyes of your guests. Their thrill of discovery and adventure rekindles your own.

You often see things you have never seen before, or just again, but in a different light. And you see the effect the natural world has on people. The guests you are taking into the wilds are diverse, involved in every imaginable occupation from across the country, indeed the world. And their experience on the trip can be transformational.

It can be a simple change like the slowing of their internal clock. Or it can be life changing, as was the case for a thirty-six-year-old linguist on the fourth day of one of our six-day trips on the Selway River.

Ellie White was originally from Cleveland, Ohio, but had spent the past thirteen years studying the language of Australia's aboriginal people. She and her parents were camped with me, three guides and eight other trip participants at Tango Bar Camp. Our location was the remnants of a past 500-year flood that had deposited tons of rock, gravel and sand below a sharp bend in the Selway River.

The flat was now anchored by several hundred-year-old cedars and Ponderosas, bordered on one side by the river, and on the other by a heavily forested, north-facing slope. On the slope was a dense stand of Douglas fir, moss and ferns – a coastal-type, biologically diverse enclave located hundreds of miles inland from the Pacific Coast. That night I had used the sand surface of the camp as a canvas, drawing out a map of Idaho to show the rivers and mountains, painting a picture of the geological forces that had formed our surroundings.

The next morning I noticed Ellie sitting by the river drinking her morning coffee, so I joined her and asked how the trip was going. "I stepped out of my tent last night," she said, "and as I looked up at the canopy of stars overhead, my soul expanded."

Having been accused at times of having a silver tongue, I was surprised to find myself unable to conjure an appropriate response. So I let it slide. All day long, rowing, steering my raft through rapids and reflective pools, I pondered her statement. How profound! What did she really mean?

That evening after dinner I found Ellie again and told her I had been thinking about her comment all day, Could you tell me more?

"I was intrigued by your presentation at Tango Bar on geology and wilderness," she explained. "You used all natural tools to paint a picture in the sand of where we are. Your discussion of an anthropocentric view of nature versus a biocentric view made me think – I am not separate from, but am part of nature, too."

"As I sat there in the still of the night, gazing up at the stars, I sensed how I fit in a larger universe. My view of myself – who and what I am, how I am connected to the natural world – expanded."

My own perspective of the time I spent with my outfitted guests was forever changed. The term recreation meant more as I came to see how the wilderness experience could lead people to truly re-create their view of life. My efforts and those of my guides were giving people an opportunity to connect with nature, to find refuge from the challenges and burdens of modern life, to experience challenge and risk, build new skills and find a sense of community with their fellow travelers.

There were other times when my responsibility for the guests' safety and well-being were brought clearly into focus. My friend Craig Vetter described just such an event in an article he wrote for *Outside*

Phyllis on the Selway River

magazine about his trip with us on the Selway:

I awoke that night to a roaring wind in the trees and the popping of something like muffled shotgun blasts. It was about four or five. I got my headlamp and clothes on and crawled out into the dark. The rain had stopped, and the popping turned out to be a corner of the kitchen tarp, torn from its heavy rock anchor by the wind that was coming straight up the river in gusts of 50 to 60 miles an hour. I walked the 20 yards to the water. The boats were slapping against one another, but holding. Then, as I squatted for a drink, I heard a long, terrible cracking of wood up among the tents. There was a huge crash, then another. I froze. There was no question that the trees had fallen in our camp, maybe even across my tent, but I could see nothing beyond the limits of my narrow beam as it passed through a hundred trees, any one of which might have been next. I listened for screaming but heard only wind.

There was no more safety where I was than up among the tents, and I decided I'd better wake anyone who was still asleep, though raising an alarm seemed somehow futile. It was nearly unbelievable that we had run Ham rapid without incident, and then had tracked this night and this wind to this campsite so that these monstrous old trees could fall on us. But we had. There was a strange sort of resignation in the realization that there was nowhere to run, nothing to do but let the odds play themselves out.

I started back up the cobbles, and when I was almost among the trees, my light caught Scott, one of the boatmen, huddled against the river side of a healthy old cedar. I started to say something, but another cracking cut through the wind. Scott braced against the tree. I stood where I was. Then the crash, close, and to our right. We gave each other a big stupid look.

I heard voices and saw flashlight beams dancing crazily through the trees above us, near a spot where a man named Bill and this three grown sons had pitched their tents. As I came up on them, I heard Sam, a senior at Yale, say, "We heard it coming but we couldn't get the zipper open to get out. The branches slapped us through the tent fabric. I just sat there and shook for about 15 seconds."

His brother, Si, who'd been in the tent with him, was running his flashlight up and down the trunk of a 70-foot cedar that lay about 18 inches from their torn and leaning tent.

The wind died as if it had finished its business, and then the rain returned, a monsoon of a storm. All of us were forced back into our tents to wait it out, to sleep if we could. That morning we inspected the damage, including a 50-foot cedar that had missed Scott's tent by five feet. Around the breakfast fire, each of us told our piece into the story. At one point Si looked at me and said, Was that you who came running up just after that tree hit and asked, "Well....did it make any sound?" It turned out to have been a businessman from Cleveland named Eddie, who swore he'd had no idea how close the tree had come when he'd made the joke.[1]

It is easy to understand the massive challenge and risk my outfitted guests found from a falling tree narrowly missing them in camp. But I also found that what might seem small risks to me could be very real and sizable to my guests. On one of my earliest outfitted trips I took a sixty-three-year-old woman name Faye and her two grown daughters down the Middle Fork of the Salmon.

When she arrived in Stanley, Idaho, to begin the trip, Faye appeared slightly frail, but up to the challenge. She handled the rigors of river camping well. On the third night of the trip we camped at Shelf Camp, two miles from Loon Creek Hot Springs, a popular hiking destination for river travelers.

At four-thirty in the afternoon, after setting up camp, Faye approached me about accompanying the rest of the group on the hike to the springs.

"How far is it?" she queried.

"About a mile," I responded, then returned to my camp duties as she and her daughters left.

Two hours later she returned and pulled me aside. "You lied to me!" she angrily declared. "That hot springs was much farther, and you knew it! Why didn't you tell me it was two miles each way?"

"I knew what a special place the hot springs is and that the trail was good and level," I replied. "I was afraid if I said two miles, you

1 Craig Vetter, "The Selway Meditation," *Outside* magazine, April 1988

Middle Fork of the Salmon River,
Survey Camp

might not go, so I fibbed a little. Now that you've been, was it worth it?"

The anger faded from her face, replaced by recollections of the scenic hike along the creek, the warm, soothing waters of the spring – a special time and place she had shared with her daughters. My intent had been met — to allow the wilderness to challenge an aging urbanite, and have her sense the rewards of pushing beyond her preset notions of her limits – to succeed in risking the unknown.

I did not know until later how an event that seemed routine to me had become a special part of the lives of Faye and her daughters. My Christmas note to past guests had brought a return letter from one daughter requesting that I remove Faye from my mail list. She revealed that Faye's frailty on our trip was for a reason. She had cancer. Despite her illness she had wanted to make the trip with her daughters.

Since the trip the disease had run its course. The letter told of Faye's passing and expressed their thanks for the experience that I had allowed them to have with their mother in Idaho's wilderness. It was a memory their mother cherished, and that her daughters, and now I, will carry for the rest of our lives.

That extra mile, at Faye's age and experience, walking in the backcountry was a major challenge – to her. I had learned that it is easy for the fit, the young, the naturally adventurous to dismiss the importance of small departures to those who do not readily or often take them.

I can safely say that twenty-seven years of river outfitting has left me with less than a handful of negative experiences on trips, but the time many years back when my guides and I took two sisters and their husbands from Miami on the Middle Fork of the Salmon left a lasting impression.

Our first night's stop was Joe Bump Camp, a wooded flat tucked on the inside of a sharp bend in the upper river. As we set camp, erected tents for the guests, put out the kitchen gear, a sister stopped me and asked, "Where is the bathroom?"

"Through the trees there, down the trail, you will see it on your left," I replied.

Minutes later she returned and said she couldn't find it. All she had found was a two walled wooden structure, but no bathroom.

"Yes, that is it," I explained. "That outhouse is what passes for a bathroom here in the wilderness."

"I'm not going there!" she exclaimed.

"You don't understand. That is all we have."

"Hrrrrrummmmph," was her only reply as she turned and departed.

Shortly she returned, this time with her sister and the biggest can of disinfectant spray I had ever seen. Which they promptly used on the structure. One sister stood guard as the other finished their visit to what surely was a new low in their life's experience of toilet facilities.

The next morning we were preparing breakfast. The chill of mornings at that high elevation, even in July, had prompted the guides to build a warming fire. Several guests were gathered round, soaking in the heat, drinking coffee and reliving the day before. One of the sisters arrived with a bundle; a towel wrapped around contents unknown, and placed it on the fire.

Odd glances were exchanged among the crew, shrugs, what was this?

I eased over and asked the sister, "What are you burning?"

"Oh," she said, "those are just our clothes from yesterday."

"Clothes?"

"Yes, we decided we didn't want to take them back and wash them. We just brought enough to change every day."

Later in the morning the guides and guests completed the chores of breaking down camp, loading all gear and personal duffel into the boats. The last guide task was always to "walk the camp" searching for any items, even down to what we call micro-litter, that might have been left behind.

Leaving a pristine camp was a major component of every pre-trip orientation talk back in Stanley. We take out everything, leave nothing, even the tiniest piece of thread or paper. It is a source of pride, important to us, and important to the Forest Service ranger who issues our permits.

When I came to the opening in the brush where the two couples' tents had been I found the surrounding area littered with trash – cigarette butts, wrappers, washcloth, even used feminine products. It wasn't my idea of how to start the day, but I carefully gathered it all, wrapped it in the discarded washcloth, and approached the offending couple.

They angrily denied it, but the evidence was clear. I wondered what they had been doing during the orientation talk.

The next morning the guides were waiting by the breakfast fire and graciously offered to help the sisters with their problem. It turned out that in the bundle each day were new clothes, worn once. By the end of the six-day trip, each of the crew had laid claim to their share of new Polo shirts, shorts, even camp pillows.

Outfitters

For days the sisters avoided me, but confined to a small group in the midst of the wilderness, it could not last. Even the hardest cases cannot resist the magic of the canyon. By day five the two couples had come around and, who knows, may have learned something.

Outfitters view this process as the freeze, thaw, freeze cycle.[2] People coming from urban environments, their own lives and jobs, arrive with a frozen rigidity born from their own knowledge of how life works. Their routine is familiar.

In the wilds it all changes – abruptly. How do we get to the river? Where will we camp? What are our tent and sleeping arrangements like? When and what do we eat? How is it prepared? And, as the sisters asked, "Where is the toilet?"

Their home landscape, determined by structures, electricity, engines, and schedules is replaced by a landscape of mystery – to be revealed to them at a pace determined by flowing water. Their ability to alter the pace, to control, is limited to a basic human strength – their guide's and their own energy transferred from muscle, tendon and bone, through a paddle or oar to the fluid beneath us. This is the thaw period. The outfitted guests are open to learn, to forge a new understanding, influenced by new experiences, and with the help of a professional guide, find a different way of looking at the natural world.

Ellie, Faye and Faye's daughters were forever changed by their wilderness experience. By the end of their trip, even the sisters understood our approach to the wilderness resource. Hopefully the experience had a positive impact on them in the future.

My life as an outfitter was made possible, like Joe Zaunmiller's experience, by early days on my uncle's farm, in the woods with my father, and on rivers and outdoor excursions with friends. Like Joe, those skills lead me to Campbell's Ferry.

Phyllis' days independently roaming her family's California ranch and trips to the river with friends brought her, too. Frances' days in rural Texas helping raise a family and later as a willing student of Harry Donahue, Jim Moore, Bert Rhoades and Joe brought to her a competency essential to her life at the Ferry.

All of us found a connection, an appreciation of where we

2 I owe my friend Richard Clark, fellow outfitter and educator, for much of my understanding of our role as outfitters in wilderness.

were and how, like Ellie, we were part, not separate from it.

Frances spoke for us all when she wrote of the Idaho Primitive Area in one of her columns in the *Idaho County Free Press*:

Back in the days when the United States was a rich nation, there were men, both in and out of Washington who did not have a cataract in their mind's eye. They could see the time coming when a tree would not be a tree, but would be 'board feet' for the saw or pulp mill. They saw in the future when a creek would not be a place to cool tired feet, nor would a river be only for men to play with fishing gear. No, they saw the time when these United States would be so poor, that creeks and rivers would only be recognized as water power, and could not be used for playthings.

Those men were not blind, nor were they stupid. They knew that the souls of men need the stillness of forested mountains and canyons. So, after long deliberation and due process of law, the Primitive Area of Idaho came into being.

It is a place where trees grow that were not planted, and a man can walk and he is not trespassing. He can spend a day or a week or as long as he wants, soaking into his being the stillness of the mountains, that brings healing peace to man. He sees the creeks running free and clear, with fish in quiet pools. While he sits on the trunk of a fallen tree and eats his lunch, he looks at all that is around him, and his mind is not closed to understanding, but listens to the voice of the stillness that is the mountains. And he listens to the story of how the half-rotten tree trunk he is using for both chair and table came to be there, at the edge of the clearing.

No, the trees are not planted in the Primitive Area, yet they grow, as the tiny little one, so small you'd think something would step on it and it would be crushed. But it has a toughness not dreamed of in nursery rows, and it will grow, each year lighting its candles to the Spring. Until the time when the tree, too, will be a monarch of the mountains, tall and straight with slender strength, asking only for its top in the sun while the rich brown dirt covers its feet. And it still grows, offering shelter from sun and storm to both two and four-legged people, and to the ones that fly and wear feathers.

The tree only grows, and asks nothing until a summer storm comes over the ridges from the high peaks and crags. Then it bows its head and prays, even as you and I:

Let not the thunder notice me and call my name, for then the lightning will find my place and use my length as a path for its journey to its marriage with earth.

Let not the wind twist my branches, for should they break and fall to earth , the nest that they shelter will be broken.

Let not the wind and rain come together, else the dirt will be washed from my roots and the wind will bend my body, and I will fall to earth no longer a tree.

Let me pass safely through this storm, as though those in the past, so that I might give shade and shelter as I have done in the past.

And the man sitting on the trunk of a fallen tree, sees the nest of a grouse in the tangled branches. He hears the squeak of a mouse that has built its home in the dry needles. And a chipmunk comes from somewhere and tells him the local gossip.

And the man takes that part of the stillness, that has soaked into his being with him, even out of the mountains.

No, it was not a wasteful United States that set aside the Primitive Area of yesterday and today and tomorrow. Even as the belly needs meat and bread, so does the soul of man need a quiet place apart from cities and people, where he can reach an understanding with his inner being.

It is for this that they made a Primitive Area. A gift for you and to your son who is not yet born, to play in and keep for all time, yours.

Chapter Twenty-Three

Wild Lands

"To the pioneer of history the wilderness was a foe to be conquered, so that he might make farms and pastures out of the endless forests. Today's pioneer has a new purpose – to preserve some remnants of that wilderness from the onrush of modern civilization. The ax and the plow will not serve us in this struggle. Today's instruments are more subtle. They are progressive law and informed public opinion – demanding that we maintain our wilderness birthright."
– President Lyndon B. Johnson, 1966

The Idaho Primitive Area so eloquently written about by Frances is a name formally given to the vast wild lands surrounding Campbell's Ferry in 1931. Creating primitive areas was the third step in an evolving public lands designation process that began with the term forest reserves in 1892, followed by national forests in 1905. The process for the lands around the Ferry would not reach its zenith until 1980.

The motivation to create sanctuaries of wild lands came from those who saw and experienced them – those who had developed a personal understanding of what was at stake, of what would be lost should the growing industrialization and modernization of the outside world continue to the point where none was left. Among the visionaries were naturalist John Muir, foresters Gifford Pinchot and Aldo Leopold, sportsman Teddy Roosevelt, and oddly, often leaders and benefactors of the industries posing a significant threat.

The industrialists who advocated wild land preservation were men who came to see that the stake was nature itself and the wildlife it supported. Judging by their story, it is clear that forces similar to those affecting Ellie, the opportunity to expand one's soul, also touched these men.

The Idaho Primitive Area idea began on trips into the same areas early prospectors had taken en route to Thunder Mountain.[1] The organizer of the trips was Harry Shellworth, an executive of the Boise Payette Lumber Company. Shellworth was commonly known as a representative of the Weyerhaeuser interests in Idaho. He was born in Texas in 1877, but moved to Idaho with his merchant father. As a young man Shellworth joined the Idaho Volunteers, sharing the Spanish-America War mission to the Philippines with our Warren Cook.[2]

Shellworth traveled the Orient after the war and came back to Idaho in 1905 to marry and work in the timber business with the company that in 1957 became Boise Cascade Corporation. His work took him into many of the forested areas of the state. He utilized knowledge gained traveling and inspecting the forests to become a guide, an arranger, a general stage manager for backcountry trips with friends and business associates. He was doing what we now call outfitting and using the trips as a way to build lasting relationships with the men of power he invited to go with him.

These trips were a factor in Shellworth becoming influential in Republican politics. In 1927, one of the more than twenty such trips he made to the Big Creek area included prominent Eastern businessmen, Idaho's Governor Baldridge, Kellogg, Idaho mining executive Stanly Easton, and District Forester Richard Rutledge from Ogden, Utah. These long-term friends, Republicans all, might at first glance be suspected of being on a reconnaissance mission for future exploit-

1 Dennis Baird and Lynn Baird, "A Campfire Vision: Establishing the Idaho Primitive Area," *Journal of the West*, Vol XXVI, No. 3, July 1987, p. 50
2 Baird and Baird, p. 53

ing activities. Had their inclination been so, what better mix of financial and political savvy and means could be brought to the task? But in this case, the magic of the wilds would trump their drive for the dollar.

A favorite campsite for the group's hunting sojourns was the cabin and homestead of *Cougar* Dave Lewis. Lewis, a former packer and scout for the cavalry on their 1879 military expeditions chasing the Sheepeater Indians in the area, had settled a flat on Big Creek just downstream from Cabin Creek, the homestead of the Caswell brothers of Thunder Mountain fame. Today Dave Lewis' place is known as the Taylor Ranch, a wilderness research station for the University of Idaho.

Harry Shellworth later wrote of the group's discussions on their trips, "Many times during this trip the topic of our evening's talk around the camp fire was the question of whether or not this Middle Fork Salmon River country, or at least that portion which is the natural winter range of game, should or should not become either a game preserve or a primitive area."[3]

The stage for the Shellworth hunting party discussions had been set by men working for the Forest Service – such as Bob Marshall, Aldo Leopold, Arthur Carhart and others. What these men were pushing for, what was needed at the time, was a vessel, a regulatory structure, a legal means to define their preservation ideals in a clear management direction for employees of the agency. The answer came in Forest Service Regulation L-20, an oddly bureaucratic moniker for a document of such importance.

In March of 1929 Forest Service Chief Robert Y. Stuart wrote a letter to his district foresters stating, "the economic desirability of preserving conditions capable of furnishing unique forms of outdoor recreation, which contribute directly and in marked degree to the maintenance of high mental and physical standards, is obvious." He spoke of the obligation of the agency to create research reserves and primitive areas, which would be, "primarily inspirational, educational and recreational, and maintain, primitive conditions of travel, habitation, subsistence and environment, conditions that would vary, sometimes that of the Indian, or in other cases the early fur trader or trapper, or the pioneer miner, or the pioneer stockman or settler, or the

---

3 Baird and Baird, p. 50

logger."[4]

The following August Chief Stuart's proposals were formalized in Regulation L-20 and approved as an amendment to the Forest Service Manual, thereby creating the category of land designation to be known as primitive area. The stated purpose of the areas was, "To prevent the unnecessary elimination of [or] impairment of unique natural values, and to conserve, so far as controlling economic considerations will permit, the opportunity to the public to observe the conditions which existed in the pioneer phases of the Nation's development, and to engage in the forms of outdoor recreation characteristic of that period; thus aiding to preserve national traditions, ideals and characteristics, and promoting a truer understanding of historical phases of national progress."[5]

Other forces in support of the preservation idea were at work as well. Teddy Roosevelt, Jr. and his fellow sportsmen at the Boone and Crockett Club pressed President Calvin Coolidge for a definite national policy on recreation. President Coolidge established a National Conference on Outdoor Recreation that met in Washington in 1924 and continued work until 1929. The conference called for a study, later published by the American Forestry Association and the National Park Association, that identified vast stretches of land as prime candidates for preservation. The largest contiguous such area was the lands around Campbell's Ferry. The organizations put pressure on the Forest Service to act.

Regional Forester Rutledge also heard from others with personal knowledge of the subject, men who, like him, had stared into the magic of a backcountry campfire and dreamed of how the experience could be saved for future generations. One, Frederick Ransom, an orchard owner from Clarkston, Washington, was a frequent writer to government officials promoting his, "idea of saving a part of this central Idaho for the propagation of its many fine species of wild life."[6] Robert Bailey, the man who had earlier made a trip through the area using William Campbell's ferry and the Three Blaze Trail (see Chapter Eight) was also an advocate.

4   Baird and Baird, p. 50
5   Gerald W. Williams, *The Forest Service: Fighting for Public Lands*, (Westport, CT: Greenwood Press, 2007), p. 23
6   Baird and Baird, p. 54

Outfitter J. P. Boyle also wrote in support. Boyle was born in 1867, the son of a Pennsylvania steel mill worker. He traveled west to work in the mining industry, first in Utah, then in Custer, Idaho, at the head of Salmon River's Yankee Fork. Boyle found good prospects near Custer and in 1920 he was renting a home in Santa Monica, California, working as a mine promoter.

Perhaps Boyle, like others, had found the best way to make money mining was to mine wealthy Southern Californians, selling them stock in his latest prospect. By 1930 Boyle was back in Stanley and had started an outfitting business. Just to the west over the hill from Boyle's mine at Custer was Loon Creek, a tributary of the Middle Fork of the Salmon. This part of the Salmon watershed was a prime candidate for inclusion in the primitive area. Boyle was at the end of the road and wanted it to go no farther.

Remarkably this idea to set aside a vast stretch of central Idaho was gaining strength in the midst of very challenging economic times. The Great Depression was in full swing and one would think it was a time when little thought would be given to restricting commercial natural resource activity. But this was an idea being promoted by the upper end of the economic scale. These were men who could sustain a downturn in business. They could set aside any economic concerns when it came to preserving their opportunity to pursue hunting jaunts into the wild. They could listen to their heart and nurture dreams of preserving future opportunities for them and their offspring to connect with nature.

The tipping point in turning a campfire idea into reality came from a contact with Idaho's Senator William Borah. Augustine Davis, a wealthy southern businessman who fell in love with the Idaho wilderness during a fall outfitted hunting trip into the Middle Fork, wrote the senator and asked what was being done to protect the country. Senator Borah contacted the Idaho Chamber of Commerce for assistance in answering the inquiry and the Chamber's president turned to Harry Shellworth for help.

The response Shellworth drafted for the Senator, along with supporting reports Regional Forester Rutledge collected from the Challis, Salmon, Idaho and Payette national forests, ended up on Governor Baldridge's desk. In the fall of 1930 the Governor asked his hunting pal Shellworth to help line up a group of their Republican friends to form the Governor's Committee on the proposed primitive area.

Since the committee was hand-picked by the Governor and Shellworth, it is no surprise that the final report was supportive of establishing a primitive area. When the local paper made the whole process public, it generated mixed responses. But there were not enough negatives among them to derail the carefully orchestrated process created to implement the plan hatched around Cougar Dave's campfire.

In January 1931, Rutledge sent the supporting documents, along with expressions of support by two sportsmen clubs and the Chamber of Commerce to Chief Forester Robert Y. Stuart. After some minor adjustments, Chief Stuart signed the final Idaho Primitive Area Report on March 17, 1931. The report set the goal for an area that would be the largest by far of those established under the L-20 regulation, "To make it possible for people to detach themselves, at least temporarily, from the strains and turmoil of modern existence, and to revert to simple types of existence in conditions of relatively unmodified nature [and] to afford unique opportunities for physical, mental, and spiritual recreation and regeneration."[7]

By creating the regulatory framework for protecting wild lands in primitive areas, the Forest Service was attempting to resolve a major conundrum for federal land management agencies. It is clear from the proceedings of the National Conference on Outdoor Recreation that at the time neither the Forest Service nor the National Park Service had clear notions about how to deal with completely unimproved areas.[8]

The Park Service was under increasing pressure from the automobile and mass recreation; the Forest Service was commodity oriented and reluctant to make irreversible decisions that would prevent future generations from drawing upon needed resources.

Despite that reluctance, the Forest Service, starting with the actions creating the Idaho Primitive Area and others, began a course of administrative action through forest plans that gradually protected millions of acres of wild lands. These were important steps in establishing a core – a core that would one day become the seed for a na-

<hr>

7 Baird and Baird, p. 56

8 Harold K. Steen, *The U.S. Forest Service, A History,* (Seattle, WA: University of Washington Press, 1976), p. 156

tionwide wilderness preservation system exceeding one hundred million acres. But it would take thirty-five years for Congress to take the legislative action needed to create the system. In the meantime, it was up to other advocates to push for more additions to primitive areas and to expand existing ones.

No one was more effective than Robert Marshall. Bob Marshall was born into wealth in 1901, the son of a successful New York City attorney. Marshall's father, Louis, had argued several cases before the U.S. Supreme Court. Louis Marshall helped lead a fight for wilderness in the Adirondack Mountains of upstate New York and instilled in his children a passion for wild places.

Bob's education included a degree from the New York State College of Forestry at Syracuse, a master's degree at the Harvard Forestry School and a Ph.D. in plant physiology from Johns Hopkins University. From 1925 to 1929, between Marshall's masters and Ph.D. he worked at the Priest River Experiment Station in northern Idaho as a Junior Forester for the Forest Service. His winters were spent in Missoula, Montana.

To say that Marshall spent time *in* a station or Forest Service office is somewhat inaccurate. He hated being indoors and often used his prodigious capacity for hiking to cover tens of miles of forests and mountains in a day.

While at Priest River Marshall wrote home to describe one day, "This dandy walk was 38 miles in length, so, of course, after a light supper I took a 2 miles stroll to make the 15th 40 mile day of my life. As a result of this day's activities, I have now enjoyed 30-mile days in 15 states."[9] Marshall was twenty-four years old at the time of this report, and during the next four years in Idaho and Montana he would add extensively to his hiking accomplishments exploring what we now call the Selway – Bitterroot and Frank Church – River of No Return Wilderness areas. His first hand knowledge of Idaho's wild lands made him a fierce and effective advocate for the protected areas we cherish today.

****

9 AnneMarie Moore and Dennis Baird, *Wild Places Preserved: The Story of Bob Marshall in Idaho*, (Moscow, ID: University of Idaho Northwest Historical Manuscript Series, 2009), p. 7

In 1932 the head of the Branch of Research for the Forest Service asked Bob Marshall to come to Washington, D.C., and produce the forest recreation section of A National Plan for American Forestry, later to be known as the Copeland Report. Marshall's efforts on the report allowed him to locate and map remaining roadless segments of the national forests. He would use his knowledge to advocate expansion of acres included in the primitive area classification, and to campaign against shrinkage of existing areas. Marshall realized that the biggest threat, the surest way to rob an area of its primitive nature was to build a road through it. And he knew that Forest Service managers often advocated construction of *protection roads*, sometimes called *truck trails* to aid in fire fighting efforts.

One such road had been identified two years earlier in the report from the Idaho Governor's Committee on the Proposed Primitive Area – "The State Highway Department had a survey by aerial photography made down the main Salmon River from Salmon City to Riggins last summer to determine the practicability and feasibility of a highway down this route. Such a road would follow the north boundary of this tract [The Idaho Primitive Area]. No interference with such a project is contemplated."[10] Depending upon the final engineering recommendations, the proposed road would have run across the flat that is now Campbell's Ferry or on the opposite side of the river through the Jim Moore Place.

In 1932 Marshall wrote the Deputy Chief of the Forest Service and drew the battle lines in what became an eight-year disagreement over the Salmon River Road. Marshall's argument was that there were not many opportunities for really large areas to be preserved. And among the few he recommended for, "a substantial increase in size was the primitive area in central Idaho. If this area were set aside, Marshall wrote, it would necessitate the abandonment of plans for the construction of the proposed road down the Salmon River between Regions 1 and 4."[11]

Marshall's letter brought a quick response from the local forest supervisors, the same ones who had earlier responded to Regional

10 R. H. Rutledge and H. C. Shellworth, Governor's Committee on the Proposed Primitive Area, 20 December 1930
11 Moore and Baird, p. 68

Forester Rutledge's request that they drum up support for the initial primitive area. They reminded their superiors that promises and assurances had been made, and now the local managers feared being accused of "double crossing and worse." The Supervisors were perceptive. Mining interests, the mayor and Chamber of Commerce in Salmon and others felt betrayed and raised a public outcry.

There were powerful natural realities on Marshall's side. The geologic forces that had shaped the canyon had left profoundly difficult challenges for anyone trying to build a road through it. The very characteristics that gave the canyon its rugged beauty, the canyon's steep walls of solid granite, were a nightmare to road engineers. But this was a nation that decades before had dug a canal across the Isthmus of Panama. And in 1932 the Forest Service had been given a large, youthful workforce, the CCC.

It was unrealistic to think that Idaho state road funds, even federal highway funds, could tackle a project of this scope in such a rural area, but the agency had a lot of youthful energy to focus on the task. The effort was begun to build what today would be called a road to nowhere.

The Forest Service, as is often the case, had varying opinions on the project, depending upon whom you asked. Region 1 forester from Missoula wrote the chief, "The Salmon River Road can be built only at a tremendous outlay of cash and physical effort to overcome the transportation difficulties in the distribution of camps and supplies. I do not believe that the Army would consider the undertaking as at all feasible…. Unless the canyon is literally stuffed with companies, little will be accomplished on that gigantic undertaking. I do not believe that the taxpayers should be assessed to conduct that sort of undertaking. Better by far feed the men at home and save money…."[12]

Region 4 forester from Ogden hedged his position stating that while the region had never supported a road through the canyon from Shoup to Riggins, it did note, "A truck trail is being built down Big Creek and it is proposed to build a truck trail down the Salmon River to the mouth of Big Creek. By such a truck trail one could get supplies, equipment and men for fire purposes to the mouth of Big Creek materially quicker than it would be possible to do so by the Big Creek trail. This truck trail would also be of considerable importance

12 Moore and Baird, p. 73

for recreation…. It would also have some importance for the mining industry…."[13] The Big Creek referenced here is what we now call Panther Creek, a tributary of the Main Salmon, not the Big Creek that is a tributary of the Middle Fork.

A 1933 edition of the *Idaho County Free Press* quoted an *Oregonian* article, "For many years men have dreamed of putting a railroad or a highway between these massive walls, which rise a sheer 1,000' in places, and let the wide world look in to see what a wealth of minerals, timber, sports and scenic grandeur Idaho is hoarding in that untamed wilderness."[14]

Idaho's Governor Ross made a different argument, "In the face of the present serious unemployment situation, if the Salmon River highway were built and not a car ever traveled over it, it would be worth while as a means to relieve the present situation." For a while, that perspective helped carry the day. It was the CCC, its seemingly limitless supply of men and its budget, that was the primary movers in keeping the road construction moving.

The CCC crews were pushing downstream from Salmon past Shoup and the mouth of the Middle Fork, and upstream from Riggins toward French Creek. Weather played a factor in support of the road project. Of the fifty-three CCC camps in Idaho, many were at higher elevations. Just as the canyon bottoms had been a better place for William Campbell's garden, they were now a place to continue CCC work away from the deep snows and harsh winter conditions of the higher camps.

In 1933 Bob Marshall left the Forest Service for a new job as head of grazing and forestry at the Bureau of Indian Affairs. The position kept him in Washington, D.C., where he utilized contacts with leaders in the federal land management agencies to continue his push for preservation of wild areas. Marshall often using the threat of a road through Idaho's Salmon River Canyon as an example of why time was of the essence. In one letter to a high official in the Department of the Interior he noted, "The largest forest wilderness in the country, embracing 3,300,000 acres in central Idaho, is in imminent danger of being cut in two by the proposed road up the Salmon River."[15]

---

13   Moore and Baird, p. 71
14   Moore and Baird, p. 76
15   Moore and Baird, p. 83

Marshall's voice of alarm was joined by Elers Koch of the Forest Service who faulted agency fire fighting activity in the Bitterroots for its role in destroying wild lands:

The Lolo Trail is no more. The bulldozer blade has ripped out the hoof tracks of Chief Joseph's ponies. The trail was worn deep by centuries of Nezperce and Blackfeet Indians, by Lewis and Clark, by companies of Northwest Company fur trader, by General Howard's cavalry horses, by Captain Mullan, the engineer, and by the early-day forest ranger. It is gone, and in its place there is only the print of automobile tire in the dust....

The Forest Service sounded the note of progress. It opened up the wilderness with roads and telephone lines, and airplane landing fields. It capped the mountain peaks with white-painted lookout houses, laced the ridges and streams with a network of trails and telephone lines, and poured in thousands of fire-fighters year after year in a vain attempt to control forest fires.

Has all this effort and expenditure of millions of dollars added anything to the human good? Is it possible that it was all a ghastly mistake like plowing up the good buffalo grass sod of the dry prairies? Has the country as it stands now as much human value as it had in the nineties when Major Fenn's forest rangers first rode into it?[16]

Ironically this call questioning the value of the Forest Service fire-fighting effort was being sounded at the same time the agency was settling on the 10:00 A.M. policy. The policy had brought the building of depots to support thousands of mules, men and trucks available at a moments notice to rush to a point as close as possible to the fire. This put pressure to build more roads to make more forested areas quickly accessible by truck. And pressure was also coming from the air. In 1940 the first smoke jump from a Travel Air was on Marten Creek, a tributary of the Selway River, leading to a post World War II buildup of smokejumper bases and assets that continue to support that role today.

In 1935 Bob Marshall and a few friends took the fight to pre-

16 Elers Koch, "The Passing of the Lolo Trail," *Journal of Forestry*, 1935, Volume 33, 1935, pp. 99–105

serve wild lands outside the agency to the general public when they founded the Wilderness Society. The organization had wilderness preservation as its only goal. The first issue of the organization's publication, *Living Wilderness*, included an article discussing the threat to wilderness posed by road construction on public lands using CCC labor for the effort. That same year Marshall had a critical meeting in D.C. with four regional foresters, including Rutledge who had personal knowledge of the Idaho Primitive Area. The notes from that meeting contain a section specific to the Salmon River Canyon Road:

Salmon River Canyon – At the present time the Forest Service is building forest development roads on both the east and west ends of the Salmon River Canyon, using CCC camps for that purpose. At the present rate of progress it will be approximately ten years, according to Rutledge, before the west-end project approaches the west boundary of the present primitive area, approximately four to five years before the east-end project approaches the east boundary of the primitive area. He expressed doubt whether the entire project through the canyon will be constructed during one's lifetime. Emphasis was laid on the fact that the Salmon River Canyon constitutes the one possible route in a north and south distance of 200 miles or more through which a water grade road can be constructed from eastern to western Idaho; which circumstance makes the construction of such a road more or less inevitable in course of time. If that is true, advantage might be taken of the present opportunity to build a part of the project. Rutledge stated that he could not make any compromise on this position as it was one of major importance and involves certain political considerations.

Marshall's position was that the Salmon River Canyon is the last wooded river canyon accessible only by water. Because of that fact he believes that the entire canyon be maintained in a primitive condition and free from roads.

By 1936 the road had been completed from Salmon, past North Fork and the mining settlement known as Shoup, downstream to the point where the Middle Fork of the Salmon enters the Main Salmon. Several Idaho politicians visited the site to support the project and at the urging of the Salmon Chamber of Commerce, pressed the Forest

Service to continue the work.

Idaho Congressman White was among those pushing the effort. He wrote the agency and heard back from the acting chief of the Forest Service who explained that the work force for such projects had begun to diminish. President Roosevelt had begun a gradual reduction in the 2,158 CCC camps.

Nonetheless, the chief assured the congressman that among the plans for that year was the construction of the Mallard Creek Road from the CCC camp at Red River to the Salmon River at what we now call Whitewater Ranch. In what appears to be an attempt to keep the Congressman's hopes for the larger road project alive, Chief Rachford noted, "This would seem to be an advantageous location for setting up a road base from which construction work in both directions along the Salmon River can be carried on."[17]

Another road was being built from Dixie down into the canyon, reaching the river near the mouth of the South Fork of the Salmon River, the location we know today as Mackay Bar. The large flat on the north bank of the river was seen as a potential site for another CCC camp. Located seventeen miles downstream of the Mallard Creek Road, it was planned as a base from which crews could work up and downstream.

The master plan was in place. Crews would push into the canyon from the Salmon end upstream, the Riggins end downstream and from two interim points at Mallard Creek and the South Fork. The battle to implement the plan continued.

It almost seems as though a "giveth and taketh away" strategy was being pursued by the Forest Service. While continuing the road work, the agency also expanded areas protected under the new primitive area designation. In July of 1936 the 1,870,000-acre Selway-Bitterroot Primitive Area was created. And 145,000 acres were added to the Idaho Primitive Area, primarily in the Pistol Creek and Indian Creek tributaries of the Middle Fork.

The new Selway-Bitterroot Primitive Area had its own road building issues. Proposals existed at the time to extend a road from Selway Falls on the Selway River up to the mouth of Moose Creek, from Paradise Guard Station on the upper river down to the mouth of Bear Creek, and also an extension of the Horse Creek Road east of the

17 Moore and Baird, p. 107

Bitterroot divide over the top and west into Bear Creek.

To the everlasting relief of current and future generations of wild river boaters and wilderness advocates, none of these plans ever became reality.

In 1937 Bob Marshall went back to work for the Forest Service D.C. office as head of the Division of Recreation and Lands where he remained until his death in November of 1939. Marshall used the time to continue to advocate expansion of primitive areas and to improve the regulatory support for their preservation in Forest Service policy. He proposed another expansion of the Idaho Primitive Area, this time by an additional 411,520 acres.

Region 4 was not totally opposed to the expansion, but cautioned that due to local sentiment, it was necessary to proceed cautiously. The region had identified 50,000 acres around Thunder Mountain and locations of mining activity in Big Creek they felt should be removed from the existing Primitive Area. They agreed to suspend road construction in Marshall's proposed addition. It appeared the region and Marshall were coming to an understanding that at some appropriate future date, a compromise based on those figures might be reached, but all knew of local resistance to any expansion.

The *Lewiston Morning Tribune* reflected local opinion when it took editorial note of Marshall's activities, "In the eastern mind, however, we are despoilers, anxious only to lay waste and exploit all of our natural resources, and their remedy is to lock up the forests as we would rare objects in a museum, rather than to use them wisely for the benefit of all people. It is unfortunate, because we have enough difficulty as it is without interference of meddlesome busybodies..."

In the end, forces far from Idaho would determine the ultimate status of the Salmon River Road. In 1939 President Roosevelt sensed the approaching war and began to downsize the CCC. In December of 1941 when the Japanese attacked Pearl Harbor it was just a matter of months before all the funding and manpower for the project were diverted to the war effort.

The final status of the upstream segment of the road was an ending four miles below the mouth of the Middle Fork, a campground and boat launch ramp known today as Corn Creek – forty-two river miles upriver from Campbell's Ferry (Map 7). At the lower end of the canyon the road comes up from Riggins to a boat ramp at Vinegar

Creek – thirty-seven river miles downriver from Campbell's Ferry. The Mallard Creek Road reaches the river four miles above the Ferry. The Dixie to Mackay Bar Road reaches the river thirteen miles downstream.

After the war, the status of the wild lands and river canyon surrounding Campbell's Ferry was in the hands of the Forest Service. But those who cherished wild lands did not trust leaving their ultimate disposition and preservation at the whim of agency managers.

****

After WWII fuel rationing ended and automobiles became readily available. The economy boomed, triggering a swell of home building and travel. The homes needed lumber and the Forest Service responded to the surge in demand by increasing the harvest on the national forests from 3.3 billion board feet in 1945 to almost 12 billion board feet by 1970. The agency also expanded their road-building program to facilitate access to the forests.

Fortunately the Salmon River Road was no longer part of the agency road program – it was too much cost for too little return. But the pressure on all wild lands continued to build. As a result virtually every review of primitive area and wilderness boundaries during this period included proposals to reduce them to accommodate the demand for forest products.

Viewed from Campbell's Ferry, the pressure of growing encroachment on their canyon Eden brought mixed feelings for Joe and Frances. They loved the solitude and wildlife supported by their natural surroundings, but the couple had to make a living. Joe had been the first to find a way to sustain a living at the Ferry. He had succeeded with a mix of work for the Forest Service, occasional sales of livestock and a growing outfitting business. But there were challenges.

Joe's Forest Service work was intermittent, reliant on agency budgets and plans – some years the agency needed contract help and had the budget to pay for it. Often it didn't.

Sale of livestock as a revenue source was marginally viable due to the distance to market, limited ground available to raise winter feed, and restricted access to public range. For outfitting Joe and Frances needed access for their hunting operations, but too much could destroy the very experience the couple was offering the outfitted public.

Since William Campbell had helped build a trail into the canyon from Dixie, access to the Ferry for supplies and outfitted clients had been a day-long thirteen-mile pack trip. The Mallard Creek Road had begun to change that. Supplies and people could be transported via truck and car to the river for a shorter pack or float to the Ferry. But if Joe could do it, so could any member of the public that wanted to access the beauty and wildlife of the canyon. The couple began to see more visitors to the area and use of the ferry to cross the river saw a mini-boom.

The river itself was also becoming a more viable access route. Just as Joe was finding success taking the public into the wild via horseback, others began to use boats to haul people down the river for hire. Among the first were Clyde Smith and his son Don. Their first descent had been in 1930 and for years afterward the Smiths ran trips as Guleke had done, moving material and supplies through the canyon in wooden scows.[18]

In 1943 the Smiths began outfitting, taking the Frederic Christian motion picture group down the river using carrier pigeons to send messages back to Salmon. The following year the Smiths contracted to guide the Army Corps of Engineers to inspect possible dam sites. A second two-and-a-half month follow-up trip was made with the Corps in 1945. On the second trip the Smiths used a power boat to shuttle the surveyors and supplies up and back as they hopscotched to survey sites, in effect running the entire river both up and back one small stretch at a time.

In July of 1947 Glenn Wooldridge of Grants Pass, Oregon showed up in Riggins with a twenty-two-foot plywood boat powered by a thirty-five horsepower Evinrude outboard motor. Wooldridge and two friends announced to the astonished locals gathered on the river bank that they planned to power up the river. They carried their personal duffel, groceries, four hundred pounds of gasoline, oil and a spare twenty-two horsepower motor on the trip.

Five days later Woolridge proved all the local naysayers wrong when he showed up in Salmon. We can imagine Joe and Frances hearing the odd sounds of a motor on the river, walking to the bank and

18 Johnny Carey and Cort Conley, *River of No Return,* (Cambridge, Idaho: Backeddy Books, 1977), pp. 54-59

scratching their heads as they watched the boat do what no one had ever done. The title *River of No Return* lost a little of its luster that day.[19]

Another type of watercraft also began to show up in increasing numbers. During the war effort the military had contracted construction of thousands of rubber rafts. Now these same boats were available as war surplus to anyone who wanted to try their hand at river travel.

The inflatable rubber boats made for an easier entry into what had once been a highly skilled endeavor. Cap Guleke and Monroe Hancock were among the few who had mastered the intricate skills necessary to steer wooden craft among the perils of river rapids. The newcomers found that an inflatable was more forgiving, bouncing off the same rocks that meant sure disaster to the wooden hulls piloted by the old timers. Operating inflatable rafts was still a significant challenge, but the game had changed forever.

In 1936 Bus Hatch, Frank Swain, Royce Mowrey and Alton Hatch, all from Utah, pioneered a run down the Middle Fork of the Salmon rowing fourteen-foot wooden boats. On reaching the Main River, they *turned the corner* and kept going all the way to Riggins. The Hatch family later changed over to the war surplus inflatables and became pioneers of the western whitewater rafting industry from the Colorado River in the Grand Canyon to Idaho's Salmon River.

In 1940 Prince Helfrich from Oregon ran the Middle Fork of the Salmon for the first time in McKenzie boats. He returned after the war and began a tradition on Idaho rivers continued by three sons, grandsons, and today a great-granddaughter.

These were the days when all you had to do to be an outfitter was just show up. If you wanted to float a river, you did. No permission was needed. Hunting outfitters like Joe Zaunmiller faced the first controls – primarily fish and game laws restricting when and where they could go. Later, as river traffic grew, float outfitters would face restrictions, too.

As the number of people turning to outfitting as an occupation grew, the need to regulate them became evident to both state and federal officials. And as the regulatory environment grew, outfitters saw a need to meet, organize and pursue dealing with the growing regula-

19 Carrey and Conley, pp. 54–59

tory challenges in a more professional manner.

Greatest among those challenges was determining how outfitters fit into the nation's evolving efforts to preserve and protect the very lifeblood of their existence – the clean, free-flowing streams and quality wildlife habitat of wild places like central Idaho.

Chapter Twenty-Four

Wilderness

"In the final analysis, wilderness is preserved not by a law engrossed on parchment but by the people themselves. Because the American people so strongly value these wild places, sharing a sense of duty to pass them unimpaired to future generations, we have a strong wilderness program backed by a strong law. Because Americans have an inborn love of their land – of their 'purple mountains majesties' – we can have confidence that wilderness will remain a part of America's long future."
The Enduring Wilderness
– Doug Scott

Outfitters come to their profession from a variety of backgrounds. Often their motivation is twofold – to find a way to make a living in the natural world they love and to escape the structure and restraints of work in an increasingly urban and industrial world. Howard W. (Bill) Guth was such a man.

Bill had learned the sheet metal trade as a youth and used it in various mining and construction jobs. During the Depression he found work at a placer mining operation on the headwaters of the Boise River near Atlanta, Idaho. Bill's job was to kill enough deer and elk to keep the miners fed. While in Atlanta he met Doris Larson of Gooding, Idaho, whom he married in 1936.[1] The marriage produced two sons, Norm and Billy, who would grow up to become icons of Idaho outfitting and have an enduring impact on the industry and the disposition of the wild lands on which it was based.

Bill later found work at the Rio Tinto copper mine near Elko, Nevada, where he was president of the miners union. "He was always in the middle of things," recalled his son, Norm. "He led all the miners out on strike once. I can remember him going back to Washington, D.C., to sit on a reconciliation panel." Political activism is a trait Bill would pass on to his oldest son.

With the onset of World War II the family moved to Bellevue, Washington where Bill used his sheet metal skills in the shipyard. In 1942 he developed medical problems with ulcers and the military released him. Bill had a brother-in-law living in the small, high mountain community of Stanley and as Norm relates, "My uncle convinced my dad that he could become an overnight millionaire in the dude business. Dad had been making good money in the shipyard and came to Idaho with $9,000 in cash. He bought a pack string – a dozen mules and a dozen horses. He had never been on a horse in his life, but my dad could do anything he put his mind to. My uncle was supposed to provide the knowhow and Dad was going to provide the money. My uncle soon found out how much work outfitting was. He didn't even make the first year."

Stanley, perched astride the headwaters of the Salmon River, had a population of 158 persons in 1940 (population sixty-three in 2010). At 6,253', the small community is surrounded by the majestic Sawtooth Mountain Range to the west, the Boulder White Cloud Range to the east and the newly created Idaho Primitive Area to the north. Dozens of nine and ten thousand foot plus peaks and high mountain lakes dot the area giving it the feel of an American version of the Swiss Alps. Stanley's high elevation setting in a bowl surrounded by mountains often produces brutally cold winters — the record low is

---

1 Norm and Kay Guth, Personal Communication, 4 April 2012

minus fifty-four. Nevertheless, a more idyllic setting to raise two boys with backcountry savvy cannot be imagined.

Bill Guth's outfitting business was a summer and fall operation. Each summer he organized two and three week pack trips into the high country – traversing the Sawtooth Range providing his clients' access to the golden, rainbow and cutthroat trout in the streams and lakes. Guth also purchased a property in the Seafoam Mine area north of Stanley where he built cabins and corrals to serve as a base for fall hunting expeditions into the nearby Idaho Primitive Area. From Seafoam Guth would pack hunters into the Middle Fork of the Salmon River country, introducing his sons to the area through seasonal fall trips in the vast Middle Fork watershed as far north as Chamberlain Basin.

As is normal in the early years of building an outfitting business, Bill found he needed to supplement his family income with regular work in the winter. He hired on with Bechtel Corporation who had a contract working on the development of nuclear power at the National Reactor Testing Station near Arco, Idaho. Arco is a small town to the south of the central Idaho mountains on the edge of the Snake River Plain. In 1955 Arco would become the first community in the world to be lit by nuclear generated electrical power.

Two boys growing up in Stanley in an outfitting family could acquire a Ph.D. in the ways of the natural world, but formal book learning was a bigger challenge. Norm Guth described his early school experience, "I spent eight years of grammar school in Stanley, Idaho. When I graduated from the eighth grade I was the valedictorian. That tells you there was only one student in the eighth grade in Stanley, me."

In 1953 Bill Guth bought the Middle Fork Lodge with other partners and moved his young family into the Idaho Primitive Area. They acquired the property from Tom and Nell McCall. The homestead had been settled in the late 1800s as a trappers cabin, and the McCalls turned it into a residence and guest ranch. They used the natural resources at hand to fashion one of the many homesteaded properties in the primitive area that evolved into access points, bases from which people could use the millions of acres of surrounding wilderness. McCall diverted water from Thomas Creek to irrigate hay fields. He also used the water to turn a small wheel to generate electric power. A natural hot springs on the property was piped into the buildings for heat. A small sawmill cut lumber for barns, cabins and other structures.

McCall's Lodge was perched on the middle of five forks[2] of Idaho's Salmon River. The Middle Fork was the core of the Idaho Primitive Area, and remains to this day the backbone of travel into the vast central Idaho wilderness. This tributary of the Main Salmon River originates where Bear Valley Creek and Marsh Creek join forty-three river miles upstream of the Lodge.

From the lodge the Middle Fork defies the map and flows north another sixty-three miles before joining the Main Salmon. McCall took note of the first pioneers of river travel passing by his lodge and joined them by adding war surplus rafts and float trips to the hunting and guest ranch services he offered his guests.

Getting to the lodge was an adventure in itself. Via land it was a full day pack trip from Seafoam. Two days were required if you came in from Landmark to the west or Myers Cove and Camas Creek to the north. The quickest and easiest access was via airplane to a landing strip cut out of a flat across the river from the Lodge – a fact not lost on young Norm Guth.

After grade school in Stanley, Norm began spending school months living with an aunt and uncle in Rupert, Idaho. He started taking flying lessons as a junior in high school. By his senior year he had saved up $3,000 for college, but his passion for flying and the backcountry won out. With his dad's agreement, he invested the college money in a four seat Aeronca Sedan that was capable of hauling over eight hundred pounds of fuel, people and supplies into the Lodge on each flight.

Norm was growing up in an outfitting family and getting a first class hands-on education in all the components of an advanced degree in backcountry living. His dad's outfit in Stanley and Seafoam taught him the art of packing horses and mules. He attained backcountry flying and river running skills during his days at the Middle Fork Lodge.

Just the physical ability was not enough. Guth had to know how to manage operations and people, and oddly enough, in the wilds of Idaho, political savvy became necessary. One might think the out-

2 The five major tributaries of the Salmon River are the Yankee, East, North, Middle and South forks.

fitter's life is one free from such burdens – after all, isn't their time just spent riding through the woods or floating down the river?

The harsh reality is the Guths and all outfitters choose a life that includes those escapes, but in truth is thoroughly regulated in most every facet by bureaucracies at both the state and federal levels. Idaho outfitters work in some of the most pristine high quality wild lands and wildlife habitat on the planet. Many people value the backcountry and they all desired a say in how it is used. It is, after all, *public* land.

The face of the federal level bureaucracy with administrative duties in Idaho is the Forest Service, to which Norm had a family connection. The uncle who had originally partnered with his father before realizing how tough the work was found a job with the agency. And Norm had a second uncle who became the ranger at Seafoam.

"When we first went there the forest ranger was next to God. He was the neatest guy in the world. The reputation of the Forest Service was absolutely gold plated. Those were the best people. They spent all summer clearing trails and fighting fires. The local forest ranger was one of the local civic leaders. That didn't change until the mid-1950s when they started to try and control everything."

At the state level Norm watched his father, Bill, and other outfitters come together to form a professional trade organization, the Idaho Outfitters and Guides Association. A few years later in 1961 Bill was involved in the state of Idaho effort to establish a state board charged with protecting the safety, health and welfare of the public that used outfitter services. The days of licensing and state regulation had begun.

Norm had seen his father lead a union, represent the miners' interests in Washington, D.C., and build a successful, multi-faceted backcountry outfitting operation. The profession was now going to need someone to shepherd it through the complex legislative and legal process that eventually defined outfitting's role in wilderness. Norm grew into that role as a leader and wilderness politician.

****

In the first half of the twentieth century pioneering wilderness advocates in and out of government struggled to find a practical way to actually protect some areas of wilderness. As they came to see it, wilderness was not some luxury or plaything but a fundamental human need, yet the American wilderness was as they expressed it, 'vanishing with appalling rapidity.' Their goal was nothing less than to preserve wilderness areas with 'a presumption of perpetuity.' As these preservation advocates came to discover other approaches could not give that guarantee of permanence, they concluded by mid century that wilderness preservation could be secured only by statutory law – by act of Congress.[3]

In 1956 Frank Church, a promising young attorney from Boise was elected to represent Idaho in the U.S. Senate. Upon arrival in Congress Church discovered that the first-ever proposed law dealing with wilderness had been introduced that same year by Minnesota's Hubert Humphrey. Given Church's own love of wild places and the proposed law's potential impact on millions of acres in Idaho, the thirty-two year old senator was naturally drawn to the legislative effort. This would lead to Senator Church playing the pivotal role of senate floor manager in passage of the final bill in 1964.

Under the 1964 Wilderness Act 9,000,000 acres were chosen to start the National Wilderness Preservation System. Idaho's Selway-Bitterroot Wilderness made up 1,200,000 of those initial acres. The vast area represented by other primitive areas in the state posed the possibility of more additions. The questions were, how much, under what conditions and when?

One provision of the 1964 Wilderness Act was a requirement that all federal land management agencies review existing primitive areas and the wild lands adjoining them to determine their suitability for wilderness designation. In 1972 the Forest Service began their review of central Idaho. The area, including the lands around Campbell's Ferry and the Middle Fork, were under pressure. Commercial interests in the timber industry and some within the Forest Service wanted less protection, not more. Some Forest Service advocates were invoking a "purity principle" desiring to include only those areas that were one hundred percent free of any signs of man.

Advocates of a larger area, ironically very close to the

3 Doug Scott, *The Enduring Wilderness: Protecting our Natural Heritage through the Wilderness Act*, (Golden, CO: Fulcrum Publishing, 2004)

2,300,000 acres that Bob Marshall had once envisioned, were willing to accept some features that were less than pure. They were less concerned with historical activities, viewing them as an asset. The system of trails and widely spaced homesteads and camps were seen as starting points for journeys into the millions of still wild, pristine, indeed pure acres surrounding them.

The purists deemed these activities as *inconsistent* or *non-conforming*.

Years later I spent six years on a task force looking at the Selway-Bitterroot Wilderness and use patterns. Of the one and one quarter million acre area, we found that less than one quarter of one percent of the land was taken by the main system of trails and administrative sites, including a couple of airfields. More than 98% was absolutely pristine, not a footprint of man on it.

The battle over wilderness preservation in central Idaho would come down to a fight between proposals to add a core 1,200,000 pure acres to the wilderness system without inconsistencies, or a larger 2,300,000 acre addition with a supporting web of access.

And what would happen to outfitting? Was it inconsistent with wilderness, a non-conforming use? When outfitters read the 1964 Act they had reason to be concerned. Section 4 (c) of the Act titled *Prohibitions of Certain Uses* states that, "Except as specifically provided for in this Act.... there shall be no commercial enterprise... Section 4 (d) 5 titled Special Provisions says, Commercial services may be performed within the wilderness areas designated by this Act to the extent necessary for activities which are proper for realizing the recreational or other wilderness purposes of the area."

The key word is *may*. While generally prohibited, allowance of commercial services is discretionary. And the discretion in central Idaho would be in the hands of Forest Service managers.

Outfitters were in a tough position. Their lifeblood, the wild lands where they operated, were, as the conservation community pointed out, under never ending pressure from development through road building, logging and mining. Some outfitters had come from those jobs. Mining had helped feed the Guth family. Outfitters lived in small, rural Idaho communities with neighbors who relied on extractive industry jobs to support their own families.

On the other hand outfitters were experiencing increased regulatory pressure from Forest Service managers who were gaining a growing say in how and how much their activities would be allowed in the backcountry. It was the proverbial rock and a hard place.

In 1972 a coalition called the Idaho Environmental Council (IEC) emerged in Idaho. The Council represented several groups, a broad range of local citizens interested in maximizing the area in Idaho that would be protected under the future wilderness law. After developing an overall plan to push for wilderness, several IEC members including Ted Trueblood met in Boise to form the River of No Return Wilderness Council with one goal: establish a 2.3 million acre RNR Wilderness area.

Outfitters sought to learn the scope of the issues facing them by participating and monitoring the IEC and RNR Council meetings and by talking to the Forest Service.

As Norm Guth explains it, "The Forest Service came over and told me and all of us on the river that we had a year or two to get everything out and off the river. We had to have all of our permanent structures down and gone."

We asked, "Why do we have to do all that?"

They said, "The Sierra Club and all these environmental outfits don't want you there."

"So Richard Smith and I went to the Sierra Club meetings and to the Wilderness Society and we found out that they didn't know anything at all about this. The Forest Service was making this all up and putting the blame on them. We ended up getting pretty close with the Sierra Club, Wilderness Society, the IEC and RNR Council."

Outfitters also heard from the purist advocates in the Forest Service. At an annual outfitter meeting in Salmon, Bill Worf, director of recreation and lands from the regional office in Missoula, spoke to the group. "He wanted us to oppose wilderness," said Guth. "He was trying to talk us into going for a pioneer area or something like that – something outside of wilderness." The idea gained some traction with the group.

Marty Rust, an outfitter with interests in the Flying B on the Middle Fork and a camp on the Owyhee River disagreed. He spoke in favor of outfitters supporting wilderness. His view was that future wilderness regulation was just a fact of life. Wilderness designation

was necessary to protect Idaho's wild lands and if outfitters wanted
to work in the backcountry they should get over their reluctance and
move on. Guth supported the argument. Deciding which way to go
was coming down to an analysis of the threats to outfitting – was it
development or regulation that posed the biggest danger. And who do
you trust?

At a meeting at Walt and Shirley Blackadar's home just outside of Salmon, Carl Hocevar of the IEC explained that he felt the
Forest Service was playing games with the various groups, pitting one
against the other so they could ultimately gain approval of their own
minimal proposal.[4] "Our chief complaint is this extreme purity crap
being pushed by the Forest Service, Hocevar said. First they try to tell
us that an area doesn't qualify if there's any significant sign that man
has ever been in the area, and then once the area has been classified,
they tell us that traditional uses such as jetboating must be stopped
and primitive hunting camps and landing strips must be removed. According to all other interpretation, this is clearly not the intent of the
Wilderness Act. We think their approach is nothing more than a cheap
stunt intended to pit the jetboaters and outfitters against us while in
reality we have the same goals. With us arguing against each other,
the Forest Service hopes to push their own weak proposal through
Congress and thereby protect their management options in the area."

Guth was in a critical position to help the outfitters make the
decision. He knew and was talking to Frank Church, Idaho Congressman Jim McClure and several other congressional and governmental
leaders who were drafting the bill. Guth was able to do so thanks to
an advantage outfitters have. The vast majority of the public lacks the
skills to access wilderness on their own. When the political leaders
from Idaho and key players in Washington wanted to gain first hand
knowledge of the places they were discussing they needed to make
trips on the Salmon River.

Senator Church was encouraging the visits. At a speech at the
University of Idaho, Church said, "Congress is not properly representing the people if concerned citizens can't turn to us and say, We think
the agency is mistaken in proposing to develop – or not develop – this
or that area. Come take a look."

4 Pete Henault, "Environmentalists Take a Stand," *Intermountain Observer*
(Boise), 10 March 1973

Church understood the power, the transformative experience a wilderness trip could bring to his efforts to pass a bill. He wrote, "I never knew a person who felt self-important in the morning after spending the night in the open on an Idaho mountainside under a star-studded summer sky." Often, the person that was spending that quality time around the campfire under the stars with the decision makers was Norm Guth.

A friendship grew that led Church to ask Guth to come to Washington, D.C. Just as his father had represented miners in Nevada, Norm made the trip and gave testimony on the wilderness bill — twice in the Senate and once in the House. Church introduced Guth to Congressman John Saylor, a Republican from Pennsylvania who sat on the powerful House of Representatives Interior Committee. Saylor had worked with Church on passage of the 1964 Wilderness Act. He was a stalwart in Congress for wilderness advocates.

When Congressman Saylor came to Idaho to *take a look* Norm had a prior commitment to a meeting in Boise during the first part of the visit. He asked his friend Harold Thomas, owner of Allison Ranch on the Main Salmon (ten miles upriver from the Ferry) to host the congressman. After his Boise meeting, Norm flew into Allison, fixed the group breakfast, and got down to the discussion of how they could secure passage of a bill protecting the larger 2.3 million acre wilderness that the IEC supported.

One of the larger issues to be addressed was how to accommodate the traditional uses on the Main Salmon River. For decades local citizens and outfitters had been using powerboats on the river. Plus there were almost a dozen private *inholdings* in the canyon. These were the old homesteads where pioneers had perfected title under the Homestead Act. Still in private hands, many were being used as points of public access to the river and surrounding wild lands. Allison Ranch where the Congressman was visiting and Campbell's Ferry were among them.

The Wilderness Act does not allow taking of private property, so the dozen deeded properties would have to be *grandfathered in.* There were also a few hunting camps that were operating under special use permit from the Forest Service, including one owned by Guth.

Years before, Norm had bought Big Squaw Creek Camp from Bob Smith as a base for fishing and hunting on the Main Salmon. The place was a bargain – an eyesore that had problems. The old, dilapidated structure hung over a small beach at the river's edge and lacked a legal waste disposal system.

The camp had been there since 1937. The Salmon Forest supervisor and Norm had agreed on a plan to get rid of the Big Squaw Creek camp and move the operation to Smith Gulch, an old mining claim and less obtrusive location a few miles downriver, back from the river where proper waste disposal could be added. The two decided it was best to wait until the pending wilderness bill was completed before making the move.

Their plan would prove to be controversial and complicated by a quirk of geography. Ever since the establishment of the national forest system, different approaches to wild land issues had often played out between the more purist leaning Region 1 on the north side of the river, and the feet-on-the-ground approach of Region 4 to the south.

Big Squaw Creek Camp was perfectly located to become a pawn in the struggle between the two styles of management. Physically, the camp was in Region 1 on the north bank of the Salmon River, the dividing line between regions. But to facilitate management of a river canyon with limited access, the Forest Service had decided to give administrative duties over this segment of the river and the camp to Region 4. Philosophical differences with poorly defined turf boundaries – a recipe for a fight.

Senator Church and many other principals working on the wilderness bill visited Big Squaw Creek Camp.[5] The Senator was aware of the agency plans for the site. Church, ever the master of compromise and legislative success, knew he could deal with it. If it was a question of including the inholdings, camps and other existing uses and have a larger wilderness, or excluding them and accepting a smaller wilderness, he favored the former.

As Guth later told it, Senator Church's, "idea was wilderness preservation, not wilderness creation. He wanted to preserve everything that was there. He wanted to preserve the traditional uses, the trail system and the way it had been. Frank knew what was going on

5 Bethine Church, the senator's widow, and Dennis Baird, head of the North
Idaho Sierra Club and leader in the Idaho Environmental Council, both would
write letters to Congress documenting the senator's knowledge and intent concerning the camp.

back there and he was all for it."

Church addressed the issue directly at the University of Idaho in 1977. In the speech for the First Annual Wilderness Distinguished Lecture Series, Church referenced Ted Trueblood, his friend and a major participant in the IEC:

Time after time when we discuss wilderness, questions are raised about how developed an area can be and still qualify as wilderness, or what kind of activities within a wilderness area are consistent with the purposes of the Wilderness Act. I believe, and many citizens agree with me, that the agencies are applying provisions of the Wilderness Act too strictly, and thus misconstruing the intent of Congress as to how these areas should be managed.

One of my longtime friends, Ted Trueblood, challenged the purity doctrine of the Forest Service in a September 1975 issue of Field and Stream. As Ted put it, the Forest Service with their purist doctrine is trying to 'scuttle the Wilderness Act. In arguing his case, Ted refers to the exclusion of deserving Idaho areas from wilderness classification because they contain minor evidence of man's prior activities, to requirements which make outfitter operations difficult, to fish and wildlife management activities which limit the enjoyment of hunters and fishermen, and – perhaps most tragic of all – to the burning of historic cabins to eliminate the evidence of earlier human habitation.

Such policies are misguided. If Congress had intended that wilderness be administered in so stringent a manner, we would never have written the law as we did. We wouldn't have provided for the possibility of insect, disease and fire control. We wouldn't have allowed private inholdings to remain. We wouldn't have excluded condemnation, as the means for forcibly acquiring developed ranches within wilderness areas – a practice allowed on ordinary national forest lands from which wilderness is created. We wouldn't have made wilderness classification subject to existing private rights such as mining and grazing.

We wouldn't have provided for the continuation of non-conforming uses where they were established – including the use of motor boats in part of the Boundary Waters Canoe Area and the use of airfields in the Primitive Areas here in Idaho. As these examples clearly demonstrate, it was not the intent of Congress that wilderness be administered in so pure a fashion as to needlessly restrict customary public use and enjoyment. Quite the contrary, Congress fully intended that wilderness should be managed to allow its use by a wide spectrum of Americans.[6]

The proposed Idaho law would establish the largest wilderness area in the lower forty-eight states, and would also protect over 125 miles of the Salmon River under the Wild and Scenic Rivers Act. To accommodate the uses on the Main Salmon it was decided that the bill would be written in a unique manner.

Normally when wilderness and wild and scenic designations overlap, the more stringent provisions of the Wilderness Act prevail. The drafters of the Central Idaho Wilderness Act included specific provisions in the law that the less stringent restrictions of the Wild and Scenic River Act would prevail in the Main Salmon River corridor. To ease concerns raised by local citizens who feared future agency restrictions on access to their favorite hunting and fishing areas, Church and Saylor provided opening language in the law regarding the vast primitive watershed of the Salmon River, which stated, "such protection can be provided without conflicting with established uses. "

It is informative for the discussion on what would and would not be wilderness in Idaho to look at the definition of wilderness included in every wilderness bill ever passed by Congress. The law defines wilderness as land that *generally* appears to have been affected *primarily* by the forces of nature with the imprint of man's work *substantially* unnoticeable. [emphasis added] The framers of the Act included these modifiers in a pointed rejection of the purist view.

****

Working with another friend, Cecil Andrus, Guth would see even higher powers brought to bear in support of the larger wilderness area proposal. Andrus, elected four times governor of Idaho, was

6 *Frank Church Collection.* Special Collections, MSS 56, Albertsons Library, Boise State University, Boise, ID

a consummate outdoorsman and master of the Idaho political scene. I once heard him described as having a small scale imbedded in his brain representing a perfect balance between the Idaho public's desire to tap local resources for jobs, yet protect the wild base of their outdoor hunting and fishing lifestyle. Andrus valued his friend Norm Guth's knowledge of the backcountry and would later appoint him to the Idaho Fish and Game Commission.

"Cece," as Andrus was known to Guth and most Idahoans, landed a job in the Carter Administration as secretary of the interior in 1977. He was in a critical position in D.C. during the years leading to passage of the Central Idaho Wilderness Act. One day in 1978 while talking to the President, Cece was surprised to be presented with a brochure about a trip on the Middle Fork and the presidential statement, "I'd like to do this."

Cece told the President it would be the best trip of his life – he should go. He also told the President that he should meet a friend that was coming to town to testify for the wilderness bill. Guth explained, "Cece Andrus had me come to his office and we go straight down to the White House and go into the Oval Office to have a meeting with Jimmy Carter and set the whole thing up."

Guth was told to keep the planned trip a secret. He had to be careful as he arranged logistics while working within the Forest Service regulatory system to get permission to launch a trip on the date the President's schedule demanded – August 20.

Guth approached the river manager and asked for special consideration to start a trip a day earlier than his permit allowed, telling him, "I have some important people from Washington, D.C., on the trip."

The ranger replied, "Every Tom, Dick and Harry tin horn politician from Washington is trying to tell us how to do our job. There is no way. I just can't do it."

Guth asked, "Well what if the guy's name is Jimmy Carter?"

The ranger still refused, so Secretary of the Interior Cecil Andrus talked to his fellow President's cabinet member, Secretary of Agriculture Bob Bergland, the boss of the Forest Service. Bergland issued the permit for the trip from Washington.

Further complications arose when the White House advance team – Secret Service, doctor, communications specialist and photographer, arrived in Idaho. They wanted to use a helicopter to scope out the two campsites on the river where the President would be staying.

Norm told them, "You are going to be four star cross ways with the Forest Service when you take a helicopter in there."

The river was still part of the primitive area, but under law was being managed as wilderness. This meant no motorized or mechanized access. There are exemptions to these restrictions in the law for administrative actions, but the ranger was in unknown territory and being cautious.

Finally the head of the advance team jumped into Guth's discussion with the ranger and asked, "Who do you work for?"

Every time the ranger answered with another person up the chain of command – from ranger to supervisor to regional forester to chief of the Forest Service to the secretary of agriculture – the advance team leader would ask again, "And who does he work for?"
Finally, the ranger acknowledged that the boss of them all was the President of the United States, to which the advance leader replied, "The President says we are going in there with helicopters. You kind

Norm Guth pilots his sweep boat down the Middle Fork of the Salmon River
President Carter and wife Rosalyn fish for cutthroat trout

of pass the word around, would you?"

On the river President Carter was an easy sell on the idea of Central Idaho wilderness. He told the group that he would sign a bill for as large an area as they could get to his desk.

The end result of the eight-year effort to pass what became the Central Idaho Wilderness Act of 1980 was an area larger than most had dreamed possible. Continued application of the vision Frank Church professed in his Idaho effort has resulted in a national wilderness system that is the envy of the world.

In his 1977 speech at the University of Idaho, Church revealed that he and other framers of the original Wilderness Act anticipated a system that would some day consist of forty to fifty million acres. As of 2012 the National Wilderness Preservation System is a total of 109,512,959 acres in forty-four states and Puerto Rico – a remarkable five percent of our nation – an area the size of California.[7] At 2,366,827 acres the area around Campbell's Ferry, the Frank Church – River of No Return Wilderness, is the largest area of unbroken wilderness in the lower forty-eight states. When you add in the adjoining Gospel-Hump Wilderness to the northwest and the Selway-Bitterroot to the north the size of the contiguous designated wilderness in central Idaho is 3,913,210 acres. Frank Church would be pleased.

Everyone didn't leave the process happy. Bill Worf, who had tried to convince outfitters that wilderness did not include them, retired from the Forest Service. He started an organization using Guth's camp at Smith Gulch as a poster child in an effort to draw more support to his purist interpretation of the Act. Using his knowledge of the agency appeals process, Worf engaged in a ten-year battle to terminate the Forest Service permit for the camp and have it removed.

When that failed, in 2000 he found a judge in Montana who supported the Worf purist view. The judge ordered the camp and two others removed. In 2003 with support from Andrus, McClure, Bethine Church (Frank's widow), Dennis Baird, a former leader of the IEC, and the author, Congress passed legislation negating the judge's decision and reaffirming Frank Church's view of how the central Idaho wilderness was to be managed.

I admire Bill Worf for his passion for wilderness and his tenac-

---

7 Current information on the size of the system and each component can be found at wilderness.net.

ity. The goals of the organization he founded are admirable. But his single-minded attack on Guth and outfitting was excessive.

The struggle to save his Idaho investment almost killed Guth, who, but for a never before tried medical treatment, would have died from a stress-induced immune system disease. He eventually sold his Idaho interests and moved to Alaska, where today he continues his lifelong role of providing public access to wild places. He runs the Guth's Lodge at Iliamna River with his sons and grandchildren.

Worf passed away in late 2011. The lodge at Smith Gulch still stands, providing another generation of Americans an opportunity to use and enjoy Frank Church's wilderness.

****

The effort to protect Idaho's wild lands through wilderness designation did not end in 1980. The activist outfitter path forged by Norm Guth was taken up by Grant Simonds, the executive director of the Idaho Outfitters and Guides Association.

Grant played a pivotal role in the Owyhee Initiative, a collaborative effort to protect Idaho's high southern desert and associated canyonlands and rivers. Simonds brought detailed knowledge of the area and a remarkable talent for collaboration to the table. Prior to a guiding career Grant had served Idaho schools as an organizer and team builder. He applied those talents to building consensus in support of protecting country he and his family knew and loved. His focus throughout the process was necessary and appropriate access for those who visit the area.

The eight-year Owyhee Initiative process ended with legislation in 2009 that added 517,000 acres of high desert and canyons in southern Idaho to the National Wilderness Preservation System – the first in Idaho to be managed by the Bureau of Land Management (BLM). The new law also added 316 miles of the Owyhee and Bruneau Rivers to the existing 481 miles of Wild and Scenic Rivers in Idaho.

The wilderness movement in Idaho continues. Congressman Mike Simpson is working to secure a solution among various proposals for new additions to wilderness in the Boulder-White Clouds region east of Stanley, Idaho. Local outfitters are involved.

.

Chapter
Twenty-Five

Ferry Life

"To the living we owe respect,
but to the dead we owe only the truth."
– Voltaire

The end of World War II brought improved economic conditions in the United States – good news for Joe and Frances' outfitting business and their financial security. Life at the Ferry took on an almost routine pace, an annual schedule of spring chores, summers of hay-making and gardening, preparations for fall hunting activities, establishment of remote hunting camps and caring for clients and stock.

Thanksgiving and the end of hunting season took on special meaning for the couple as their outfitted guests left for Dixie and points beyond. The couple enjoyed their outfitted guests, building what would become lifelong friendships with several, but like family visiting for the holidays, it was great to see them arrive, and nice to see

Porch and water source

them go.

The couple had fashioned a home in the log cabin built four decades earlier by Warren Cook. The structure sat inside a fairly new picket fence that enclosed a small garden. From the gate a short path led to a covered porch that faced south to enjoy the down-canyon view.

The irrigation ditch from Trout Creek ran under the fence, in front of the porch and under the outhouse before slipping over the edge of the yard to find the river below. The ditch, which resembled a small creek, was aesthetically pleasing and provided a ready water source. Split firewood was stacked neatly against the cabin wall.

From the porch a thick wooden door swung into a rustic eighteen by eleven-foot kitchen. Cupboards flanked each side to serve as a pantry and to store dishes. A double-oven Great Majestic wood cookstove sat against the south wall. Pots and pans were suspended from hooks set into the log ceiling joists above. Across from the stove was a work counter that topped three large drawers, a flour bin, and a small storage area.

Great Majestic woodstove

An eighteen by twenty-one foot main room served as a living and dining room, and part of the year as a bedroom. A small door hid extremely narrow, steep stairs that led to two attic bedrooms, their sloping ceilings mirroring the steep

278

Upstairs in the Cook Cabin
1958

roofline. Heat from the kitchen stove rose through the single plank floor to the upstairs, much appreciated during the winter but grueling during summer.

Downstairs, a smaller window on the north wall looked down into a small gully in back of the house. A woodstove sat in the corner. Simple rustic furniture included a table, chairs, and desk.

The cabin was fairly spacious for its time, simple and rustic but clean and neat. Uninsulated windows and somewhat porous construction made it challenging to heat during extreme cold but a series of rugged individuals had made it work. The thick log walls kept the downstairs surprisingly cool in the summer heat.

With no indoor plumbing, occupants washed their dishes, clothes, and themselves in wash tubs with water heated on the woodstove or, during warm weather, in the ditch itself. The only toilet was a four by eight-foot "two-holer" outhouse perched on the edge of the embankment above the river about fifteen yards from the cabin.

With revenue brought by outfitted clients, the couple was able to establish a savings account, the first Joe or Frances had experienced since arriving in the Salmon River Canyon. They had money to last the winter and build a nest egg.

Ferry Life

We know much of the four post-war decades at the Ferry through Frances' weekly columns published in the *Idaho County Free Press* newspaper, her private letters written to family in Texas, and the memories of family members who visited often.

In 1950 Frances' sister Doris, her husband Johnney Pollan, and their children Rebecca and Johnney, Jr., loaded into the family Studebaker and drove from San Antonio to Whitewater Ranch. Other family members had visited beginning in 1947, the first of many such visits over the next thirty-eight years. Joe would meet the family with a string of horses and mules to take everyone and their luggage the four miles of trail downriver to the Ferry.

One year Johnney Sr. showed up at Whitewater with two huge watermelons, hauled all the way from the Pollan home in Texas. A proud Texan, Johnney had often kidded Joe about the small watermelons in the Ferry garden. Joe took one look and asked, "How do you expect me to get those to the Ferry?"

"I got them all the way from Texas. The next four miles are your problem!"

Joe's packing skills were up to the task.

The kids loved Joe. "He was an amazing old man," said Becki. "Very strong, hard working, cantankerous, rolled his own cigarettes, always had a pouch of tobacco and papers in his pocket."[1]

Joe's language, like most packers, was colorful. Becki's Aunt Frances warned the children, "Remember when Joe talks to the mules that is mule talk."

"Joe really loved horses and mules. Cars were not his forte. When he learned to drive it was hard to learn to use the brake," explained Becki. "He kept trying to stop it by hollering, Whoa, goddamn it! When they would go out to town someone else would drive."

Life at the Ferry was an adventure for the kids. "We would take our baths in the kitchen in a # 2 washtub," said Becki. "She would crank the old washing machine up on the porch. It was loud. I loved running the ringer."

"Aunt Frances was a great cook. She always had stacks of hot-cakes, butter, syrup, home-made jelly, applesauce, biscuits, bread. We would stay in Elk City the night before we came in and the lady would call Frances to tell her we were coming. She would place an order for

1 Becki Pollan Godfrey and Johnney Pollan, Jr., Personal Communication, 2008

us to pick up. Aunt Frances always wanted a large stick of baloney and 'store bought' bread. She cut thick slices of baloney and fried them and put them on the store bought bread. She was tired of her own, but we loved the homemade bread. That was always our first lunch when we got there."

Mary Eisenburg, Frances' niece, remembers being fed canned cougar. "We called it Kitty Burgers!"

Texas watermelon at the Ferry

Becki Pollan Godfrey recalls, "We had elk steak, big skillets of home fries, sliced tomatoes, fresh vegetables from the garden – fresh greens, onions, potatoes, and corn. After she had cooked for several hours she would always go and clean up, put on a long skirt, makeup and lipstick – show up at the table, dressed for dinner. She made us kids at least go wash off some of the Idaho dirt before we ate."

"Joe was rough on the edges, but had a good heart. It was still dark when he got up, lit a fire in the corner stove, made a cup of very strong coffee. He added a touch of Irish whiskey to his first cup. Then he would go up to the barn to check on the stock, back to the blacksmith shop, then to the woodshed to get some wood for the stove. He would sit and talk to Dad or whoever was in the kitchen."

Every day at the Ferry

Becki and Joe – 1956

was an adventure for young Johnney, Jr., "Frances would get up and start breakfast, pancakes the size of a plate, any way you wanted eggs. She was always heating water for cleaning. When she finished cleaning up after breakfast she would get dough out to let it rise and go work in the garden. About noon she came back to do her baking – three to five loaves of bread baking. The cabin was heaven when she was baking! She had to make a lot because we would just devour one loaf just as it came out of the oven. In the heat of the day we would take a nap. Frances would read, or write."

"At the beginning of the day, depending on what she was going to prepare, for instance apple pies, cobbler, or applesauce, she would give us instructions and tell us to go out and get a five gallon pail of apples. We would go out and pick, wash, cut them all up and get them ready for her to use. Sometimes it would be raspberries or eggs. She directed and we did. You learned real quick what you could and could not do with Frances. You did not want to upset her. She would go to the cellar and get canned meat – elk, bear, whatever. She always made gravy with Pet milk, home fried potatoes, vegetables, collards, chard."

"The guys got to go do fun things – move the stock, set out salt, chopped wood," said Johnney Jr. "The girls stayed back to heat water and clean the kitchen. The only light they had was kerosene lamps, so when it got dark you went to bed."

"Joe had a salt lick where he got his meat. He would set up at the back of the barn and make a thirty-five yard shot. He wasn't going to do unnecessary work. He was very efficient. He was small of stature, but stout. He never took a day off. When it was raining he would sit on the porch and fix tack."

"Uncle Joe and Aunt Frances had a marriage of convenience" said Johnney. "She was there to help him and he was there to help her. They survived. They got along and loved each other."

Frances often wrote of the wonderment and solace she drew from her surroundings and rural lifestyle. The river, the couple's constant companion, prompted Frances to write, "She strains and roars in pain and anger – trying to draw the high snow out of the mountains so summer can be born – and the high grasses can turn green and grow. Once the birth of summer is a fact and the new year is here, then she will quietly go about her business of being a place for fun and relaxation. She'll run, cold and clear and green as a pine tree. Instead of growls and roars, her voice will soften to a soft sh-sh-ing murmur, except for the rapids that she keeps to remind us that the Salmon is a 'red-headed woman, but she is no lady."

Frances wrote of the regular back-breaking chore of raising and harvesting hay as good for the body and spirit. "I guess one reason the hay grows so fast is because Joe and I both like haying. Some people tell us we are old fashioned and do our work the hard way. Maybe so, but it's fun to work in a field of sweet smelling clover and it's fun to move it back into the barn until you can't get another forkful in, and then to build a stack. And in the fall when the snow starts creeping down the ridges, it is food for my soul to look at the stock and the hay and know there is plenty. Some of my neighbors feel sorry for me in the hay field, but they don't know what they are missing. Once, to keep what my generation called 'in shape' I played tennis and volleyball. I get the same exercise with a hayfork. Of course if all women did as I do, the corset and girdle section of the catalogue would be thrown out and maybe Sears, Roebuck can't afford that."

By November the sun, which had arced high over the homestead through long summer days, now would not reach the Zaunmiller's little cabin until 11 A.M. For five brief hours the sun barely skirted the southern rim of the canyon. In December, with the arrival of the winter solstice, that time would shrink to just three hours. January and February brought bone-chilling cold and snow with nighttime temperatures periodically dipping into single digits, even below zero.

Taking care of the ferryboat, a year round daily chore for the couple, became an especially challenging task when the river froze over, as described by Frances in her column, "When the cold came, the river dropped. A couple of days of mixed rain and snow, the river raised. Ice-bound, the ferry cannot rise with the water, for the mush ice holds everything fast to the bottom, including the edges of ice bridges. When the river raises in winter the water runs over the ice. Unless the ferry is freed, water will pour in and then there is a cold, hard job of work to do."

"So New Years day was the day that the ferry had to be taken care of. A little bit of 'know how' – a lot of time – and some muscles that never get a chance to get fat – that is all it takes to take care of the ferry in winter. One and a half manpower, each with an axe, cut the ice all round the boat. He had the long side to cut free, while she

Harvesting hay at the Ferry

cut free the shorter front and rear. Ice a foot or more thick is 'such fun' to cut – and always just as the axe goes through, water gushes into the hole you have made, and splatters all over you."

The problems with a frozen river were compounded when it thawed, sending a torrent of ice flows downriver, "When that huge junk of ice went grinding downstream, everything in the river or along the bank was in trouble. Ice and more ice – small pieces no bigger than a house being shoved on the bank for they had no place to go in the river, and the poor old ferry was shoved up on the bank, too. That was a mess if ever there was one. There was the ferry about thirty feet from the water, huge cakes of ice piled on her, and she was on top of more ice."

During the spring runoff the ferry brought more troubles, but not so much that the couple couldn't pause to enjoy a small miracle provided by nature, as Frances reported in a letter home:

The ferry is like a senile person. It requires constant attention, especially during high water. At the present stage of raise, about 15 feet above normal, we make four trips each day to take care of the ferry. Tonight we had to push the boat out, so it would not rub against the rocks – with my back against a rock and my feet against the pole that would hold the boat out, I was pushing with all my 135 pounds. Slow but steady the pole slid down the face of a rock and the ferry moved into safe water.

I was watching the pebbles roll in the water's edge when a large hellgrammite came out of the water. We quickly pulled tight the ropes that hold the boat in place, then both Joe and I watched a salmon fly be born. The hellgrammite got a tight grip on the rock, then it rested, but not for long. The miracle began to take place. We were so still but had we shouted or thrown rocks the birthing would have continued as it struggled and the back began to split. We could see the beautiful salmon colored body of the fly and I ached with its straining. With much neck twisting and arching of the back, the head finally pulled free of the shell, then the body started emerging until part of the wings were out. The legs came next, then slowly with many pauses for rest, the rest of the complete fly emerged and only a soft gray shell remains of the hellgrammite.

The ferry icebound in winter

Ferry Life

Chapter
Twenty-Six

The Ferry
Retires

"Bridges become frames
for looking at the world around us"
– Bruce Jackson

While working on the Ferry in the spring of 1955 an accident occurred that began a course of events destined to bring major changes to the ranch and all future travelers who sought access to the wilderness from the north. It would trigger Frances' first time in the role of public activist, the first of many:

This spring Avon Hill and Gene Mott helped Joe get the ferry out of the water. As soon as the boat dried Joe and I worked – we cleaned it and gave it a coat of tar. I crawled under and found the big worm holes and plugged them with caulking compound. We were proud of the old boat for not falling apart as we worked on it. Yesterday we were ready to put her back into the water. Joe and I have worked together so many years that it never entered my mind we should get someone to help us. I had the simple job of easing the slack on the cable. We were using a 3-block tackle. Of course once in a while a pulley would bind and I would get it unstuck.

Never again will I work around a steel cable wearing jersey gloves. It hurt like the end of the world when my hand was jerked into the pulley and pinned there. Pain! It took some doing but my Joe got me free. Two fingers had been caught – one was not hurt, the other was a strange looking thing – as thin as a silver dollar, but not flat – it had the curve of the groove of the pulley. I looked at it and wanted to be sick.

I think Joe hurt more than I. He wanted me to hurry to the house and do something about it. But the ferry was half in the water, so we finished launching the boat. Then the finger got all the attention it needed. Lucky me, our medicine chest is a real one.

The column reporting damage to Frances' right hand to readers of the Free Press was signed Lefty Zaunmiller.

Later that year, Frances wrote Idaho Senator Henry Dworshak telling him about the ferry and asking that a bridge be built to replace it. "The first ferry was built about 1890," Frances wrote in her typical exaggerated style, "and from then 'til now, the only way to cross the river is on the ferry. We cross the river only 4 or 4 ½ months in a year. The rest of the year – the water is too high in summer, and the ice stops the crossing in winter. Have you ever been on a ferry when the river was too high, and felt the floor tip, saw the water start to curl over the bow into the boat and prayed that the cable would break so the boat could rise level again and not be sucked under? I have, and it was a wild ride."

The bully pulpit of her weekly column helped Frances generate a rising tide of public support for a bridge to replace the ferry. Senator Dworshak responded with congressionally mandated financial support for the project in the Forest Service budget.

To build a bridge in the canyon the Forest Service had to find ways to move the necessary materials, men and supplies to the remote site. The Mallard Creek Road to Whitewater Ranch had to be extended the last quarter mile to the bank of the river. The existing four-mile trail from road's end to the bridge site was too narrow, climbed high above the river and had inadequate drainage. Rock slides could close the route at any time and winter often created an impassable frozen surface. A crew with a gas powered drill and dynamite were tasked with building a new route closer to the river, a route engineered to be passable year round.

With agency support, Joe turned the property's hay meadow that ran up the slope of the canyon wall into a viable landing strip. Irrigation ditches that crisscrossed the meadow were filled in to smooth the surface. Trees that blocked the approach path were removed. When Joe was done, Bob Fogg with Johnson Flying Service of Mc-Call, Idaho, hiked in to examine the work, pronounced it passable, and returned two days later in his Super Cub to make the first landing.

The new runway brought a remarkable change in life at the Ferry. Frances reported to her readers, "It is not the best landing strip in the canyon, in fact maybe it is one of the worst, but it will let supplies come in for the bridge crew. With supplies will come the mail. It seemed odd to walk out to the meadow and get the mail. Wonderfully new and I like it."

The Zaunmillers now had improved access to the outside world, a route over which they had control. The landing strip was private and permission to land would be granted only to pilots of their choosing – not just the ones bringing mail, but also periodic flights for supplies and clients for the hunting and fishing business.

The new runway brought peace of mind as well. As Warren and Rose Cook had experienced half a century earlier, slow access to medical care could take a heavy toll on canyon residents. All were reminded of this fact in the summer of 1954 when two pioneers of commercial river running, Ralph and Red Smothers, were floating the river with one of the canyon's first parties of paying tourists. The group stopped upstream of the Ferry at Richardson Bar to spend the night with their friend Okie Grogg. As Frances described it, "They found him in bed with the covers pulled up round his shoulders, asleep. He had been asleep for about ten days."

****

The logistics of building a suspension bridge in a remote wilderness canyon were complex. The new landing strip provided relatively easy access for men, their food and personal gear. The heavy materials were the biggest challenge. How do you move tons of cement mix, thick steel cables, steel bridge pylons and deck supports from the end of the road to the bridge site four miles downstream? The river route might be an option, but two major rapids, Elkhorn and Growler, are located in the four-mile stretch.

For the answer the Forest Service turned to Monroe Hancock. As the lead boatmen for the large wooden scow that had brought the National Geographic Society group down the river twenty years be-

Tex Mott and Don Nitz delivering bridge materials

fore, Hancock had personal knowledge of the challenges. On the National Geographic trip he had steered his heavy scow onto the rocks in Growler and spent hours struggling to free his craft. Decades later, he was now the wise old man of river transport. He proposed a plan to the Forest Service to move the gear with a large rubber raft mounted with sweeps front and back. Hancock recommended two men he knew were up to the job – Tex Mott and Don Nitz.

A crew was stationed at the end of the road at Whitewater to load the raft, another at the bridge site to unload, and yet another near Mackay Bar where the road from Dixie came to the river. Each day for a week and a half the boat was loaded with material, run the four miles to the Ferry, unloaded, then run empty another thirteen miles down-river to Mackay Bar. Here the raft was deflated and sweeps dismantled and loaded on a truck. The gear was hauled up out of the canyon to Dixie, almost to Red River, then back down the Mallard Creek Road to Whitewater – a forty-five mile trip, one way that took four hours.

A man named Hunter owned a sawmill near Dixie next to the route, and after the truck went passed several times pulling a raft, he came out, stopped the driver and asked, "Where the hell are you getting all those rafts?"[1]

Among the materials delivered to the site were tents and equipment necessary to establish a kitchen and chow hall. The crew built a wooden platform on the south bank of the river just upstream from the bridge location to create a feeding station large enough to support the twelve-man crew. Lodging for the crew was provided in a large tent bunkhouse previously built by Joe to house his hunting and fishing clients.

The project became a year round effort. The first task was building the concrete abutments to support each end of the bridge deck. A cable was strung across the river with a carriage on it so the men could cross back and forth for work on each side. Two anchors (*dead men*) were buried underground in several feet of concrete on each side to hold the twin suspension cables that ran from tall steel-beam bridge towers on each bank.

The work proceeded in fits and starts, often interrupted by the brutal winter of 1955–56. The young men of the bridge crew, restless after idle days brought on by heavy snow, had snowshoes and skis brought in. There was no lift, but that did not deter the burning of youthful energy to snowshoe up the Campbell's Ferry runway, strap the shoes to the back, ski down, swap the skis for snowshoes, and back up the hill again.

When good weather returned, the crew began to hang stringers – smaller cables that ran from the large suspension cables down to six inch I-beams placed crossways to hold the wooden deck. At the north end of the bridge next to the tower, the stringers were as long as the tower was tall. As each pair was hooked to the suspension cable the lengths of the stringers were gradually reduced until the center,

1 Zeke West, Personal Communication, 2011

Frances christening the bridge – 1956

low point was achieved, then lengthened again as the south bank and tower was reached. Wooden decking for the bridge was cut from trees felled on site using a small gasoline powered sawmill brought in by the Forest Service just for this project.

As the bridge neared completion, an unusual cargo came on one of the regular supply flights piloted by Bob Fogg. C. J. (Chet) Olsen, regional USFS forester from Ogden, Utah, who had approved the bridge project, was a close friend of noted historian Bernard De-Voto, a native of Ogden. DeVoto was a well-known western historian, winning a Pulitzer Prize for *Across the Wide Missouri,* one of several books he wrote about the fur trade and the settling of the American West. He received wide acclaim for his 1953 abridged edition of the *Journals of Lewis and Clark.*

DeVoto had spent months of his work on the journals camped on the trail along the Lochsa River, some seventy-five miles north of the Ferry. When DeVoto died in November of 1955 the family informed Olsen that he had requested that he would like his ashes spread on the Idaho section of the Lewis and Clark Trail. Olsen contacted Bob Fogg to request that he join a flight to the Ferry when feasible and extend the flight north over the Bitterroot Mountains. On April 16,

1956 Fogg and Olsen, bearing DeVoto's final remains, landed at the Ferry. The two unloaded supplies for the bridge crew, then proceeded north on a mission they named Operation Lochsa.

Joe and Frances, two bridge crew and Chet Olson, far right

Olsen returned to the Ferry when the bridge was completed, attending a ceremony where Frances broke a bottle of champagne on the structure to mark the occasion. Joe was in attendance, but moving slowly. At age sixty-five, Joe was using a cane, showing the toll that decades of backcountry work had taken on his knees.

Joe was not the only Zaunmiller with a health issue. He and Frances both were regular smokers and that summer she detected a problem in her throat. A trip to the doctor in Grangeville revealed a malignancy. Surgery was scheduled and remarkably, given the state of cancer medicine at the time, Frances was cured. Despite the fact that she refused to give up smoking (she claimed the Doctor told her she should continue smoking "to keep her throat open"), she survived another thirty years.

In the spring of 1956, with Joe and Frances both back at the Ferry and feeling better, they said goodbye to an old friend. "The old ferry boat made it thru the winter – but it was so tired of holding back the water until finally the old boards just let the water thru, like a piece of fine screen. While she was still afloat the water was knee-deep. The man and woman salvaged pulleys and cables and then they turned her loose. Somewhere on the river she will find her grave, perhaps in the rapids below the house."

The old ferry did not want to leave. Men with long poles pushed to get her to go. Even then she hugged the bank – hit rocks and rested a bit before turning into the current. At the rapids she lodged on a couple of boulders as though she wanted to wait and see another high water at the Ferry. The last ferry eventually ended up on a gravel bar just upstream from Riggins. The cables and pulleys the Zaunmillers salvaged from the ferry boat remain on the property today, part of the historical display used to share the history of the site with visitors.

The last ferry is shoved off on its final journey

Chapter
Twenty-Seven

New Owners

"Dreams have only one owner at a time.
That's why dreamers are lonely."
– Erma Bombeck

Frances' illness and surgery caused a major setback to the family's finances. Their savings were wiped out and the two were left with debts to both the doctor and hospital. On August 11, 1958, Frances wrote her sister Billee with news:

Joe's birthday is today, 67, and he is celebrating by shoeing mules. I finally convinced him that I'd much rather share the wealth of this ranch while he is alive to help him enjoy it with me – for I could not run it alone if a widow. So we have put it up for sale. Not a big advertising deal, but quietly let the word drift around that we would sell, keeping the house, garden and orchard for our use during our lifetimes. In less than a week the first prospect was here talking price and terms to Joe.

Once again exaggerating, Frances wrote,

If you know someone who wants to own the last privately owned homestead in the Idaho Primitive Area – and it is the last one – four miles from the nearest road, with a mail route that comes each Tuesday in summer and twice a month in winter – a good trail to the road and a packbridge (horses, no cars) across the river – landing strip for small aircraft on the ranch – if you know such a person and he has about 30,000 dollars to pay for the ranch – then tell him about it.

Sounds high for a little more than 80 acres – but less than 30 acres is cleared, and the rest is loaded with the big timber. Between a million and a million and a quarter feet of first grade timber are growing on the ranch. Enough to sell for a nice piece of money, or to use in erecting the cabins and lodges that are necessary for a dude ranch to get into the big time so far as making money is concerned. There is even a sawmill here to convert the timber into lumber.

I want Joe to sell, so he can stop working so much. He won't slow down at all, but 67 is time to start slowing. I thought that I had better let you know that is in the breeze, cause when we sell, we are going to spend a winter in Texas – Joe says that we will go south at the first frost and not come home 'til the last snow is gone – me, I give him two months at the most and he'll be nuts to get home. Personally, I'd rather let Texas come to Idaho, still it might be nice to see the changes, as long as I could come home when I got thirsty for a drink of water.

****

John Crowe

The prospect that Frances referenced was John Crowe of Redding, California. John was originally from Boise, an engineering graduate of the University of Idaho. He was the nephew of Frank Crowe, an engineer of national fame. Frank had led the building of Arrowrock Dam on the Boise River east of Boise where he perfected a cable, tower and rail concrete delivery system that made large dams possible. Frank later headed the six-company consortium, including Morrison Knudsen of Idaho, that built Hoover Dam.

During college John worked part-time with his uncle Frank on Deadwood Dam in Idaho and on Hoover Dam. After graduation John followed Frank to work full time on the Parker Dam that formed Lake Havasu downstream of Hoover Dam on the Colorado.

John married his college sweetheart, Mary and raised four children. The two shared a love of the outdoors. He took Mary squirrel hunting on their first date. After college and working for his uncle, John formed a construction company of his own that cleared the reservoir for Shasta Dam in California, the site of Sea-Tac airport in Seattle, and railroad tunnels in Oregon.

Tired of the travels demanded by John's engineering career, the couple purchased a cattle ranch near Redding, California, and branched into an equipment and air charter service. But Idaho remained their favorite hunting grounds and retreat. They longed for a place to connect the kids to their love of Idaho.

The Crowes knew other Idaho enthusiasts from the Redding area and frequently hunted with one, Loren Hollenbeak, who owned land north of the old Caswell Ranch on Cabin Creek. Other Redding residents who bought into Idaho were Sid Hinkle – the Selway Lodge, Mallard Creek and Dixie – Frank Santos – Croofoot and Bryant Roberts – James Ranch. It was on a hunt at Cabin Creek that the Crowes first met Joe Zaunmiller. John remembered that Joe's packstring had some of the biggest mules he had ever seen.

While en route to one hunt Crowe met Warren Brown, a friend from college, at the McCall airport. Brown had recently purchased Yellow Pine Bar on the Salmon River and knew about the Zaunmillers' plans to sell the Ferry. John jumped at the opportunity, engaging his friend Rex Kettlewell as a partner. John flew into the Ferry and made a deal with Joe on the spot. Part of the deal included Joe and Frances staying on to care for the place. Kettlewell's interest turned out to be short lived. He sold to the Crowes two years later.

Initially the Crowes would stay in the large tent Joe had set up for hunting clients and the bridge crew. In 1960 John and Rex refurbished the old sawmill the Forest Service had left after the bridge project. Calling themselves Thick and Thin Lumber Company, they built a sturdy sixteen by twenty-four foot one room cabin that is still

John Crowe and Rex Kettlewell milling the lumber for the Crowe Cabin

Crowe Cabin under construction

New Owners

Mary Crowe

Rex Kettlewell and John Crowe reassemble the tractor
flown in by Bob Fogg in a Travel Air 6000

standing.

John respected Joe Zaunmiller and the years of effort he had put into the place. He began looking for ways to make Joe and Frances' life easier.

The biggest improvement the Crowes brought was in Joe and Frances' finances. The Crowes paid the Zaunmillers $30,000 for the Ferry with $8,700 up front and the balance to be paid in $2,130 annual payments plus five percent interest over ten years. The steady revenue stream from the note made the next decade financially secure, but struggles would return. The down payment easily paid off the couple's medical bills with money left over for a project Frances had long desired – a fireplace for their cabin. She had to wait almost a year for construction to begin, claiming that qualified stonemasons, "were booked up like a debutante."

Joe's work load was reduced dramatically when the Crowes disassembled a 1953 Farmall tractor from their Redding cattle ranch and contracted with Bob Fogg of Johnson Flying Service to fly it to the Ferry. Johnson's Travel Air 6000 handled most of the parts easily, but the large tractor tires were a special problem. The tires had to be taken off the rims and folded in half to fit into the plane.

Immediately the burden of annual hay and grain production at the Ferry was significantly reduced. The horsepower of the tractor, lovingly named Lucille by the appreciative Joe, replaced animal power. All Lucille needed was a barrel or two of gasoline Joe would pack in from the end of the road at Whitewater Ranch. For a man with aging knees and joints, the occasional trip upriver for gas was a small price to pay for the big help Lucille became at the ranch.

Frances' response to the Crowes' help was not as positive. Her problems were twofold. Frances often talked about how nice it was to get the chance to talk with a woman since during most of her time at the Ferry she was the lone female. But that worked best when the visiting woman understood her role. All went well as long as the visitor looked up to the pedestal Frances had claimed in her self-assigned role as the owner of the canyon.

Frances, in her view, was Ferry royalty – all knowing in all matters. Of course Frances was due some deference. She lived a life that most romanticized – self reliant, strong, and knowledgeable in the ways of the wild. Mary Crowe respected that, but had some strengths of her own.

More than Frances' equal, Mary Crowe was quite superior when it came to worldliness and education. With a college business degree, Mary became the bookkeeper for the couple's multiple businesses. Mary was well traveled, an accomplished hunter and could hold her own in the outdoors. Near Frances in age at forty-seven, she was a very attractive woman.

According to Mary Crowe, "Joe was great to talk to, but Frances would interrupt and take over. Joe would tell her, 'Oh, Frances, you sound like a broken record,' and go outside to tend stock and get a chance to talk with John."[1]

"I enjoyed Frances in some ways," said Mary. "She was a good cook and could can produce and fruit from the orchard. But none of the kids liked her very well. Neither did John or I. You could never tell her anything or advise her in any way. She knew everything."[2]

When the Crowes brought in a small generator and wired the Zaunmillers' cabin for lights, Frances ran it for one night. The noise was too much, so charging radio and phone batteries became its sole use. A kerosene powered refrigerator, a considerable improvement over keeping items cool by soaking them in ditch water, should have been welcomed for the major improvement it was. It was used off and on for several years, but on one trip to the Ferry the Crowes found it sitting on the front porch, door off, being used as shelving. "It used too much kerosene," was Frances' comment.

Frances acknowledged being set in her ways. In one of her columns she had written prior to the Crowes' arrival:

The places on the river should get new owners more often – then in a few years they would be as nice as anything in town. You can go to the ones that have had the same owner for generations and while the place will be clean and comfortable, still it shows that the ones who live there found a way of living that suited them and settled to that, resisting any hint of a change – and a lot of times a bit of a change would make that way of living so much better. The Ferry is like that.

For years Joe has wanted to put running water in the house,

1 Mary Crowe, Personal Communication, 2008
2 Crowe, Personal Communication

but she doesn't want it. Running water would make a lot less work, but Joe does not guarantee that the little water ditch that talks its way past the kitchen door would not be taken away – so she will keep the ditch and listen to the water tell its tales of the places it has been. You should listen to it brag sometimes.

Another thing about running water piped into the house – that means a bathroom and no matter where she tried to place a bathroom: she cannot get the view that is now enjoyed from the little building over the hill. Maybe we should let someone else 'have the place' for a few years. They would not be bound by sentiment and would do all those things that should be done.

Frances maintained a civil relationship with the Crowes. Although years later she would chastise them for not, in her opinion, doing more for the place. She encouraged them to sell to someone, "who would do more than just own it." In a personal letter to John and Mary she asks, "When did your interest in Campbell's Ferry die?"

John and Mary had not lost interest. The Crowes were getting on in age, as was Frances. Frances wanted help, but only on her own terms.

Chapter
Twenty-Eight

Lost Love

"Though lovers be lost
love shall not"
– Dylan Thomas

In the winter of 1961–62 tragedy visited the Ferry. Nine days after Christmas on the afternoon of January 3, 1962, Joe Zaunmiller walked out of the back bedroom and suddenly collapsed on the living room floor. A massive heart attack had taken the rugged, seventy-one-year-old patriarch of the Ferry.

Joe's death came too late in the day to get help. After notifying the neighbors in the canyon via the Forest Service phone and over the backcountry radio, Frances spent her last night at the Ferry with Joe. The next day a Piper Cub on skis was dispatched from Grangeville to pick up Frances, and returned for a second flight to bring out Joe's body. He was buried several days later in the Prairie View Cemetery in Grangeville.

According to a column informing her readers of Joe's death,

Frances spent the next two months in town, taking care of funeral and estate matters, writing a new will and recovering from a bout of pneumonia.

After Joe's death, Frances wanted time to herself, and asked for privacy:

It was the sixth of March when the plane brought me home. Different friends wanted to be with me. They were afraid for me to come alone to this empty house. Poor ones. So kind and yet not one realized their concern was misplaced. Sooner or later each would return to her home. I would go with them to the plane and then I would return alone to my empty house.

So I asked each to let me return alone. I also requested that no guests visit me until I asked them to do so. For I knew that I must learn to live in my house alone, without my Joseph, before I could share my house with other people. I did not even want those who would stay just an hour or two drinking coffee while they visited. I needed the complete privacy that can only be obtained here at the Ferry. To grieve for my Joseph.

But the grief is more for myself. I am so lucky that I had those nineteen years as his wife. But I never wanted it to end. I know I was not the first wife, nor the last that was so content in her life with her husband that the years before her marriage were like a dream. It seemed we had been married always and would continue to be so. He was not a perfect man. Instead he was a most human kind of person. A few people could not understand how I could come again to the Ferry to live alone. But he made this house where we lived together the way I wanted it.

There seems little doubt of the sincerity of Frances' love for Joe. Twenty-two years prior she had arrived in the Idaho backcountry running from her first husband, Charles Gamble, whose criminal actions were too much for her to bear. In the Salmon River Canyon she met and married a man who, like her father, had faced and beaten the challenges of difficult times. Joe had forged a rewarding life among the beauty and majesty of the Idaho wilderness and Frances had willingly shouldered her share of that effort.

There were times when she chafed at the stern German bearing that ruled Joe's house, but in the larger scheme of her life in the canyon, it didn't matter. She didn't know immediately what her life would be like after Joe. "A widow is a most unthinkable condition, she wrote to a friend. Wife, but non-wife. She hugs her wifehood close and the closer she clings the more the non-wife is there. Grief, yes. Joy of all that was, a joy of being wife and a non-belief of non-wife. To me, the most horrible word in any language is 'widow.' I am Joe Zaunmiller's wife. He is not dead. He has just gone on a trip and I could not go, too."

Over time, just as she had often with stories of her own life, Frances spun tall tales about Joe's death. Norm Close, son of Frances friends Tom and June Close, was told an amazing tale. The reason for her obfuscation is unknown, but Norm says that Frances told him, "Joe got really sick and they couldn't get any help. So when he died she wrapped him in a manty and dragged him out to the woodshed. He froze there. The ground was frozen so she couldn't bury him. The pack rats started chewing on him, so she dragged him into the downstairs basement and closed the door so the rats couldn't get him. He stayed there through the winter until they could bury him or get him out."[1]

Part of Frances' struggle after Joe's death was how to present a proper public view of her life while giving in to a rising tide of passion at her very doorstep. On the one hand her rural Texas upbringing in a Methodist home required she show a sense of propriety. Widows must wait at least a year before entertaining a new life. But deep in the wilds of Idaho, with almost no one around, time was short.

It seems to have begun in the spring. Friends had come to help, and all left – except one. Vern Wisner lived at the Ferry, a short walk across the orchard in the Crowe Cabin. The Zaunmillers both knew Vern well. He was a fixture in the canyon. During the Great Depression Vern had drifted into Idaho from Nebraska. For a while he worked for an uncle who was a contractor in Payette, Idaho. In 1942 he registered for the draft in Elk City where he had found part time work with the Forest Service. Like many others he was drawn to the river and canyon. He befriended Floyd Dale who at the time owned what is now called Whitewater Ranch.

At various times Vern settled into the Polly Bemis place, spent

1   Norm Close, Personal Communication, 10 March 2013

time in the mining town of Dixie, and lived in a small cabin at the mouth of Little Elkhorn Creek. On hikes to and from roads end at Whitewater Frances had stopped to visit and admired Vern's "neat, compact little house." The two shared wildlife stories and late evening strolls in the orchard to watch the bears eating fruit.

On Christmas Day, 1961, Vern, John and June Cook enjoyed dinner with the Zaunmillers. It was a happy time with no hint of the

Vern Wisner, Joe Zaunmiller, and June Cook
Christmas, 1961

tragedy that would strike nine days later.

After Joe's death Vern took care of the Ferry while Frances was in town dealing with the loss. Some time after her return on March 3 Frances offered another dinner invitation to Vern.

In early June, Vern had to leave the canyon. The Crowes were coming in and needed their cabin, and Vern had a medical problem. A nerve in his face was causing intense pain, symptoms that sound like the condition Trigeminal Neuralgia. The pain is described by some as the most intense pain known to mankind – so intense the condition is sometimes called the suicide disease. After receiving medical advice and medication, Vern stayed in Elk City, struggling with the decision of what to do next. But he could write, and he poured his heart into a series of letters.

Elk City, Ida
June 8, 1962
Dear Frances

I was out to Grangeville today and just got back. I am going to take a few days treatment and if that don't help enough to suit me I am going to go to Boise first, then maybe on to Salt Lake and have that nerve cut out, but that is a brain surgery job. But this morning I couldn't take even a drink of water and hadn't been able to eat anything since I ate breakfast with you but I have taken four pills two doses and I just had a hamburger steak, hash brown potatoes and coffee and did all right so that might slow it down and I will be down before I go to the hospital for with brain surgery I might never come back. That is all I have to say. I am shaky now.
Vern

June 9

To my Darling Frances – my lovely Indian Maiden. I am so happy I can't do anything but sit in this cabin and think of you my Angel. It won't be long until I see you because I am going to try that trail between the 8 and 10. Those pills are making me better but slowly. Maybe I am in too big a rush but the pills don't know I am about crazy to see my sweetheart of the mountains and if I die trying so what, for if I lose you I think I would make one good shot with the old 44 for you are truly my one and only real love of my life.

I did not know what love could do to a man until I found my angel by the stove. I began to love you after you came back in and I saw how hurt and alone you was. You don't know it but I spend many a sleepless night and did not dare to let you know but that short sweet kiss you gave me when I left for McCall made me know I just had to try and now I want you to know you are worth more to me than all of the gold in the hills. I will show up there as soon as I can and I would rather die at your feet than lose you or tell you one little lie or hurt you in any way. My sweetheart I read your long letter 2 or 3 times every day and it makes me feel so happy I don't know what to do. I just forget the nerve in my face and feel much better.

June 13
Dearest Frances,

My amado – my carino por siempre [my love, my sweetheart, forever]– can I say more? I can think of all the nice things I want to say to you. I will never live long enough to say it all for I love you so much it hurts me. I only have one thing in mind – if I could only come home to my angel.

I want you to decide what I should do about that nerve in my face – should I go have it cut off or take medicine for it – that is what is hard for me to makeup my mind – it is a lot better now. I hardly notice it but if you say go I will do it for you because I give up my life for you. I am glad to do it.

June 14

There is more. I must see you. I think I will go to the hospital at once as I am worse this morning and something has come up that I should talk to you in person only. I don't know which to do but I love you more than anything in the world and am afraid this is the end of me yet I can't say or do anything against you for you are my sunshine and my very life and may God, if there is one, be good to you and let only the best things happen to you.

June 15

Think I had better shut up and take this to the mailbox.
Love,
Vern

June 22

To Frances My Darling,

My Angel, I am so nervous and shaky I can hardly write because I love and need you so much. If you would only be mine I would try so hard to get well and give you the love and affection you and I have both been longing for so long. It is a terrible thing to want to be with and keep in my arms some one and know they can't return your love. It don't matter how soon I reach the end of the trail if when I do you could only be holding my hand I would not mind.

My face is much better the last few days but the medicine I am taking makes me act like I was drunk and if I try to walk down the trail I might go over the bluff into the river but before long I am going to try for I can't wait much longer to see you and take in my arms the most beautiful body in the world that I have ever seen. I wish I had never left there till you ran me away. My face is getting better but my heart is sick. I sit in this little cabin and every corner I look in I see you standing there and it is hell and I am yours and yours only until I die.

I can't think of any news except Hank hasn't a chance in the world to get well. I saw John Cook. He is on the way in to the river and will tell why I haven't been down. Please take good care of yourself and be the real Frances and don't lose any more weight and if my prayers will do any good you will always have the best.
Yours Only Forever,
Vern

June 24
To My Darling Frances My Angel,
I must tell you this. If you will be mine I will give you love beyond your wildest dreams for I now know you are the only woman I ever loved this way. If I can't have you this is the end of me for life. It would be hard to bear and there is no pain on earth like the one in my heart. We could love and live so happily together on my income and your money would be yours to save or spend on yourself alone and my last years would be heaven for me and I could come to a perfect end with you to close my eyes. Why oh why don't you tell me you will and I will go to Boise and get that nerve fixed and come right back to you and you can go to Texas and I can stay there and wait for my darling knowing she will come home to me. I can hardly stand this place. It makes me nervous and shaky to just sit here and dream of my sweetheart. Please don't make fun of me for this love is real - just one love life. This is a lifetime and I can-

not change it. I can do a lot of things I didn't do while I was there and it will make me happy to do them and besides we can fish and fish and enjoy life in the hills and you could have your paper and weather station and be truly happy.

June 25

Please answer my letters and tell me how you are and what you are doing and darling be the real Frances that you can be if you want to. That is the Frances I love so much. I told you I would have nothing to do with any other woman and I will keep my word and I do hope you will do the same for me. I don't feel quite so well today. Those pills are working on all my nerves and I act just like I am drunk.

June 27

Well here is another day. I am much better but those pills still make me shaky. I wish I could just lie on your couch and get well and hear the voice of the real Frances I love and pet you some more and whisper nice things in your ear and see you move around. I could say it a million times. It always comes out the same – My Darling Angel, I love you.
Vern

June 29

To My Darling Frances

I got your long letter and I don't know how to tell you how much it meant to me the loving words you wrote. Oh please my wonderful angel, don't change. For some years ago I decided to hate all women, but now you have made me see what one good and precious woman, my sweetheart is worth and how dumb I have been all these year. But how lucky I am to wait till a jewel like you should say you love me. You say you love your chief but I think I am the weakest buck in the tribe for my heart is so full of joy. I let a few tears of joy fall on the paper as I was read-ing and am glad and proud to tell you no one could love you more. I will get down there as soon as I think I can drive that road to the place at the end of the road. I will let my darling go

anywhere she wants and I will keep a light burning in my heart waiting for her return even if my arms hurt from wanting you in them every night or how long the days and nights may be till she returns. I am getting better every day but slowly. Maybe I am in to big a hurry to see my beautiful baby and hold that perfect body close in my arms again. I wish I had 50 years to show you. I am not much good with words, but I will do my best at loving. And I see now that is the thing that counts for to think of you makes me warm all over and nothing matters to me but you my wonderful woman. Why oh why do I have to sit in this cabin and stay away from perfect heaven when most of my pain is being away from you.
I say it a million times, carino mio I love you
Vern

The feelings Vern expressed were returned in letters Frances wrote.

Dear, when you do go to Boise, please let me know thru the radiotelephone. I do so want to know where you are. Darling, do you realize the Boise deal may take more than just a day or two – and the longer you wait the longer it will be before you can come a courting. (I get the nicest warm all over glow, every time I think about my Chief coming courting).

My Dear, I have a question – and it must be answered. When a woman is trying to catch a chief for her man does she call him Sir or your Highness – or would it be OK if she just followed her heart and call him Darling and My Dear? Now you tell me – for I know a woman who is sort of dumb but anxious to learn. She certainly wants to land the Chief.

I'm getting sleepy Dear – take care of my love – good care Darling.

Cook was teasing me today – but that can wait until tomorrow. Cook isn't so dumb.

Friday
I've been washing windows, Dear, and thinking of you, us. We needed this time away from each other – so we would be

forced to think a bit – and so far as I am concerned, the separation has been long enough. Please Dear, don't make it any longer than necessary – for me, Dear, if not for both of us.

And Dear, I am so glad I am not the first woman in your life. But Darling, I am the last one in your life – whether we have just these few days, or be it years. And dear, I'm so glad there were many between the first and me, because I – I don't know how to say it on paper Darling – but

A year later, Frances would write her sisters to introduce them to Vern. She tried to put the proper Methodist spin on what was happening at the Ferry and reinvent the man she now loved. "Vern was an old friend of Joe's," she wrote. "He meant no more to me than anyone else who came to visit Joe. They would talk guns or hunting or trapping or horses. I would cook and wash dishes and get away from the house all I could to let Joe talk his man talk but also because there was no place in the conversation for me. But other than his name and that he liked sugar but no cream in his coffee, I did not know Vern. Nor, did he know me. We did not begin to get acquainted until Joe was gone nearly a year."

"Vern was brought up differently from Joe," Frances continued. "His father was Scot. His mother was a full blood Sioux of the tribe of Sitting Bull. His mother was also a school teacher – must have been a good one – a superintendent of schools in Wichita for twenty years."

Frances' story of Vern's Sioux heritage is a fairy tale. Like many, including Frances, Vern had come to the Salmon River Canyon for reasons he wished to forget. Vern may himself have believed the story of his Indian origin. Perhaps it was family lore told to him as truth. The census records tell a different story.

Allen Vernon Wisner's father, Edward, was born in New York State, the son of German immigrants. His mother, Mary, was born in Illinois and is listed in the 1890 census as white. When Vern was born on December 25, 1894, in Lexington, Nebraska, his father's occupation was listed as laborer and his mother a teacher.

His parents divorced in his early teens, sending Vern, his mother and twin sisters to live with her parents. At age 18, in September of

1913 Vern enlisted in the Navy in Buffalo, NY, and became a water tender on the battleship *U.S.S. Kearsarge*.

This was the era of the Great White Fleet, the large group of steam-powered battleships sent round the world by President Teddy Roosevelt to project American power. The large boilers in the massive ships required constant attention to assure that water levels did not get too high, losing the ability to produce steam, or too low and lead to overpressure and explosion. Vern's job was in the engineering department on the ship, part of what was called the black gang who lived and worked below the main deck and seldom saw the light of day.

During his Navy career Vern earned enough shore leave to marry fourteen-year old Beryl G. Wisner from Baltimore, Maryland. The couple had two children, a daughter, Edith, born in 1915 and a son, Otis, born in 1917. Beryl's maiden name was Wisner and may have been his cousin.

Vern's four-year hitch in the Navy ended September 25, 1917, but eleven months later he was inducted into the Army infantry for World War I. He served a tour of duty in France as fireman on a locomotive hauling freight to the troops. On May 13, 1919, at age twenty-four the 5'8" young man with sandy hair and fair complexion was honorably discharged.

When the 1920 census was taken, Vern, Beryl and son Otis were not recorded, but their five-year-old daughter was living with Beryl's parents twenty miles northwest of Baltimore. Four years later Vern and Beryl are found in the Baltimore city directory living near the port, with Vern working as a fireman.

We do not know the circumstances surrounding his actions, but some time after his discharge from the military Vern left his wife and children in Maryland and moved west to start a new life. The 1930 census shows him working as a laborer on a cousin's farm in Nebraska before the Depression took him to Idaho.

****

Frances' new relationship did not sit well with her friends. Alice Wilson Rickman had come to the Salmon River Canyon in 1935 and settled on Jackson's Bar with her father, Howard *Haywire* Wilson, mother Nellie and five other Wilson siblings.

Lost Love

Haywire was known in the canyon for his ability to make most anything mechanical work. He got to know Joe Zaunmiller by helping him with his original sawmill. Later the two built what would be the last ferryboat. Frequent visits to Campbell's Ferry by the Wilsons led to a lifelong friendship between Frances and Alice, but the events of 1962 strained the relationship.

"Joe Zaunmiller was a smart man," said Alice. "He could conjure up things, like digging ditches with no levels – he put in all the irrigation ditches at the Ferry. He built the barn. He could sure handle horses. He was a very strong man who could do a day's work. He was a hero to us Wilson kids. We just loved him. When Frances married Vern Wisner so soon after Joe died I really had my nose in a kink for a while."[2]

"We thought Vern was a bum, that he had married Frances for a place to live and free room and board. He must have been good in bed. We couldn't see that he was good for anything else. We never saw him work. But she really loved him. I finally accepted it after several years."

Mary Crowe had a similar view of Frances' new husband, "Vern Wisner was an old guy, the kind of guy who lives along the river, does something, not much, probably lived off a small pension. I don't think he worked. I don't know of anything he did except a little in the orchard."[3]

Frances' family had a different view. "The first time we flew into the Ferry Frances had just married Vern," said niece Becki. "It was strange to us that Joe was not there."

"I always felt that Vern was more Frances' intellectual equal. He had traveled a lot, was well read and spoke well. Uncle Joe was more used to the mules and his four letter words. Frances always wanted to present herself as a lady, most of the time. She could use four letter words, too."

"But Vern was very nice to us. It was a different atmosphere at the Ferry that summer. Things were more laid back. Aunt Frances wasn't as busy cooking, cleaning and taking care of things. It was more enjoyment. Frances was starting to enjoy her life. We were

2 Alice Rickman, Personal Communication, 2010
3 Mary Crowe, Personal Communication, 2009

314

thankful that she had someone."[4]

After their romance blossomed, to the couple's great relief, Vern's medical problems abated. Frances followed her heart. On May 2, 1963, she and Vern traveled to Asotin, Washington, and tied the knot. For the next eight years the couple enjoyed the life both had sought – Frances dived into her writing and causes with a passion, enjoying her new, true companion.

Vern had been a canyon resident for decades, scratching out a living hunting, fishing, and trapping. Some thought him lazy, but that is unlikely. At the Ferry he handled chores as he could, given his frequent medical problems.

In one of her columns Frances described their typical day:

One of the nicest things a husband can do happens every morning at the house at the Ferry. Your Frances has no idea just when Vern gets up to build the fire in kitchen stove. She rarely hears the clatter as cups and saucers are placed on the coffee table. Snug in bed, she is catching up on the sleep she missed

Vern

4 Becki Pollan Godfrey, Personal Communication, 2008

when she walked out in the night to listen to the night birds. Not until the coffee pot is placed on the little table is she wakened with a "coffee's ready."

She sips her coffee and watches night leave the orchard. As she sips a second cup the thought comes that she is a very lucky woman. After dressing, she feeds the chickens and takes the morning weather readings, calls them in on the radio and starts standard Ferry breakfast – sourdough pancakes, hash browns and bacon or ham. Dishes are stacked for later. She gets wood from the shed to restock for the fireplace and kitchen stove, taking time to enjoy the birds, deer and elk grazing in the orchard and at the salt lick. Grain is given to Old Jack, the mule.

Lunch is leftovers, then a short nap, reading aloud until time for the afternoon weather, another cup of coffee from the second pot Vern has prepared, then a trip to the garden to dig spuds and artichokes. The evening meal varies, any time between 5 and 8 P.M., followed by more reading to Vern until he is ready to call it a day. She washes dishes, cleans the kitchen and lays out a supply of cooking wood and kindling next to the stove so the man who cannot see can build a morning fire and make the special pot of coffee, used every morning as bait to get a sleepy wife out of bed with "coffee's ready."

Throughout the first seven years of their marriage, Vern made frequent trips to the VA hospital in Boise, treating a variety of ailments. In 1970, he received bad news. Frances reported, "Vern went out for a very thorough checkup and learned he had man's dreaded affliction, hardening of the arteries. It was so advanced 'nothing can be done for it,' said the doctors. And so, he came home."

Vern was quiet for a few days, talking very little, but thinking a lot. Once the ever-present company was gone, he asked Frances to sit down for a family conference. He told of the medical verdict he had received, and his own decision to go to the Old Soldiers Home. Frances listened, and replied, "I'll order the plane for you, if that is what you really want. But before I do, listen to my side of the situation. I am going to stay here at the Ferry, with you, or without you and without you it would be damned lonely."

"I did not marry you to be a bother," Vern said.

Lost Love

"We would have to get someone to come in to get the wood in and saw it up. I can split it, and it does not take any more wood to keep two people warm than it does to keep one. All the other chores, it is me who would have to teach a helper how to do them."

Frances asked for a winter – all her way, and she got it. That winter was not hard on Frances, but it was the roughest Vern Wisner ever spent. "For sheer difficulty to endure," Frances wrote, "it beat any war time duty, or winters at putting that little cat over the snow-road to Dixie and running a trap line was child's play in comparison."

For months Vern did little more than lift a coffee cup and slow walks to the outhouse. By mid-January he had the strength to come out for the daily feeding of the stock, but it was then that Frances realized how bad his sight had become.

While petting a mule Vern asked, "Which one is it?"

By spring of 1972 Vern's vision began to return – enough to help friends who came to help them replenish their wood supply. "He has a sighted space about five feet in front of the left wheel of the tractor. So he can drive around the ranch in the well known places."

In a February 13, 1974 column Frances wrote, "Vern has been

Vern and Frances – 1971

an invalid for four years. There were bad days as well as others when the world was all roses. Until this January when each day was bad. It seemed that each yesterday was better than the today. There was no pain and no fever. He had had blackouts before, months apart, now they returned unpredictable and frightening. At the outset of a blackout Vern would not faint in a ladylike swoon. He fell backwards, swiftly. She was more scared of his head hitting hard object than the blackout."

When the blackouts became almost constant Frances panicked. She radio-telephoned the doctor but was told more tests were all they could do, if he could come to Boise.

"Four years before when the disease was first diagnosed Vern was told that his hardening of the arteries was too advanced, too extensive and that he should 'go home and let Nature take its course.' Frances was told that he would not make it through the winter and a nursing home was recommended. Frances would not have the love of her life reduced to a chart and a bed number, so the Ferry became an extended care facility with Frances head nurse."

Frances took advantage of advice from doctors who stopped while floating the river. They told her that the improvements Vern experienced in 1971 were rare for those with his condition, to not get their hopes up. Toward the end, when breathing became difficult, Frances stacked quilts around him so he could sleep sitting up. Trips to the Blue Room were impossible, so coffee cans and a bedpan became part of everyday routine.

Zeke and Marlene West from Whitewater Ranch made frequent stops to help with chores and check on the couple. "It was one of Vern's bad days that Marlene rode up, untied a gunny sack from behind her saddle, and grinned that she wanted to show Vern something."

Marlene hurried into the house. Minutes later Frances set aside her wood splitting and followed, pleased to find Vern awakened from his misery by the unexpected visit. As he ran his hands over the hide of a large mountain lion, the sharing of tales of past hunting adventures with Marlene and Zeke brought Vern to his feet for a

Zeke, Vern and Marlene

short trip into the bright sun of a snow-covered winter day.

This was Vern's last day outside, except for the brief March 1st trip up to the landing strip for a flight to the VA hospital in Boise. Two weeks later Frances followed, arriving at the hospital in time to spend a final afternoon with the love of her life.

From his bed Vern reached out to touch her dress.

"It is the red one you like," she whispered.

One finger touched her nylon clad knee and she told him, "They are new, not a broken thread."

"Which shoes?"

"The red ones, heels that high."

The flame still burned. The same that had flared so brightly fourteen years before on the night Vern had walked across the orchard, accepting the dinner invitation of the newly widowed Frances.

At the VA Hospital the couple shared stories and an update on the critters, wild and domestic, that shared the Ferry home they loved. Shortly after five, Frances made a quick trip away for dinner, returning at six to the doctor's news that Vern was gone.

Vern was given a military funeral in Grangeville. He was laid to rest next to a vacant plot where one day the two lovers would be reunited.

Chapter
Twenty-Nine

Activist

"An activist is someone who makes an effort to see problems
that are not being addressed and then makes an effort
to make their voice heard. Sometimes there are so many things
that it is almost impossible to make your voice heard
in every area, but you can sure try"
– Joanne Woodward

In 1961 Frances first published her view of the ongoing efforts
to change the millions of acres of national forests and primitive area
surrounding the Ferry to a new designation – wilderness. As always,
Frances held strong opinions, backed by her twenty-one years in the
canyon. She explained to her readers, "she has learned the laws of the
primitive area by contact."

Frances had seen success in advocating for a bridge, a new
trail to the bridge and extension of the backcountry air mail route to
include stops at the Ferry. Emboldened, she launched a multi-year
campaign of letters and advocacy among her readers. She urged them
to help fight what became the Wilderness Act of 1964, the Wild and
Scenic Rivers Act of 1968 and the Central Idaho Wilderness Act of

1980.

There was a fundamental flaw in Frances' position. She supposed that there was a law of the Primitive Area that offered legal protection for the lands she had so eloquently written about (see the end of Chapter 22). Frances wrote her state and federal congressional representatives, as well as the President, asking for copies of the Primitive Area law.

Senator Church and others informed her there was no such law. The Primitive Areas had been created by administrative action of the Forest Service, not Congress. If the Forest Service created the protection, they could remove it, and had done so in some cases. Wilderness advocates, with good reason, did not trust Forest Service managers. They viewed this lack of legal protection as a primary reason new laws were needed to protect wild places for future generations.

Among Frances' fears was one that the Wilderness and Wild and Scenic Acts might remove existing homesteads, including Campbell's Ferry and its residents. There was also the threat of eliminating existing backcountry landing strips that provided access to backcountry users and residents. But the greatest threat she saw was a proposal put forth by the North American Water and Power Alliance (NAWPA).

In the 1950s a California engineering firm had developed a plan under NAWPA, to divert water from Alaska, Canada, Montana and Idaho to the desert Southwest. A series of dams, reservoirs and tunnels would move the water. In Idaho dams would be built on the Clearwater, flooding twenty-nine miles up the Selway and twenty up the Lochsa.

On the Salmon River a dam below the mouth of the Middle Fork would flood up the Middle Fork, Big Creek, North Fork and the main river almost to the town of Salmon. Another, the 725 foot high Crevice Dam, would be located thirteen miles above Riggins. It would inundate Campbell's Ferry and back water ten miles up the South Fork of the Salmon.

Today, we can see such a proposal as nonsense due to costs and environmental concerns. But in Frances' day it was not as far fetched. She lived in the heyday of western dam building. The Colorado River project was becoming a reality. Congress held hearings on NAWPA in 1964.

A section in the Wilderness Act titled Special Provisions was the focus of Frances' fears. Section 4 (d) (4) gave the President power to, "as he may deem desirable, authorize prospecting for water resources, the establishment and maintenance of reservoirs, water-conservation works, power projects, transmission lines, and other facilities needed in the public interest..."

Frances saw this provision as trumping the core of the Act. Her fears were not abated when she learned one candidate for President in 1964 was a senator from the desert Southwest, Barry Goldwater of Arizona.

Ultimately, Frances' fears were misplaced. She found herself on the wrong side of history.

The opening line of the Wilderness Act states, "In order to assure an increasing population accompanied by expanding settlement and growing mechanization, does not occupy and modify all areas within the United States and its possessions, leaving no lands designated for preservation and protection in their natural condition, it is hereby declared to be the policy of the Congress to secure for the American people of present and future generations the benefits of an enduring resource of wilderness."

The Act is a powerful law for preservation, made even more so by the existence today of what Aldo Leopold called for in *A Sand County Almanac*, "a militant minority of wilderness-minded citizens ..... on watch throughout the nation and available for action in a pinch." That cadre exists today, built by decades of visitors to America's wild places, and even more who care, even if they never set foot in wilderness.

Nevertheless, Frances did not trust the new law, stating her position as, "the river and its canyon left as it was, and as it is. Wild, unruly at times, with a few of the hardships taken out."

She published her own plans for the area. Included was an all weather road the length of the canyon, out of sight above the north rim, complete with periodic campgrounds, scenic turnouts, lodges, apartments and dormitories. The Mackay Bar Road would be improved and a new road brought into the canyon at Black Creek. The Whitewater Road would remain as is. A trail would be constructed the length of the canyon accompanied by a phone line, complete with periodic pay phones in weatherproof boxes. She also proposed helicopter logging in the canyon.

Activist

We are fortunate that Frances' bully pulpit failed her this time.

****

In the early 1960s Frances took up the cause of hunting practices. Al Tice, her neighbor, fifteen miles downstream at Mackay Bar, had built one of the largest hunting operations in the state. He brought in a small dozer and improved the landing strip at Mackay Bar to accommodate his own planes and those of his clients. Traditionally, the planes were just a tool used to transport clients to and from his base at the confluence of the Main and South Fork of the Salmon.

Tice soon realized that he could use his plane to spot game, increasing the chance of success for his well-heeled clientele. It was legal to do so, but many thought that Tice was crossing the line of ethical practice. Especially when word got out of his use of a helicopter.

Elk hunting among the steep cliffs of the Salmon River country is a challenging activity. The real work starts once the near half-ton animal is dead on the ground. The usual method of getting the meat and trophy rack back to camp is a pack string of sturdy mules.

On one occasion, a Tice client had dropped a bull on the edge of a steep precipice and the animal slid into a deep, narrow canyon inaccessible to mules. A radio call back to camp brought out a new tool belonging to a wealthy visitor to Mackay Bar. The client's helicopter hovered over the canyon and extended a long rope that the guides attached to the carcass for the quick flight back to camp. To one of Tice's guides, this became "the day I saw the mules smile."

Frances, Vern and one of their hunting clients at the Ferry didn't see it that way. Frances began a letter writing campaign to members of the legislature and the Idaho Department of Fish and Game, requesting that the use of planes and helicopters in the pursuit of game be outlawed. She wrote the Idaho Outfitters and Guides Association, of which she and Tice were members, and told them that she intended to come to their December 1962 meeting in McCall and "raise hell."

She did, and the board of the group, led by Paul Filer from Shepp Ranch with Al Tice as treasurer, unanimously passed a resolution stating, "Any gross, unfair advantage to the hunter automatically interferes with critical and necessary conservation of the species. We oppose use of any helicopter or radio to purposely enhance the hunter's odds of spotting game from the air, circling or hovering over said game to aid in directing ground parties, or in the use of radio to guide the hunters to the known hiding place of game."

Frances used her regular column in the *Free Press* to rally her readers to write the legislature and back a bill introduced to outlaw the practice. State Senator William Dee, representing Idaho County, had written the bill. He was also Frances' attorney on private matters.

The bill was passed unanimously in March 1963 with Frances sitting in the gallery of the Legislature in Boise.

Activist

Chapter Thirty

Visitors Welcome Or Not

A Free-Loading Friend
of Frances

can come, stay, eat, sleep and play
FOR NO PAY

At Campbell's Ferry, on the
Salmon River

As the popularity of river travel grew, Frances struggled with the rising tide of people washing upon the shores of the Ferry. To deal with the influx she issued *Freeloading Friend of Frances* cards to a select group. The back side was numbered and signed by Frances. She meant it. For those not included, it was touch and go on what type of reception they would receive at the Ferry door.

Her thoughts on visitors was a balancing act in Frances' own mind. For years in her columns she encouraged visitors, especially when she and Joe were selling fishing and hunting trips. When she began tending to ailing husbands and later when she was on her own, she was much more private.

In those later years she needed help. As she wrote in her column, "Frances measures each approaching pair of masculine shoulders with unfinished chores in mind."

She knew what she didn't want. Ten miles downstream was a well-known example. Sylvan Hart, known to most as Buckskin Bill, was a showman who reveled in entertaining visitors. Not Frances. "Lord how I would hate to have this place and people turned into another Buckskin Bill item," she wrote. "One is enough. Let Bill have it. Please deliver me from those who barge in with the air of, 'We are here, entertain us."

At one point she got on the radiotelephone and complained to all her canyon neighbors that someone "is telling floaters to stop at Campbell's Ferry. Go up to the house and you'll see an interesting old woman, as though Frances were a tid-bit on a tray to amuse the tourists."

Watching the degradation that occurred across the river at the Jim Moore Place also shaped Frances' opinion of river floaters. "I dislike the word vandalize, or vandalism, or vandal. I call them thieves. The tourists are very good people at home but when they come down the river on their summer trips they're a long ways from home and they seem under the impression that no one will realize how far back they've been unless they take a part of the canyon with them. Jim's place was wrecked."

On one occasion Frances was startled by a rock thrown through her cabin window. Charging outside she unleashed a torrent of "mule talk" to the surprised group of young men accompanied by a few adults. One of the adults said a youth in the group had thrown the rock and gave the lame excuse that they did not know the cabin was occupied.

"That is what happens when the general public is turned loose," wrote Frances. "I don't like them."

Frances understood the value of a river experience to the public. "I'm glad they can come. I think anyone who lives his life and has not seen that beautiful canyon, not looked down in that clear water that's so clear it's green, have watched the white froth in the rapids, and slopes with trees and grass and beautiful rocks, I think the person who lives his life and does not see that is cheated. But that is as people. As tourists, oh, brother. Ah, they're good people but they're a long ways from home."

****

In 1973 Frances received a visit from Cort Conley, one of Idaho's best-known river guides and historians. At the time while working as a guide for Shepp Ranch, Conley had the editor of *Smithsonian Magazine* as a client. The editor was working on a book about the Snake River Country and had a chapter about the Salmon as a tributary of the Snake. He had heard about Frances and wanted to meet her. Conley told him, "We haven't made any arrangements, but just the two of us can go up and see how it goes. The rest of you people stay in the rafts. She has a dog and a thing about visitors. We don't want to leave the gate open."

The two men went up and knocked. Frances came to the door, looked right past them and said, "Who left that gate open?"

Conley turned around to find all the people had followed them up, left the gate open and the dog was out!

Frances barked an order, "Step inside."

Vern was in the back on the bed. She said, "What do you mean coming up here?"

Conley apologized, explained that he had told the people to stay at the boat, and would go out and tell them to get the hell back to the boats.

Pulling on her cowboy boots Frances said, "I can tell them better myself."

Conley watched amazed as Frances came out, but instead of telling the group off, she was nice, "She said hi, how are you? And visited with them and told them they really should go over and see Jim Moore's buildings across the river. When the people left she was very pleasant."

Conley recounts, "I went over to Jim Moore and spent some time walking around. Back then there were artifacts everywhere. The blacksmith shop was filled with old blowers, lots of tools, cans and horseshoes. I told everyone, Don't take anything. Leave it as we found it. Later, at the takeout near Vinegar Creek I was on the ramp, moving bags up to the bus. I dropped one bag and it was open enough for a can to come out onto the ramp. It was an old coffee can, in perfect shape, that Jim Moore had cut and put a wick in to use as his oil lamp. Despite everything that had been said, one of our clients, this son-of-a-bitch from San Diego, a wealthy restaurant owner, had stolen it. I looked at him and thought, Do I take this from him?"

Not willing to risk offending his boss and one of his well-heeled clients, Conley relates, "I didn't. I just let it go. So somewhere in San Diego is Jim Moore's lamp."

"I can understand how bitter Frances was and why she blamed it on the river people, says Conley. You must wonder what it must have been like then, taking care of an invalid husband, on the homestead with no electricity, wondering what the future held. You don't have anything except the value of the land, a life estate, and wondering what happens when you can't split wood or carry water."

Later that year Frances refused Conley's written request for an interview as part of the Idaho Bicentennial Commission Oral History Project.

She wrote, "I do not allow the working press on the ranch for any reason."

Frances informed Conley that she was a member of the Press and, "When my knowledge of the Old Timers and Idaho Back Country is published, whether by tape or in print, it will be under my by-line."

In a later letter she wrote, "I've found that the visitor who wants to talk is allergic to taking part in daily chores."

Conley attempted to correct Frances' misconception of his role, stating he was not part of the working press, and his efforts to preserve Idaho's oral history would not be published or used for financial benefit, only stored at the Idaho Historical Society. The interview would not to be released without the subject's permission.

He also wrote, "I work as hard as a flat-tailed beaver and would be willing to work at any labor you'd care to put in front of me for a week in return for conversation."

Nothing worked to change her mind.

In 1976, after interviewing John and June Cook as part of the Oral History Project, Conley had a marker made for the grave of Rose Cook, John's stepmother, who had died in childbirth at the Ferry. John Cook wrote a letter of introduction asking for permission for Conley to install the marker.

Frances refused, speculating that it would increase the number of visitors who came up from the river to see the grave. She was offended that Conley had failed to ask her permission before making the marker. She insisted that if there was to be a marker, Dave Cook was going to chisel it in a large rock that would be placed on the grave.

The issue was not resolved until after Frances' death when Conley brought the marker to the Ferry on one of his many float trips through the canyon.

Despite the disagreements, Conley respected Frances and included her in his excellent book, *Idaho Loners*, which chronicles the lives of many backcountry characters.

"We had a love/hate relationship," said Conley, "but she hated me."

****

Others who came up from the river had a better chance at a good reception. "Pity the able bodied males who stop at the Ferry and ask if there is anything she needs done," wrote Frances. "Pity, too, those who do not ask, for they shall not be welcomed at second coming. Of course there are others – nice, thoughtful men – who never ask if there is a heavy chore waiting for a strong set of muscles. Instead, those kind, thoughtful ones just get busy and do the chores. Never asking. And the coffee is fresh brewed for them."

Dr. Omer Drury and his family were among those who earned a Friend of Frances designation. Drury owned a rafting business on the river, making several trips each year. On one occasion he and his crew brought Frances several bags of coal, which became her emergency heat source in the winter. At every stop Dr. Drury would inquire about Frances' health, offering medical help with her various maladies.

Another outfitter who developed a friendship with Frances is Wayne Johnson of Salmon River Rafting Company. Their relationship got off to a rocky start when several of Johnson's rafting guest decided to hike up to the Campbell's Ferry landing strip without first asking permission.

Johnson, who had stayed back at the Jim Moore Place to assist a handicapped client, was unaware of the trespass until Bob Smith told him of Frances' displeasure.

Johnson wrote Frances a letter of apology, "for the intrusion upon your privacy and the violation of basic principles of courtesy." He took, "full responsibility and blame for the event," and assured Frances it would not happen again.

Frances was impressed with the letter, promptly writing Johnson a five-page response explaining her feelings about most float groups.

She told Johnson how, one summer in the mid-1970s, a group of "kayakers – seven of them – were in my living room, drinking my coffee, when a female Master Sergeant type seriously asked, Now that you are a widow – how do you handle your sex life? Wayne, that little bit of crudity slammed my door tight. It stays shut."

In a later note she explained the mail schedule to Johnson and granted permission for his groups to come watch and film the plane's arrival. She did caution that the property was "saturated with bear" from August through October and no dogs were allowed.

Johnson's respectful approach to Frances earned him a Freeloading Friend of Frances card, a rarity among floaters.

****

In the summer of 1975 Frances looked up from her rocking chair on the front porch to see a handsome, lean, bearded young man approaching her home. Gary Kraus was looking for permission to camp on the beach under the bridge and for directions for the first of many hikes he made into the backcountry.

Kraus had grown up a surfer in Florida and was not experienced in backpacking, but after a tour in Vietnam as a Navy Seal, he decided to pursue a dream.

While serving his country, Kraus had read *The Last of the Mountain Men* by Harold Peterson, a romanticized account of the life of Sylvan Hart. Intrigued by the account of someone still living off the land in the wild, Kraus had followed the crude map in the back of the book to Dixie, then down the primitive road to Mackay Bar Ranch.

There he inquired if they knew Buckskin and was told, "Sure we know him. He just had a heart attack. He is in Boise."

Disappointed, Kraus headed upstream, stopping briefly at the vacant cabin at Rhett Creek that belonged to Reho Wolfe. Seeing the old cabin, meeting Frances and fascinated by the vast stretches of wild lands surrounding the Salmon River, Kraus decided to spend any spare time he could scrap together exploring the Idaho wilderness.

Over the next ten years he took on jobs in Wyoming, Montana, and went back to school in Florida. Every break he would head to Idaho's backcountry. After the first couple of short trips the next dozen were at least three months, and twice he spent the entire winter in a cabin he built up Trout Creek, a short distance from the Ferry:

Gary Kraus

In my first encounter with Frances she was neutral. I didn't know a lot about her at the time. She wasn't unfriendly. She was pretty arrogant. As I spent time back here I got to know her fairly well. When I got to know Zeke and Marlene at Whitewater and Harold and Phyllis at Allison Ranch, they would tell me, "If you go by Frances' stop and see if you can give her a hand with anything."

I helped her a lot. She was getting on in age. I would help her with the ditch and firewood.

Frances was good about feeding you if you did some work for her. When I would come by she would be in the kitchen and have her feet propped up on the stove, reading a book. I stayed over every once in awhile. We would be having dinner, sitting in the kitchen talking. It would get to be late and dark. She knew I was camped some distance away. She would say, Just throw your sleeping bag down and you can get going in the morning.

She lived in the kitchen in the winter. It was too hard to heat the whole place. The fireplace didn't do much good. She used it to burn trash.

She never got really friendly. Kind of standoffish. I think her past was always in the back of her mind. It was like she was always looking over her shoulder.[1]

The cabin that Kraus built was a marvel for someone with no building experience:

I read Thoreau early in my life and was fascinated with the concept of building a cabin. It took five months total, half for the building and half for the fireplace. It was ten by thirteen – Thoreau size.

The first log I cut – I had never cut a tree down before. I cut it about thirteen feet, went to pick it up and geez, I couldn't even lift it. So it had to be made with smaller trees.

For the roof I tried to make shakes, but it was a skill I didn't have. I tried flaking some out and they all came out twisted. It just wouldn't work. I was about to give up — maybe find some plastic or something, perhaps hike up to Dixie and see what I could scrounge up. I was about to give up when one day I was walking down by the middle of the ridge and saw a pile, walked over, and it was a pile of shakes.

Frances told me that when the old timers put up a cabin it was usually good for twenty years. Over that time period they would find a tree with straight grain and they would limb them so as they grew they would not have knots in them. About ten or twelve years in they would cut them down, season them and stack them into bolts so when the roof went they would have re-placement shakes. What I had found was someone's old shake pile.

Gary had help with the project. Back in Florida he had met Lorrie Wilkes, a graduate student at the University of North Florida. Hearing tales of the wilds of Idaho, Wilkes decided to come see for herself. After taking an Outward Bound course in the Three Sisters Wilderness in Oregon she and her seven-year-old daughter, Katie, flew into the Ferry with Ray Arnold.

1 Gary Kraus, Personal Communication, 2010

The Kraus Cabin on Trout Creek

Kraus did not know when they were expected, and they did not know the location of his cabin. So the first week Wilkes and Katie stayed with Frances. For the next two weeks the couple worked on the cabin:

I used mud for mortar. I cut wood with a one man crosscut saw. I built a bed about a foot and a half off the ground with slats and a pine needle cushion. I put an old Army blanket on top of the needles. I made a five foot fish weir using small roots but never had much luck with it.

The basics you need to survive are shelter, food, fire

Inside the Kraus Cabin
Note the table, fireplace, and fish weir made from small roots

and water. After I got the cabin built food was always an issue. I would hike up to Bargamin Creek, catch a bunch of fish and dry them. I would make a lattice work of thin sticks and hang them off the ground. It would take about 24 hours to dry, so it was an overnight trip. I hoisted them up in a tree to keep the bears from getting them.

I hunted in the fall. Early in the season I would dry the meat. Later, I would just hang a quarter in the cabin. The fireplace was so inefficient it was cold enough in there to keep meat. After the bears were in hibernation, you could hang it outside. With meat inside, I had a good door to keep them out and when I was not there I would put brush in front of the door. A couple of times I came back to find claw marks on the door, but they couldn't get in.

Wilkes went back to Florida to complete her training as a pediatric nurse. The following summer Gary taught tennis at a camp in South Carolina where Wilkes was the camp nurse. They married while at the camp and returned to Idaho in August.

Wilkes worked as a hunting camp cook's helper at Whitewater while Gary finished the cabin. In November, after hunting season Wilkes and Katie returned to the cabin, but found it too cold, and her relationship with Gary had foundered.

The two split, but both retained a connection to Idaho. The following year Wilkes came back to work at Whitewater, making frequent trips to visit Frances. The warm welcome she had received earlier turned sour as Frances began to see Wilkes as a threat to her status as ruler of the canyon.

"She was the river gossip queen," Wilkes remembered. "Whatever she could say derogatory about people, she would. She would stir things up - keep people upset, hurt their feelings — she was a master at it. She liked to keep people on the river in upset mode — whatever she could come up with for the day to say about someone, particularly women. Marlene used to call her 'Queenie of the River.' She didn't want any competition."[2]

Kraus made many trips back to Idaho, frequently coming in via Dixie or catching the mail plane. On occasion he tried different

2 Lorrie Wilkes, Personal Communication, 2013

routes to see more country:

One April I decided to come in from the east. I rode a Greyhound bus from Florida to North Fork, Idaho. From there a friend and I hitchhiked to the end of the road where the rafts are launched on the river. We crossed the river on the Stoddard packbridge, which led to a long series of switchbacks almost straight up the canyon wall.

Shortly after we reached the canyon rim the trail disappeared under a blanket of snow stretching to the horizon. I looked at the map, at the snow, and my friend and said, OK. Here is the deal. We are not going to see anymore trail until we head back down to the Salmon River. Are you up for that? She said, Let's go for it.

It turned into a death march. We had no snowshoes and were just plugging through the snow. Nine days later I climbed a tree, and spotted the familiar landmark of Chamberlain meadows. When we got to the meadows we were shot – almost dead, near out of food, exhausted.

Sitting there with our shoes off we heard a voice, 'Hey. What are you guys doing up here?' It was a man in a Forest Service uniform from the ranger station. He couldn't believe we were there. His wife took our socks that we had been wearing for nine days, washed them, gave us some coffee and cookies and asked where we were going. We told her, Dixie. She told us we had thirty-six miles to go, gave us a bag of cookies and sent us on our way.

We hadn't gone a quarter mile before all the cookies were gone. That was the roughest trip I ever did out here. We got to Dixie, got resupplied and came back to the cabin on Trout Creek.

Once when Kraus was visiting Frances told him, "My vet is coming down the river today. He is going to fix Gretchen." Gretchen was Frances' one-year-old German Shepherd. A couple of hours later a float boat group came up, including a vet from Grangeville.

"He threw a tarp down on the ground just outside the garden fence, gave Gretchen some anesthesia, turned her over, cut her open, tied her tubes, sewed her up and said, She'll be fine in a couple of days."

Frances also had a Boston Bull Terrier, Ruben, that she adored. She also had cats, but when one got in a fight with Ruben, according to her niece Mary, "She killed it. But first she gave it a last meal. She didn't have any cats after that."

Kraus relates, "Ruben had respiratory problems and had gotten to the point that he had a really hard time breathing. He was to the point that he was weak, could hardly get up. He needed to be put down, but she couldn't do it. I happened to be passing through and she said, 'I can't do it. Will you do something with him?' I thought, Please, I don't want to put him down, but she was so shaken she couldn't do it. So I took him out to water ditch. She buried him in the garden."

****

Dave Cook tells another story revealing Frances' personality. Dave is the son of John and June Cook, grandson of Warren Cook. He and his parents were good friends of Frances and frequent visitors to the Ferry.

"A lot of people loved Frances.....that didn't know her," said Dave. Frances could be very cantankerous:

If she had an opinion, everybody knew what it was, whether you agreed with her or not, you knew what Frances thought. She had an opinion on every subject. No matter if she had any facts, she had an opinion.

Years ago there was a big controversy in the backcountry about giving salt to the elk. They found that the elk were covered with thousands of ticks. The way you keep ticks off of cattle is to give them sulfur salt. The Game Department figured they could fly over the backcountry and throw salt blocks out – it was an easy, simple way, and the elk would shed the ticks.

But some of the game biologists said Mother Nature has been taking care of these animals for eons, and we might upset the apple cart if we go in there and introduce something that hasn't been there before. This should be studied before we do it. Everybody in the country took a hard position, either anti-salt or pro-salt – no reconciliation. Frances was very pro-salt. And she was very vocal about it.

338

It is the custom of the backcountry if people come visit, you feed them supper. One time the Forest Service ranger and the head of Fish and Game landed at the Ferry and Joe Zaunmiller invited them to stay for supper. The Fish and Game had just decided that they were going to delay the salt feeding program, which had riled Frances something awful.

So they came down for supper and she put on a big kettle of boiled potatoes. There was no salt on the table.

Mark Twain said, Salt is what makes potatoes taste bad, if you don't put it on.

So they all took some boiled potatoes and started to eat. At first no one said anything.

Finally Joe spoke up and said, "Frances, don't you think we need just a little salt here?"

"No, by God. If the elk don't need salt, neither do these guys. Now eat!"[3]

****

Maurice Hornocker, world renowned expert on large cats, also visited the Ferry and got a healthy dose of local perspective on the species he dedicated his life to study.

Frances disagreed with him on game management – specifically mountain lions. "Frances wondered why her attitude is labeled emotional simply because her opinion of the need for the big cats is based on watching the game herds shrink to small bunches, even loners. While his approach is labeled 'intellectual' simply because he made a 'study' of the cats – got a doctorate as one result of that study."

While Hornocker deplored that two men up-river had taken seventeen or eighteen big cats that winter, Frances was elated to hear it. She wished the men had been hunting near the Ferry – to protect "her deer and elk."

****

In a letter to John and Mary Crowe Frances tells of an unwelcome visit by a reporter from the *L. A. Times*. "He was not here at

3 Dave Cook, Personal Communication, 2009

Phyllis Thomas, Tom Close, Frances, Harold Thomas and Gretchen 1984

my invitation. As soon as I realized he was the press I sent him back to the plane. I thought I made it clear that I did not want to be splashed on the pages of the *L.A. Times* — so the article was a surprise to me."

The article was printed in newspapers across the country, prompting a flood of fan mail and a call from *The Tonight Show* with Johnny Carson. "On the phone I told Carson NO — and in reply to his letter wrote the same NO. This is the way Press began on Buckskin. And he – for fun – allowed interviews – went out to be on talk shows – and ended up with no time when free of darn dudes. I'll not let it start. I got a few nice letters from people it might be fun to know but most were from pure nuts and kooks. I rate the marriage proposal as kooky nut. Fame? Who wants it? It's a pain in the neck, or somewhere."

Frances also turned down requests from ABC's *Good Morning America.*

****

Harold and Phyllis Thomas purchased Allison Ranch in 1973 and settled in to the canyon community. Harold is an experienced pilot, using his own plane for flights in and out of his ranch. He would frequently check with Frances to see if she needed anything. The answer was usually, yes, earning them a Freeloading Friend of Frances membership.

Among the chores they found at the Ferry in 1977 was a new outhouse. The old privy was perched on the edge of the front yard of Frances' cabin, and had a unique *self-flushing* feature. The small ditch that ran in front of the cabin had been routed under the outhouse to take the product of the facility over the hill down to the river.

Norm Close remembers it as a two-holer. "I always thought it was a nice. You could do your business on one side and fish through the other. Maybe you would catch a brown trout!"

When the old facility collapsed over the hill, Harold and Phyllis took on the task of building a new privy. Harold designed the new structure, cutting the needed sheets of plywood into two-foot wide sections so they would fit in his airplane. After the building was complete, Frances decided to paint it.

Late one afternoon a tall young man came up the trail from the river and found Frances, brush in hand, applying a bright blue paint to the outhouse. Bill Bernt of Salmon, Idaho is the owner of Aggipah River Trips. He and his brother had finished their camp chores at the Jim Moore Camp and slipped away from their clients to call on Frances.

After a brief hello, Frances said, "You're tall. You can paint while we talk," and handed him the brush.

After a while Bernt got up the nerve to ask Frances, "Why the garish blue color?"

"I want the Sierra Clubbers to be able to see it from the river!"[4]

---

4 Bill Bernt, Personal Communication, 2006

The Blue Room

Chapter
Thirty-One

End of an Era

"Life is pleasant. Death is peaceful.
It's the transition that is troublesome"
– Isaac Asimov

On the morning of October 28, 1983, at 8:01A.M. while sipping her morning coffee in her nightgown, robe and slippers, Frances heard a strange rattling noise and turned to see dry beans dancing as though boiling in water in a clear glass jar on the shelf. Except there was no water. The floor of the 1905 cabin began to heave. Frances called her German Shepherd, Gretchen, grabbed the lighted candle and hurried out the front door into the yard. The layers of walnut leaves coating the ground were suspended in the air, then began to ripple in waves like surf approaching a beach.

Frances started back into the cabin to dress, but an aftershock changed her mind. Instead she went to take the weather, away from any structures. An hour after the first shock she returned to the house. The counter tops and floor were littered with beans, rice, coffee, macaroni and the shattered remains of glass containers. Broken dishes and tumbled containers were mixed among the fallen debris. In the living room books had cascaded from their shelves, drawers were half open and a dry fish tank used to store knitting yarn was in shards on the floor. A map had fallen from the wall and was soaked by the contents of a broken kerosene lamp.

The following day, during a visit to the Blue Room, Frances felt the entire structure rock back and forth, threatening to toss the building and its occupant over the edge toward the river. Later, a trip to the cellar underneath the cabin found her shelves of canned goods intact, but a major support beam had dislodged and was lying across the entry. Another aftershock sent Frances scurrying out of the cellar. For two nights Frances made her bed outdoors away from any structure.

The Borah Peak Earthquake, though centered near Mackay, Idaho 125 miles away, was strong enough to rattle nerves and cause structural damage at the Ferry. At 6.9 on the Richter Scale, it was the largest quake ever recorded in Idaho. Years later as restoration work was begun on the historic cabin, much of the underpinning had to be replaced to repair the damage.

****

The early 1980s was a time of increased visitation and support from Frances' network of canyon friends and family. Sisters, nieces and nephews from Texas made extended annual trips to Idaho to help. Canyon neighbors were in constant touch with the elderly widow living alone at the Ferry.

The old Forest Service telephone lines had been abandoned by the agency, but the canyon residents kept it operating for the daily conversation it allowed. It was a critical life line should problems arise. Zeke West, who had a hunting and fishing business at Whitewater, became a close friend of Frances, checking on her on a daily basis. Zeke says it was easy to know when all was well – she talked non-stop.[1]

"Frances liked a good listener. When she talked to you on the telephone, she would talk as long as she could hold the conversation,

1 Zeke West, Personal Communication, 2011

Frances – 1980

but as soon as you started talking, she had something to do. I had an old cowboy caretaker down here. One day Frances called up while he was doing dishes. Frances started talking so he just laid the receiver down and went back to his dishes. When he was finished, he picked up the phone and Frances was still talking! She never even missed him!"

If there was any sign of trouble, Zeke would drop whatever he was doing and check on Frances. "I'd been out to town and came back in and asked the neighbors how everyone was doing. They said they hadn't heard from Frances for a couple of days. I said, You haven't heard from her at all? No."

I'm thinking why in the hell didn't somebody go down there. The snow was about thirty inches deep and was crusted. It wouldn't hold you up on snowshoes. Just as you would get going, down you would go. Then climb out and down you would go again. I wasn't too young then either. But I couldn't get her on the phone or on the radio. There was nothing to do but head out.

I was about halfway down there and I was pooped. I didn't know if I could make it there, but it was just as far to turn back.

End of an Era

I finally got up to the cabin exhausted. Frances sat me down in a rocking chair in front of the fireplace, built a big fire, wrapped me in blankets and handed me a bottle of whiskey. She said, This will perk you up. I sat there and drank a bit of the whiskey and warmed up after a bit.

The radio didn't work. She claimed it was batteries. And the phone line was broken. On the way down I had found the break in the phone line and patched that back together. That was a tough trip down there. The next day I had to go back, so I put on the snowshoes and said, I'll walk the river ice - to heck with the trail. The trail was all slid in, just ice chute down to the river in a lot of places. I had to crawl across those places coming down, so I figured I would walk on the river ice. I started out and fell into a crack. I couldn't get that dang snowshoe out. I had a heck of a time getting out. So when I did, I got off the river. That was enough of that. I got back on the trail and made it home. That was quite a trip.

Zeke was concerned about Frances being alone at the Ferry with wildlife roaming the place. Once, Frances called up when Zeke had a hunter at Whitewater.

She said, "A cougar came by here last night."

He asked, "How do you know that?"

"I heard him."

"Every once in a while he would let out a kind of squall. He was looking for a mate or something. I know it was a cougar. You come down here and get after him."

Zeke loaded up a couple of horses and headed to the Ferry. "We cut the track right up where the Chamberlain Trail crosses the ferry, between Frances' cabin and the Crowe cabin. We got him."

Another time Frances was having trouble with bears. The berry crop in the mountains was bad, so dozens of bears were feeding in the Ferry orchard.

Cougar

End of an Era

Frances told Zeke, "There are forty of them coming in here. I know them all."

On her daily trips to the chicken coop, barn and garden, Frances devised a way to scare the bears away. "Some of the bears were aggressive, said Zeke, So she took two of the old square five gallon kerosene cans and rattle them together to make a sound the bears didn't like."

But she couldn't do her chores while carrying the cans, "So she recorded the sound, tied her little recorder to her waist and played it as she went about her chores. That way her hands were free to carry things, get her work done and the bears stayed away."

"She told me she killed nine bear that summer. She only killed the ones that stood their ground and snapped their teeth at her. I asked her what she was doing with the bears and she said she was taking them out behind the chicken house."

Zeke asked, "How did you do that?"

"She had a garden cart that was kind of tub shaped. She would roll up next to the dead bear, reach over the handles and grab a couple of handfuls of hide and fall backwards. When she landed she would be sitting on the ground on her rear end and the bear was in the cart."

"Frances left the dead bear behind the chicken coop and pretty soon the other bears would clean it up."

A steady supply of wood for the winter became an annual task for Zeke. "I found out that she was just picking up fallen branches, what she called squaw wood, for her wood supply. So every fall I would have a few guys in here at Whitewater with a couple of extra days or so and we would load up our chain saws and gas, ride down there and start that old tractor up. We would fell timber and skid it. We would whack the heck out of that timber down there, have her about ten cords of wood. She never did burn it all. She would cook up a big meal for us. She was a heck of a good cook. I always looked forward to meals down there. She made up a beef stew with canned meat. She let me pasture my fifteen head of horses and mules down

Black bear

Frances – 1984

there for cutting the wood."

Ray Arnold would visit every week flying the mail plane. Carol Arnold would fix a special treat for Frances, taking a half gallon of ice cream from the freezer, cut it in half, and wrap it well enough to last for the forty minute flight to the Ferry.

Frances and Gretchen would meet the plane at the airstrip with a bottle of Kahlua and a spoon. With no refrigeration to save it, Frances sat next to the plane and ate what she could, giving the rest to Gretchen. When Frances became too frail to make the hike up the hill to meet the plane, Ray would bring mail and supplies down to her.

Throughout Frances' life at the Ferry she had dealt with numerous health issues. In 1956 she went to Lewiston twice for surgery for thyroid cancer. In 1978 on a trip down the hill to meet a jetboat she fell and broke a leg. In 1979 she had all her teeth pulled. In 1980 sister Billee and niece Mary Key came from Texas to take care of the Ferry while she was out getting new teeth. In 1985, Frances' cancer returned.

On a mid-December day several attempts to reach Frances on the phone had brought no response, so Zeke once again made the trip to the Ferry to check on her. Marlene West describes what he found, "When he entered the cabin there was Frances laying on a bed she had made in the middle of the floor. The fires in the stove and fireplace had gone out and Gretchen was laying on her feet, trying to keep her warm."

Frances was in pain, unable to walk, so Zeke got on the phone and called for Marlene to come help. She saddled a mule, struggled with the snow and fallen timber blocking the trail, and finally arrived. While Marlene tended to Frances, Zeke cleaned up, washing dirty dishes that were piled in the cupboards.

"I couldn't help her," said Marlene. "Finally everybody was just trying to talk her into going out."

"She didn't want to go out," said Zeke. "It took quite a bit of talking."

Frances' closest personal friend in the canyon was Tom Close from Allison Ranch. "We got him on the phone," said Zeke. "Tom was a big influence. She finally said she would fly out if Tom would come down and look out for the Ferry and Gretchen."

Zeke went back to the Ferry the day when the plane was coming. Frank Hill flew in from Grangeville and brought Alice Rickman to help.

Tom Close and Frances – 1984

"Frances had these plastic toboggans that she pulled stuff around on, so we rolled her up in a bunch of quilts and put her on one of those toboggans. I was pulling and Alice Rickman was pushing. We had to take her clear to the top of the runway. It was quite a tussle. Alice finally gave out and I had to pull her all by myself."

Frances said, "I don't weigh but 135 pounds."

Zeke replied, "They are all there today, Frances!"

The plane took Frances to Grangeville, but they could not help her, so she was transferred to Lewiston. She requested that Zeke ride in the ambulance. As they drove with Marlene following, Frances kidded Zeke, "Isn't this something! Zeke and Frances headed down the road with Marlene in hot pursuit!"

At the Lewiston hospital a young male friend came by to visit, "Frances, I'm so sorry you're sick."

She replied, "Hell, I'm not sick. I'm dying!"

"That was Frances," said Linda Karki.[2]

Frances was determined to spend her final days at the Ferry, constantly urging her friends to make the necessary arrangements. Linda relates, "Frances and I were having a conversation with the doctor about what we would do when she was back at the Ferry. The doctor asked what would I do when she died. I said I could dig a hole in the snow, wrap her in canvas and wait until we could get a plane in. The doctor thought that was a pretty good idea."

But Frances spoke up and said, "Oh, hell, just open up the window!"

"We could have gotten her back to the Ferry," said Linda. "At the hospital they were using an orange and a syringe to teach me how to give her morphine if I had to. When we got to Grangeville the weather was awful. There was delay after delay. When there was a break in the weather Frank Hill would find a reason to delay more. We just didn't want to do it."

As the end neared, Frances held on. She had made up her mind to wait until her final Social Security check arrived. Linda Karki and Alice Rickman were taking turns sitting with Frances. Each day she would ask, "Has the check arrived?"

On the morning of January 6, 1986, Linda stopped at the post office on her way to the hospital.

Check in hand, she entered the room, leaned over the matriarch of the Ferry and whispered, "The check is here. You can go now. Vern is waiting."

Frances died that afternoon.

At Allison Ranch Tom Close was sitting enjoying his daily libation when Gretchen began to howl. It was the afternoon of January 6th. A week later, Gretchen passed peacefully in her sleep.

2 Linda Karki, Personal Communication, 2011

End of an Era

Frances and Gretchen,
waiting for the mail

"She was a great old gal. I miss her."

– Zeke West

From the air, this great canyon
Must be especially beautiful during Christmas
With the pine and grass covered slopes
Now frosted by snow and ice
An emerald ribbon
Which is the Salmon River
Ice decked in holiday dress
Faint wisps of wood smoke from chimneys
Chimneys so many miles apart
No smoke from one
Joins that of another

Frances Zaunmiller Wisner

Chapter Thirty-Two

Preservation

"So much of our future
Lies in preserving our past"
– Peter Westbrook

A small child dipped a ladle into the cool clear water flowing in the ditch placed here by pioneers almost a century before. A crowd of visitors milled about Warren Cook's now empty 1905 log cabin. Many sought refuge from the summer heat in the shade of the majestic quarter-century-old English walnut tree that dominating the yard.

Some had been here two years prior and felt they owned, in their hearts and in actual artifacts, part of the place. Some had items left to them in Frances' will. Others had purchased personal items and artifacts auctioned off by the executors to pay her final expenses. This day they had come to learn what would happen to the property, the cabin, barn, blacksmith shop and other structures sitting on eighty-five acres surrounded by wilderness – a place they all knew simply as the Ferry.

Many were worried, with good reason. Bob Abbott, the first to speak, wore the familiar Forest Service green uniform of a district ranger. The agency had a reputation for cabin burning. The gathered friends of the Ferry knew of many specific examples of similar historic structures in the Salmon River Canyon that were no more – burned, victims of an agency wilderness purity movement. Would these historic buildings suffer the same fate?

Bob Abbott

Abbott began his talk to the group by introducing Donna McBain. McBain represented The Trust for Public Lands (TPL), a land conservation organization from California that was now the owner of Campbell's Ferry. McBain explained to those gathered that the future of the Ferry would be controlled by an agreement struck between John and Mary Crowe, the Forest Service and her organization.

The first step in creating the agreement had been TPL's purchase of the property from the Crowes. With the purchase had come a deed, the legal document that transfers ownership. Legal ownership in America generally includes the right of the owners to do with the property as they see fit. McBain told the gathering how this deed was unique. It was drawn in a way that would control what future owners of the Ferry could do.

John and Mary Crowe with
Donna McBain

The next step after TPL's purchase, McBain explained, had been TPL's sale to the government, represented by the Forest Service, of something called a conservation easement.

The easement is a legally enforceable land preservation agreement that becomes part of a deed and removes some of the property owner's rights.

354

Preservation

One way to look at property rights is as a bundle of sticks, where each stick represents a right to use the property in a certain way. The most valuable sticks are the rights to develop a property, to subdivide it, use it in a commercial venture, or to mine or farm it.

By attaching a conservation easement to the deed, by the government paying to take away rights, any future owner of the property is restricted in what they can do with the Ferry. The entity chosen to enforce these restrictions was the Forest Service.

"What the conservation easement does," McBain explained. "What we sold to the Forest Service is really a responsibility. The easement is a responsibility to make sure that after the TPL is no longer the owner, the next owners cannot subdivide the property, they can't cut down the trees on the property, they can't make any substantial grazing or agricultural use. What remains is a snapshot of what is here. What you see here, with some minor improvements and upkeep, is really what will be here in perpetuity."

Somewhat naively, McBain went on to say, "The Forest Service, being one of the most stable federal government entities around, is the logical entity to hold that responsibility. With the easement they now have that right and responsibility to help the public make sure that this property stays as it is."

The third and final step, yet to be done at the time of the gathering under the walnut tree, was to sell the restrictive deed held by TPL to a steward for the property, a conservation buyer.

McBain told the gathering, "We would like to find a suitable steward that can help lead up the effort to assure that this structure [Cook Cabin], the barn, the Crowe Cabin, and all the other historic buildings around here, stays standing."

"The property needs somebody, preferably local, that will take the lead and share the responsibility to co-manage the property, see that it is preserved and secure a stable source of funding for that. And use it also as a place to bring the public up from the river to learn a very valuable and interesting piece of history on the Salmon River — so that the Salmon River doesn't just become trees and a beautiful river, so that very important historical aspects of the river are maintained for everybody to enjoy."

******

The plan that Donna McBain and TPL revealed that day looked great on paper, but actually implementing the agreement on the Ferry's future has proven difficult.

Bob Abbott, as the district ranger with authority over this portion of the Salmon River Canyon, was in charge. Had those gathered under the walnut tree been able to look into Abbott's heart their immediate concerns about his intentions would have been relieved.

Bob had known Frances well. Despite her frequent criticism of his employer, Bob respected her iron will and tenacity demonstrated over decades of life at the Ferry. Abbott was one of the few Forest Service people Frances had granted regular visitation rights to her home.

Near the end, he had stopped to see Frances in the Grangeville hospital. Abbott listened to her dying request – that a footbridge be constructed across the dangerous crossing of nearby Rhett Creek. Two years later the bridge was built.

The clearest evidence of Abbott's feelings for Campbell's Ferry can be seen during a visit to Abbott's modest private home perched on the edge of the Camas Prairie just outside Grangeville. A painting of the Cook Cabin and walnut tree, the very setting where he now spoke, is prominently displayed over his living room mantle. The painting was a retirement gift from his staff who knew of his love for the place.

The task of getting agreement between TPL, the Crowes and the government and funding the easement had not been easy. Bob Abbott later explained, "The 1980 Central Idaho Wilderness Act had authorized money to buy properties in the canyon, but you don't see a dime of that until Congress makes a specific authorization. It would have been perfectly legal for John Crowe to sell the place to the highest bidder. I was concerned it might be turned into a Coney Island. That bothered me a lot personally."[1]

There had been prior attempts to buy the Ferry. In 1987, a year after Frances' death, Larry Garner, an outfitter who worked out of Cold Meadows in Chamberlain Basin, had approached the Crowes and struck a deal to pay $639,000 for the property. The deal fell through when Garner failed to make payment, so the Crowes took it back.

1 Bob Abbott, Personal Communication, 2011

Joe Scott, an heir to the Albertsons fortune, had also approached the Crowes. They had a deal, but at the last minute John Crowe requested a lifetime estate interest that would allow him to come to the property anytime until his death. Scott was willing to extend invitations to visit, but would not put it in the deed, so the deal fell through.

Soon after that Bob Abbott contacted John Crowe. He had an idea of how to get the Crowes their money and meet their common goal of preserving the place.

With Crowe's blessing Abbott contacted TPL. He began to push the Trust to send someone over to see Campbell's Ferry. "I got Zeke West to pick me and Donna McBain up at Vinegar Creek. We took her to Campbell's Ferry, up the river past Salmon Falls, then back to overnight at Whitewater Ranch. We wined and dined her and got her to fall in love with the river, too."

Abbott's plan was to use TPL as an intermediary. TPL would front the money to buy the place from Crowe. The agency would then buy an easement from TPL allowing them to get most of their money back. The balance would be taken care of when a conservation buyer was found to pay TPL for the deed with the restrictive easement.

Abbott had the players lined up, but getting the money from the agency's budget was a problem. Abbott's district and the Nez Perce Forest had no money appropriated for easements, but that didn't stop this old ranger who was savvy in the complexities of agency budgets.

Abbott discovered that Idaho Senator Jim McClure had secured an appropriation to buy easements on the upper river on properties between North Fork and Corn Creek. Forest Service managers there had been unable to make a deal with property owners in their area and the money was not spent.

Abbott pulled strings and twisted arms to get access to this pool of Salmon National Forest's easement funding. That is not as easy as it sounds. Within the massive agency bureaucracy each forest and district jealously guard its turf – especially the money. In 1989 Abbott pulled it off and paid TPL $569,000 for the conservation easement on Campbell's Ferry.

Along with the easement, Abbott secured veto power from TPL over who the conservation buyer would be. "I exercised that power twice. One group that was interested was some family in Chicago that I thought was connected to the Mafia – they had plenty of money, drug money for all I know. I dumped that one real quick. Joe Scott, the Albertsons heir, contacted me, but the easement wouldn't allow him to build a fancy retreat so that went nowhere."

At the December 1989 annual meeting of the Idaho Outfitters and Guides Association I met Bob Abbott to talk about buying the property.

I already knew Bob well. As President of the outfitter organization I had built good relations with many agency personnel through the organization's efforts to build a partnership between outfitters and managers. And many managers knew me through my outfitting business. The agency respected my track record of professional, safe operation. And they liked the way our guides made educating our guests about wilderness a key component of each trip.

With Bob's approval, Brad Janoush and I concluded the purchase with TPL and became the new owners, the conservation buyers of Campbell's Ferry. We paid TPL $65,000 and made a $10,000 donation to the Idaho Heritage Trust (IHT). IHT had been set up as part of the Idaho State Centennial celebration with a mission to preserve the historic fabric of Idaho. IHT agreed to use the funds we donated to facilitate historic preservation, part of it to be invested in restoration of the Cook Cabin at the Ferry.

******

Brad and I thought we had a good deal. We owned a special piece of Idaho history. We could float, fly or hike to the property, enjoy it, hunt, fish, and just relax far from the demands of our business lives. Looking at the deed, we were in total agreement with the purpose stated in the easement, "to provide for and protect the natural, scenic, open-space, fish and wildlife, historic, cultural values (collectively the 'conservation values') of the property."

We saw in the easement that Forest Service managers, who I knew well and trusted, had discretion and the authority "to perform such other scenic, aesthetic, historical, fish and wildlife, sanitation, restoration or other work deemed necessary or desirable to protect and promote the values."

Yes, there were a lot of restrictions on use of the place, some very harsh. But we were in general agreement. We didn't want to see it developed, or changed. We just wanted to be able to go there and play a role in taking care of it.

What we did not see, nor understand, was the range of challenges that faced both the agency and us as we tried to preserve and protect a historic property in remote wilderness. We would learn the hard way.

What Brad and I and our other partners did not count on was the near collapse of what Donna McBain had said was "one of the most stable Federal Government entities around."

The Forest Service, one of the four principal federal land management agencies, with 35,000 employees and a proud history of caring for the forest was increasingly becoming a bureaucratic nightmare. Supportive managers who wished to get things done were hamstrung. And then there were other agency personnel who outright opposed preserving the Ferry. Indeed, some would just as soon see the historic homestead burn!

To understand why the agency is struggling we have to look at the history of the Forest Service, and who better to explain it than a man who had been brought in to fix it – retired Chief of the Forest Service, Jack Ward Thomas. It is, according to Thomas, an agency with an uncertain mission that has changed and become too complex.[2]

During the initial, or Custodial Era of the agency, from 1905 to 1946, the Forest Service mission was focused on the establishment of boundaries, regulation of grazing, mining, and water flows to enhance settlement. Only limited timber harvest was allowed for local needs.

After the massive fires of 1910 in Idaho and Montana, wildfire suppression was added as an emphasis, justified as an effort to protect the forest until they could later be harvested for the good of the nation in what many believed would be a future timber famine.

After World War II timber demand increased dramatically. A growing population, booming economy, and millions of men and women returning from military service unleashed a pent-up demand for housing. Multiple federal programs like the GI Bill encouraged home ownership. As the agency was ramping up to meet the demand for wood products, Congress passed the Multiple Use and Sustained

2 Jack Ward Thomas, "Uncertain Trumpet," *Fair Chase*, (Missoula, MT: Boone and Crockett Club, 2012)

Yield Act of 1960, adding recreation and fish and wildlife purposes to the agency's existing timber, watershed and range mission.

District rangers, once deemed the most powerful persons in the agency with autonomy over decisions in their district, found their authority constrained by an ever growing cadre of wildlife and fisheries biologists, ecologists, soils scientists, social scientists, recreation managers, law enforcement officers, and other specialists. New laws were giving new voices a say in how the agency operated.

Also during this period the Forest Service increasingly moved from the traditional practice of cutting individually marked mature trees to clear cutting. The process was simpler, more efficient and maximized revenue to both the timber companies and the agency.

To the public and advocates of the new recreation, watershed and fish and wildlife elements of the mission, clear cutting was deemed ugly and destructive.

In response Congress gave critics of the agency more and more tools to fight them - the National Environmental Policy Act (NEPA) in 1970, Endangered Species Act of 1973, and the Freedom of Information Act (1974). Another law, the Equal Access to Justice Act ended up enabling and encouraging challenges by allowing those who sued to go to court and have the government pay their legal fees.

When invoked and interpreted by judicial decision, these laws combined to produce an impossible legal and regulatory Gordian Knot for agency managers.

In an attempt to placate the various groups with an interest in their increasingly complex mission, the agency supported the National Forest Management Act of 1976 which directed each of the 154 national forests to prepare regular ten-year management plans with public input.

The intent of the law was to give clarity to Forest Service actions and build consensus. The exact opposite occurred. The end result was more time, effort and cost — so great that by 2010, thirty-four years later, the Forest Service could not point to a single national forest plan that had been executed in its entirety.

Analysis Paralysis became the norm with appeals and legal challenges made to virtually every significant action undertaken by the agency.

In 1990 I visited Dale Robertson, then chief of the Forest Service in Washington, D.C. I had become friends with Robertson in my role as President of the Idaho Outfitters and Guides Association and as a member of the board of the American Forestry Association. I often traveled to Washington, D.C., with the chance to discuss mutual challenges with the chief.

As I entered his office, set in the corner of the historic, ornate 1878 Auditors Building with an impressive view of the Washington Monument, I was greeted by two construction pallets set just inside the office door. Each was stacked chest high with paper. The piles of paper were the current workload of appeals and legal briefs pulling the agency away from its stated mission of caring for the land and serving people.

The constant battles for the agency's soul became politicized and in 1993 Robertson was fired, only the second chief to be so treated (Gifford Pinchot was the first).

Jack Ward Thomas, a research biologist with experience dealing with the endangered spotted owl issue, took Robertson's place. In 1994 the Clinton administration did an early buyout of senior agency managers, significantly reducing the experience and brainpower pool necessary to navigate the complex administrative landscape given the agency by prior administrations and Congress. Two years later, frustrated, Thomas retired.

As one might expect, and many had hoped for, the level of timber harvest from the National Forest System fell from nearly thirteen billion board feet of timber to three. The collapse of the timber program destroyed the Forest Service budget base.

What funds were available were increasingly taken up by the growing need to fight wildfires. As noted earlier, the Rattlesnake Fire that surrounded the Ferry in 2007 cost the agency $17 million, and it was just one of many large high intensity fires occurring on an annual basis.

The effect of all this on the Forest Service workforce is predictable. By reducing the pool of talent necessary to implement complex timber sales, harvest was reduced, but the reduction also restricted the ability to get anything done.

Morale plummeted. In 2009 a study of federal agencies that looked at employee satisfaction and commitment ranked the Forest Service 206 out of 216.

Preservation

This was the organization that had been entrusted with the future of Campbell's Ferry.

******

It hurt to see the rug pulled out from under my friends in the Forest Service and witness the frustration they felt as they watched a once proud *can do* agency dissolve to an organization retired Chief Thomas labels *dysfunctional*.

I found them dedicated to a job they were drawn to for the same reasons I had been drawn to outfitting – to work in an environment that fed a love of the woods, mountains and rivers.

Many more have now retired. Among those left some still try very hard to make the agency work. But as another retired Ranger explained it, employees often approach tasks "with their career anticipation light on." Within the agency there is a term, "retired in place," to describe the all too common practice of taking no risks and waiting for the day your pension is funded so you can go on to a more rewarding endeavor.

Prior to his retirement Bob Abbott, one of the remaining can

Porch restoration work – Cook Cabin

do rangers, took several actions regarding Campbell's Ferry. He commissioned artist Nancy Dreher to create a bronze plaque commemorating the pioneers who had called the Ferry home and mounted it on a large boulder next to the trail from the river.

Abbott secured the help of Bruce Dreher, a retired Forest Service employee with extensive experience restoring fire lookouts and other historic buildings. With Bruce's lead and funds for materials from IHT, a crew of volunteers, owners and friends worked to restore the porch, foundation and sill logs of the Cook Cabin.

Foundation and sill log work – Cook Cabin

In Abbott's last year on the job he budgeted an extensive refurbishing of the packbridge and held a dedication ceremony, renaming it the Frances Zaunmiller Wisner Memorial Bridge.

Abbott's replacement was Jack Carlson, another ranger I had met in the outfitting industry's Partners Afloat and Partners Astride program. When I approached Jack Carlson to discuss what I was learning in our efforts to care for the Ferry, I found a receptive ear.

I began by telling Jack of the problems we had encountered in the first ten years of trying to keep a caretaker on the property. The results were mixed at best. It is easy to find people with romantic thoughts of going back to nature and living a primitive life style. In reality, it was hard to find the next Joe Zaunmiller.

****

One young couple invested almost an entire year at the Ferry. Shaun and Critter had a passion for the rugged life style the property demanded. With minor support from the owners they put in a garden and spent countless hours cleaning, fixing and tackling the never-ending list of tasks necessary to survive at the homestead.

When winter arrived the couple had to leave due to the provision in the easement prohibiting year round occupancy. A lack of financial support eventually forced them to pursue other endeavors.

Another couple that professed the skills to survive came in one spring with a small child. The owners provided them seeds for a garden, chickens and staples. During a fall visit a partner found the couple barely hanging on with no garden, the chickens eaten instead of laying, no firewood for the approaching winter and the cupboard bare.

Eric Lym, who lived with his family in Riggins, Idaho, seemed to be a good fit for the caretaking job at the Ferry. Having grown up in the canyon, his kind disposition, willingness to work, and enjoyment of the primitive surroundings bode well for a long-term stay.

Eric had a physical disability, the result of a Jeep accident at age nine. His disability had left him with an unsteady gait and speech pattern. It did not prevent him from hard work. He was known in Riggins for the helping hand he gave his grandmother and other elderly widows, doing chores, cutting and stacking firewood.

Eric struggled with social interactions and turned to alcohol. In 1991 Reho Wolfe, a friend of Eric's grandmother, offered him a place to stay where he could use his abilities away from the temptations of town.[3] After a couple of years at the Wolfe homestead at Rhett Creek, Eric heard that we needed help at Campbell's Ferry, and hiked the four miles upriver to meet Joe Denton, one of the owners at the

3 Kathy Deinhardt Hill, *Spirits of the Salmon River,* (Cambridge, ID: Backeddy Books, 2001), pp.76–80

time, who was in for a visit.

Eric brought his German Shepherd, Sam, and settled in to life at the Ferry. For a year, all went well. Eric benefited from periodic help from his family and his ability to spend winters in Riggins.

In his second year at the Ferry Eric returned to his drinking ways. During peak float season he began to visit river camps, looking for booze. In sober daylight Eric came across as a friendly, though somewhat odd mountain man, but his shaggy appearance and uneven gait presented a scary image when he would suddenly emerge from dark woods into the flickering light of a group sitting round a campfire.

During the day Eric discovered that he could sit on the bridge, wait until a float group came by and shout an offer, "I'll jump for a beer!"

When the owners heard of Eric's activities we became concerned. Guides, worried about their clients' reaction to Eric, had begun to change their camp schedules to avoid staying near the Ferry. We worried about our liability and decided to terminate our relationship.

Eric returned to Rhett Creek. The following summer he heard that some friends were floating the river and decided to hike up and surprise them with a jump from the bridge. The night before he slipped onto the Ferry property and found a case of beer cooling in the irrigation ditch.

Jumping from the bridge at the Ferry is a common activity among floaters. The water is deep and the 30-foot height is usually manageable. However, when you add an alcohol impaired state to an uneven landing in cold water you have a recipe for disaster.

On August 6, 1995, the Salmon River was flowing at an unusually high 8,370 cubic feet per second. With his friends watching in horror from the beach just below the bridge, Eric leapt and splashed into the river.

Eric and Sam

He briefly surfaced, struggled and sank as he was swept downstream in the unusually strong current. Efforts to locate him proved futile. A week later his body was recovered four miles downstream in an eddy near Rhett Creek. Eric was buried on his family's property next to the Little Salmon River in Riggins.

****

In 2002, after more than a decade of struggles to care for the Ferry the partners met and decided to approach the Forest Service with a proposal. We first reported on the work we had done to date – general cleanup of grounds and buildings, rebuilding the porch and foundation of the Cook Cabin, shore up a collapsed corner and repair of the barn and restoration of the irrigation and water supply ditches.

Next we set forth our concerns that the conservation values were at risk of declining for several reasons. We had been unable to sustain an oversight presence on the property. There had been multiple instances of vandalism. Human waste and waste water disposal did not meet state codes. With inadequate means to mow the grounds we feared loss of the buildings in a future wild fire.

The partners proposed to add a small room to the back of the Crowe Cabin for bath and toilet facilities. Water for the cabin would be provided by a small water reserve fed by existing ditches and piped downhill. Gray water and sewage would be disposed in an up to code septic system. We also requested clearing of the area around the buildings, thinning of the forests on the property and that the agency utilize prescribed fire to reduce wild fire risk in the surrounding national forests.

We believed that the agency had authority to take such action under the provision in our easement stating they could perform "sanitation, restoration or other work deemed necessary or desirable to protect and promote the conservation values."

The challenge the Forest Service faced were other provisions that generally prohibited cutting any live trees or plants, disturbing the soil, rocks, and water flow and making any changes to the buildings.

This conflict had been written into the easement by Bob Abbott. What were we to do? This would be our first face to face encounter with the Forest Service's Gordian Knot.

Preservation

Ranger Carlson informed us that what we were requesting was difficult at best. If we did wish to pursue it we would need to submit our proposals to an Easement Review Board. The Board had come into being as a result of the agency's efforts to deal with the complexity of the challenges they faced.

Decisions that had once been the purview of a ranger now had to be passed through a six-person interdisciplinary committee. As I sat in the 2003 meeting, accompanied by retired Ranger Abbott, trying to explain to the group what we wished to do, I could not help but visualize the process our proposal faced.

Each committee member would view it from his or her discipline's perspective. Each would return to an office with bookshelves lined with binders and reports filled with documents laying out how any decision must pass the gauntlet set forth by the myriad laws, regulations and legal precedents brought to their turf by decades of battles over use of the nation's forests.

Each had their own strands of fibers that made up the thickening rope tied in the Forest Service's Gordian Knot. I feared the rope would now be used to hang us and our efforts to preserve the Ferry.

The Review Board's answer came back with a decision fairly quickly – no. At that point I suspect the usual outcome would be surrender. Instead, I saw the meeting with and rejection by the Easement Review Board as an opportunity to learn their objections, develop a way to address their concerns, and live to fight another day – as it turned out again, and again, and again.

In early 2004 Ranger Carlson wrote a letter to his forest supervisor and the regional office in Missoula. His letter stated, "the existing Easement may be contrary to the very purposes for which it was acquired, to protect the conservation values of the property."

Encouraged by Carlson's letter, the owners proposed that we meet to discuss the challenges, not at a Forest Service office, but at the Ferry on the porch of the 1905 cabin that was the linchpin of the conservation values. Sitting in one of Joe and Frances' rocking chairs with the Salmon River whispering in your ear, surely we could come to a common understanding of what to do.

Prior to the meeting in May 2005, I got word of who was coming. As expected, the group included Salmon River District Ranger Carlson. Accompanying Carlson were Daryl Mullinex, lands officer from the Nez Perce National Forest, Heather Berg, easement administrator, and Ron Erickson, lands officer from the regional office.

To my surprise Allen Campbell, Office of General Counsel and a representative from the Idaho U.S. Attorney's office were included. It appeared the agency was willing to discuss what could be done, but were they viewing this as a possible enforcement action?

I decided to ask my attorney friend Murray Feldman of Holland and Hart in Boise to attend. Murray's knowledge of wilderness, wild and scenic river and agency management issues is extensive. Murray and I were flown from Boise to the Ferry by Joe Corlett, one of the owners. Joe is an experienced backcountry pilot and real estate appraiser. He had appraised the Ferry prior to its purchase by the Trust for Public Lands, as well as many other backcountry properties. We were ready.

I began the discussion with a review of the purpose of the easement and what we viewed as the barriers to achieving it as posed by the many conflicting and contradictory restrictions. As example, I stated, "There is a provision in the easement that prohibits cutting any live tree or plant, which means that we cannot legally cut the grass."

"Well, don't," said Daryl Mullinex.

"If we don't," I remarked, "Your fire staff tells us that the place will burn up and we will lose the historic buildings."

"That is an acceptable outcome to us," said Mullinex.

To our amazement, Heather Berg spoke up and said, "Yes, that would be acceptable to us."

Murray, Joe and I were shocked to learn that key persons responsible for administering the document controlling the fate of the Ferry would agree with its destruction. Luckily, this view was not held by all agency personnel in attendance.

It must have come as a surprise to the government attorneys that such blatant disregard existed for the values the agency was charged with protecting. The balance of our time with the group was spent walking around the property with Ron Erickson and Allen Campbell.

I found encouragement that the regional office representatives seemed interested in exploring ways to address our challenges.

Ms Berg, on the other hand, spent her time sneaking around the cabins looking for what, to her, were egregious violations of the existing easement. She found a pipe we had run from the sink of the

Crowe Cabin into a French Drain in the ground for gray water disposal.

She also found four-wheeler tracks and later claimed they had created the wagon trails on the property — tracks that had existed for more than half a century.

The four-wheeler became a component of the struggle to agree on how to care for the Ferry. Among the biggest challenges the partners and caretakers had long faced at the Ferry was moving materials and supplies and mowing the extensive meadows in the orchard and surrounding the buildings.

Bringing goods up from the river was a strenuous quarter-mile slog uphill, as was the trip to the airstrip for propane, fuel and supplies. Joe Zaunmiller had moved materials and mowed with horses, mules, a wagon and later with Lucille, the tractor. He also had a three-wheeler the Crowes brought in. A 1907 McCormick-Deering sickle-mower remains functional to this day, but it requires a source of propulsion.

The partners brought a four-wheeler in for the task, taking the position that a four-wheeler did not violate the easement prohibition of *motor vehicles*, and constituted an historical use of the property. The Forest Service disagreed and demanded its removal.

The partners were encouraged by Ranger Carlson's engagement in looking for solutions. We began to provide him with detailed responses to their concerns and documentation of how we saw the problem. We made it clear, "The owners do not wish to make any changes that would degrade the conservation values, allow any new structures, allow any commercial activity, or make any changes visible from the Salmon River."

I submitted a detailed interpretive and educational plan for the property that included signage telling the history of the property and proposed utilization of the Cook Cabin to display artifacts and framed vignettes of each past resident with pictures and their stories. This helped the agency gain a clearer understanding of our vision for the homestead, and our commitment to its preservation.

In April of 2007 the partners were encouraged to receive a letter from Carlson stating he had secured support from the regional forester and Office of General Counsel from Missoula to "initiate conversion of the existing Scenic Easement to a Reserve Interest Deed."

A reserve interest deed was a relative new legal construct the agency had come to prefer as the way to define shared rights in a property. The existing conservation easement had a negative construct – meaning it gave a long list of things the owners could not do. Anything not listed was allowed.

Over time this structure had caused problems for the Forest Service at other properties. As people developed new and better, formerly unknown ways to do things, it became difficult for the managers to stop some undesirable actions.

The reserve interest deed (RID) is instead a positive construct, requiring the owners and agency to set forth in detail what actions were necessary to accomplish the deed's purpose, and any actions not positively listed were not allowed – a mirror image of the existing conservation easement.

Carlson proposed that the basis of the proposed new deed would be to shift the responsibility to restore and interpret the historic structures at the Ferry from the agency to the partners. In return the partners would be allowed to add eight feet to the Crowe Cabin for toilet facilities with a State approved septic system, install a micro-hydro system with water storage for power, and allow use of a farm tractor.

The Ranger's letter further stated, "There are many details to be discussed and negotiated. My staff is working on a preliminary list of tasks, associated costs and timelines for this project. We should have this by the end of April." Jack also noted that the government expected the partners to pay for the work on the new deed.

In July, Phyllis and I stopped by the Kooskia office of Heather Berg. We had just completed our company's Selway rafting season and took the opportunity to stop and check on her progress on the promised task list, cost and timeline.

Berg seemed very uneasy with our visit, apologized for her tardiness and promised action by the end of August. In September, while on a raft trip down the Lower Salmon to hunt chukar, we were surprised to see a young BLM river patrol guy float up to our camp.

He was accompanied by Berg, who, shocked to see us, nervously laughed as she told us she knew she had not done her work, but could not pass on the opportunity to float the river. We wondered why a Forest Service person with responsibility for an upstream section of the Salmon and the Clearwater Rivers was here. It didn't seem funny to us.

****

During 2006 and 2007 our discussions with the agency were done in the context of massive wildfires that visited the canyon and threatened the property (see Chapter Eighteen). We were encouraged by the actions of our local district ranger, but nervous after hearing from others with a say in the future of the Ferry that they wished to see its historic structures gone. We decided to put an additional barrier in the way of such feelings.

The partners committed the funds necessary to have Campbell's Ferry placed on the National Register of Historic Places. We knew that agency managers are driven by laws and regulations, but public opinion plays a role in their actions as well.

When wildfires rage and limited resources are available to fight them, it is hard to ignore a place formally recognized by the government as a National Historic Treasure.

To get the listing we turned to Suzanne Julin, a Ph.D. and Public Historian from Missoula. It wasn't hard to get her support. The Ferry did the sales job for us. Just as TPL had been won over by a trip to the canyon, Suzanne's Campbell's Ferry visit sealed the deal. Phyllis and I did the legwork, utilizing documentation gathered as sources for this book. Suzanne knew how to speak the language of the bureaucratic process.

In February 2007 the listing was granted recognizing that Campbell's Ferry, "made a significant contribution to the broad patterns of our history," and is, "associated with the lives of persons significant in our past. Campbell's Ferry is significant due to its association with the Thunder Mountain gold rush, one of the last gold rushes in the American West. The site also represents ferry transportation, a mode of travel that was crucial to the settlement of the entire country in general and Idaho in particular. The ranch at Campbell's Ferry illustrates the lives and lifestyles of backcountry settlers who dealt with the hardships created by the isolation and ruggedness of the Salmon River country. Finally, Campbell's Ferry is significant as the home of Frances Zaunmiller Wisner, who chronicled day-to-day life there, and by doing so left a record that allows readers to understand the realities of life in the wilderness in the mid-twentieth century."[4]

What agency employee would want the destruction of such a national and state historical treasure on their resume'?

We continued to build the components of a hoped for revised agreement with the Forest Service. In October of 2007 the Idaho Heritage Trust hired Keith Jones of AHJ Engineers of Boise to produce a Structural Assessment document. The plan contained therein is now the basis for all future preservation and maintenance work on the historic buildings.

The end of 2007 brought another milestone in our Forest Service relationship when Jack Carlson retired.

In August of 2008 Mike Cook and Joe Bonn, representing the Nez Perce National Forest, and Alan Campbell, OGC, Region 1 and Ron Erickson, lands officer for Region 1, visited the Ferry.

As we settled around Frances' dining table in the Cook Cabin the first words from Mike Cook were, "Doug, you have been patient long enough. We need to get this done by the end of the year." Phyllis and I thanked Mike for the comment, then sat back and listened as the agency representatives discussed among themselves how they could *get this done*.

It was an interesting insight into the struggles of caring people working for a near dysfunctional agency. As each component of an agreement was raised one or the other would suggest someone on some district or forest in the region who had demonstrated an ability to work through the complexities they faced.

I gave the group a draft of a new RID I had made using examples from Shepp Ranch and Mackay Bar. We then walked around the property looking at our proposals for a water system for fire protection, domestic consumption and power, the addition to the Crowe Cabin for up-to-code toilet facilities, preservation work on each building and the placement and content of interpretive and educational signs. As the group left Phyllis and I were encouraged that progress was being made.

Later in August we received a letter from Ranger Darcy Ped-

4   Campbell's Ferry, National Register of Historic Places, # 356036, Listed February 8, 2007

ersen, Jack Carlson's replacement. Pedersen resolved the long-standing disagreement over the four-wheeler by authorizing the use of a farm tractor on the property.

In December we were able to take advantage of the unsettled markets of 2008 brought on by the near collapse of the economy. The John Deere dealer in Nampa, Idaho, sold us a tractor very close to his cost, saving $5,000. We promptly turned around and gave the five grand to Salmon River Helicopters in Riggins.

In February, when all is quiet in the canyon, our neighbors Heinz and Barbara at Five Mile Bar, ten miles downstream, looked up to see a tractor flying up the canyon. Hooked to a long tether below a Huey,

Tractor delivery to the Ferry

the latest version of Lucille was on its way to the Ferry, quickly followed by a second load with backhoe, mower and other attachments.

The backhaul to Riggins removed the four-wheeler.

Spring of 2009 brought a surprise to all the residents of the canyon. A letter arrived informing us of a meeting to be held in Riggins in May. The Forest Service and Idaho County wanted to talk to us about a program called Fire Wise. The idea was to help the residents thin and clear around structures and create on site water systems to make the properties more resistant to wild fires.

Idaho County had secured federal grant money to help the effort. The county had a track record of success with the program in the Clearwater River Canyon. The Forest Service liked the plan because the Rattlesnake Fire of 2007 had put a $17,000,000 hole in their budget, and a few thousand dollars here and there to reduce future cost seemed like a good investment.

When the Riggins meeting had been proposed within the agency, the staff expected half a dozen or so attendance at the meeting. To their surprise more than thirty showed up. All of the participants had recently stared the wild fire monster in the face. They had our attention and any effort to help was welcome.

During the discussion of the Fire Wise program I questioned the agency about how we might handle provisions in easements on the properties that conflicted with the action needed to implement the program. The response was they would work it out. And they did.

Representatives from the Nez Perce Forest and Idaho County came to the Ferry and reviewed our plans to thin and clear around the buildings and put in a water system. In August we received a letter from Ranger Pederson saying ordinarily under the easement cutting of live trees and plants were prohibited, but also cited provisions stating the agency, "may authorize specified activities to protect and promote the Conservation Values of the property. She called the work, necessary and desirable." We were pleased. Our new ranger was stepping up and making a decision.

Idaho County gave us a grant of $4,100 for labor to thin and clear the brush and small trees that had accumulated downhill of the Cook Cabin and around other structures.

In 2010 Ranger Pedersen acted again, granting us authority to proceed with our plans to install a water system. Fred Sillge's 1917 drawing of the property showed a ditch from Trout Creek to the uphill side of the property that had been put in by

Before thinning and clearing

After

the early pioneers. Now we would take advantage of their handiwork and use it to fill a small pond and two 1,600 gallon tanks.

With the help of the tractor, backhoe and friends, we dug over three thousand feet of trench to hold four and two inch pipe to bring water from the tanks downhill to the Crowe Cabin, orchard and meadows. The tanks were 185 feet elevation higher than the orchard which, thanks to the laws of gravity, produced 90# psi at the end of the pipe.

The ability to run sprinklers around the buildings and throughout the orchard brought real peace of mind during the hot, dry days of summer. The place was green, an oasis, an Eden among the dry fire-prone slopes and forests of the surrounding canyon.

We spent $15,000 on pipe and materials to create the new irrigation system. Idaho County came through again, this time with a $9,400 grant for labor to install the system.

Ranger Pedersen had demonstrated an understanding of the needs to protect and preserve the Ferry. She moved the process forward while acknowledging the challenges we faced. She referenced, "the many changes occurring in the Forest's and Region's organization," stating that, "I can't accurately predict a completion timeline" for the new deed.

That is the frustrating part of dealing with a near dysfunctional federal agency. There is no predicting when things will happen. But as long as there are dedicated employees like Abbott, Carlson and Pedersen, we can continue to work within the system. Eventually, we will achieve the new deed, and formalize what both the agency and the partners know is needed to accomplish our mutual goal of protecting Campbell's Ferry's conservation values.

The agency continues to experience a high rate of turnover in key positions. In some cases that process works to the Ferry's benefit. In 2011 a new easement administrator was appointed.

This time it is someone who has the same passion and love for the canyon that Bob Abbott had. And important to the property owners, he shows a respect for the role we play in providing the sweat equity to preserve historic properties. Most recently we have been working with a talented and knowledgeable person in the regional office who has taken on the task of finalizing the RID. If you visit her office in Missoula, you will see a picture on her desk of Frances, swinging a bottle of champagne as she dedicated the bridge in 1956.

Preservation

There is, in the canyon, in the agency and among the American public what Aldo Leopold called, "A cadre of wilderness minded citizens" available to work to protect the Salmon River Canyon. Not just its remarkable natural values, but the historical and cultural values which Congress made part of the purpose of wilderness and wild and scenic designation.

Working together we can, as the Wilderness Act says, "secure for the American people of present and future generations the benefits of an enduring resource of wilderness" – a resource that includes the special values that are Campbell's Ferry.

Clyde Smart and Doug Tims
Installing the new fire suppression and
irrigation system

Chapter
Thirty-Three

21st Century
Ferry

"In dwelling, live close to the ground.
In thinking, keep to the simple"
– Lao Tzu

The high mountains of the Idaho wilderness are still covered in snow, casting a blanket of stillness over the landscape. Our small plane's engine pierces the silence, winds down the South Fork of the Salmon River, leading us once again to the Eden of Campbell's Ferry. As we round Lemhi Point and drop below 5,000' the snow gives way to clumps of green, the first signs of spring returning to the canyon. We circle the homestead as Ray checks the runway for critters, thankful that this time the deer, elk and turkey, hearing the plane overhead, have sought the sanctuary of the forests, clearing the way for our return.

As it was on our first trip to the Ferry, Phyllis and I once again begin the process of reawakening the Ferry from its winter sleep. As

I hike to the barn, she opens the Crowe Cabin to see if our effort to prevent it becoming a seasonal home for rodents has been successful. We have help.

Thanks to Nabil and Samir, two cats from the shelter in McCall that make the Ferry their year-round home, the days of a cabin with chewed up contents mixed with droppings are no more. The eight months supply of cat food we left in the feeder under the Cook Cabin has more than carried them through. Both are sleek and fat, just a little shy as they adjust to sharing their lair once again with humans. The cabin is as clean and neat as we left it six months ago.

In the barn are stacks of lumber, left drying through the winter. Time, sweat and an Alaska mill are all that was needed to turn beetle killed pine trees into the boards needed to maintain and repair the historic buildings and a future bathroom addition to the Crowe cabin. Next to the lumber sits our small John Deere tractor, a four-foot high mound of snow nearby, the last remnants of a winter's worth of snowfall sliding off the barn roof.

I reattach battery cables, fill the tank with diesel and smile as the engine springs to life. The days of wheelbarrows and sleds to haul supplies from the river and landing strip are gone. I know how happy Joe Zaunmiller was when he first discovered the joy of having a tractor to help with chores.

As we walk across the orchard, daffodils line the walkway; Frances' ditch talks, welcoming us home. The air is sweet with the scent of blossoms from apple, pear and peach trees.

The increased springtime flow of Trout Creek feeds the diversion ditches that flow to and give life to the Ferry. Their course to the Ferry has not changed since the days William Campbell first dug them. Although in this twenty-first century version of the homestead, all I need do to restore water to the cabin and irrigation system is to walk the upper ditch, move a few rocks, and send water flowing to the pond and tanks at the top of the runway. From there the three thousand feet of buried pipe, put in place for the Fire Wise program, delivers water under pressure to our sink, outdoor shower, and the sprinkler system for the orchard and garden.

I light the propane refrigerator/freezer so Phyllis can unpack the box of frozen meats, fish and vegetables we brought from town. This box is one of ten we filled during our annual epic spring trip to

Costco in Boise. Nine remain in the walk-in freezer at Arnold Aviation in Cascade, ready to fly in with the mail every two weeks or so. Later, come mid-June, our garden, perched on the same flat as William Campbell's over a hundred years before, will produce and replace frozen vegetables with fresh. Dry goods and staples soon fill the shelves, the same shelves Frances once stocked in the back room of the Cook Cabin.

Our firewood supply waits, stacked in front of the Crowe Cabin prior to last fall's departure, ready to feed the wood stove and cut the chill of cool spring days and nights.

On the outside uphill wall of the cabin I open the cabinet that houses the control panel for our power system. For years we had relied on a small generator and barrels of gasoline flown in by air taxi. Now, with the flip of a few switches, our system springs to life, showing batteries fully charged, held up through the winter by a small bank of solar panels.

Mostly the sun powers our lights, computer and satellite modem. Someday, soon we hope, the bulk of our remaining carbon footprint will be eliminated by a micro-hydro system powered by the ample supply of diverted Trout Creek water flowing downhill.

As the sun approaches the canyon rim in the western sky, my last task of the day is fetching the iron bell from the barn and mount-

ing it on the post at the top of the trail from the river. The bell will remain silent today and for weeks to come.

For now, snow blocks the road from Elk City into the canyon. The river is cold, holding back the tide of floaters that begins mid-June. It will be a month or more before we polish up our history talk and greet the small groups of wilderness travelers who stop to hear stories of the Ferry. Phyllis and I have the Ferry to ourselves, drenched in the blessed solitude of early spring in the Salmon River Canyon.

To celebrate we build a fire in the pit in our front yard and watch flames dance among the animal cutouts as evening shadows move across the orchard.

The Authors

Doug Tims is Chairman of the Board and CEO of Maravia Corporation in Boise, Idaho, semi-retired splitting time between Campbell's Ferry Ranch on the Salmon River and Tucson, Arizona. He had a twenty-seven-year career in outfitting on the Middle Fork of the Salmon and Selway Rivers and in leadership of state and national outfitting organizations. Today he is in charge of ditches, mowing, and maintenance at the Ferry. Doug has two daughters and five grandchildren living in Boise. Rita, a Vizsla, who came to the Ferry at seven-weeks, is an avid quail and chukar hunter, guards the property and greets our guests.

Phyllis is retired Dean of the College of Fine Arts and Associate Vice-President for the Arts at the University of Utah. She had a thirty-year professional career in dance interspersed with roles in dance education and leadership on the national level, later moving into university administration. Her passion today is Campbell's Ferry, gardening, physical fitness, writing, and enjoying Idaho and Arizona sunsets. Phyllis often leads our visitors on tours of the homestead, telling stories of the lives of Ferry pioneers.

Contact

Doug Tims
doug@rivertraveler.com
208-344-7119

Phyllis Tims
phyllis@rivertraveler.com
520-780-7680

Ferry Media
602 E. 45th Street
Boise, ID 83714

Timeline

1892 – First forest reserves established

1897 – William Campbell arrives in Salmon River Canyon
Bitterroot Forest Reserve established

1898 – Caswell brothers discover Thunder Mountain

1900 – Warren Cook joins Idaho Volunteers in Spanish-America War

1903 – William Campbell disappears

1905 – Warren and Rose Cook move to Campbell's Ferry
Rose Cook dies
U. S. Forest Service established

1906 – Oscar Eakin buys Campbell's Ferry

1907 – Fred Sillge buys Campbell's Ferry

1909 – Town of Roosevelt wiped out by flood

1917 – Sillge files homestead application

1921 – Sillge drowns in the Salmon River
Sam Myers moves to Campbell's Ferry, dies en route to Dixie

1922 – Bob Hilands buys Campbell's Ferry from Sillge estate

1927 – Hilands completes homestead process, is granted title

1929 – The beginning of The Great Depression

1931 – Idaho Primitive Area established

1933 – Hilands sells half interest in Campbell's Ferry to Joe
Zaunmiller

1935 – National Geographic visits Campbell's Ferry

1938 – Bob Hilands gives up and moves to Pennsylvania
Emma Zaunmiller dies in a horse accident

1940 – Frances Coyle is hired by Joe Zaunmiller

1942 – Jim Moore dies
Joe Zaunmiller and Frances Coyle marry
Joe and Frances move to Walla Walla

1944 – Joe saves enough money to move back to Campbell's Ferry

1945 – Frances writes a letter that begins her journalism career
Norman Wolfe is buried at Campbell's Ferry

1949 – Lloyd Lindholm arrives at Campbell's Ferry

1952 – Lindholm buys half interest in Campbell's Ferry from
Hilands estate

1955 – Zaunmillers buys Lindholm interest

1956 – A pack bridge is built to replace the ferry

1960 – John and Mary Crowe purchase Campbell's Ferry
1962 – Joe Zaunmiller dies
1963 – Frances marries Vern Wisner
1964 – The National Wilderness Preservation System is created by
Congress
1968 – The Wild and Scenic River System is created by Congress
1974 – Vern Wisner dies
1980 – Central Idaho Wilderness Act creates the Frank Church -
River of No Return Wilderness and designates the Salmon
River a wild and scenic river
1986 – Frances Zaunmiller Wisner dies
1988 – Trust for Public Lands (TPL) buys Campbell's Ferry from the
Crowes
1989 – TPL sells a conservation and scenic easement to the Forest
Service
1990 – Doug Tims and Brad Janoush purchase Campbell's Ferry
from TPL
Four additional partners are brought into ownership
2006 – Doug and Phyllis Tims retire and begin spending half of
every year caretaking Campbell's Ferry
Large wildfire threatens Campbell's Ferry
2007 – Campbell's Ferry is placed on the National Register of
Historic Places
A second wildfire threatens Campbell's Ferry
2013 – Merciless Eden published